the

Dunamis

project

The Healing Ministry of Jesus

by
**Zeb Bradford Long, Rinda Dean,
Victor Matthews, Bob Whitaker**

**Presbyterian - Reformed Ministries International
Revised August 2000**

PRMI DUNAMIS PROJECT
IN THE SPIRIT'S POWER

TABLE OF CONTENTS

The Healing Ministry of Jesus Christ

Preface

I. ROAD MAP OF THE MATERIALS – HOW CAN WE EVER COVER SO MUCH?

This massive manual only just begins to touch the area of healing ministry. It is impossible to cover the entire manual during the five-day intensive equipping event. Each Dunamis equipping team will have to carefully discern the direction of the Holy Spirit as well as the needs of the people in selecting the topics.

The manual has four basic sections

1. Basic introduction to healing ministry: This includes the biblical and theological framework for healing and our preparation for healing ministry.

2. The spiritual, inner, and relational healing ministry of Jesus Christ and our participation in it.

3. The physical healing ministry of Jesus Christ and our participation in it.

4. Implementing and nurturing healing ministry in the local congregation.

It is strongly recommended that the Basic Introduction to Healing Ministry be covered at each Dunamis event. This is foundational. After this, the group may be led to focus on either the second unit or the third with a summary wrap-up of the fourth. Another option is to strive for some balance in covering both the second and third by not going the full depth in each of them.

To help the teaching team select which topics should be presented we have included a road map of the manual.

As these selections are made, in addition to the needs of the people, one need to take into account what the Holy Spirit is doing. For instance, there have been events where the Holy Spirit seemed to be majoring in physical healing. At other times, it has been in the area of inner or relational healing.

The second aspect of choosing topics is the gifting and anointing of the teaching team. Some people are especially anointed for certain topics. For instance, some individuals bring relational healing and others physical healing. In putting together the team these differences in gifting and anointing need to be balanced. At the same time it is also acceptable if, because of the gifting of the teachers, the specific event is weighted in the direction of their anointing.

To deal with the inevitable frustration of not covering in equal depth all sections of the manual we suggest the following:

1. The manual is provided for continued study after the event.

2. Often the teaching in the manual only becomes relevant and meaningful after actually entering ministry following the Dunamis event. When this begins to happen the manual may be studied with increased benefit.

3. The full teaching charts are provided to make the materials easier for you to use in a small study group. By actually teaching the materials yourself you will have the opportunity to continue to grow with them and in your understanding of the actual practice of healing ministry.

4. PRMI will be offering in-depth equipping events on these specific topics. These events will be for those called into more specialized forms of ministry.

II.   THE PURPOSE IS TO EQUIP PEOPLE FOR HEALING PRAYER MINISTRY

From the very start we must be completely clear as to the purpose of the Dunamis Project and this unit on healing.

First, what we are seeking to accomplish:

> To equip clergy and lay people for biblically sound, Christ-centered, Holy Spirit empowered prayer ministry.

> To help clergy and lay people cultivate the art of cooperating with the Holy Spirit in doing Jesus' ministry of spiritual, inner, relational and physical healing.

> To develop spiritual leaders who are called by Jesus and empowered by the Holy Spirit to introduce healing ministry in their churches by modeling it.

> To equip spiritual leaders who are anointed to teach and to equip others to participate with Jesus in His ministry.

> In all this, the focus is on prayer ministry.

What we are NOT offering in this course:

We are NOT providing a method of counseling or therapy. We are providing a way of praying for people that seeks to be led and empowered by the Holy Spirit.

We are NOT competing with or replacing therapeutic methods. One may be led into prayer, either before, after or even during therapy. These may be complimentary but are not the same.

We are NOT making guarantees that our approach will work. Rather, we are presenting the Holy Spirit who works and is responsible for the results.

We are NOT promising physical or inner healing to those who attend the events. Rather, we provide the context in which the Holy Spirit may work and trust Him to do His gracious will among us.

We are NOT equipping you to do medicine in any form. Rather, our purpose is to teach you how best, through prayer, to cooperate with Jesus Christ who is the great physician.

III. ABOUT ILLUSTRATIONS AND TESTIMONIES

In this manual there are many testimonies used. Their purpose is as follows:

To build up faith and expectation that Jesus Christ actually does work today through the Holy Spirit to do healing ministry.

To encourage us to take the risk of following the guidance of the Holy Spirit to pray for others.

To demonstrate specific aspects of the dynamic of cooperating with the Holy Spirit in Jesus' healing ministry.

To provide the means that the Holy Spirit may use to touch those similar broken places in the participants of the Dunamis event and thus lead them into experiencing Jesus' healing work.

All of the testimonies are real and represent the first hand experience of the authors. Most of them took place in the context of ministry rather than in the clinical setting. We have always tried to link the reported results to objective verification, but these reports in no way represent scientific studies of the effectiveness of healing prayer ministry.

Some of the testimonies have been given publicly and are included in the text with the permission of the person. When this is the case, the person is named. Most of the time, in order to protect confidentiality of the people involved, the testimonies represent a collage of many specific cases put together in order to demonstrate a specific aspect of how the Holy Spirit works.

We have drawn from hundreds of actual cases to put together the stories in this manual. If it should seem like we have named a particular case that you were involved in, this is an unintended coincidence or due to our common humanity and common ways of being wounded. For instance, we have dealt with many cases of sexual abuse. After a while one begins to see certain patterns emerge. Each case is tragic and personal but often share features that are common to other similar cases. These common features may connect deeply with one's own situation.

In all cases we have done the utmost to protect the confidentially of those who have been wounded and are in process of being healed.

PART I

Introduction

The Creation – Fall - Redemption Framework of the Healing Ministry of Jesus Christ

By Brad Long

The Dunamis Project
Presbyterian-Reformed Ministries International

Romans 18-19:22
Romans 3- 9-19
Romans 2 - 8:28&30

Exdoes 34
Ravelatims 22
2 Corenth(5)5 -17-20

I. GOD'S ORIGINAL VISION FOR HUMANITY

To gain a biblical understanding of Jesus' healing ministry we must begin at the beginning of God's intentions for humanity as revealed in the opening chapters of Genesis. Without this framework we will understand neither the full extent of our need for healing or the extraordinary depth and breadth of Jesus' healing work.

God's original vision for humanity was a set of harmonious relationships forming a divine human community that embraced the created order.

This vision is glimpsed in the creation story:

> 26   Then God said, "Let us make man in our image, in our likeness, and let them rule over the fish of the sea and the birds of the air, over the livestock, over all the earth, and over all the creatures that move along the ground."
> 27   So God created man in his own image, in the image of God he created him; male and female he created them.
> 28 God blessed them and said to them, "Be fruitful and increase in number; fill the earth and subdue it. Rule over the fish of the sea and the birds of the air and over every living creature that moves on the ground."
> 29   Then God said, "I give you every seed-bearing plant on the face of the whole earth and every tree that has fruit with seed in it. They will be yours for food.
> 30   And to all the beasts of the earth and all the birds of the air and all the creatures that move on the ground-- everything that has the breath of life in it-- I give every green plant for food." And it was so.
> 31   God saw all that he had made, and it was very good. And there was evening, and there was morning-- the sixth day. (Genesis 1:26-31, NIV)

God's original intention was for there to be a divine, angelic, human, animal and plant interconnected community. The key to the harmony of these relationships was their proper ordering under the sovereignty of God.

The setting for this ideal community was the Garden of Eden, which God commanded the human beings to keep and to till. In regards to the animals, with whom we could communicate with, we were given responsible dominion.

To understand why it is even possible for human beings to need healing we must fully grasp the way God created us and the plan that He had for us.

A. HUMAN BEINGS ARE MADE IN THE IMAGE OF GOD FOR A LIVING RELATIONSHIP WITH GOD

Of God's creations on earth, human beings are unique in that we have a spiritual nature that is in accord with God's nature and thus makes possible communication with the realm of the Spirit. Human beings uniquely span the spiritual and material realms. Andrew Murrey describes our nature as follows:

> The spirit quickening the body made…a living person with the consciousness of himself.
> The soul was the meeting-place, the point of union between body and spirit. Through the
> body, man, the living soul, stood related to the external world of sense; he could
> influence it, or be influenced by it. Through the spirit he stood related to the spiritual
> world…[where] he could be [both] the recipient and the minister of its life and power.
> Standing thus midway between two worlds, belonging to both, the soul had the power
> of…choosing or refusing the objects by which it was surrounded, and to which it stood
> related.[1]

Later we shall explore this spiritual, body nature of man and add the dimension of the conscious
and subconscious. This will be gathered together under the biblical understanding of the human
heart. This unique construction of the human being flows from the astonishing fact that we are
made in the image of God.

When He made us in His image the fundamental result is that we have been made for
relationship with God. This relationship defines our ultimate purpose for our existence, as well
as the ultimate source of a human beings health, purpose and happiness.

St. Augustine in the opening book of his confessions establishes our relationship with God as our
ultimate purpose for our existence and the true meaning of our life.

> Thou movest us to delight in praising Thee; for Thou hast formed us for
> Thyself, and our hearts are restless till they find rest in Thee?

The one in whose image we are made is love. This means that not only are we restlessly seeking
God's love but God is reaching out to us in love. God loves us and wants us healed and set free
to love Him. He loves us and wants us to be able to love others.

Our being created in the image of God with the capacity for love and to be loved, gives human
beings a unique capacity to be wounded in their heart. We shall see that this most fundamental
wounding takes place around our most basic capacity for fellowship with God.

B. HUMAN BEINGS ARE CREATED IN THE IMAGE OF GOD FOR DOMINION OVER THE EARTH

In creating us in His image for dominion over the earth, God gave us certain extraordinary
capabilities. We were intended to be powerful and immensely gifted creative artists like God.

The tools that all human beings have been given to share in creation and dominion are summed
up at the Wright Brothers memorial in North Carolina. This is a monument celebrating one of

---

[1] Andrew Murray, *The Spirit of Christ* (Fort Washington, Pa.: Christian Literature Crusade, 1964),
pp. 227-228. Quoted by George Otis Jr. *In The Twilight Labyrinth: Why Does Spiritual Darkness
Linger Where it Does?* (Grand Rapids, MI: Chosen Books) pp. 93-94.

humanities greatest achievements.

"In Commemoration of the Conquest of the Air by the Brothers Wilbur and Orville Wright, Conceived By Genius, Achieved By Dauntless Resolution and Unconquerable Faith."

> 1. **Conceived** - This suggests the creative imagination that is the capacity for vision, which enables us to conceive the not yet and to grasp new unseen possibilities. (Genesis 6:5, 8:21, 11:6)
>
> 2. **Genius** - This rational facility enables us to analyze and to plan.
>
> 3. **Resolution Or Will** - Directs our energies toward an end.
>
> 4. **Faith** - Grasps the vision and connects us to natural and supernatural powers needed for fulfillment.

These capacities are deduced from the remnants of the image of God that remain in us after the fall. George Otis based on scripture inference and contemporary scientific observation speculates that Adam and Eve in their original glory may have had the following capabilities:

- Command a virtually unlimited and flawless memory;
- Communicate with other species;
- Perform instant and accurate analyses;
- Process external stimuli through all or most of his senses simultaneously;
- "See" remote places and events mentally;
- Transfer his thoughts into other minds without verbalizing them;
- Manipulate external objects with his mind
- Instantly teleport himself to other locations. [2]

I recognize that this is all a little beyond our normal thoughts about our first parents whom most of us have relegated to the realm of myth. Consider for a moment that they may have actually been real. George Otis from the results of recent scientific studies on the capacities of the human psyche provides an update on what Adam and Eve's actual mental capacities as summarized by John Calvin's reflections on the image of God. This suggests that the human heart may contain unfathomed depths that can only be understood with models drawn from the Bible and modern depth psychology.

Being made in the image of God for relationship with God and for dominion has left us with a unique nature that will be affected in specific ways through sin. Human beings are a whole composed of a mind, spirit, soul and body. This will make it possible for us to be inwardly wounded by sin. As we shall explore later, this unique nature will also require some specific processes for its restoration.

---

[2] George Otis Jr. p. 101.

C. MALE AND FEMALE WERE MADE TO BE HELPMATES TO ONE ANOTHER AND TO SHARE IN RESPONSIBLE DOMINION OVER THE EARTH

Much inner hurt is related to our sexuality and to broken relationships between men and women. None of this hurt is comprehensible unless we see God's ideal that is still etched in our hearts.

God's original intention for male/female relationships was one of mutual co-equal helpmates created in His own image. Together in the context of the marriage covenant, male and female were to share in responsible dominion over the earth.

We get a glimpse of God's intentions in the following places:

> 27 So God created man in his own image, in the image of God he created him; male and female he created them.
> 28 God blessed them and said to them, "Be fruitful and increase in number; fill 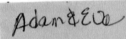 subdue it. Rule over the fish of the sea and the birds of the air and over every livi[ng] moves on the ground." (Genesis 1:27-28, NIV)

It is clear from these verses that God intends that being made in His image is something that both men and women share together. God's original vision was of male and female in the covenant of marriage sharing mutually together in dominion over the earth.

Some have argued that because Adam was created first or because Eve was the first to lead the couple into sin, then God's original intention was for Adam to be superior to Eve. This is a post-fall interpretation justifying the results of sin rather than grasping the glorious vision of how God intended things to be. We find a compelling argument for equality and mutuality between male and female in the following verses.

1. The first argument is Genesis 1:27-28 as stated above. There is an emphatic inclusion of both male and female in being created in the image of God and in having dominion. Any differences between male and female required for the fulfillment of the mandate to "multiply and fill the earth" are a matter of biological function rather than of their nature or authority.

2. The next line of argument comes from the manner in which Eve was created.

> 20 So the man gave names to all the livestock, the birds of the air and all the beasts of the field. But for Adam no suitable helper was found.
> 21 So the LORD God caused the man to fall into a deep sleep; and while he was sleeping, he took one of the man's ribs and closed up the place with flesh.
> 22 Then the LORD God made a woman from the rib he had taken out of the man, and he brought her to the man.
> 23 The man said, "This is now bone of my bones and flesh of my flesh; she shall be called 'woman,' for she was taken out of man."
> 24 For this reason a man will leave his father and mother and be united to his wife, and they will become one flesh.

25   The man and his wife were both naked, and they felt no shame. (Genesis 2:20-25, NIV)

From the Bible account it is definitely true that Adam was created first. However, if we read the Genesis story carefully we find that there was no suggestion at all that this gave headship or leadership to Adam. Rather what is noted, as the result of having been formed first, was that Adam was lonely and incomplete! Despite an exquisite garden filled with animals, which the man had named, the text emphatically states the fact: *"But for Adam no suitable helper was found."*

In the Bible, the term "suitable helper" is a term strongly suggesting equality and comparability. The Hebrew word "helper" is used in the Old Testament as a stronger party coming to the aid of a weaker party, as in God helping Israel.

While it is certainly true that woman was taken and formed from Adam's rib, the choice of a rib which is from the middle part of the man also suggest equality. Some have further questioned the choice of the translated term "rib." The actual Hebrew word is more often translated in scripture as "side" or "chamber." This fuller meaning of "rib" further reinforces the idea of equality. [3]

Most important of all is the man's reaction when God brings the woman to him. There is the cry of identification, *"This is now bone of my bones and flesh of my flesh..."* Then note that in marriage the man is to leave his own family and become one flesh with the woman. If Adam was the superior should not the woman leave her family and be joined to the man?

3. The next argument for equality and shared dominion comes from the curse of sin. Here it does clearly establish that men will rule over women.

> *16   To the woman he said, "I will greatly increase your pains in childbearing; with pain you will give birth to children. Your desire will be for your husband, and he will rule over you."*
> (Genesis 3:16, NIV)

The curses that follow our first parent's disobedience represent a reversing or corrupting of

---

[3] In the 1800's Katherine C. Bushnell advocated for women in spiritual leadership in her then radical book, "God's Word to Women." She makes the following observation that from examination of the Hebrew seems to hold up. Lesson 5 -

> I do not profess to manipulate the Hebrew a single step in advance of the possibilities of any student who may possess the Englishman's Hebrew Concordance (also the Young Analytical Concordance) but the word "rib" seems to be a mistranslation. The Hebrew word translated "rib" in both the Authorized and Revised versions occurs 42 times in the O.T. and in this instance ALONE is it translated "rib". In the majority of cases it is translated "side" or "sides", in other places "corners" or "chambers", but never rib or ribs. It is only translated that way in these two verses describing the separation of Eve from Adam. In the Septuagint version, which was the Scripture quoted by our Lord, the word is "pleura" which in Homer, Hesiod and Herodotus is used for "side", not rib, and, in the Greek of the N.T. is invariably translated "side". There is a word in the O.T. the true translation of which is "rib" and nothing else, and it occurs in Dan.7:5, but this is a totally different word from the word translated "rib" in the Genesis passage. Had God taken only a rib from Adam, the latter would not have exclaimed "she is flesh of my flesh, and bone of my bone" but merely, she is "bone of my bone".

God's original good order.

God's Original Intention	The reversing effect of the curse which was the result of sin.
Gen 1:28-30 28 God blessed them and said to them, "Be fruitful and increase in number; fill the earth and subdue it. Rule over the fish of the sea and the birds of the air and over every living creature that moves on the ground." 29 Then God said, "I give you every seed-bearing plant on the face of the whole earth and every tree that has fruit with seed in it. They will be yours for food. 30 And to all the beasts of the earth and all the birds of the air and all the creatures that move on the ground-- everything that has the breath of life in it-- I give every green plant for food." And it was so. (NIV)	Gen 3:14-15 14 So the LORD God said to the serpent, "Because you have done this, "Cursed are you above all the livestock and all the wild animals! You will crawl on your belly and you will eat dust all the days of your life. 15 And I will put enmity between you and the woman, and between your offspring and hers; he will crush your head, and you will strike his heel." (NIV)
Gen 1:27-28 27 So God created man in his own image, in the image of God he created him; male and female he created them. 28 God blessed them and said to them, "Be fruitful and increase in number; fill the earth and subdue it. Rule over the fish of the sea and the birds of the air and over every living creature that moves on the ground." (NIV) Gen 2:23-25 23 The man said, "This is now bone of my bones and flesh of my flesh; she shall be called 'woman,' for she was taken out of man." 24 For this reason a man will leave his father and mother and be united to his wife, and they will become one flesh. 25 The man and his wife were both naked, and they felt no shame. (NIV)	Gen 3:16 16 To the woman he said, "I will greatly increase your pains in childbearing; with pain you will give birth to children. Your desire will be for your husband, and he will rule over you." (NIV)
Gen 1:29 29 Then God said, "I give you every seed-bearing plant on the face of the whole earth and every tree that has fruit with seed in it. They will be yours for food. (NIV) Gen 2:8-9 8 Now the LORD God had planted a garden in the east, in Eden; and there he put the man he had formed.	Gen 3:17-18 17 To Adam he said, "Because you listened to your wife and ate from the tree about which I commanded you, 'You must not eat of it,' "Cursed is the ground because of you; through painful toil you will eat of it all the days of your life. 18 It will produce thorns and thistles for you, and you will eat the plants of the field. (NIV)

d made all kinds of trees s that were pleasing to the \	
den were the tree of life ood and evil. (NIV) ..nd the LORD God commanded the man, r ou are free to eat from any tree in the garden; 17 but you must not eat from the tree of the knowledge of good and evil, for when you eat of it you will surely die." (NIV)	Gen 3:19 19 By the sweat of your brow you will eat your food until you return to the ground, since from it you were taken; for dust you are and to dust you will return." (NIV)

From this, we may conclude that in a fallen world the man is the ruler over the woman. However, this is the shattering result of sin and not God's ideal. God's ideal was harmony among the creatures, equality and shared dominion among male and female, and immortality for human beings.

The fact that the results of the fall for the women includes pain in childbirth and being ruled over by her husband, is strong evidence that this was not at all God's intention just as the death that resulted from sin was the opposite of what God intended for us which was life!

4. Some have argued that there is built into the prefall created order male headship over female. It is noted that Adam did give Eve her name. (Gen 2:23, 3:20) This is certainly true he did.

Nevertheless to conclude a rigid headship of authority of all men over all women at all times and places is contrary to the previous sweeping statements made by God of shared dominion, equality and mutuality. (Gen. 1:27-28, 2:18,21) Worst, this ridged approach represents the perpetuation and institution of the hurtful results of the Fall that we see in nascent form in God's statement to Eve in Gen 3:16. It is a way denying women their rightful expression of dominion in church and society that has been promised to them by God as creatures made in His image. If we follow the logic of this approach then society is robbed of the gifts of female judges, teachers, CEO's, military officers, etc. All of these positions and a myriad more are positions of authority. (If you want to see such a society then visit the Talibon ruled Afghanistan.)

5. Adam being created first and naming Eve does provide some basis for male headship in the limited context of the marriage covenant. To fill out what this Headship means in the actual practice of a marriage between a man and woman who are "in Christ" which is overcoming the effects of the Fall, we must reach beyond the Genesis story to observations made by St. Paul. There we find an extraordinary concept of Headship that is contrary to the usual social forms that are post Fall. Paul paints a picture of headship "in Christ" that is governed by love, mutual dependence and mutual submission. (1 Cor 11:3-12)

5. The final argument for God's original intention for men and women is seen in the Kingdom of God as brought by Jesus Christ. Through Jesus, in the Kingdom of God, there is a process of

restoring the original intentions of God to creation.

a. We see this first in the way Jesus treated women. In the patriarchal, male-dominated Hebrew society Jesus treats women with extraordinary dignity and respect. He welcomed women as his disciples and even sent them as the first witnesses of the resurrection.

b. Second, in the prophecy of the outpouring of the Holy Spirit which has happened at Pentecost, it is emphasized that the Holy Spirit will fall upon all flesh and that both men and women, both sons and daughters will be empowered by the Holy Spirit. (Acts 2:17-18)

c. Finally there is Paul's extraordinary declaration of the results of our being new creations in Jesus Christ.

> 26   *You are all sons of God through faith in Christ Jesus,*
> 27   *for all of you who were baptized into Christ have clothed yourselves with Christ.*
> 28   *There is neither Jew nor Greek, slave nor free, male nor female, for you are all one in Christ Jesus.* (Galatians 3:26-28, NIV)

Given the original intention of male and female sharing in dominions over the earth together, both with the faculties of the image of God, we may now grasp how it is possible for our sexuality to be distorted and for there to be deep hurt around male/female relationships.

In addition the structural inequality in dominion between male and female that has been built into all fallen societies which is the result of the curse of sin is contrary both to God's original intentions and our original nature. Thus, the arrangement itself is hurtful to both male and female, as it is a continuation of the effects of sin and disobedience.

D. UNDER ADAM AND EVE'S RESPONSIBLE DOMINION THE ANIMALS WERE TO BE IN COMMUNICATION AND IN COMMUNION WITH EACH OTHER AND WITH HUMAN BEINGS

There is the suggestion in Genesis that there was to be community and communication between human beings and the animals. God's original plan seems to have been that all the animals that Adam named would not kill one another, but would live on plants. Likewise, Adam was given the plants as food as well, saving him from the necessity of killing animals for food. This lack of killing for food in God's original plan was part of the structure of "responsible dominion" that the Adam and Eve were given over the earth.

Perhaps it is mere hopeful fantasy on the part of those who truly love animals, but the Genesis story seems to have assumed that at least some of the animals could talk. The Bible, without the slightest surprise, reported an extended dialogue between the snake and the woman. In the garden it must have been normal for the first couple to have discourses with at least some of the animals that were "clever."

This distant memory of a time when humans and animals could communicate would certainly account for the way human beings have so often embraced pets as part of their households and talked to them as if they were children. It would also account for the distant longing awakened in us through books such as C.S. Lewis's *Chronicles of Narnia* in which animals can talk.

This original capacity for community and communication with the creatures placed under our dominion also provide another whole sphere where human beings have both special needs, as well as unique capabilities to receive wounding. It is true that among the animals Adam did not find a helpmate suitable for him, but they were a part of Adams and Eve's original harmonious community.

E. HUMAN BEINGS WERE ORIGINALLY CREATED WITH PHYSICAL BODIES THAT WERE HEALTHY, VIGOROUS, UNAFFECTED WITH ILLNESS OR DISEASE AND MADE FOR IMMORTALITY

Modern Christians generally have not given much attention to the actual physical attributes of Adam and Eve. We have tended to dismiss the story of two actual people in a garden as a myth. Suppose, however, we take seriously what the Bible does reveal about their actual physical bodies. This will shed light on why sickness and death are emotionally experienced by human beings as such an anomaly. This suspension of our scientific disbelief will also bring us to the reasons why Jesus' healing work is not just spiritual and emotional, but physical as well.

George Otis in his book, *The Twilight Labyrinth: Why does Spiritual Darkness Linger Where it Does?* makes the following remarkable observations.

> While Scripture is not explicit about Adam's size, it does offer several indirect clues that point toward great physical statue. The first of these is God's expectation that Adam would "take care of " and "work" a vast garden (Genesis 2:15). Given the data provided in verses 9 – 11, we may assume that this mandate would have required extraordinary strength and stamina.
>
> Another indicator of Adam's statue is found in the reference to the mysterious Nephilim, or giants, that resulted from the union of the "sons" of God with the "daughters of men" (Genesis 6:1-2). In these direct descendants of Adam, also described as "heroes of old" and "men of renown" (verse 4), it is likely that we are glimpsing characteristics possessed by their progenitor.
>
> We must also remember that immortality was an integral part of Adam's original blueprint – a fact that should not be shrugged off as relating to his spirit alone. Adam was created with a body, and if sin had not entered the world, his body would not have known death. Given this fact, we may be forgiven our curiosity over just what kind of body it was.
>
> The proposition that Eden's abundant fruit (Genesis 2:9, 16-17; 3"1-6, 11-12) provided Adam and Eve with resistance to disease and again receives support from at least two Bible passages. In one of them, the Godhead reasons that fallen man "must not be allowed to reach out his hand and take also from the tree of life and eat, and live forever"

(Genesis 3:22). In the other passage, the apostle John refers to a heavenly tree bearing life-giving fruit and healing leaves (see Revelation 22:2). P. 96

After the Fall when Adam and Eve were driven out of the garden and sin begin to bring its devastation, it took a number of generations for human beings to lose their health and vitality. We see this in the extraordinary longevity of the generations immediately following Adam and Eve. It seems to have taken human beings a while before the effects of eating the tree of life wore off. (See Genesis 5:1-32.)

Consider too that these aged people were not wasting away in nursing homes. Sometime after his 500th birthday Noah, with his three sons, began the colossal ark project.

For us why is it necessary to cast this backward glance at the long lost immortality and physical health of our first parents? The thesis of this manual on healing is that in Jesus Christ the Kingdom of God has broken into this fallen world. In this Kingdom, through the working of the Holy Spirit, there is the initiation of processes that are reversing the effects of the Fall. Since the Fall effected us physically, as well as spiritually, this process of restoration will include physical as well as inner healing.

F. SUMMARY – GOD'S ORIGINAL VISION OF HUMANITY

In summary: Human beings as male and female being made in the image of God for communion with God and for dominion over the earth required certain physical, mental and spiritual facilities. These characteristics have left us with specific needs and vulnerabilities that in a sinful world provide the occasion to receive various types of wounding. These characteristics left from our original nature will also be important for understanding not only how we may be hurt, but also to understand our process of redemption and healing.

We may picture this system of relationships in the diagram below. The solid lines with dual arrows point to community and interrelationships between the different levels of beings.

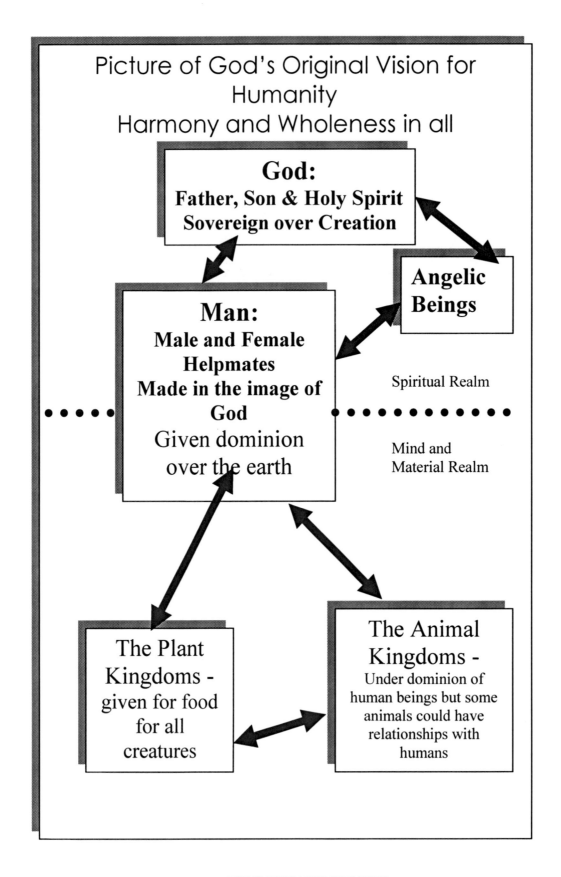

II. THE ULTIMATE SOURCE OF HURT AND BROKENNESS IS SIN

This original, God-intended reality was destroyed when human beings sought, through disobedience, to be "like God." We all know the dismal story first hand in the suffering in our own hearts and families.

The results are listed in God's words to Adam and Eve after they have sinned. Essentially this is a shattering of relationships between all parties and the terrible consequences.

> *14   So the LORD God said to the serpent, "Because you have done this, "Cursed are you above all the livestock and all the wild animals! You will crawl on your belly and you will eat dust all the days of your life.*
> *15   And I will put enmity between you and the woman, and between your offspring and hers; he will crush your head, and you will strike his heel."*
> *16   To the woman he said, "I will greatly increase your pains in childbearing; with pain you will give birth to children. Your desire will be for your husband, and he will rule over you."*
> *17   To Adam he said, "Because you listened to your wife and ate from the tree about which I commanded you, 'You must not eat of it,' "Cursed is the ground because of you; through painful toil you will eat of it all the days of your life.*
> *18   It will produce thorns and thistles for you, and you will eat the plants of the field.*
> *19   By the sweat of your brow you will eat your food until you return to the ground, since from it you were taken; for dust you are and to dust you will return."*
> *20   Adam named his wife Eve, because she would become the mother of all the living.*
> *21   The LORD God made garments of skin for Adam and his wife and clothed them.*
> *22   And the LORD God said, "The man has now become like one of us, knowing good and evil. He must not be allowed to reach out his hand and take also from the tree of life and eat, and live forever."*
> *23   So the LORD God banished him from the Garden of Eden to work the ground from which he had been taken.*
> *24   After he drove the man out, he placed on the east side of the Garden of Eden cherubim and a flaming sword flashing back and forth to guard the way to the tree of life.*
> (Genesis 3:14-24, NIV)

A. THE FUNDAMENTAL RESULT OF SIN IS SHATTERING THE IMAGE OF GOD

John Calvin describes the effects of the Fall upon our being made in the image of God as follows.

> But now [after the fall], although some obscure lineaments of that image are found remaining in us; yet are they so vitiated and maimed, that they may truly be said to be destroyed. For besides the deformity, which everywhere appears unsightly, this evil also is added, that no part is free from the infection of sin. (Commentary on Genesis)

For human beings who are made for fellowship with God, with each other and the animal world this is an intrinsically hurtful situation. We may be wounded not only in the physical body which is now subject to death, but also in the mind, soul and spirit which is the seat of relationships.

The fall and the corrupting effects of rebellion against God started first in the heavens and spread to earth through human beings. The corruption has been driven from heaven and now infects the spiritual realm. Thus human beings must not only deal with brokenness within themselves and their relationships, but also with fallen angels (Revelations 12:9).

B. HURTING INDIVIDUAL PEOPLE - THE PERVASIVE NEED FOR INNER AND PHYSICAL HEALING IN THE WORLD AND IN THE CHURCH

Go to a hospital or just walk the streets of a third world country and one is overwhelmed with the wretchedness of the human condition. Once in a slum in Brazil, as a microcosm of the whole of humanity, I saw little children starving, people with terrible untreated physical illnesses, and women selling their bodies just to get something to eat. I saw a man beating his wife and people listlessly sitting around with no work to occupy their minds or hands. The whole place stank of death and seemed in the grip of demonic spirits who fed on the human misery.

In that dark place I saw how the church was preaching Jesus Christ and there were sparks of transforming light going forth. But among Christians there is also sickness, brokenness and bondage. People in the churches are hurting. They may be strong believers, have come into a personal relationship with Jesus, have been filled with the Spirit, and are active in the church's ministries, but may also often be overwhelmed by unhappy behavior that is very contradictory to their confession of faith. Despite diligent use of the means of grace, despite tearful apologies and repeated surrender to the Lord, fear, anger, self-hate and compulsives seem to come out of nowhere to take joy and peace from them and their relationships. Such people are even found abundantly in churches that stress sanctification, death to self, deeper life truths, and victory in Christ. Usually such people are hurting emotionally from what has been done to them through significant relations and by their responses.

All of this emotional hurt and spiritual hurt goes back to our unique nature as having been created in the image of God.

C. THE CORPORATE EFFECTS OF SIN – FROM DYSFUNCTIONAL FAMILIES TO WARRING NATIONS

When we step beyond the individual to include systems of human relationships from families to nations, we find the same phenomenon of hurt. The Bible with brutal clarity reveals the effects of sin that like an aggressive cancer contagion spreads first in the individual, then to the family system and then to the whole human family.

Between men and women in their most intimate relationship of marriage instead of helpmates and shared dominion, we find the curse of sin. Man rules over the woman and her pain in childbirth has been greatly increased.

We find dysfunctional families, broken marriages, racial hatred and warring nations. The inner hurt within individuals finds corporate expression and creates systems of hurt. The effects of sin pervade all levels of human life.

This development is documented in the whole Bible. However right after the Fall we find it documented in the following stories:

1.   Cain killing Abel (Genesis 4:1-16)

When Cain murdered his brother it not only represented a break down of harmony within the family but also demonstrates the further alienation of human beings from the land and from God. Cain is cursed to wonder the earth but builds a city in the land of Nod which is outside the presence of the Lord.

2.   Heaven and earth and both corrupted (Genesis 6:1-4)

In this strange account of the sons of God who are angelic beings having sex with human females there is the hint that great evil is affecting both heaven and the earth. These unions that crossed spiritual boundaries did produce the Nephilim who were great heroes. I have often wondered if Greek Mythology does not record in more detail this forgotten age when there was an intermingling between human and divine beings. Nonetheless, the contagion of sin persisted to spread and not only was Satan among the company of heaven (Job 1:6) but the corruption of the human race exceeded all bounds.

3.   The corruption of the human race and the flood (Genesis 6-8)

The state of the human heart and the cooperate expression of sin at that time is so terrible that it can only be summed up by God's own words:

> 5   The LORD saw how great man's wickedness on the earth had become, and that every inclination of the thoughts of his heart was only evil all the time.
> 6   The LORD was grieved that he had made man on the earth, and his heart was filled with pain.
> 7   So the LORD said, "I will wipe mankind, whom I have created, from the face of the earth-- men and animals, and creatures that move along the ground, and birds of the air--for I am grieved that I have made them." (Genesis 6:5-7, NIV)

So God cleansed the earth of what He had made. Only Noah and his family were preserved.

Why did Noah find favor with God? Was it in his behavior and purity of heart? Was it because Noah and his family were of pure human lineage from Adam and Eve unmingled by these angelic marriages?

4.   The arrogance of human beings and the scattering of the people (Genesis 11:1-9)

The story of the Tower of Babel is one more expression of human cooperate sin that persists even after the flood.

5.   Sin effects the animals and the earth. (Genesis 9:3-5, Romans 8:19-22)

Most of the focus in the Bible has been upon the results of sin upon the human beings and their relationship with God. There are a number of hints however that sin also pervades the created order as well with disastrous results.

After the flood God now grants human beings the right to kill and to eat animals. This must recognize a concession to the working out of the consequences of sin. This profoundly changes the relationship between the nature of human beings dominion over the animals.

> *3   Everything that lives and moves will be food for you. Just as I gave you the green plants, I now give you everything.*
> *4   "But you must not eat meat that has its lifeblood still in it.*
> *And for your lifeblood I will surely demand an accounting. I will demand an accounting from every animal. And from each man, too, I will demand an accounting for the life of his fellow man.* (Genesis 9:3-5, NIV)

The dominion that God has given human beings by the perversion of sin has become rape of the land and the destruction of the ecological systems that sustain life. In Romans, Paul suggests that just as the image of God in human beings has been overturned by sin so too the created order has been infected.

> *19   The creation waits in eager expectation for the sons of God to be revealed.*
> *20   For the creation was subjected to frustration, not by its own choice, but by the will of the one who subjected it, in hope*
> *21   that the creation itself will be liberated from its bondage to decay and brought into the glorious freedom of the children of God.*
> *22   We know that the whole creation has been groaning as in the pains of childbirth right up to the present time.* (Romans 8:19-22, NIV)

There follows a chart of the results of the Fall and the devastating consequences of sin upon all dimensions of life.

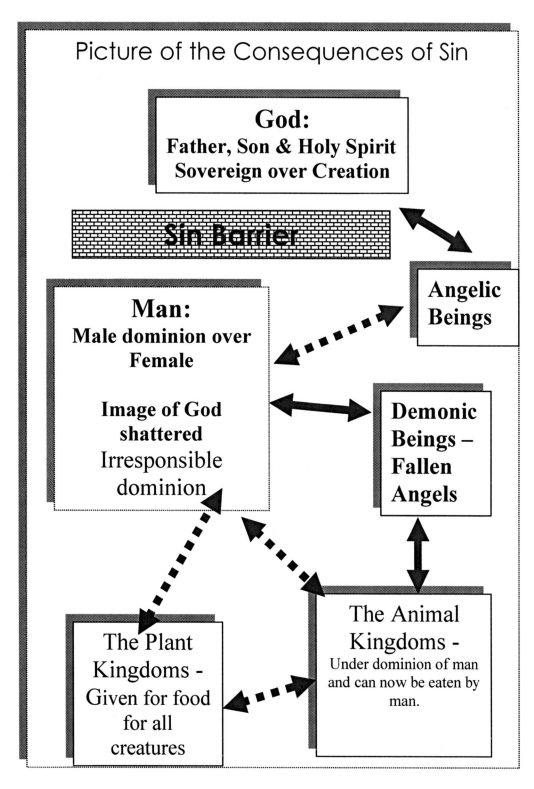

Picture of the Consequences of Sin

God:
Father, Son & Holy Spirit
Sovereign over Creation

Sin Barrier

Man:
Male dominion over
Female

Image of God
shattered
Irresponsible
dominion

Angelic
Beings

Demonic
Beings –
Fallen
Angels

The Plant
Kingdoms -
Given for food
for all
creatures

The Animal
Kingdoms -
Under dominion of man
and can now be eaten by
man.

In the chart above, the dotted arrows show broken relationships. The relationship between God and human beings is destroyed. It is now blocked by the "Sin Barrier." On the other hand, human beings may now have a direct relationship with the fallen angels who with Satan were cast out of heaven.

By the unique nature of who we were created to be, we now have the potential for hurt and wounding extending from our hearts that are created for fellowship with God all the way to our relationship with the created world in which we were to have responsible dominion. St. Paul describes our overall wretched condition that cannot redeem itself despite the fact that through the Law revealed to Moses and the guidance of our conscious,[4] we know the ideal of what we should have been.

> *9   What shall we conclude then? Are we any better? Not at all! We have already made the charge that Jews and Gentiles alike are all under sin.*
> *10   As it is written: "There is no one righteous, not even one;*
> *11   there is no one who understands, no one who seeks God.*
> *12   All have turned away, they have together become worthless; there is no one who does good, not even one."*
> *13   "Their throats are open graves; their tongues practice deceit." "The poison of vipers is on their lips."*
> *14   "Their mouths are full of cursing and bitterness."*
> *15   "Their feet are swift to shed blood;*
> *16   ruin and misery mark their ways,*
> *17   and the way of peace they do not know."*
> *18   "There is no fear of God before their eyes."*
> *19   Now we know that whatever the law says, it says to those who are under the law, so that every mouth may be silenced and the whole world held accountable to God.*
> *(Romans 3:9-19, NIV)*

Jesus Christ entered this fallen world to save and to establish the transforming reality of the Kingdom of God. Now we are ready to understand the full significance of Jesus Christ and the vast extent of His healing ministry.

III. HEALING AS PART OF OUR SALVATION IN JESUS CHRIST

Jesus Christ, the Son of God, has entered this fallen system in order to redeem and transform it. According to St. Paul, the First Adam's sin has brought death into all levels of God's good creation. Now Jesus Christ, as the second Adam, heals the fundamental relationship with God the Father and sets in motion the way of life.

> *6   You see, at just the right time, when we were still powerless, Christ died for the ungodly.*
> *7   Very rarely will anyone die for a righteous man, though for a good man someone might possibly dare to die.*
> *8   **But God demonstrates his own love for us in this: While we were still sinners,***

---

[4] Romans 2:13-15

Christ died for us.

9   Since we have now been justified by his blood, how much more shall we be saved from God's wrath through him!

10   For if, when we were God's enemies, we were reconciled to him through the death of his Son, how much more, having been reconciled, shall we be saved through his life!

11   Not only is this so, but we also rejoice in God through our Lord Jesus Christ, through whom we have now received reconciliation.

*12   **Therefore, just as sin entered the world through one man, and death through sin, and in this way death came to all men, because all sinned--***

13   for before the law was given, sin was in the world. But sin is not taken into account when there is no law.

14   Nevertheless, death reigned from the time of Adam to the time of Moses, even over those who did not sin by breaking a command, as did Adam, who was a pattern of the one to come.

*15   **But the gift is not like the trespass. For if the many died by the trespass of the one man, how much more did God's grace and the gift that came by the grace of the one man, Jesus Christ, overflow to the many!***

16   Again, the gift of God is not like the result of the one man's sin: The judgment followed one sin and brought condemnation, but the gift followed many trespasses and brought justification.

*17   **For if, by the trespass of the one man, death reigned through that one man, how much more will those who receive God's abundant provision of grace and of the gift of righteousness reign in life through the one man, Jesus Christ.***

*18   **Consequently, just as the result of one trespass was condemnation for all men, so also the result of one act of righteousness was justification that brings life for all men.***

*19   **For just as through the disobedience of the one man the many were made sinners, so also through the obedience of the one man the many will be made righteous.***

(Romans 3:9-19, NIV)

This section from Romans is quoted in its entirety because it establishes the relationship between Christ and Adam. It also clarifies the ultimate work of Jesus Christ. By His obedience on the cross a process of redemption was set in motion. C.S. Lewis sums up the redemptive work of Jesus Christ it in *The Lion, The Witch and the Wardrobe* –

"It means," said Aslan, "that though the Witch knew the Deep Magic, there is a magic deeper still which she did not know. Her knowledge goes back only to the dawn of Time. But if she could have looked a little further back, into the stillness and the darkness before Time dawned, she would have read there a different incantation. She would have known that when a willing victim who had committed no treachery was killed in a traitor's stead, the Table would crack and **Death itself would start working backwards**…"[5]

The river of life now runs through creation, the image of God starts to be restored and we begin the process of being recreated according to the original design. This happens by the working of the Holy Spirit. Now in the Kingdom of God, "Death itself is working backwards!"

---

[5] C.S. Lewis, *The Lion, the Witch and the Wardrobe: A Story for Children* (New York: The Macmillan Company, 1950), pp. 159-160.

St. Paul again spells out for each of us who are justified the results of the cross of Christ revering the effect of the Fall.

> 28 And we know that in all things God works for the good of those who love him, who have been called according to his purpose.
> 29 For those God foreknew he also predestined to be conformed to the likeness of his Son, that he might be the firstborn among many brothers.
> 30 And those he predestined, he also called; those he called, he also justified; those he justified, he also glorified. (Romans 8:28-30, NIV)

Paul says we will be glorified! This means that the results of the Fall would have been undone and we will be a part of the New Heaven and New Earth. We see the final vision of this restored creation in the book of Revelation. (This is what happens when Death has run backwards as far as it can go. We end up with eternal life!)

> 1 Then the angel showed me the river of the water of life, as clear as crystal, flowing from the throne of God and of the Lamb
> 2 down the middle of the great street of the city. On each side of the river stood the tree of life, bearing twelve crops of fruit, yielding its fruit every month. And the leaves of the tree are for the healing of the nations.
> 3 No longer will there be any curse. The throne of God and of the Lamb will be in the city, and his servants will serve him.
> 4 They will see his face, and his name will be on their foreheads.
> 5 There will be no more night. They will not need the light of a lamp or the light of the sun, for the Lord God will give them light. And they will reign for ever and ever.
> (Revelation 22:1-5, NIV)

Does this not sound familiar? Has not the Bible taken wandering humanity in a full circle? This is Eden! But now richer, deeper and more wonderful then before because of the blight of sin and death that had to be overcome by the blood of the Lamb. In the end the image of God will be restored, our bodies restored to their intended glory, our relationships with one another and the creation the way God intended them. In this redeemed condition, our full dominion will be restored. And we will reign with God forever and ever!

A. THE KINGDOM OF GOD

This new reality of redemption and transformation, that has been planted like a seed in the fallen world, is known in the Bible as the Kingdom of God.

The Kingdom of God is the context where Jesus, through the Holy Spirit, is redeeming humanity from sin and healing the effects of the Fall. The vision of God's Kingdom provides a framework big enough to embrace the spiritual, emotional, physical, cooperate, and cosmic dimensions of Jesus' healing work.

Healing is part of the practical working out of our salvation in Jesus Christ. In the life, death, resurrection and ascension of Jesus Christ there is a restoring of God's original intentions for humanity and for creation. As was said by the saints of the Church, "The glory of God is manfully alive."

The nature of the human beings who need this healing is presented in the Bible is of a holistic unit. Some, starting with Augustine, would neatly divide up human beings into spirit, mind and body. There certainly are different aspects of human beings that we must acknowledge if we are to form an adequate understanding of our nature. This however, reflects more of a Greek view of human nature than a biblical Hebraic view. This holistic view in which neat demarcations dissolve into gray areas is more consistent with our actual experience of the interconnection between mind, body and spirit.

The different dimensions of our being, however, will determine different aspects of healing as they take place in the Kingdom of God. For the sake of convenience, we will distinguish between the following foci of Jesus' healing work. These will provide the manual organization.

1.   Spiritual Healing

This is the restoration of our fundamental relationship with God the Father.   This is the most basic form of healing and the beginning of all other healing.

> *17   Therefore, if anyone is in Christ, he is a new creation; the old has gone, the new has come!*
> *18   All this is from God, who reconciled us to himself through Christ and gave us the ministry of reconciliation:*
> *19   that God was reconciling the world to himself in Christ, not counting men's sins against them. And he has committed to us the message of reconciliation. (2 Corinthians 5:17-19, NIV)*

To be reconciled to God takes place through the death of Jesus Christ and through our being born again through the Holy Spirit.

b) Inner Healing

Inner healing is part of the process of undoing the hurtful effects of sin. This includes the results of our own sin and being sinned against. It is a process of restoring to wholeness the shattered image of God within us. This process begins for an individual when, through faith in Jesus Christ, they are born again into the new evolving reality of the Kingdom of God. The completion of this process is not in this world and in this time, but at the end of time when the Kingdom is fulfilled.

> *17   Now the Lord is the Spirit, and where the Spirit of the Lord is, there is freedom.*
> *18   And we, who with unveiled faces all reflect the Lord's glory, are being transformed into his likeness with ever-increasing glory, which comes from the Lord, who is the Spirit. (2 Corinthians 3:17-18, NIV)*

> *22   But the fruit of the Spirit is love, joy, peace, patience, kindness, goodness, faithfulness,*
> *23   gentleness and self-control. Against such things there is no law.*

> *24   Those who belong to Christ Jesus have crucified the sinful nature with its passions and desires.*
> *25   Since we live by the Spirit, let us keep in step with the Spirit.* (Galatians 5:22-25, NIV)

Inner healing is that transformation of our heart through the Holy Spirit that overcomes the hurt of sin and enables us to reflect the character of Jesus Christ. As our character is changed we shall yield the fruit of the Holy Spirit and be able to "keep in step with the Spirit."

c) Physical Healing

Physical healing takes place as God is restoring us to our originally intended health and immortality. This process will be completed with the resurrection. Jesus Christ, who is the first to be resurrected from the dead, has promised all who believe in Him eternal life starting now.

> *25   Jesus said to her, "I am the resurrection and the life. He who believes in me will live, even though he dies;*
> *26   and whoever lives and believes in me will never die. Do you believe this?"* (John 11:25-26, NIV)

Through Jesus we are brought into the river of life now. The physical healings that we may experience now, through natural and supernatural means, are signs of God's original design for human life, and harbingers of the abundant life in the Kingdom fulfilled in the New Heaven and New Earth.

d) Relational Healing

Relational healing takes place as Jesus heals our web of fallen relationships. This starts with the most basic relationship between male and female. It then extends, as in ever expanding spheres, to include the healing of injustice between social classes and to the healing of the nations. This work will be completed with the restoration of the Holy City through which will flow the River of Life, on the banks of which will grow the trees whose leaves are for the healing of the nations.

The result of relational healing will be as St. Paul foretold.

> *26   For ye are all the children of God by faith in Christ Jesus.*
> *27   For as many of you as have been baptized into Christ have put on Christ.*
> *28   There is neither Jew nor Greek, there is neither bond nor free, there is neither male nor female: for ye are all one in Christ Jesus.*
> *29   And if ye be Christ's, then are ye Abraham's seed, and heirs according to the promise.* (Galatians 3:26-29, KJV) [6]

e) Restoration of the Created Order

In the Kingdom of God this will be a process of healing the brokenness between human beings

---

[6] I have chosen the King James Version because it uses the term "children of God" instead of "son's of God" the Greek may be translated either way – children or sons. Clearly, the meaning of the verse is "children."

and the animals. Even the land itself will be returned to its fruitfulness and abundance. There will be harmony and peace and no longer the ravages of death among creatures, the land and human beings. There will be a restoration of human beings having responsible dominion over the animals and the natural world. The prophet Isaiah saw a vision of this type of healing we have already started to experience in the Kingdom of God.

> 6   The wolf will live with the lamb, the leopard will lie down with the goat, the calf and the lion and the yearling together; and a little child will lead them.
> 7   The cow will feed with the bear, their young will lie down together, and the lion will eat straw like the ox.
> 8   The infant will play near the hole of the cobra, and the young child put his hand into the viper's nest.
> 9   They will neither harm nor destroy on all my holy mountain, for the earth will be full of the knowledge of the LORD as the waters cover the sea. (Isaiah 11:6-9, NIV)

f) Deliverance and Exorcism

When Jesus walked on the earth a major part of His ministry was casting out evil spirits. This was due to the interference of evil spirits at every level of creation. Jesus' work of restoring humanity and creation to God's original purposes involved Him in the necessary warfare of overcoming and driving out these enemies of our redemption.

> 37 You know what has happened throughout Judea, beginning in Galilee after the baptism that John preached--
> 38 how God anointed Jesus of Nazareth with the Holy Spirit and power, and how he went around doing good and healing all who were under the power of the devil, because God was with him. (Acts 10:37-38, NIV)

Today, through the Holy Spirit, as we share in Jesus' healing ministry we may find ourselves also having to engage in the ministry of deliverance and exorcism. This is the negative necessary work of removing blocks to the advancement of the Kingdom of God.

g) A Holistic Vision of Human Nature and of Jesus' Healing Work

Let us return to the fundamental principle. We have addressed different dimensions of human nature as well as the different forms of healing. It must be recognized however that, in fact, our nature is like a tightly woven cloth. The separate threads may tease out, but they have their full meaning only as a woven unity. In actual practice these various forms of healing are completely interwoven and interdependent. While it may be convenient to start with physical or inner healing, we are called to engage with Jesus in restoring the whole person in the whole Kingdom of God. This will involve us in all dimensions of their being. Only a "systems" approach that is connected with the overarching motif of the Kingdom of God is big enough to embrace the full wonder of Jesus' healing ministry.

D. The Kingdom is NOW but is in a process of fulfillment.

The healing ministry of Jesus in all its forms must be understood as a part of what it means to be in the Kingdom of God. This Kingdom, through the Holy Spirit, is present and real now. Nevertheless, it is incomplete. We still live in a world where there is sin and death. The result is that while spiritual healing of restoring our relationship with God is completed by the sacrifice of Jesus on the cross, the rest of our healing is in process.

Our complete healing from the effects of the Fall awaits the completion of the Kingdom of God at the end time when there shall be a New Heaven and a New Earth.

This accounts for the disturbing phenomena of why Christians may still get sick, be emotionally wounded, suffer loss, and still must face physical death. It also helps us understand why miracles of healing do happen but for others healing is a long process completed only in the resurrection.

New birth as the only way into the Kingdom of God, is thus the beginning place for healing prayer ministry in the name of Jesus. Once a person is birthed into the Kingdom, healing will be a process that will contain the following intermingled spheres.

1. The restoration of the relationship with God – spiritual healing.

2. The restoration of the shattered image of God within us – emotional and physical healing.

3. The pushing back and overcoming the demonic.

4. The restoration of the core male/female relationship as helpmates in marriage.

5. The healing of brokenness between peoples.

6. The healing of nations.

7. The restoration of human beings responsible dominion over the animals and the natural world.

2.   What about the role of medical science, psychology and healthful practices?

The only way into the Kingdom of God is to be born again. Does this mean that there is no healing and health outside of a person having been born again?

No! God in His grace and love of humanity has built into the universe both moral and spiritual laws. When these are followed, there may be a measure of overcoming the results of the Fall. We are also left with the facilities of reason, rationality and responsible choice. These are the tools for dominion that God has given all human beings. We must use these to the best of our abilities for the good of humanity. This means that there is room for medical science and psychotherapy in overcoming disease and emotional hurts.

It is the conviction of the *Dunamis Project* that the supernatural working of the Holy Spirit in the Kingdom of God for healing is not at all in conflict with these natural means of health and healing. God, as creator, has established both ways and works through all ways.

Complete redemption that not only transforms this world, but also transcends it, will take place only as a person is born again into the Kingdom. The process of God's healing, which will lead to a perfect restoration of His original vision glimpsed at in the garden, begins with new birth. It ends with glorification and eternal life in the New City of God – the redeemed Eden. No human methods of healing and health can offer this final redemption.

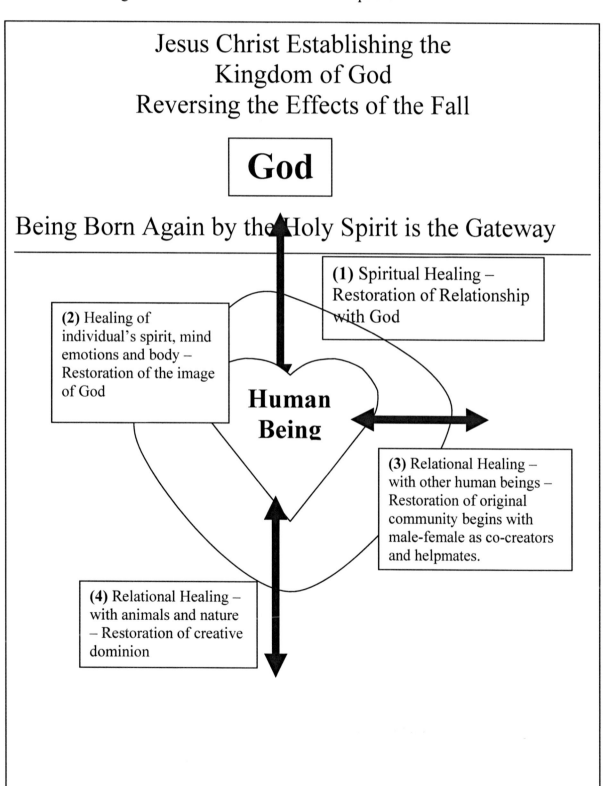

Jesus Christ Establishing the
Kingdom of God
Reversing the Effects of the Fall

God

Being Born Again by the Holy Spirit is the Gateway

(1) Spiritual Healing – Restoration of Relationship with God

(2) Healing of individual's spirit, mind emotions and body – Restoration of the image of God

Human Being

(3) Relational Healing – with other human beings – Restoration of original community begins with male-female as co-creators and helpmates.

(4) Relational Healing – with animals and nature – Restoration of creative dominion

IV. THE PURPOSE OF CHRIST'S HEALING AND OUR BEING HEALED

This Creation – Fall – Redemption framework brings us to a final issue that must be dealt with before moving into the manual. What is the purpose of Christ's healing ministry and our involvement in His ministry?

The answer is ultimately found in the mystery of God's love. He redeems us and begins to heal us simply because He loves us.

Out of this same love of God, our redemption and healing is for the purpose that we may be participants in Jesus' work of redemption. In summary, our healing whether, spiritual, inner or physical is so that we may get up and follow Jesus and then be His witness.

We see this dynamic of being saved and healed in order to be sent through Jesus' ministry of healing and also in some of the summary theological statements made by Paul about the purpose of our salvation.

The man who experienced deliverance and inner healing through Jesus is sent as a witness.

> *18 As Jesus was getting into the boat, the man who had been demon-possessed begged to go with him.*
> *19 Jesus did not let him, but said, "Go home to your family and tell them how much the Lord has done for you, and how he has had mercy on you."*
> *20 So the man went away and began to tell in the Decapolis how much Jesus had done for him. And all the people were amazed.* (Mark 5:18-20, NIV)

We have been reconciled to God in order that we may become ambassadors of reconciliation.

> *17 Therefore, if anyone is in Christ, he is a new creation; the old has gone, the new has come!*
> *18 All this is from God, who reconciled us to himself through Christ and gave us the ministry of reconciliation:*
> *19 that God was reconciling the world to himself in Christ, not counting men's sins against them. And he has committed to us the message of reconciliation.*
> *20 We are therefore Christ's ambassadors, as though God were making his appeal through us. We implore you on Christ's behalf: Be reconciled to God.* (2 Corinthians 5:17-20, NIV)

This means that our focus can never be just on healing ministry - that would divert us away from God's whole redemptive purposes.

We are to engage in healing ministry so that people may be:

➢brought to salvation in Jesus Christ,

➢empowered by the Holy Spirit,

➢discipled into maturity

➢ and sent out as witnesses.

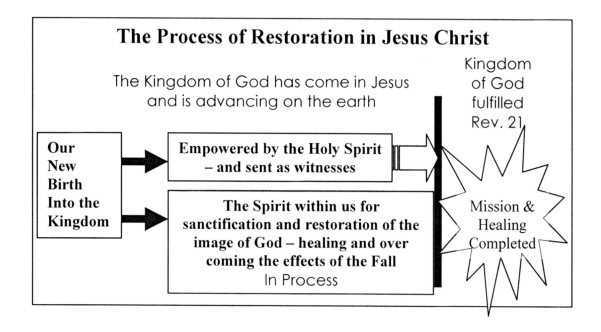

Teaching Charts

Part I

The Creation – Fall - Redemption

The Dunamis Project
Presbyterian-Reformed Ministries International

GOD'S ORIGINAL VISION FOR HUMANITY

Genesis 1:26-31

A. HUMAN BEINGS ARE MADE IN THE IMAGE OF GOD FOR RELATIONSHIP WITH GOD.

Thou movest us to delight in praising Thee; for Thou hast formed us for Thyself, and our hearts are restless till they find rest in Thee.

B. HUMAN BEINGS ARE CREATED IN THE IMAGE OF GOD FOR DOMINION OVER THE EARTH.

"In Commemoration of the Conquest of the Air by the Brothers Wilbur and Orville Wright, <u>Conceived By Genius, Achieved By Dauntless Resolution and Unconquerable Faith.</u>"

C. MALE AND FEMALE WERE MADE TO BE HELPMATES TO ONE ANOTHER AND TO SHARE IN RESPONSIBLE DOMINION OVER THE EARTH.

27 So God created man in his own image, in the image of God he created him; male and female he created them. 28 God blessed them and said to them, "Be fruitful and increase in number; fill the earth and subdue it. Rule over the fish of the sea and the birds of the air and over every living creature that moves on the ground." (Genesis 1:27-28, NIV)

D. UNDER ADAM AND EVE'S RESPONSIBLE DOMINION THE ANIMALS WERE TO BE IN COMMUNICATION AND IN COMMUNION WITH EACH OTHER AND WITH HUMAN BEINGS.

Genesis 3:1- The snake talking to the woman.

E. HUMAN BEINGS WERE ORIGINALLY CREATED WITH PHYSICAL BODIES THAT WERE HEALTHY, VIGOROUS, UNAFFECTED WITH ILLNESS OR DISEASE AND MADE FOR IMMORTALITY.

Genesis 3:22 - In the garden was food for immortality.

Genesis 5:1-32 - It took human beings several generations for the tree of life to wear off.

35

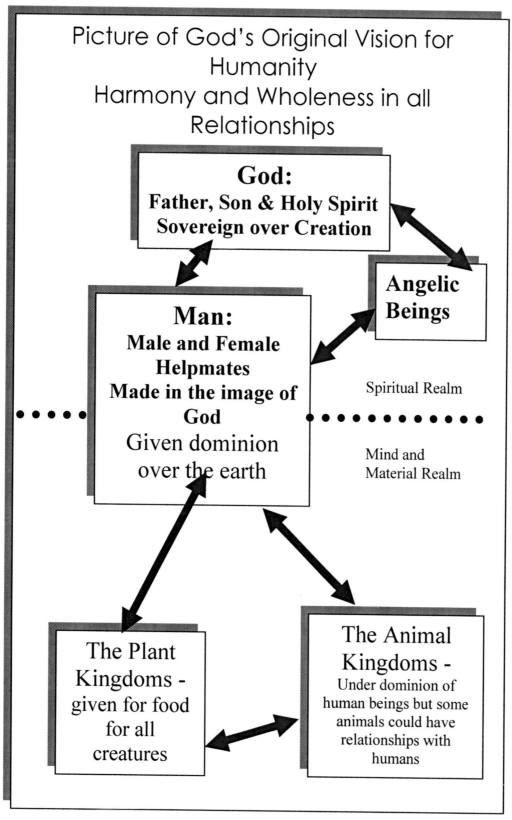

Picture of God's Original Vision for Humanity
Harmony and Wholeness in all Relationships

God:
Father, Son & Holy Spirit
Sovereign over Creation

Angelic Beings

Man:
Male and Female
Helpmates
Made in the image of God
Given dominion over the earth

Spiritual Realm

Mind and Material Realm

The Plant Kingdoms - given for food for all creatures

The Animal Kingdoms -
Under dominion of human beings but some animals could have relationships with humans

THE PRMI *DUNAMIS PROJECT*
JESUS HEALING MINISTRY
PART 1 CHART 2

THE ULTIMATE SOURCE OF HURT AND BROKENNESS IS SIN

Genesis 3:14-24

A. THE FUNDAMENTAL RESULT OF SIN IS SHATTERING THE IMAGE OF GOD.

B. HURTING INDIVIDUAL PEOPLE -
THE PERVASIVE NEED FOR INNER AND PHYSICAL HEALING IN THE WORLD AND IN THE CHURCH.

C. THE CORPORATE EFFECTS OF SIN- FROM DYSFUNCTIONAL FAMILIES TO WARRING NATIONS.

D. THE SHATTERED RELATIONSHIP BETWEEN HUMAN BEINGS AND THEIR ENVIRONMENT.

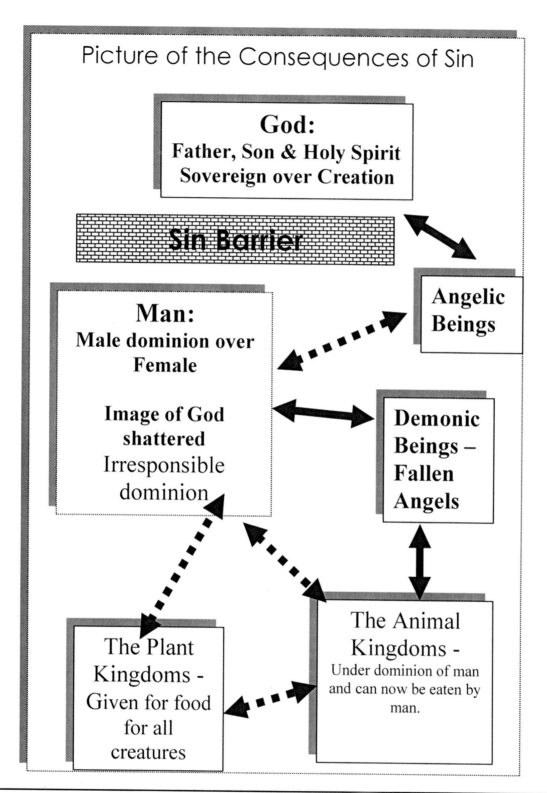

Picture of the Consequences of Sin

God:
Father, Son & Holy Spirit
Sovereign over Creation

Sin Barrier

Angelic Beings

Man:
Male dominion over Female

Image of God shattered
Irresponsible dominion

Demonic Beings – Fallen Angels

The Plant Kingdoms - Given for food for all creatures

The Animal Kingdoms -
Under dominion of man and can now be eaten by man.

HEALING AS PART OF OUR SALVATION IN JESUS CHRIST

Romans 3:9-19 - Christ is the new Adam

C.S. Lewis - Death itself would start working backwards

Romans 8:28-30 - Because of the work of Jesus Christ we will be glorified

Revelation 22:1-5 - Restoration of the Garden of Eden with the River of Life and the tree of life.

THE KINGDOM OF GOD AND JESUS' HEALING

a) Spiritual Healing

17   Therefore, if anyone is in Christ, he is a new creation; the old has gone, the new has come!
18   All this is from God, who reconciled us to himself through Christ and gave us the ministry of reconciliation:
19   that God was reconciling the world to himself in Christ, not counting men's sins against them. And he has committed to us the message of reconciliation.
(2 Corinthians 5:17-19, NIV)

b) Inner Healing

17   Now the Lord is the Spirit, and where the Spirit of the Lord is, there is freedom.
18   And we, who with unveiled faces all reflect the Lord's glory, are being transformed into his likeness with ever-increasing glory, which comes from the Lord, who is the Spirit.
(2 Corinthians 3:17-18,NIV)

22 *But the fruit of the Spirit is love, joy, peace, patience, kindness, goodness, faithfulness,*
23 *gentleness and self-control. Against such things there is no law.*
24 *Those who belong to Christ Jesus have crucified the sinful nature "with its passions and desires.*
25 *Since we live by the Spirit, let us keep in step with the Spirit.* (Galatians 5:22-25, NIV)

c) Physical Healing

25 *Jesus said to her, "I am the resurrection and the life. He who believes in me will live, even though he dies;*
26 *and whoever lives and believes in me will never die. Do you believe this?"* (John 11:25-26, NIV)

33 *The whole town gathered at the door,*
34 *and Jesus healed many -who had various diseases. He also drove out many demons, but he would not let the demons speak because they knew who he was.* (Mark 1:33-34 NIV)

d) Relational Healing

26   For ye are all the children of God by faith in Christ Jesus.
27   For as many of you as have been baptized into Christ have put on Christ.
28   There is neither Jew nor Greek, there is neither bond nor free, there is neither male nor female: for ye are all one in Christ Jesus.
29   And if ye be Christ's, then are ye Abraham's seed, and heirs according to the promise. **(Galatians 3:26-29, KJV)**

e) Restoration of the Created Order

6   The wolf will live with the lamb, the leopard will lie down with the goat, the calf and the lion and the yearling together; and a little child will lead them.
7 The cow will feed with the bear, their young will lie down together, and the lion will eat straw like the ox.
8   The infant will play near the hole of the cobra, and the young child put his hand into the viper's nest.
9   They will neither harm nor destroy on all my holy mountain, for the earth will be full of the knowledge of the LORD as the waters cover the sea. **(Isaiah 11:6-9, NIV)**

f) Deliverance and Exorcism

3 7   You know what has happened throughout Judea, beginning in Galilee after the baptism that John preached—38   how God anointed Jesus of Nazareth with the Holy Spirit and power, and how he went around doing good and healing all who were under the power of the devil, because God was with him. **(Acts 10:37-38, NIV)**

g) A Holistic Vision of Human Nature and of Jesus' Healing Work

1   Then I saw a new heaven and a new earth, for the first heaven and the first earth had passed away, and there was no longer any sea. **(Revelation 21:1, NIV)**

D. THE KINGDOM IS NOW BUT IS IN A PROCESS OF FULFILLMENT

All forms of healing will also be a process.

The Dimensions of Healing in the Kingdom of God

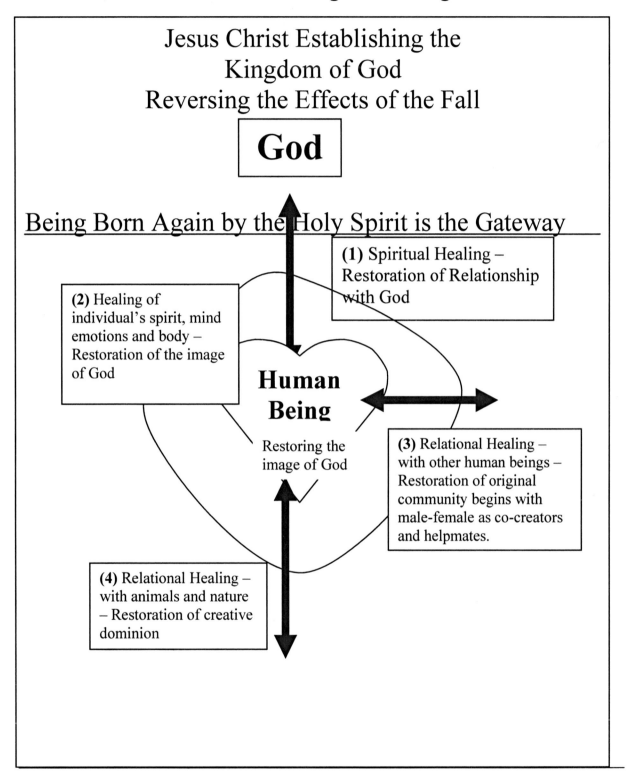

Jesus Christ Establishing the
Kingdom of God
Reversing the Effects of the Fall

God

Being Born Again by the Holy Spirit is the Gateway

(1) Spiritual Healing –
Restoration of Relationship
with God

(2) Healing of
individual's spirit, mind
emotions and body –
Restoration of the image
of God

Human Being

Restoring the
image of God

(3) Relational Healing –
with other human beings –
Restoration of original
community begins with
male-female as co-creators
and helpmates.

(4) Relational Healing –
with animals and nature
– Restoration of creative
dominion

The Purpose of Christ's Healing and Our Being Healed

A. MARK 5:18-20 --The man who experienced deliverance and inner healing through Jesus is sent as a witness.

18   As Jesus was getting into the boat, the man who had been demon-possessed begged to go with him.
19   Jesus did not let him, but said, "Go home to your family and tell them how much the Lord has done for you, and how he has had mercy on you. "
20   So the man went away and began to tell in the Decapolis how much Jesus had done for him. And all the people were amazed.
(Mark 5:18-20, NIV)

B. 2 CORINTHIANS 5:17-20 -We have been reconciled to God in order that we may become ambassadors of reconciliation.

17 Therefore, if anyone is in Christ, he is a new creation; the old has gone, the new has come!
18 All this is from God, who reconciled us to himself through Christ and gave us the ministry of reconciliation:

19 that God was reconciling the world to himself in Christ, not counting men's sins against them. And he has committed to us the message of reconciliation.
20 We are therefore Christ's ambassadors, as though God were making his appeal through us. We implore you on Christ's behalf: Be reconciled to God. (2 Corinthians 5:17-20, NIV)

C. We are to engage in healing ministry so that people may be:

o brought to salvation in Jesus Christ,

o empowered by the Holy Spirit,

o discipled into maturity

o and sent out as witnesses.

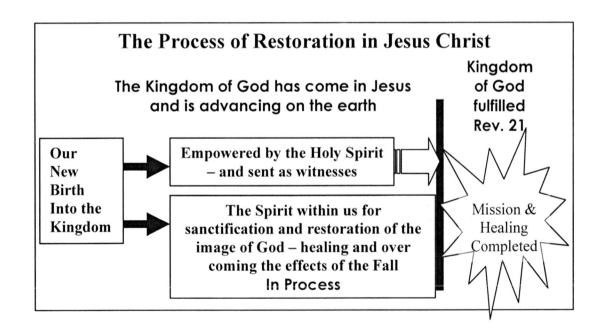

The Process of Restoration in Jesus Christ

The Kingdom of God has come in Jesus and is advancing on the earth

Kingdom of God fulfilled Rev. 21

Our New Birth Into the Kingdom

Empowered by the Holy Spirit – and sent as witnesses

The Spirit within us for sanctification and restoration of the image of God – healing and over coming the effects of the Fall In Process

Mission & Healing Completed

PART II

**Biblical and Theological
Foundations for Healing Ministry**

By Bob Whitaker

The Dunamis Project
Presbyterian-Reformed Ministries International

This section written by Bob Whitaker was the introduction to the original *Dunamis Project* manual on healing. I have moved it to become chapter 2 following the first chapter that lays out the "Creation – Fall – Redemption Framework as the context in which Jesus' healing ministry takes place. There is some duplication of material in these two chapters. Nevertheless this chapter further develops the Creation – Fall – Redemption framework for understanding Jesus' healing ministry.

I. Healing in the Old Testament

God is revealed in the Old Testament as the merciful healer whose purpose is to make all people whole through a right relationship with Him.

1. Genesis 1:27-28 states that God made our first ancestors in His image; this implies that humankind was made to be whole in every way from the beginning.

2. Genesis 1:31 asserts the goodness of what God made; the rest of the Hebrew scriptures clearly state that the body, as well as, the human spirit is good-the whole being is treasured because God made it. Dualism does not exist. (In the Old Testament God's redemptive purpose is directed toward the whole community rather than just to souls.)

3. Genesis 3 teaches that the tempter and sin spoiled man's harmonious relationship of wholeness and happiness with God, and the result was alienation, pain, torment and death which began as spiritual and then physical. In death's train came the inevitable manifestations of disease, disordered emotions, weakened will, and distorted perceptions. As a result of being out of harmony with God, the true center and source of all life, everything was thrown into chaos. (Dis-ease literally means to be out of harmony with God, self and others. The body, mind, and spirit interact improperly.)

 4. The Genesis 3 account of the fall of man is the first of many passages which teach that disease and death are God's punishment for sin, particularly the sin of disobedience. (See also Leviticus 26:14-16f.) Conversely, health is one of God's rewards for obedience to His revealed will. (See Deuteronomy 28 for a summary of this doctrine.) Consequently, the Hebrews believed that all disease was due to sin on the part of the individual or his ancestors. (This view was modified by Jesus.)

5. Through the call of Abraham and the formation of the covenant community, God sought to overcome sin and its consequences. As He led His people out of Egypt and through the wilderness, and as they sought but found only polluted water at Marah (Exodus 15:23f), He showed Moses how to heal the water and revealed Himself as "the Lord, your healer." (Interestingly, God showed Moses a natural or herbal remedy to purify the water rather than healing directly through Moses' prayer.)

 6. In giving the law, God gave specific rules for the prevention of the spread of disease and the maintenance of health among the Jews far in advance of anything known at the time in other nations. These included: the sanitary disposal of excrement (Deuteronomy 23:12-13), the

washing of body and clothes in running water after contact with disease or dead bodies
(Leviticus 14:50 and Numbers 19:11-22), the concern for pure water supply (2 Kings 2:19-22),
the isolation and quarantine of persons with infectious diseases (Leviticus 12:1-4), the dietary
regulations (See a Bible dictionary under "food."), the care about bodily discharges such as
sputum (Leviticus 15:8), sexual morality, etc. (See S. McMillen, *None of These Diseases*, 1963.)

7. Just as God gave an herbal remedy to Moses in answer to prayer, He also gave medicine and
physicians. The Talmud tells us that a physician was appointed to minister to the priests in the
Temple. 2 Kings 20 shows that after God told Isaiah to tell Hezekiah that He would heal him in
three days and add fifteen years to his life, Isaiah ministered healing to him by putting a cake of
figs on his boil!

The apocryphal Book of Ecclesiasticus shows the Jewish attitude towards doctors:

> *Honor a physician with the Honor due until him for the uses which ye may have of him:
> for the Lord hath created him. For of the most High cometh healing... The Lord hath
> created medicines out of the earth; and he that is wise will not abhor them... With such
> doth he heal (men), and taketh away their pains... My Son, in thy sickness be not
> negligent; but pray unto the Lord, and he will make thee whole. Leave off from sin, and
> order thine hands aright, and cleanse thy heart from all wickedness... Then give place to
> the physician, for the Lord hath created him: let him not go from thee, for thou hast need
> of him. There is a time when in their hands there is good success. For they shall also
> pray unto the Lord, that he would prosper that, which they give for ease and remedy to
> prolong life."* (Ecclesiastes 38:1-15, A.S.V.)

2 Chronicles 16:11-13 indicates, however, that we are to seek the Lord first of all, rather than to
rely primarily upon physicians.

8. The teaching that God sends sickness to those who are disobedient to His laws (Deuteronomy
32:39) is challenged in the book of Job. What is intimated in Genesis 3 is made explicit. God is
not directly the sender of sickness; Satan caused Job to be sick. Furthermore, Job was righteous
according to the law, but nevertheless suffered, and God allowed it for Job's purification. (Here
the teaching of the New Testament concerning suffering is anticipated.)

9. The Old Testament looks forward to a Messiah who would not only save from sin, but also
from disease. Isaiah 35:5-6, 53:4-5, 61:1 and Malachi 4:2 show that the Messiah will be a
healer.

10. The main prescriptions for health in the Old Testament is basically trust and obey.
Marvelous passages in this vein include: Deuteronomy 28, II Kings 5:1-14, Psalm 107:17-20,
and Proverbs 4:20-22.

11. Numbers 12:10-15 and Ecclesiastes 3 provide an important insight for healing ministry:
Often a timing is involved; a person may not be ready to be healed until certain events, such as
new insights on repentance or obedience transpire.

II. Jesus' Ministry of Healing

A. Salvation and Healing

The name Jesus literally means, "Jehovah is salvation." In the New Testament the term for "save" occurs over one hundred times. There are fifty-four references in the Gospels. The term save can be translated either, "to save," "to make whole," or "to heal." Less than one-third of the references to salvation refer to the making whole of bodies, minds, and emotions. They show that Jesus was typically Hebrew--His saving activity included healing the whole person. The majority of the New Testament references deal with salvation as deliverance from sin and death (Romans 1:16, Matthew 1:21, John 3:16-17). This shows that while Jesus came to make us well, in every sense of the word, His priority was to save us from sin and reconcile us to God eternally.

B. God's Will Revealed in Christ

When wrestling over God's will for the sick and whether to pray, *"If thy will be done,"* simply look at Jesus. He is the image of the invisible God; He shows us what God is like, and He perfectly does the will of God. By word and deed He shows that God's will is to heal the sick. If we suppose that God intends for us to be sick, then Jesus is in opposition to God because He goes about eradicating sickness. One-half of the content of the synoptic Gospels, up until the last week of Jesus' earthly life, is about healing. Twenty-six individuals are reported to be healed by Jesus and over ten times we are told of group or mass healings. (There are only four stories of moral or ethical transformations reported.) In five places in the Gospels He gives specific instructions to His disciples that they are to heal in His name and makes impressive promises about their ability and equipment to do so.

Consider the following observations from the Gospels:

a. Every sick person who sought healing from Jesus received it, and He healed physical, mental and emotional diseases of all types (See Matthew 15:30-31, Mark 7:31-37).

b. When parents sought healing for their children or when others brought the sick to Jesus, the children or the sick were healed.

c. Even when ministering to crowds, He usually healed **all** of the sick, *"every disease and infirmity,"* or *"as many as touched Him."* The least that is said about His ministry to the crowds was that *"many"* were healed. (Luke 7:21 and Mark 3:10)

d. In a few cases He spontaneously found and healed someone who did not seek healing from Him, like Peter's mother-in-law. (See also John 5:2.)

e. Jesus did not discourage the health seekers. He did test the faith and purpose of the Canaanite woman (Matthew 15:21f) and the nobleman from Capernaum (John 4:47f), but

He never said, "you're supposed to suffer sickness," "it's good for you to bear it" or "it's not God's will for you to be healed." Nor did He tell them that they were being punished by God. He did not build barriers of "confess first," or, "promise to be good," but rather He encouraged them to believe and respond in faith. (Mark 5:35, 9:14f)

f. Jesus normally healed in response to sincere faith. The faith may have been in the sick person, or in friends and relatives, or in the community,[1] and/or in some or all of the above. Faith is usually a crucial element. He praised exemplary faith (the Centurion Matthew 8:5, the Syrophoenician woman Mark 7:24). He encouraged people to believe (Mark 5:36, Mark 9:14f), and He stated that healing would be, "according to our faith" (Matthew 9:29), and credits some healings to faith, for example *"Your faith has made you well"* (Mark 5:34).

When His disciples failed to heal the epileptic boy, Jesus rebuked their lack of faith. He went on to say that if they had just a little faith they could move mountains. (Matthew 17:14f)

When Jesus failed to heal more than a few people in Nazareth, He did not blame it on God's will, but rather on the people's lack of faith! (Mark 6:5)

g. Relevant to the Old Testament emphasis on obedience to God's commands is the way Jesus normally healed through a word of command. In **six** cases the people were healed as they obeyed in faith what Jesus told them to do. (Mark 2:9, the paralytic; Mark 3:1, man with a withered hand; Luke 17:11, ten lepers; John 4:46, nobleman's son; John 5:2, impotent man; John 9:1, man born blind.)

h. Healing people was so important to Jesus that on several occasions He healed on the Sabbath in the synagogues, even though by so doing He infuriated the authorities who regarded healing as a breaking of the Sabbath laws against work. He could have postponed meeting those needs until the next day, but He saw it as a service more important than watering one's animals; it was a "doing good," and a way to show the worth of a person. (Matthew 12:9f)

---

[1] Perhaps we have failed to see how important it is for friends or relatives of the community to have faith for healing. In the Gospels, nine of Jesus' healings are accomplished through the faith of such persons. (Mark 1:30, Mark 2 the paralytic, Mark 5:22 Jairus' daughter, Mark 7:24 daughter of Syrophoenician woman, Mark 7:32 deaf and dumb man, Mark 8:22 blind man of Bethsaida, Mark 9:14 father of the epileptic boy, Matthew 15:30 crowds bringing their sick, John 4:46 son of Capernaum official.)

Luke 9: 23-24

III. Theological Issues

*✱ Daily - die to yourself &
your agenda!*

A. The Sources of Sickness

In the view of Jesus and the New Testament, we do not need to accept sickness. Rather it is something bad, an enemy to overcome. In the Gospel records, Jesus never attributed sickness to God, although the Old Testament emphasis on sickness being sent by God as a punishment for sin is present in Acts 5:1-11, 12:23, 13:8f, and Revelation 2:21.

1. The devil

It is significant that the first encounter of Jesus with a hurting person, according to Mark, was with a man with an unclean spirit in the synagogue at Capernaum. He is not called a sick person, and the cure is not called a healing. We might call it a healing even though the Gospel writers always distinguish between healings and the casting out of evil spirits. But this first encounter is the first Gospel answer about the source of illness. Jesus was well-known as a powerful exorcist. He viewed the deliverance of demoniacs as a sign of the Kingdom of God coming in (Luke 11:20 and Matthew 12:28). The healing mission of the seventy was viewed by Jesus as the downfall of Satan (Luke 10:17-18). The healing of the woman bent over for eighteen years was described as a victory over Satan who was the basic cause of her misery (Luke 13:16).

2. Sin

The second (or third after the healing of the leper) major healing recorded by Mark is of the paralytic carried by four men. (Mark 2:1-12) It is clearly intimated that Jesus perceived the root of the man's paralysis to be sin and guilt. Therefore Jesus first pronounced him forgiven of his sins, and then He raised him up from his bed. Similarly, in John 5, Jesus raised up a paralyzed man at the pool of Bethsaida. Afterward, the source of his sickness is revealed when Jesus says to him, *"See, you are well! Sin no more, that nothing worse befall you."* (John 5:14)

The healing ministry went hand in hand with the preaching ministry. The preaching was a declaration of the Kingdom of God breaking in and was followed by a call to repentance. While some healings may have set the stage for preaching and repentance, it seems likely that many healings followed repentance for sin, as in James 5:16.

3. A Fallen Universe

Much sickness and misery is not caused by personal sin. In Luke 13:1-5, Jesus said that the Galileans killed by Pilate and the eighteen upon whom the tower of Siloam fell were not worse sinners than others. But He goes on to exhort, *"Unless you repent you will all likewise perish."* We conclude from this that calamity of any kind is not necessarily the result of outstanding sin. This conclusion is confirmed by Jesus in John 9:1-3, where Jesus stated that the man born blind was not blind because of his sin or his parents' sin, *"But that the works of God might be made manifest in him."*

There is a mystery here. We can't presume to know all that Jesus is suggesting, but at least we can conclude that God allows sickness to happen because it is an opportunity to show His healing mercy and love to us. Jesus never reflected on the fall and its results. But it is legitimate to remember that God allowed our first parents to sin, and planned or permitted consequences to follow in terms of alienation, pain, sickness, and death in order that He might show His redemptive love.

Jesus realizes that all are caught in a web of evil that we did not weave. We are victims but it is our responsibility to choose life. *"When He saw the crowds, he had compassion for them, because they were harassed and helpless, like sheep without a shepherd"* (Matthew 9:36). He sees that we are like fish caught in a net (Luke 5:1-10, Matthew 13:47-50). He also sees us as enslaved captives, blinded, oppressed and unable to set ourselves free (Luke 4:18). Far more than He exhorts people to repent, He acts to cut the cords, break the chains, and open prison doors. This all implies that much of human sickness is caused by an Egyptian-like enslavement and a Babylonian-like captivity that is the consequence of the fall.

4. Suffering and Sickness

Jesus does not suggest that we accept sickness as the will of God. Rather, He calls us to accept the suffering of self-denial and cross-bearing and to lose ourselves in sacrificial service for others and the Gospel.

Our Calvinistic heritage leads us to interpret all of the New Testament calls to suffering and trials as calls to accept sickness stoically as willed by God for our discipline. (By some strange twist of reason, it is all right to alleviate the sickness through medicine but not all right to seek healing through prayer or spiritual healers!)

But Jesus saw that there was enough suffering willed by God without adding the additional burden of sickness, which is the curse of a fallen world where an enemy steals, kills and destroys. As our substitute, Jesus bore our sin and sickness for us, and gave us the cross of bearing patiently the hurts and troubles of others, overcoming evil with good. To live and work lovingly with difficult persons, to be faithful in an unsatisfying covenant relationship, to give sacrificially, to witness heroically, to do good to those who hurt us, to forgive the despicable deed -- this is the call of suffering love which we are to accept. Meanwhile, we are not to passively accept sickness, but we are invited to ask and to receive whatever we need in His name (remembering that He is the great Healer) that our joy may be full (John 15:7, 16:23-24).

5. St. Paul's understanding of suffering

St. Paul is a good example of this attitude toward suffering. He cheerfully bore all manner of suffering and adversity as a missionary for the sake of Christ (See 2 Corinthians 6:3-10, 11:23-

33). But when he faced either demonic attack or sickness, he did not passively accept it as the will of God. In the case of 2 Corinthians 12:7-8, three times he earnestly asked that it be taken from him. Apparently, he sought healing or deliverance until he was assured that God would give him grace to rise above the problem rather than to remove it from him.

Whenever we talk about God's will concerning healing, someone will raise the issue of Paul's thorn recorded in II Corinthians 12:1-10. No other passage is more used to blunt the healing mandate than this passage. Therefore we need to look at it carefully.

"And to keep me from being too elated by the abundance of revelations, a thorn was given me in the flesh, a messenger of Satan, to harass me, to keep me from being too elated."
(II Cor. 12:7)

> 1. Thorn - this word is used three previous times in the Old Testament. It is used in the plural each time:

> "But if you do not drive out the inhabitants of the land from before you, then those of them whom you let remain shall be as pricks in your eyes and **thorns in your sides**, and they shall trouble you in the land where you dwell." (Numbers 33:55)

> "For if you turn back, and join the remnant of these nations left here among you, and make marriages with them...know assuredly that the Lord your God will not continue to drive out these nations before you; but they shall be a snare and a trip for you, a scourge on your sides, and **thorns in your eyes**, till you perish..." (Joshua 23:12-13)

> "You shall make no covenant with the inhabitants of this land; you shall break down their altars. But you have not obeyed...So now I say I will not drive them out before you; but they shall become **thorns in your sides**, and the gods shall be a snare." (Judges 2:2-4)

> Paul was a Hebrew of the Hebrews; he knew what a thorn was - it was an enemy - a personal enemy of the faith. It is not surprising therefore that the early commentators, including the most distinguished ones (St. John Chrysostom and St. Augustine) believed that the thorn was a person opposed to Paul's faith. Who tormented him at every turn, who sought to discredit his apostolate, who undermined his message, and who did he have to fight more than the legalistic Judaizers? Perhaps there was one who dogged his steps everywhere.

> 2. In the flesh - it has been assumed by some in modern times that this refers to the literal body of flesh. That is a possibility, and if so it could mean, in the context, that Paul is referring to a demon or evil spirit who was afflicting him with some physical malady. But the phrase is also characteristically used by Paul, especially in Romans, to refer to our weak human nature so prone to sin. If this is the case he could be saying, "This Judaizer really gets to me, and triggers my worst self."

> 3. Messenger of Satan - The word messenger is another translation for angel. It certainly sounds personal; it doesn't sound like a disease or affliction. The word "angel" is used 188 times in the New Testament; whether they are good or evil angels, the word is never used in connection with the bringing of sickness except possibly in Acts 12:32 where an angel of God smote Herod. Most interesting is that whatever it is, an enemy or disease, it is not from God. Paul does not regard it or him as something to welcome or accept easily. Some have thought that the devil was attacking him with evil thoughts, or terrible temptations.

But the immediate context in chapter eleven that provoked him to defend his apostleship was that he was complaining about false apostles who were enslaving the Corinthians (11:13 & 20), and he returns to this theme in 12:11. The messenger of Satan could be the ring-leader or a particularly obnoxious false apostle who was dragging the Corinthians back to the law, even as he sought to do in other churches founded by Paul.

4. <u>To harass me</u> - literally "to keep punching me" (with the fist) This word is used to describe the beating that the Sanhedrists gave Jesus after they condemned Him, "they spat in His face and <u>struck</u> Him." (Mt. 26:67) This doesn't sound like a disease; it sounds like the attack of an enemy -- it could be taken literally or figuratively.

5. <u>"to keep me from being too elated"</u> - Paul opens and closes verse seven with this explanation for the thorn. Unquestionably illness can keep us humble. Certainly illness can always serve a good purpose by so doing. But constant attacks from an opponent who throws mud on our person and our doctrine can even more serve the purpose of keeping us humble.

6. "Three times I besought the Lord about this, that it <u>should leave me</u>." The "this" and "it" refer back to the subject "thorn," which is as it should be, because "messenger" is only the elucidating opposition in vs. 7. The word here can be translated, "go away," "keep away" or "depart." That sounds like strange language for a healing of a disease, but very appropriate for a human or demonic enemy.

7. "but he said to me, `<u>My grace is sufficient for you, for my power is made perfect in weakness.</u>'" (II Cor. 12:9)
In verse nine Paul refers back to this thorn or problem as "weakness," and "weaknesses." The Greek noun means literally "without strength." Paul uses it 13 times; he also uses the adjective form of the word 13 times; Paul never translated it "sickness." (However, the word is used sometimes in the Gospels with the meaning of sickness, and the verb form is used three times out of seventeen by Paul to refer to sickness.) (Philippians 2:26 & 27, II Timothy 4:20)

In I Corinthians 11:30 Paul uses the adjective "weak" (referred to above) and uses another word, "arrostos" for "sick." Thus, in II Cor. 12 if he wanted to indicate that he suffered from some sickness he could have used another word instead of "weakness." I believe he was saying, "I am very vulnerable to being constantly opposed and contradicted; as you know I have a history of being very angry with anyone who disagrees with my faith; I was once a persecutor of the church; since my conversion I've had to fight all comers - pagans, occultists, Jews, Gentiles, heretics, but most of all those dogs of the circumcision party who keep trying to seduce my converts. One of them has been a constant thorn in my side; he's a messenger of Satan destroying the work of grace. Every time he attacks my churches I feel like I'm being punched in the face. I've asked God to take him out of my hair, to do away with him, but He says, don't let it get you down, keep your eyes on Me, My grace is sufficient for you."

While the context, words used, and manner of expression, plus the history of interpretation (before the modern era), all weigh heavily against the theory that the thorn was an illness, there is an outside chance that it was. If it was, God's grace must have been enormously sufficient. One need only read Acts 9:30 to the end, then I Cor. 4:10-13, II Cor. 4:7-18, 6:3-10, 11:23-29. It doesn't sound like a sick man in ministry. It sounds like the power of God at work incredibly through a human being made whole in Christ!

Luke 10:13-15

I personally agree with Bob's interpretation. However many other scholars have interpreted the "thorn in the flesh" as some recurring physical aliment. Here is the evidence offered to support this point of view.

THORN IN THE FLESH

> (thorn) (skolops te sarki): Paul thus characterizes some bodily ailment which afflicted him and impaired his usefulness <2 Cor 12:7>. The data are insufficient to enable us to ascertain its real nature, and all the speculations on the point are therefore inconclusive. All that we are told is that it was a messenger of Satan; that thereby he was beaten as with a fist, which might be figurative or actual; that it rendered his bodily presence unattractive. It appears that the infirmity recurred, for thrice he sought deliverance; but, by the help of God, he was able to glory in it. Sir W. Ramsay sees in it some form of recurring malarial fever. It was something that disabled him <Gal 4:12-15>; hence, Farrar supposes that it was ophthalmia, from the reference to his eyes, from his inability to recognize the high priest <Acts 23:5>, from his employing amanuenses to write his epistles, and his writing the Galatian letter in large characters with his own hand <Gal 6:11>. Krenkel has at great length argued that it was
> (from International Standard Bible Encyclopaedia, Electronic Database Copyright (C) 1996 by Biblesoft)

6. Priority of the Eternal Relationship

As indicated, soundness of body and mind was not the first priority in Jesus' ministry on earth. He came to preach the reign of God, to call people to repentance and to bring them to a right relationship with God and one another through His redemptive death and resurrection. There were times when He left scenes of healing without healing all those in need in order that He might resume His itinerate preaching ministry in preparation for His cross. (Luke 4:40-44) In John 5 there was a multitude of invalids at the pool of Bethesda waiting, we assume, to be healed. Jesus ministered only to one.

His parables, which portray the essence of His message, have nothing to say about healing. They deal with the ultimate issues of life and death, heaven and hell, righteousness, mercy and forgiveness. His overwhelming burden was to save us from guilt and condemnation, to teach us to love abundantly God and neighbor, and to prepare us for the life to come where there will not be pain, sorrow, or suffering.

Jesus clearly believed that the Kingdom of God was coming into the world through Him and that His healing ministry was evidence of it. But He also taught that the full realization of the Kingdom was in the future. He announced, *"The Kingdom of God is at hand"* (Mark 1:15), *"The Kingdom of God is in the midst of you"* (Luke 17:21). But He also taught us to pray for the coming of the Kingdom and taught about His own coming in glory as the commencement of its fulfillment. There is a direct parallel: the Kingdom has come, but it has not come fully; we are saved through faith in Christ, but we are being saved (sanctification), and hope to be saved fully when the Kingdom comes fully. Therefore, we can conclude that healing through Christ is a present reality to be received and enjoyed, but no one is perfectly healed in this life anymore than anyone arrives at sinless perfection, and we must all "wait for adoption as sons, the (final and perfect) redemption of our bodies." (Romans 8:23)

It is important as we seek to be healed and to be instruments of healing that we keep this reality in mind: we have, and we have not yet; we are citizens of a healing Kingdom, but we look forward for the radiance of that Kingdom to engulf us fully. *Glory by the Father, Jesus Lord!*

B. Motive for Healing

What was Jesus' motive for healing in the Gospels? One explanation that was common in the church of my boyhood was that Jesus healed to prove that He was the Messiah and/or that He was divine. Certainly His mighty works indicated a closeness to God and did fulfill the Messianic expectation, but they were not unique to Jesus--these works were also found in the prophets, especially Moses, Elijah, and Elisha, and they were repeated in the apostles. If He performed the works to prove divinity, why did He tell the healed ones not to publicize it? (Mark 1:45) If He wanted to prove His Messiahship to the Jews, why did He make an issue of healing on the Sabbath, an act which outraged the Jews and convinced them that He was not the Messiah because He had broken their understanding of obeying the command to rest on the Sabbath?

Another explanation for the healing ministry is that the healings were done as signs and object lessons to prove the spiritual message.

As already indicated, Jesus saw the deliverance of demoniacs and the healing of the sick as a sign and portent that the Kingdom of God was breaking in and that Satan and sin were being overcome. Clearly the healing of lepers points to the cleansing of the leprosy of sin through the redeeming Christ. John's gospel refers to the mighty works as signs and relates these works in such a way as to point to eternal theological truths implicit in their happening. But one has to sift the record exceedingly fine to find anything to indicate that Jesus' motive in healing was intentional dramatization of the message. The healings flowed out of who He was--the Savior, in the total meaning of the word. The actions, like the words, poured out of a heart that is God's heart.

Jesus' heart-motive is nowhere more revealed than the Sabbath day healing in the synagogue of a man with a withered hand (Mark 3:1f). The authorities did not care about healing the man; they were captives to their Sabbath rules. Jesus was angered and grieved by their hardness of heart; His heart, full of mercy, goodness, salvation, had to be expressed! Most of the healings were cases of a need to be met, and Jesus did the merciful and loving thing. In three cases the subjects appealed to His great mercy--the father of the epileptic boy, blind Bartimaeus, and the ten lepers. In five cases the healings are clearly motivated by compassion--the leper (Mark 1:42), the multitudes (Matthew 9:36, 14:14 and 15:30), and the widow of Nain's son (Luke 7:11).

Matthew indicates that after the healing of the man with a withered hand, crowds followed Jesus *"And he healed them all,"* and then told them not to speak about it. Matthew then states that this was to fulfill Isaiah 42:1-4 which is a depiction of incredible gentleness and sensitivity. There it is: gentleness, mercy, and compassion. Jesus healed because He is the merciful lover of hurting people. He is the incarnation of God's total love for the total person.

1. Obedience and Timing

His supreme love for the Father, as expressed through obedience, motivated Jesus, not merely His love of people. As a result, healing for some was not offered or it was postponed. Right after the healing of the paralyzed man at the pool of Bethesda (only one was chosen for ministry, out of many who were suffering) Jesus began to emphasize, *"The Son can do nothing of His own accord, but only what He sees the Father doing; for whatever He does, that the Son does likewise."* In many such statements He underscored His total reliance on the guidance and direction of the Father. This meant that He left scenes where people were seeking Him for healing in order to go and proclaim the Gospel in many towns before He died.

John 11:1-6

In the case of Lazarus (John 11) it meant that when He heard Lazarus was ill, **because** He loved him, He delayed going to heal him. He knew that God had a greater purpose in mind by allowing Lazarus to die and, manifesting His glory through Jesus, raising him from the dead.

How many times have we found that while God wills to heal us, the healing often tarries despite Herculean efforts? Is it not true, that for reasons best known to God and for His ultimate glory, many healings await the resurrection? Consider the martyrs.

By Christ's example we are taught that we are not called to pray for immediate healing for everyone. We are called to be sensitive to the voice of God. At times He cautions us to wait; at other times we may pray first for repentance or salvation from sin, reconciliation, restitution, or preparation for death. There are also times when the healing does not occur for a long time, perhaps because the reward to the person and the glory to God will be greater as a result of the added time.

Consider what this means for praying "in the name of Jesus." Jesus promised, *"If you ask anything in my name, I will do it."* (John 14:14 - See entire context of John 14-16.) The name sums up His character and spirit and all that He was and did. To truly pray in His name we must abide in Him and listen to Him (John 15:7), even as He was in union with His Father and constantly listening to Him. Surely this means to be guided concerning whom we pray for, when, and how.[2] It seems to me that the times when I didn't discern a healing it was because I was not in harmony with this truth.

I remember praying frantically to keep an older woman from dying, and I urged my congregation to join me in praying her well. Earlier I had assured her husband that God would heal her; I did not want to be wrong, and I did not want to disappoint him. Pride and fear clouded my ability to hear God. Inexperience was also a factor. I assured him of healing because he sincerely reported that after praying a long time, he had an experience of hearing the voice of God say, "I will heal her." This has occurred a number of times in my ministry. I have concluded that the people did hear from God, but He meant the ultimate healing of heaven. Often we are so fixated on this worldly healing that we do not hear what He is saying.

2. Disparity Between Jesus' Ministry and Ours

Jesus normally healed by word of command and, with one exception (Mark 3:22-26, the blind man of Bethsaida), He healed instantaneously. The same was true of the apostles. Why is it then that in the churches today most healings seem to happen more gradually? This will be discussed in detail later but for the moment consider Agnes Sanford's answer. Sanford, a great pioneer in modern healing ministry, believed that Christ's perfect relationship with the Father and His total reliance upon the power and wisdom of the Holy Spirit, made Jesus a perfect channel of God's healing. There was not any hindrance nor blocking in the instrument and conduit of healing, light, and love. However it is otherwise with us.

Though the power of God is great, it is constricted and impeded as it comes through us. It is similar to a huge surge of voltage trying to channel through an ordinary household wire. I would add that most of the great healers I have known and studied were simple, humble people who were disciplined and purified through much earthly poverty and suffering. Today, in South America, Africa, and Asia there are an increasing number of ministers whose ministry more closely approximates that of Jesus. Yet, most of us in the western world have been comparatively spoiled and pampered by life to the point that our ministries are less effective.

3. Reality of Demons

In the twentieth century in the western world, most who went to seminary were well exposed to the view that demons may have been a first century way of speaking about psychological complexes. According to this view, Jesus accommodated Himself to the primitive view about

---

[2] Since Jesus normally healed all who sought healing from Him, and since the scriptural norm is healing, I normally pray for healing of some kind for all who ask it. But at the same time I am mindful of the "checks" in my spirit when God is saying, "not yet," or "not this way," or "pray this way."

the devil and hosts of evil spirits in order to communicate with people in terms they understood. But He did not believe in such entities. In other words, His teaching about the demonic and the stories of His commanding evil spirits to depart from people need to be demythologized, or explained in psychological terms. It was further suggested that the church may have reported the deliverance ministry of Jesus in terms of their primitive worldview, but that He Himself did not speak and act in a manner that endorsed the reality of demons. Such ideas have been promoted by many modern theologians whose philosophy is closed to any good or evil realities which they have not experienced or which they cannot conceive of in their rationalistic and human-centered approach to reality.

My Own Belief I was heavily influenced by such thinking. It seemed to me positively unbelievable that evil was personified in a powerful evil personage called the devil or Satan. It seemed to be a fairy tale that he was once a great angel who rebelled against God and led a host of lesser angels into rebellion with him. And I felt embarrassed that the New Testament actually taught that demons were fallen angels (Matthew 25:41 and Romans 8:38), especially since I considered angels to be as real as tooth fairies. I was incredulous when I read that demons speak (Matthew 5:9 and 12), believe (James 2:19), exercise their wills (Luke 11:24), know about their future fate (Matthew 8:29), recognize Jesus as the Son of God (Mark 1:24), obey His commands (Mark 1:23f), and can even inhabit animals as well as humans (Luke 8:26-33).

Change of View My inability to believe in the demonic in New Testament terms was part of a larger problem--the inability to believe in the historicity of supernatural happenings in the Bible. However, all of this changed when I experienced an infilling of the Holy Spirit similar to that described in Acts 2. The supernatural power of God became very real and present. To my great surprise, the outpouring of the Holy Spirit was soon followed by a temptation experience in which the devil manifested himself in a way which convinced me of his reality in accordance with the biblical description. Other encounters caused me to be convinced. As Calvin said, "Scripture makes known that there are not one, not two, nor a few foes, but great armies, which wage war against us...frequent mention of Satan or the devil in the singular denotes the empire of wickedness opposed to the Kingdom of Righteousness." (*Institutes* I, 14, 13) In the thirty years since, I have spoken with hundreds of "liberal" ministers who, like me, had a change of view once they had a power encounter with the Holy Spirit.

Illiberal Education My liberal education was not so liberal. Not one professor seriously presented or defended the scriptural and classical view of the demonic which was consistently believed by all the great thinkers of the Church until this last century. Missionary stories of encounters with spiritism, witch doctors, or demon-possessed people were not investigated or discussed with any seriousness. Luther's throwing of an ink bottle at the devil was mentioned in such a way as to suggest that he was a very superstitious person. The classical treatises on demon-possession were not required reading. We never heard anything like the following from any of our theological role models: "Evil is not merely a lack of something, but an effective agent, a living, spiritual, being, perverted and perverting, a terrible reality...It is contrary to the teaching of the Bible and the Church to refuse to recognize the existence of such a reality...or to explain it as a pseudo-reality, a conceptual and fanciful personification of the unknown causes of our misfortunes..." (Pope Paul VI, 1972).

Lopsided Theological Education I am suggesting that our problem is, in large part, a one-sided theological education that needs to become conversant with the fathers of the Church, the history of missions, the worldview of the third world, and especially needs to be in dialogue with the best evangelists and healers in the fastest growing segment of Christianity -- the Pentecostal-Charismatic community.

Spiritual Anemia Further, our problem is a deficiency in spirituality, a superficiality in prayer and a lack of in-depth knowledge of the Holy Spirit.

Confused Thinking There is also a lack of clear thinking. Why would Jesus accommodate Himself to the first-century worldview about demons if He believed the theory to be false? He did not hesitate to challenge their false views about sin and sickness (John 9); He corrected their false view of defilement and uncleanliness (Mark 7); He corrected their superficial understanding of the law (Matthew 23); He rebuked Peter for seeking to turn Him away from the cross (Matthew 16:23). If He spoke the truth in such crucial matters, why would He hesitate to correct prevailing views of good and evil if He thought that they were wrong? The issue was and is fundamental and not simply speculative; humans are not solely responsible for their predicament in Jesus' view; they are also victims of Satan and his hosts and so need to be rescued from disabling oppression (See Luke 4). They are captives of a strong man fully armed who must be overcome before they can be delivered (Luke 11:21-23).

C. S. Lewis once said that if you find it hard to believe something, try believing the opposite, and Morton Kelsey said:

> "If evil has no reality, then either man's ills must come from the direct action of God or one must end in denying that God has power to act. Either God becomes a monstrous being, somewhat less moral than man...or else man finds himself in a meaningless world, with no real answer for his physical or spiritual sickness...In the long run there seems to be no alternative when people are unable to see the reality of evil."[3]

Isolation A possible reason for our disbelief about the demonic is that as an upper-middle class denomination we have isolated ourselves from the desperate masses so much that we have almost eliminated the chance of encountering a demon.

The Mystery of Evil The question about the reality of demons is part of the greater question of how a good God could allow evil to exist in His good creation and why He permitted it to gain such a terrible control and to crush innocent children. There is much we would like to know that we cannot now know, but we look forward in trust that what is now obscure will someday be clear when the Perfect has come. (1 Corinthians 13:10 and 12) Meanwhile, we have enough revelation in Scripture to be delivered from evil.

---

[3] Morton Kelsey, *Healing and Christianity* (Harper & Row, 1973) p.330.

Part of that revelation is that the evil one is a liar (John 8:44); he is extremely subtle and deceitful (Genesis 3:1-7) and is adept at making evil appear good and good appear evil (2 Corinthians 11:3). He is adept at disguising himself as an angel of light (2 Corinthians 11:14). Like a rat, he hides himself and makes us think he does not exist or at least that he is not around our church. Where the preaching and praying are anemic and the faith is eviscerated and bloodless, he lies low and breathes his lifeless soporific. But if revival comes, he cannot stand the climate; he must react vociferously.

He must destroy the new life without exposing himself and risking his own destruction. Thus he stirs up a commotion or sows seeds of division and destruction by dripping extra poison into jealous, ambitious, or proud hearts (James 3:13-18). He is such a master at hiding himself that we fall into fighting each other instead of fighting the instigator (Ephesians 6:12).

Only if the revival becomes strong in the Lord and in the strength of His might, only if the Spirit of wisdom, counsel, might and discernment is poured abundantly into our hearts do we begin to see more clearly through the darkness and perceive the rats hiding in our midst and see how to drive them out. Until then it is easy to disbelieve in demons, for their nature is to hide. A church that has prided itself on its intellectual knowledge and cultural wisdom is particularly vulnerable to being duped.

4. Faith and Healing

Isaiah 57

Faith in the healing ministry of Jesus normally plays an important role, sometimes crucial role, in many of the New Testament incidents. But it is not an absolute; some, then and now, are healed unexpectedly, sovereignly, and sometimes seemingly with little or no faith on the part of the one healed. (Of course we often find that a loved one or friend, for example, did have faith and was praying for healing.)

Other Factors There are other factors which are as important as faith, and which sometimes maybe even more so. 1 Corinthians 13:13 states, *"So faith, hope, love abide, these three; but the greatest of these is love."* Agape love is the greatest healing tonic in the universe. *"Love covers a multitude of sins"* (1 Peter 4:8), and one of those sins is a lack of faith. Specifically, forgiving love is often the key to healing. Anyone who has been active in healing ministry for long knows of cases of people who sought healing with great faith, but the healing did not come until they forgave a close relative or friend who had deeply hurt them. It is significant that when Jesus talked about faith to move mountains and emphasized what is often called the prayer of faith, He concluded the teaching on such faith by saying, *"And whenever you stand praying, forgive, if you have anything against any one; so that your father also who is in heaven may forgive you your trespasses."* (Mark 11:25) Further confirmation of the cruciality of forgiving is found in Jesus' teaching on the Lord's prayer, as in Matthew 6:9-15. James, in his fifth chapter, also emphasizes confession of sin *"in order that you may be healed"* (James 5:16).

The Prayer of Faith When Jesus and the apostles ministered to the sick, the healing usually took place through an authoritative command, *"Be opened"* (Mark 7:34), *"Be clean"* (Luke 5:13),

"Rise and walk" (Luke 7:23). Often the command was accompanied with touch. The word of command is called, "the prayer of faith." It is mentioned in James 5:15, *"and the prayer of faith will save (heal) the sick man, and the Lord will raise him up."* It is vividly demonstrated by Jesus when He says to the fig tree, *"May no one ever eat fruit from you again"* (Mark 11:14). The next day the tree was withered away to its roots (Mark 11:20). Jesus then used this as an object lesson on the prayer of faith. He began by saying, *"Have faith in God."* The Greek construction of that exhortation can just as well be translated, "Have the faith of God." The faith that dramatically changes the fig tree or moves mountains is a faith which comes from God Himself; it is God's faith, *"that does not doubt in his heart but believes that what he says will come to pass"* (Mark 11:23). It is the same supernatural faith that spoke the world into being and raised Lazarus from the grave.

Gift of Faith This faith is clearly a gift; we don't ordinarily have it. When we have this faith that comes from God, there is not any doubt in our hearts; we do not have to pump it up; we believe that what we say has already been given; we are sure that God has granted our request and the word of faith that flows from it (Mark 11:22-24). This is the gift of faith that Paul mentions in 1 Corinthians 12:9 and 13:2. It is more than the regular faith by which we are saved; it is mountain-moving or miracle-working faith.

We can pray for it. We can exercise it in faithful ministry, and I believe we can grow in it through faithful obedience in ministry, but it is a gift. We will find that we cannot make it happen when, where, and how it pleases us. There will be people we desperately want to see healed, perhaps precious loved ones, but we are not able to pray the prayer of faith with power. There will be other times when it does not make a difference subjectively whether we do or do not. The Spirit will move upon us powerfully, and we will rebuke the sickness, or say, "In the name of Jesus, be healed," and it will happen before our eyes. Jesus never missed in His exercise of the prayer of faith because He was perfectly in tune with His Father. He was always listening and obeying, and wherever He went, He only did what the Father prompted, and only spoke as the Father spoke to His own heart. He was completely free of false motivation, such as wanting to impress people, of being insecure, of having to prove His authority, or of trying to get people to listen to Him. He was a perfectly yielded instrument of divine love and grace.

5. Atonement and Healing

In Matthew 8:14-17 the healing ministry of Jesus is said to be a fulfillment of Isaiah 53:4, *"He took our infirmities and bore our diseases."* In the RSV the words are translated, *"Surely he has borne our griefs and carried our sorrows,"* and in the margin the alternative readings are "sicknesses" and "pains." In keeping with the Hebrew understanding of a salvation for the whole person, Matthew certainly understood the prophecy as being inclusive and applicable to the healing ministry of Jesus. In 1 Peter 2:24 we read, *"He Himself bore our sins in His body on the tree, that we might die to sin and live to righteousness. By His wounds you have been healed."* The meaning of the atonement is related to dying to sin and living in righteousness. The word "healed" seems to be referring to the spiritual dimension of salvation. But for the early Hebrew Christians and all Gentile converts schooled by the apostles, the word healed would have been understood in the broadest and most inclusive way. The first Adam's sin led to a total death--

spiritual and physical; but the second Adam's act of righteousness led to acquittal and life for all who believe. Paul emphasizes the abundance of that life resulting in a victory over the world, the flesh, and the devil (Romans 5:12-21). When speaking of the Lord's Supper in 1 Corinthians 11, he confirms the healing benefit of the Lord's death by saying that those who fail to discern the body and blood of the Lord have suffered weakness, illness and death. When we study the fathers in the first three centuries, this view is further confirmed (See section on church history).

How did Jesus view His death? One significant clue to this question is found in John 3:14-17. Jesus likens His death to the lifting up of the serpent on the pole in the wilderness (Numbers 21:4-9). It is a healing image. The people were dying of snake bites, but if they looked to the bronze serpent on the pole, they were revived and lived. We, too, are dying of sin and sickness from the fiery serpent, but if we look to Jesus crucified for our wholeness, there is wonderful life and healing.

Therefore, it is thoroughly biblical to see in the atonement a provision for our healing; death and condemnation are vanquished and all of the consequences of the fall have been borne by Christ in His suffering. We have been forgiven and healed. To appropriate that healing may take a lifetime or may wait until heaven, but it is provided, no less than forgiveness in His death and resurrection.

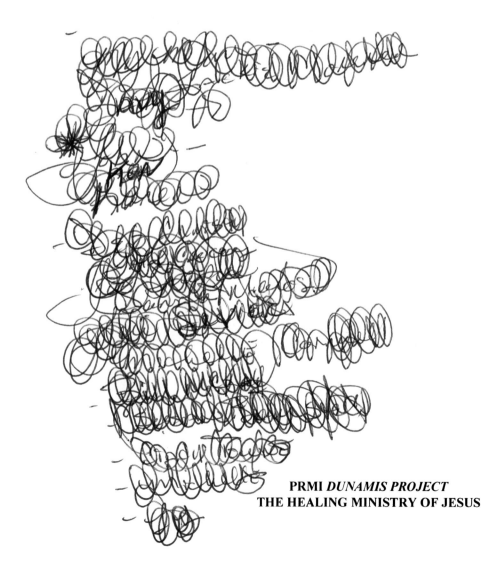

Teaching Charts

Part II

Biblical and Theological Foundations for Healing Ministry

The Dunamis Project
Presbyterian-Reformed Ministries International62

HEALING IN THE OLD TESTAMENT

1. In the beginning human beings were created whole, good, and in relationship with God.

   Genesis 1:27-28 - Made in the image of God

   Genesis 1:31 - Goodness

2. Sin brought death in all forms

   Genesis 3

3. God has made a covenant with His people - death and disease are God's punishment for disobedience, life and health are the rewards for obedience.

   Genesis 3

   Deuteronomy 28, 32:39

   (Challenged in the book of Job, and revised by Jesus)

4. The Law provides a basis for health.

- Sanitary disposal of excrement - Deut. 23:12-12

- Washing of body and clothes in running water after contact with disease or dead bodies - (Leviticus 14:50 and Numbers 19:11-22),

- Pure water supply - (2 Kings 2:19-22),

- The isolation and quarantine of persons with infectious diseases - (Leviticus 12:1-4),

- The dietary regulations

- The care about bodily discharges such as sputum -(Leviticus 15:8),

- Sexual morality - (Leviticus 20:10-21)

5. Hebrew culture honored the physician as given by God - but we are to seek God rather then rely upon physicians.

Ecclesiastics 38:1-15

2 Chronicles 16:11-13

6. The Old Testament looks forward to a Messiah who will save from sin and also disease. The Messiah will be a healer!

Isaiah 35:5-6, 53:4-5, 61:1

Malachi 4:2

Jesus Christ the Messiah Provides a Theological Framework for Healing

A. Salvation in Jesus Christ included the whole person and the whole cosmos

B. God's will is revealed in Jesus to be to heal the sick

C. Sources of sickness

    1. The devil

    2. Sin

    3. A fallen universe

D. Jesus' priority of the healing process

    Spiritual to cosmic - a process moving to completion

E. Healing flows from Jesus' nature and from the advancement of the Kingdom of God

F. Healing fits with God's timing and ultimate purposes

PART III

A Brief History of Healing Ministry
In the Church of Jesus Christ

By Bob Whitaker and Brad Long

The Dunamis Project
Presbyterian-Reformed Ministries International

I.   THE CHURCH'S EXPERIENCE WITH HEALING

A. THE APOSTOLIC PERIOD

1.   Jesus Commissioned His Disciples to Heal

Matthew 10 states, *"He called to Him His twelve disciples and gave them authority over unclean spirits, to cast them out, and to heal every disease and every infirmity...preach as you go saying, "The kingdom of heaven is at hand. Heal the sick, raise the dead, cleanse lepers, cast out demons. You received without pay, give without pay."* At first, this mission was to the Jews only.

In Mark 6:7f and Luke 9:2f, this commission to the twelve is again recorded without the limitation "to the Jews only."

In Luke 10 the apostles and 70 laymen were appointed to go two by two into every town where Jesus was about to come. They were told to heal the sick and to say to them, *"The Kingdom of God has come near you."* When the apostles and laymen returned to report amazing success, Jesus reminds them of the authority that He has given them; *"Behold, I have given you authority to tread upon serpents and scorpions, and over all the power of the enemy; and nothing shall hurt you."*

Before His crucifixion Jesus reminded His disciples: *"Truly, truly I say to you, he who believes in Me will also do the works that I do; and greater works than these will he do because I go to the Father. Whatever you ask in My name I will do it, that the Father may be glorified in the son."* (John. 14:12)

After His resurrection, Christ gave the disciples the Great Commission. *"All power in heaven and on earth is given unto Me. Go therefore and make disciples of all nations, baptizing them in the name of the Father and of the Son and of the Holy Spirit."* We tend, however, to overlook the next phrase, *"teaching them to observe **all that I have commanded you"*** (Matthew 28).

Mark's gospel is even more specific; it shows that Jesus went on to say, *"these signs will accompany those who believe: in My name...they will lay their hands on the sick; and they will recover"* (Mark 16).

The Church has always used the above passages as her authority to preach, teach and baptize. With equal authority they authorize the Church to continue Jesus' mission of healing.

2.   Jesus Empowered His Disciples to Heal

In the Gospels Jesus promised to empower the disciples to continue His ministry. In the opening chapter of Acts the risen Lord reminded them of the promise of being baptized with the Holy

Spirit. He told them to wait in Jerusalem for this power to bear witness to Him. Then, after His ascension, the disciples *"with one accord devoted themselves to prayer"* (Acts 1:14) to prepare for the coming of the Spirit in fullness. Ten days later came the mighty outpouring of the Spirit that gifted and equipped the whole Church for powerful witness and ministry (Acts 2).

Initially the witness of the Church came in terms of miraculous worship and praise that attracted a crowd. Then followed the Spirit-filled preaching of Peter that resulted in the conversion of 3,000 and the birthing of a transformed and transforming community of faith. In Acts 3 the healing ministry flowed forth through the disciples. There are nineteen examples of healing in Acts: ten individual and nine mentions of multiple healings. Most occurred through the apostles, but some occurred through laity. For example Ananias, Acts 9; Stephen, Acts 7; and Philip, Acts 8, were deacons and instruments of miracles and healing.[1]

Paul makes it clear that the power to heal and to perform miracles was given by God to the church to carry on the ministry of Jesus. In 1 Corinthians 12:18 and 28, as He discusses the gifts and ministries (including healing), he uses a word which means these gifts were "set," "fixed," "placed," "appointed," and "constituted" in the church by God. Thus they were not given just to launch the church, or until the New Testament was written in its present form, but were made a permanent part of the body of Christ.

B. THE POST-APOSTOLIC PERIOD

The power to heal was never withdrawn by God. We know from the writings of the Apostolic Fathers, who came after the apostles, that during the first three centuries the Church continued to manifest abundantly the healing grace of Christ. Irenaeus, one of the best of the early theologians, writing in the second half of the second century said, "Those who are in truth His disciples, receiving grace from Him, do in His name perform miracles... For some do certainly and truly drive out devils. So that those who have been cleansed from evil spirits frequently both believe and join themselves to the Church. Others have foreknowledge of things to come; they see visions, and utter prophetic expressions. Others still heal the sick by laying hands upon them, and they are made whole. Yes, moreover, the dead have been raised up and remained among us for many years. And what shall I more say? It is not possible to name the number of the gifts which the church, scattered throughout the whole world, has received from God, in the name of Jesus Christ...and which she exerts day by day for the benefit of the Gentiles." (*Against Heresies*, Book II, Chap. 32, Sec. 4)

This testimony is not an isolated one; the continuance of the healing ministry in the second and third centuries is amply attested to by Justin Martyr, Origen, Tertullian, Hippolytus, Novatian, and other lesser known writers. [2]

---

[1] The predominance of apostolic healings, rather than a description of lay ministry of healing, may be due to Luke's editorial purpose which may well have been to prove that Paul is equal in apostolic performance.

[2] See *Christian Healing* by Evelyn Frost for abundant references from the Ante-Nicene Fathers, or *Healing and Christianity* by Morton Kelsey, (Harper & Row, 1973.)

1.   Resurrection Life

The emphasis of the fathers' thinking on healing was paramount during the resurrection. It could be summed up in the words of Romans 8:11, *"If the Spirit of Him who raised Jesus from the dead dwells in you, He who raised Christ Jesus from the dead will give life to your mortal bodies also through His Spirit which dwells in you."* The fathers never cease to marvel and argue that since Christ is risen from the dead, we are living in a new creation; the power of the risen life has become victorious; and the signs of this victory are transformed lives, miracles of healing, and unbelievable courage and peace in the midst of persecution and martyrdom.[3]

2.   St. Augustine – A builder of a Christian worldview that was open to healing ministry [4]

Augustine laid the foundations for the older western worldview that was open to the power of God expressed in healing. He explored three ways of building a worldview, and discovered a philosophy based on Christ to be the best one. Before he arrived at the Christian view, he tried three others:

a) New Age (Manichaean) philosophy

As a youth and an intellectual, Augustine was fascinated with occult; Gnostic teachings that claimed to have been revealed by spirit guides from the spirit world. The knowledge revealed to Mani and Zoroaster, among others, seemed to have great power and wisdom, especially when compared to the Bible, which seemed to him simple-minded. But in the end Augustine tired of it:

> Among the Manichees our credulity was mocked by a promise of certain knowledge, and then so many most fabulous and absurd things were imposed to be believed, because they could not be demonstrated.[5]

Augustine began to question whether the claims of Mani were really true. This led him to ask, "How can we know anything to be true or false?"--the question of epistemology.

b) Science (Academic philosophy)

Augustine began to question everything that anyone believed about anything whatsoever. He became a skeptic, a habitual doubter:

> There half arose in me a thought that those philosophers whom they call 'Academics' were wiser than the rest, for they held, men ought to doubt everything.[6]...I wished to be made just as certain of things that I could

---

[3] Ibid.

[4] This section about St. Augustine has been added by Brad Long.

[5] Augustine, *Confessions*, translated by John Ryan (New York: Doubleday, 1960) VI.7. Ryan's translation has been used throughout.

[6] Augustine, VI 8.

not see, as I was certain that seven and three make ten.[7]

The search for certain knowledge led him to the same method for discovering truth that Rene Descartes later proposed: rational deduction and observation. Augustine eventually rejected this epistemology as too narrow. Life could not be lived under such a method, which rejects credible witnesses and all human and divine authority. The rational mind becomes the only credible witness.

3.   Platonism

Augustine started to explore the philosophy of Plato. Plato had discerned the nature of God – the supreme reason, the efficient cause of all things, eternal, unchangeable, all-knowing, all powerful, just, holy, wise and good. Clement of Alexandria said of Platonic philosophy that "it was to the Greeks what the law was to the Jews – a schoolmaster to bring them to Christ."

As Augustine began to apprehend God through the writings of Plato, his worldview began to admit biblical paradigms. Yet he soon realized that Platonic philosophy was incomplete. By itself, though it had some truth, it had no power.

It was over his battle with sexual lust that Augustine was driven from powerless philosophy to the reality of Jesus Christ. In Jesus Christ was found the power of God to change his life. He also found a revelation of truth beyond reason.

This worldview had real impact on Augustine's expectation and experience of God working in healing ministry.

Book 22, Chapter 8 of the City of God is entitled:

> OF MIRACLES WHICH WERE WROUGHT THAT THE WORLD
> MIGHT BELIEVE IN CHRIST, AND WHICH HAVE
> NOT CEASED SINCE THE WORLD BELIEVED

In this chapter there are a number of accounts of extraordinary healings that St. Augustine witnessed first hand. Here are two of the shorter ones recorded.

> The miracle which was wrought at Milan when I was there, and by which
> a blind man was restored to sight, could come to the knowledge of many;
> for not only is the city a large one, but also the emperor was there at the
> time, and the occurrence was witnessed by an immense concourse of
> people that had gathered to the bodies of the martyrs Protasius and
> Gervasius, which had long lain concealed and unknown, but were now
> made known to the bishop Ambrose in a dream, and discovered by him.
> By virtue of these remains the darkness of that blind man was scattered,
> and he saw the light of day. P. 1022

---

[7] Augustine, VI 6.

In the same city of Carthage lived Innocentia, a very devout woman of the highest rank in the state. She had cancer in one of her breasts, a disease which, as physicians say, is incurable. Ordinarily, therefore, they either amputate, and so separate from the body the member on which the disease has seized, or, that the patient's life may be prolonged a little, though death is inevitable even if somewhat delayed, they abandon all remedies, following, as they say, the advice of Hippocrates. This the lady we speak of had been advised to by a skillful physician, who was intimate with her family; and she betook herself to God alone by prayer. On the approach of Easter, she was instructed in a dream to wait for the first woman that came out from the baptistery after being baptized, and to ask her to make the sign of Christ upon her sore. She did so, and was immediately cured. The physician who had advised her to apply no remedy if she wished to live a little longer, when he had examined her after this, and found that she who, on his former examination, was afflicted with that disease was now perfectly cured, eagerly asked her what remedy she had used, anxious, as we may well believe, to discover the drug which should defeat the decision of Hippocrates. But when she told him what had happened, he is said to have replied, with religious politeness, though with a contemptuous tone, and an expression which made her fear he would utter some blasphemy against Christ, "I thought you would make some great discovery to me." She, shuddering at his indifference, quickly replied, "What great thing was it for Christ to heal a cancer, who raised one who had been four days dead?" Pp. 1025-1026.

It is clear that this chief architect of the Christian western worldview did not believe that healing miracles had ceased. To the contrary Augustine took with great seriousness the power of God in Jesus Christ to bring all forms of healing – spiritual, inner, relational and physical.

(For more on St. Augustine please see *The Collapse of the Brass Heaven: Rebuilding Our Worldview to Embrace the Power of God.* Chapter 6 by Zeb Bradford Long and Douglas McMurry, Chosen Books, 1994)

Church leaders continue to tell about healings in the fifth century and following. The healing power is especially prevalent among the monastics, the missionaries, the great saints, and the renewalists of every age. But it is generally conceded that the power of the first centuries died down considerably after the third century.

4.   The Reformers [8]

Most of us involved in the *Dunamis Project* are from the Presbyterian and Reformed stream of Christianity. We must take one quick look at John Calvin's attitude toward the healing ministry.

During the Reformation, Luther (an Augustinian monk) and Calvin quoted Augustine more

---

[8] This section was added by Brad Long.

frequently than anyone else but Jesus himself. They all accepted his basic understanding of the world in which we live. John Calvin at least does not however seem to have held Augustine's firm conviction and experience that miracles of healing have continued. To the contrary he seems to suggest that the gifts of healing have ceased.

> But that gift of healing, like the rest of the miracles, which the Lord willed to be brought forth for a time, has vanished away in order to make the new preaching of the gospel marvelous forever. Therefore, even if we grant to the full that anointing was a sacrament of those powers which were then administered by the hands of the apostles, it now has nothing to do with us, to whom the administering of such powers has not been committed.[9]

I suspect there are several reasons for Calvin's position that healing has ceased.

A. First was his own life experience. First he lost a child and then his wife died. We usually think of Calvin as a cold man with no feelings. But the loss of his wife whom he loved deeply was devastating. He wrote:

> Calvin thus writes to Viret on the death of his wife: "I repress, as much as I am able, the sorrow of my heart. With all the exertions of my friends, I effect less in assuaging my grief than I could wish; but I cannot express the consolations that I experience. You know the tenderness of my mind, or rather with what effeminacy I yield under trials; so that without the exercise of much moderation I could not have supported the pressure of my sorrow."[10]

Calvin himself was of a feeble disposition and died of some ailment of his stomach. His own experience was not of God's healing power but the grace to endure these terrible personal afflictions.

> How, it may be asked, did Calvin comfort himself under his wounded affections? He knew and felt that his light afflictions, which were but for a moment, were working out for him a far more abundant, even an eternal weight of glory. The following extracts from his letters prove that he relied on no comfort but that of his gracious Savior.
>
> "The Lord," he writes to Farel, "has spared us to survive Caurault. Let us be diligent to follow his example; and watchful to tread in the path of increasing light, till we shall have finished our course. Let no difficulties dismay us, or any weight of earthly sufferings impede our progress towards that rest, into which we trust he is received. Without the hope of this glory to cheer us in our way, we shall be overcome with difficulties, and driven to despair. But as the truth of the Lord remains firm and unshaken, so let us abide in the hope of our calling, until the hidden kingdom of God be made manifest." After the death of his wife, he writes to Farel: "I now suppress the sorrow of my heart, and give

---

[9] John Calvin, (Trans by F.L. Battles), *Institutes of the Christian Religion* (Philadelphia: Westminster, 1975) p. 1467. This is about the most negative text found in Calvin against the continuation of the gifts of the Holy Spirit. I believe he is speaking in reaction against the Anabaptists and the Catholics. There are many other references from Calvin that shall appear in these materials that support the continuation of the empowering work of the Holy Spirit.

[10] .Theodore Beza, *The Life of John Calvin*, p. 70.

myself no remission from my official duties. May the Lord Jesus strengthen me in this so great calamity, which would inevitably have overpowered me unless he had stretched forth his hand from heaven, whose office it is to raise the fallen, to strengthen the weak, and to refresh the weary."

The power of the Holy Spirit was seen in the work of transforming one's heart in the face of suffering.

> Viret, in his answer to Calvin on the death of his with, thus writes: — "I admire the influence of that divine Spirit which operates in you, and proves himself by his fruits worthy of the name of the true Comforter. Justly may I acknowledge the power of that Spirit in you, since you bear with so composed a mind those domestic misfortunes, which must intimately affect, with the greatest possible severity, your heart, that was always so readily involved in the calamities of others, and so accustomed to feel them, as if they were your own…" [11]

There is one reference however that suggests that some around Calvin did believe in the power of prayer for healing.

> In the following year, Calvin, in consequence of his imprudence, was attacked with a tertian fever when preaching and obliged, contrary to his inclination, to leave the pulpit. This circumstance gave rise to many false reports, which were so acceptable to the Roman Catholics, that a solemn procession was held at Noyon, his native city, and the canons returned public thanks to their idols for the death of our reformer.

There is no reference to how serious this illness was but it must have been cause for concern if it stirred up reports of Calvin's imminent demise as well as the prayer of God's people.

> But the prayers of the pious prevailed, and Calvin was so far from falling a victim to the disease, that he seemed, as it were, to be renewed in strength, and commenced an unusually long journey to Frankfort, where he had been invited for the purpose of terminating the disputes of the French Church. [12]

While we should avoid reading too much into this report. It does demonstrate that God answering the prayers for healing has not ceased but indeed continues.

B. Another reason for Calvin's lack of focus on healing ministry may have had a lot to do also with his own gifting and anointing. It was for preaching and teaching the word of God and for pastoral and administrative church leadership. Calvin's anointing was essentially "apostolic" in that he established the church on the basis of the Word of God. Restoring the priority of the Word of God was also the purpose of the Reformation as a whole. The Catholic Church had so focused on the miracles of the saints and the veneration of relics that there had been a loss of the power of the Word of God. The primary manifestation of the Holy Spirit's power during the

---

[11] Ibid. p. 71.
[12] Ibid. p. 40.

Reformation was in reestablishing the Scripture as the Word of God and justification through faith in Jesus Christ as the way of salvation. In this context it is not surprising that physical healing was not high on the Holy Spirit's agenda during this era of church history. This, however, does not mean that healing has ceased all together or that there may not be occasions in church history when it is the Holy Spirit's primary means of advancing the cause of Jesus Christ.

C. REASONS FOR DECLINE OF HEALING MINISTRY

- It must first be realized that the decline of healing ministry was part of a larger problem--the waning of vitality and spiritual power in the Church.

- Increasing heresy, and especially the Gnostic heresy, caused schism and controversy to increase in the Church-- this problem began in the first century and reached its height in the middle of the second.

1.   Gnostics

 The Gnostics were super-spiritual. They were negative about the created world and flesh. They could not accept a real incarnation and maintained that Jesus only seemed to die or suffer. They denied that the Savior died for our sins to win our redemption; they taught that He came to impart a secret knowledge that would liberate us from the evil world of matter and give us a clear consciousness of the ideal spiritual world. Since flesh was evil, they had no concern for healing it; they wanted to escape it. They denied the resurrection of the body because they believed it was an unspiritual concept. Most of them denied the gifts of the Spirit -- they were the perfect spiritual elite who felt they had arrived spiritually and did not need gifts.

They were typically Greek -- Hellenists in their distaste for the body and for an incarnation - atonement - resurrection spiritually. They infiltrated the young struggling churches (their beginnings are evident in Paul's letters where he combats them and especially in 1 John), and even though they were gradually weeded out, they left a taint, or inclination, to de-emphasize the healing of the body. The holistic Hebrew emphasis of salvation for the whole person was definitely weakened.

2.   Results of Controversy

Gnosticism was not the only controversy; there were several nasty ones. Later in the third century began the terrible Arian heresy that discredited the full divinity of Christ. Inevitably, the climate of arguing and battling over important beliefs reduced the atmosphere of brotherly love and peaceful union in Christ. That was not conducive to a healing ministry.

3.   Institutionalization

The process of institutionalization is always inevitable and necessary for a powerful and growing movement, but in reaction to heresy and schism, the Church tended to overreact in tightening control. Originally every Christian was a witness; many laypersons spontaneously healed and exorcised persons in the name of Jesus. Everyone was a minister. To combat abuses, the leaders firmed up the structure of bishops, elders, and deacons. Increasingly, ministries were concentrated only in the hands of officially appointed and ordained persons reporting to bishops. Councils were called; rules were drawn up, and the clergy were developed as a professional elite who could be trusted to do the ministry more effectively than the laity.

4.   Asceticism

This movement encouraged the view that it was good for the body to suffer. Strange as it may seem, originally the movement towards a life of solitude, self-denial, and prayer, which began in the late third century, was a charismatic renewal movement. The early monks, like Antony and Pachomius, were men of great spiritual gifts and famous for the miracles that happened through them. However, the self-denying emphasis became a severe mortification of the flesh that in effect became a hatred of the body and moved into self-torture and punishment. This resulted in many early deaths. The idea easily developed in the Church (with no little help from the Gnostic influence) that it was good for the body to suffer. An accompanying tragedy for the future of healing was that the idea grew that only very holy men and women, like the monks, were worthy to have spiritual gifts and to do miracles.[13]

5.   Growing Popularity and Worldliness

Until the reign of Constantine over the Roman Empire (A.D. 311-337), Christianity was periodically persecuted with more or less severity depending upon time and provincial leaders. Some of the persecutions were almost universal and terribly cruel. The last one under Diocletian (A.D. 303-311) was a final terrible effort to destroy the Church. In God's providence, the persecutions did the opposite--they purified the Church. They forced the nominal believers and hypocrites to stay away and caused the main body of Christians to depend on the Lord more than ever.

6.   A Shift in World View: moving from Plato to Aristotle

"There was a major shift in theological thinking, in which Plato's worldview was replaced by that of Aristotle; this resulted in a rationalistic outlook which had little place for any direct contact between God and man, hence little room for healing." This statement by Morton Kelsey in his book, *Healing and Christianity* (p.201) represents a major thesis that he developed in the 1960's. He shows how all of the great Christian thinkers before the barbarian and Arab invasions of the Roman Empire were very open to dreams, visions, and gifts of the Spirit and revelations of God. But by the time of Thomas Aquinas, the thinking had shifted and Thomas systematized this new worldview which was to dominate the Church until the 20th century.

With Thomas, God was to be known through reason based on past revelation rather than through

---

[13] Francis MacNutt, *Healing* (Ave Maria Press), pp. 64f.

direct experience. He felt there was no need for direct encounters between God and man as a usual occurrence, and that it was not desirable to expect them. Such things could happen only to very saintly people under extraordinary conditions.

Though the main body of Catholic believers, and even Protestants, shared deeply in Thomas' view, in the Catholic Church there continued a popular pursuit of miraculous healing centered on shrines of the saints and relics. These movements tended to be uncritical and superstitious. Separated from mature theological leadership, it became more and more exaggerated in practice and in its reports, and lost its credibility. It was this popular movement that the reformers probably reacted against. They made no attempt (with the exception of Luther in his later life) to restore the apostolic ministry of healing, and it seems never to have occurred to Calvin to call for the elders to anoint him and pray the prayer of faith during his many grievous illnesses.

(For a detailed account of the development of a western worldview that has excluded the power of God to work miracles of physical healing please see the book, *The Collapse of the Brass Heaven: Rebuilding Our Worldview to Embrace the Power of God*, by Zeb Bradford Long and Douglas McMurry, Chosen Books, 1994.)

D. THE MODERN CHURCH REDISCOVERS HEALING

1.   John Gaynor Banks - The Order of St. Luke

Early in the 20th century the Order of the Nazarene was started by an Episcopal priest to carry the ministry of healing to the churches. The Rev. John Gaynor Banks became the leader of this Order. He then founded the Interdenominational Order of St. Luke in 1946. By the early 60's there were 500 Episcopal churches with regular healing services listed in the Order of St. Luke magazine called *Sharing*. There were a sprinkling of Presbyterian ministers and services listed also. This order spread the good news of healing in a very balanced and disciplined way. One of the first Presbyterian ministers to hold regular healing services in his church was the Rev. James H. Brown at Upper Octorara Presbyterian Church near Parkesburg, PA. They began in 1952. Later in the 50's Brown became the first mainline denominational pastor to hold regular charismatic praise and prayer meetings in this church.

2.   Glenn Clark and the Camps Farthest Out

During the 30's Glenn Clark, a Presbyterian Sunday School teacher, began to hold prayer fellowship retreats that became known as Camps Farthest Out (CFO). The camps became nurturing centers for hungry Christians who wanted more of God. They grew and proliferated all over America, meeting in beautiful outdoor campgrounds, especially in the summer. Some of the camps specialized in healing beginning after World War II, and others became discovery and training experiences in the life of the Spirit. Some became empowering places where ministers like Jim Brown and Tommy Tyson (Methodist) prayed for persons to be baptized in the Spirit. They were, and are, launching sites for dynamic spiritual living that have fed the healing renewal.

3.　Agnes Sanford

A Presbyterian woman is the spiritual mother and grandmother of many leaders in the healing movement today. Agnes Sanford was the daughter of Presbyterian missionaries in China. Later she married an Episcopal clergyman, Edgar Sanford, and identified with his church. She wrote, lectured, and counseled extensively to promote the healing ministry of Christ. Because she was gifted intellectually and spiritually, she influenced many. In the 50's she began schools of pastoral care for ministers. They lasted for three to five days, were held at retreat centers, and were taught by teams of spiritually astute leaders along with Agnes. In these schools Agnes imparted the concepts and methods of spiritual renewal and healing ministry. An early Presbyterian leader in the Order of St. Luke and pastor of First Presbyterian Church, Rye, New York, worked closely with Agnes in the Schools of Pastoral Care. He was the beloved Dr. Joseph Bishop.

4.　Synod of Ohio Pioneers Healing Ministry in 1960

In the Presbyterian Church U.S.A., the Synod of Ohio pioneered in 1960 by having a Synod Committee guide the churches in the development of the healing ministry and annual healing conferences. The United Presbyterian Church of Canton led the way in the establishment of this ministry because of the prodding and direction of a prominent eye surgeon, Dr. Claire King. Dr. King's concern for a spiritual healing ministry was prompted by two experiences:

1.　He had scheduled cataract removal surgery for Frank Fluno of East Liverpool, Ohio. After prayer and the laying on of hands by the Rev. Rudolph Miller, Presbyterian Pastor at East Liverpool, the cataracts disappeared. Fluno's vision was 20-20 in one eye and 20-22 in the other. Dr. King cancelled the surgery.

2.　The other case involved an eight-year-old boy whose eye was so badly injured in an accident that the iris was protruding through a ragged cut in the cornea. Dr. King treated the eye preparatory to surgery the following week. When the mother brought the boy in, Dr. King observed in the manner of the boy and mother that something wonderful had happened. On Sunday they had been persuaded by friends to attend Kathryn Kuhlman's spiritual healing service in Youngstown, Ohio. The mother and son said the eye was healed. Dr. King examined it and found it to be in perfect condition with no sign of ever having been injured.

These two experiences convinced Dr. King that spiritual healing was more than a myth.

(Dr. King died in 1986 at age 93.)

5.　Pastor Don Bartow

No one followed through more on the concern of Dr. King than Pastor Don Bartow who retired from Westminster Presbyterian in Canton. Bartow held his first public healing service in 1959.

Since then he has held twice-a-year-healing conferences to impart the vision and implementation of the healing ministry in every church for thirty years. He also regularly held healing services at Westminster. In 1970 the Lord gave him a vision to encourage the establishment of healing services in every Presbyterian Church. He has published many books and tapes toward that end.[14]

6.   Presbyterian Charismatic Communion - (PRMI)

The charismatic renewal movement was, and is, the strongest impetus to the renewal of healing in all of the churches. In 1966 it surfaced as a fellowship of Spirit-filled ministers in the Presbyterian Church and grew rapidly in the late 60's and early 70's. In the mid-seventies some 10 percent of Presbyterian ministers in the United Presbyterian Church U.S.A. were members of the Presbyterian and Reformed Ministry. The emphasis on the empowerment and gifting of the Holy Spirit to renew the Church inevitably caused a strong desire to heal in Jesus' name. Other streams of renewal, together with PRMI, have caused a gradual shift in the thinking and ministry of Presbyterians. The new Directory for Worship has excellent provisions for a Service of Wholeness.

7.   Delores and Bill Winder

Since 1977 no one has done as much for healing ministry in the Presbyterian Churches in the U.S.A. and New Zealand as Bill and Delores Winder. Bill and Delores have traveled widely among the churches conducting healing missions. They have ministered in many small rural and mission churches where the people sometimes cannot cover their travel expenses. They are loving individuals who stay up late at night praying for the last person who needs their personal attention. They have brought about amazing changes in the experience and attitude of Presbyterian churches that used to be lukewarm toward the healing Lord.

"Their ministry has come about as the result of Delores' miracle healing in 1975. The story of this healing has been told briefly in Dr. Richard Cadorph's book, *The Miracles*, and by Delores herself in her book, *Jesus Set Me Free*. It has been called `one of the great miracles of the 20th century.' She was near the point of death after suffering for nineteen and one-half years from an incurable degeneration of the bones called pseudo-arthrosis.

"Delores had had several spinal fusions and, most importantly, two `percutaneous cordotomies,' which are procedures normally reserved for terminal patients, to relieve pain by the burning or deadening of spinal nerves. The procedure is irreversible and also results in the loss of control of bodily functions. She was in a full body cast for 15 years, and after the cordotomies retained feeling only in the upper left half of her body. She was not totally paralyzed and had some movement in her limbs and also continued to have some pain in the areas that had been numbed and severe pain in her left shoulder and back.

---

[14] See Appendix for Bartow's books and teaching seminars on the healing ministry.

"Near death, with every organ in her body losing its function, she was literally a drug addict, taking not only pain relievers and tranquilizers but medications for heart, kidneys, herniated esophagus, etc. She was a Christian and a 'good church member,' had been a Sunday School teacher and active in the church until her disease made that impossible, yet no one had ever told her that Jesus still heals today.

"She was fully prepared to die and, indeed, looked forward to death as a release from her pain. Her only concern was for her teenage adopted son and how he would manage emotionally after she was gone.

"Through the prayers and urging of a servant of God who heard of her condition and wouldn't take `no' for an answer, she finally agreed to go to hear Kathryn Kuhlman speak at a Methodist meeting. At the time, her only prayer was that God would give her something to help her son. In great pain and discomfort and extremely upset about being `conned' into attending such a meeting, all she wanted was a word from the Lord, and then to get out.

"With no faith in healing, an outright dislike for Ms. Kuhlman's `showmanship,' and the continuing desire just to die and get it over with, she was hardly a candidate for healing from the human point of view. Yet within the space of about 15 minutes, God reached down and totally healed her. Feeling was restored to her limbs, her back was straightened and restored, all internal problems were healed, pain was taken away, and she was delivered from drugs.

"This healing did not, however, make an `instant believer' out of her. She was shocked to find that now she had to live, instead of going to be with the Lord as she had dreamed of for so many years. It created tremendous tensions in a marriage that for years had been centered on her illness and eventual death. What was especially difficult to understand was the fact that many of her church friends, instead of rejoicing over her healing, turned their backs on her because they couldn't deal with it.

"When she subsequently received a prayer language and the word of knowledge, she was shunned further. God was out to enlist her in His service, but she fought Him for months. All she wanted to do was stay home and live a normal life, but the Lord and her husband Bill, more obedient than she at this point, continued to force her into testifying publicly, and gradually into the healing ministry.

"Finally, she gave up and submitted to God's plan, and today she and Bill travel almost constantly, sharing her testimony, teaching from the Word, and ministering healing, very often through the word of knowledge and accompanied by strong manifestations of the Holy Spirit. She is a careful teacher and either she or Bill always tries to explain what is happening, for the benefit of those who are as surprised at these manifestations as she initially had been. Unlike Ms. Kuhlman, she is not a `one woman show:' not only does her husband minister with her, but she encourages church elders and other lay people to help with the laying-on of hands, anointing with oil, and ministering to those who are receiving healing."

by Jackie Foulon, Burbank, CA

Teaching Charts

Part III

A Brief History of
Healing Ministry in the Church

The Dunamis Project
Presbyterian-Reformed Ministries International

A Brief History of the Healing Ministry in the Church

I. The Apostolic Period

    A. Jesus commissioned His disciples to heal (Matthew 10:1-8)

    B. Jesus empowered His disciples to heal (Acts 1:8)

    C. Resurrection life (Romans 8:11)

II. St. Augustine - A builder of a Christian worldview that was open to healing ministry

    A. God still works miracles just as He did in the Bible

    B. Many miracles are recorded in Book 22, Chapter 8 of the City of God.

III. Reasons for Decline of Healing Ministry after the Apostolic Age

A. Gnostics

B. Results of Controversy

C. Institutionalization

D. Asceticism

E. Growing Popularity and Worldliness

F. A Shift in World View: moving from Plato to Aristotle

IV. The Reformers

A. Martin Luther

B. John Calvin

V. The Modern Church Rediscovers Healing

A. John Gaynor Banks - The Order of St. Luke 1946

B. Glenn Clark and the Camps Farthest Out 1930's

C. Agnes Sanford 1950's

D. Synod of Ohio Pioneers Healing Ministry in 1960

E. Pastor Don Bartow 1959

F. Presbyterian Charismatic Communion - (PRMI) 1966

G. Delores and Bill Winder 1977

VI. The Healing Ministry of Jesus Christ Continues in the Church Today

PART IV

Our Equipping for Sharing in Jesus' Healing Ministry Today

By Bob Whitaker and Brad Long

The Dunamis Project
Presbyterian-Reformed Ministries International

I. Our Call To Share With Jesus In Healing Ministry (Brad Long)

From the beginning of Jesus' earthly ministry, He called others to join Him in ministry. First He sent out the twelve disciples, especially commissioning them to share with Him in healing ministry.

> *"And he called the twelve together and gave them power and authority over all demons and to cure diseases, and he sent them out to preach the kingdom of God and to heal."*
> (Luke 9:1-6) The disciples were sent out - given authority over all demons, to heal and to preach.

In Luke 10:1-20 (Matthew 9:37-38, 10:1-7-16) Jesus sent out the 70 to heal the sick and to proclaim the coming of the Kingdom, and they returned rejoicing that demons were cast out in His name.

While it is clear that this call is extended to the first disciples is it also extended to us? We are convinced that He also calls us to follow Him in power ministry. While it is true that some may have special areas of giftedness, this call to share with Jesus in healing ministry is extended to all those who are called into salvation. This is not just for the first disciples, nor for the great saints of the Church, but for " *... every one whom the Lord our God calls to him*" (Acts 2:39).

A. We Are Called and Equipped to Share in Jesus' Ministry Empowered by the Holy Spirit

1. Jesus promised in John 14:12-14 that those who believe will do the works that He did--in fact, greater works.

> *12   I tell you the truth, anyone who has faith in me will do what I have been doing. He will do even greater things than these, because I am going to the Father.*
> *13   And I will do whatever you ask in my name, so that the Son may bring glory to the Father.*
> *14   You may ask me for anything in my name, and I will do it. (NIV)*

2. Jesus received the Holy Spirit's power, not just for Himself but also to equip us for power ministry.

> *"He on whom you see the Spirit descend and remain, this is he who baptizes with the Holy Spirit."* (John 1:33)

B. The Promise of Jesus' Presence, Power and Authority Always Accompanies the Commissioning

When Jesus was resurrected and the Lord appeared to His disciples, He gave them a commission that applies also to us.

> *"Peace be with you. As the Father has sent me, even so I send you."* And when he had said this, he breathed on them, and said to them, `Receive the Holy Spirit. If you forgive the sins of any, they are forgiven; if you retain the sins of any, they are retained.'"* (John 20:21-23)

> *"You are witnesses of these things. And behold, I send the promise of my Father upon you; but stay in the city, until you are clothed with power from on high."* (Luke 24:48-49)

> *"All authority in heaven and on earth has been given to me. Go therefore and make disciples of all nations, baptizing them in the name of the Father and of the Son and of the Holy Spirit, teaching them to observe all that I have commanded you; and lo, I am with you always, to the close of the age."* (Matthew 28:18)

C. We Are Called to Follow Jesus into Empowered Ministry Doing the Works That He Did

Jesus came to fulfill the office of prophet, priest, and king. Each of these offices had a power dimension to it and was also related to healing ministry. Through the Holy Spirit upon us, we are commissioned to continue Jesus' work of prophet, priest, and king.

In addition to being in Christ and being empowered by the Holy Spirit, there are special ways that we may be prepared to share with Jesus in healing ministry.

II. Ways To Be Equipped For Healing Ministry Today (Bob Whitaker)

A. Investigate

Find a vital healing service or a lively prayer group where people are being touched. Attend, observe, participate, and interview some of those involved. Faith catches; go where it is. Healing of body, mind or spirit is especially available in a group which is really open to God and expects that He will draw near and affect noticeably those who ask.

B. Listen

By interviewing healers, leaders of healing services, or people who have been healed, your faith will be kindled to be healed and to be an instrument of healing. If living witnesses are not readily available, read magazines with testimonies or books or listen to tapes.[1]

C. Study

Attend Christian conferences on healing, or take courses on healing offered by churches or Christian groups. Let your questions drive you to seek creditable answers.

D. Cultivate Expectancy

In most historic denominations the level of faith is very tame. Very few expect God to do much and they are therefore seldom surprised. Something must burst open our horizons and give us a new vista of what can happen through faith. "*All things are possible to him who believes*" (Mark 9:23). The first three paragraphs above are designed to give us a faith lift, but they are tame. Some of us are in a rut of respectability and stained glass decorum. It would help to go to a Pentecostal revival on the other side of the tracks, or to a Benny Hinn meeting, or to take in the powerful preaching of Mario Murillo with signs following. Every Presbyterian could benefit from a week of John Wimber meetings or Vineyard services and then go to the prayer room and ask to be prayed over. Ask where the power of God in Christ is being manifested and go. As a young seeker I went to such things and was caused to realize that "*eye has not seen, ear has not heard the things which God has prepared for those who love Him.*" (1 Corinthians 2:9 paraphrased)

E. "Rekindle the Gift of God That is Within You"

"*Rekindle the gift of God that is within you...; for God did not give us a spirit of timidity, but a spirit of power and love and self-control*" (2 Timothy 1:6). The Holy Spirit indwells every believer, but the flame is often low. Turn to the Lord with humility and truth. Keep saying to Him, "I have not sought you with a whole heart; I have known you and followed you only in part; come and inhabit me fully with your Spirit; cause me to do your works boldly and wisely." Meditate and pray concerning the promises of Scripture regarding the enablement and enduement of the Holy Spirit. Dwell especially on the following: John 7:37-39, 14:12-14, 14:18-24, 15:1-11. Luke 10:1-9, 17-20, 11:5-13, 24:49. Acts 1:1-14, 2:1-47, 4, 8, 10, 19: 1-7. Galatians 3:1-5. Reread the Gospels focusing on the healing ministry of Jesus. Seek the Lord with all of your heart, mind, and strength until you have had a personal revival and a fresh anointing of His Spirit. If you are not getting anywhere, join fasting with Scripture and prayer until God breaks through in your life.

---

[1] See Appendix for lists of such materials.

F.   Conquer Fear

Because we are immobilized by fear, we need a power encounter with God where His love breaks through. We need to be flooded with something big enough to drown the fear. The thought, "What will they think if I step out of the usual role and dare to be like Jesus?" is ever present. The fear of criticism and censure must be overcome. More important than the affirmation of Presbyters and fellow pew-sitters is the exclamation of Peter, *"We must obey God rather than men."* A power encounter makes us awestruck with God--so much so that we fear Him more than any person (Matthew 10:28). If a power encounter is not enough, we need to seek out a person or team that ministers in inner healing and receive counseling and prayer until the root of fear is torn out.

G.   Know Yourself

If you are not in touch with your own feelings and are not aware of hurts that have been healed and are in the process of healing, you will not make an empathetic listener. If you have similar unhealed hurts as the person for whom you pray, you may over-identify with them. At the same time, you will be at your best mediating healing to someone who has the same hurts as those that have been healed in you.

You need to know how God works best through you and what your strongest gifts are so that you know when to speak forth and when to let God work through others. You learn these things by doing, and it is better first to learn them as an apprentice or listener and helper rather than as a leader.

H.   Keep Sacred an Unhurried Time with God Daily

1.   Take the Time

You cannot have power with God with a firecracker prayer life. The saints have long ago established the principle: the secret of a fruitful life is union with the Lord. (John 15)
You must take time to meditate on His written Word and to hear specifically what He is saying to you. You need to take time to respond in praise and thanksgiving and to express love to Him for His own sake. You will need to intercede faithfully for those to whom you minister and for all ministry occasions. I have a cordless power drill that enables me to quickly accomplish a lot on building projects. But the drill has to be plugged into a charger nightly if it is to operate with maximum efficiency. We are the same way; we must have an unhurried plug-in-time if we are to operate with maximum effectiveness.
Included to guide you with this is a powerful method of Scripture meditation, guidance on hearing the voice of the Lord, and a prayer pattern.

2.   A Transforming Method of Scripture Meditation

Scripture meditation is not new. It is based on the discipling methods of Ignatius Loyola, founder of the Jesuits. The principle: what captures the imagination captures and motivates you. This teaching is not New Age, but rather it comes from hundreds of years of Christian saints being spiritual. Visualization is not wrong; everyone fantasizes or visualizes if their imagination isn't dead. The issue is, "What does your imagination feed on?"

Take a passage daily from the Gospels, and read it carefully. Go over it until you have the details in mind. Try Mark 1:40-44. After you read it, shut your eyes. Picture the whole scene-- see Jesus coming down the dusty road with His disciples in their robes and sandals. Imagine your feelings; you've heard about Him and you need Him desperately. You have a loathsome disease, you're in rags and filthy, and you're so scared but so desperate you haltingly move toward Him, and then you drop down on your knees before Him. They're all looking at you, but you're too miserable and desperate to care.

Imagine yourself pouring out your hurt to Jesus. Say aloud, "Please Lord, if You will You can make me clean." Then see Jesus looking at you, picture Him with a look of tender compassion on His face, see Him reaching out to touch you, see His lips move, hear His voice say, "I will, be clean." Imagine healing light and virtue pouring into your whole being. Begin to thank Him for healing love. Express your devotion to Him.

Picturing the scriptural events will enable the Word to penetrate your heart with life-changing effect. It is much more effective than simply reading or studying. One wonderful aspect is that with certain passages you will find that what begins as active imagination becomes a vision experience in which the Lord breaks through and you commune with Him in Spirit and in truth. It is beautiful and transforming. Practice this discipline and you will find your mind constantly renewed and centered on Christ. (See Romans 12:1.) (See also chapter on scriptural basis for emotional healing.)

3.   Pray This Way - Matthew 6:9-13

The Lord's prayer is a pattern for daily relating to God in the most fulfilling way.

Note: **First we are taught to center on Him** instead of self. The first half of the prayer is about God. It makes sense doesn't it? If you want to be friends with someone, you start out by noticing him or her, appreciating them, expressing friendship and love, and then you unload your concerns.

Therefore: First we think about or **contemplate** who He is--whom we are relating to, i.e., The Healer. Next we **praise** Him and express appreciation and gratitude. A good way to do this is to sing psalms, hymns, and spiritual songs. Then we **petition** and **intercede** that He will come and reign in our lives, relationships, homes, churches, jobs, communities, and world as the healing Lord of love, truth and joy.

In the second part of our prayers we are taught to pray for our most **basic needs**, such as bread. Jesus taught us to be bold and specific. Many have never received healing because they have never seriously asked with faith for healing of the particular hurt.

In the Lord's Prayer, Jesus most emphasized forgiveness. We are to **confess** our sins, the most therapeutic and saving thing we can do. We are to **repent** of all resentment, anger and hate by forgiving everyone else. If we are thorough here, we will be amazingly whole, clear, unclogged channels for healing love to others.

Finally, we are to face the enormity of ever present evil, ("*When I want to do right, evil lies close at hand*" Romans 7:21). We pray that we be led on the narrow path of righteousness right through the swamp (instead of into it), and be delivered from the dragon who is seeking to devour us with death, sickness and lies.

I.   *Hearing the Voice of God*

1.   The Lord Promises to Guide Us

We need to discern what God is saying to us for our everyday life and for ministry. In terms of whom we are to minister to and how, we need to be particularly sensitive. Learning to listen to God is especially important for being about to share with Jesus in healing ministry. Here are some principles:

The Lord promises to guide us.

> "*My sheep hear my voice and I know them, and they follow me.*" (John 10:27)

> "*If any of you lacks wisdom, let him ask God who gives to all men generously and without reproaching, and it will be given him.*" (James 1:5)

2.   Seek an Attitude of Submission to the Will of God

> "*If any man's will is to do His will, he shall know whether the teaching is from God.*" (John 7:17)

> "*The meek will He guide in judgment; and the meek will He teach His way.*" (Psalm 9)

At the beginning of each day we are to tell the Lord that, whatever the cost, we are ready and willing to obey His voice. We may then expect Him to guide. Remain humble; don't look for great things, but rather look for simple loving ways to please Him.

3.   Cultivate an Inner Quietness that Listens for His Voice

We need to shut off the radio and television, avoid a frantic, rushed schedule, find a refuge (sometimes the bathroom is the only place) and learn to be *"still and know."*

The whole life needs to be formed by the written Word of God, for He will not speak contrary to His Word. We must also live according to conscience, which is normally God's prompting. (See Acts 24:16, 1 Timothy 1:15, 19, 3:9, 1 Peter 3:16.) And we should follow common sense in our daily life.

4.   The Sound of His Voice

By cultivating an inner quietness, we can hear "the still, small voice" (1 Kings 19:12) which comes as a spontaneous, creative, gentle prompting, or hunch. (*"He shall not cry or lift up His voice"* Isaiah 42:2 and Matthew 12:19.) When the little, gentle, quickening comes, it often leaves you with a eureka feeling -- it's a neat idea. But avoid impulsiveness. If a gentle inclination/conviction is from the Lord, we can ask Him if it is of Him, and if it is, it will grow on us with a sense of rightness, peace, and a freedom to act on it.

The most suspect guidance is a sudden strong impulse, an overwhelming emotional flight, an overpowering vision, and an imagination that caters to our ego and selfishness. The devil can manipulate these things to make fools of us and bring discredit to the work of God. Ordinary inspiration is the surest; the gentle inclination of love and mercy cannot be counterfeited by Satan.

In Philippians 2:13 God promises to work in us to will of His own good pleasure. As a result, His commands come to us as good desires springing up, like a light rising within. Jeremiah 31:33 states that He writes His laws on our hearts so that we desire to do what we ought. We are drawn rather than driven.

5.   Obey What You Know To Do

If it seems good and right, and there is a growing sense of peace as you pray about it, begin to move in faith to do it. Elbert Hubbard said, "Go as far as you can see and when you get there you'll see further." For example, if you are moved by compassion to pray for a woman or a man, ask her or his permission and then proceed.

6.   Confirmation and Counsel

If the leading is of God, circumstances will confirm it, provided that we act in a right spirit of humility, love, and truth. All of nature and humanity is God's servant, and so the way opens. *"Light rises in the darkness for the upright."* (Psalm 112:4)

If we are unsure, we are wise to seek godly counsel. *"In the multitude of counselors there is safety."* (Psalm 11:4) Feedback and evaluations by objective Christians are invaluable checks.

7. Remember: the Lord Leads Gently, Like a Shepherd

He is never in a rush, nor is He impulsive, rude, or irritating. On the other hand, Satan pushes, shoves, agitates, and makes frantic; he has no time to wait.

8. The Acid Test of Guidance

"And the effect of righteousness will be peace." (Isaiah 32:17) - *"Let the peace of Christ rule in your hearts."* (Colossians 3:15) - *"The kingdom of God does not mean food and drink, but righteousness, peace, and joy in the Holy Spirit."* (Romans 14:17)

III. Moving into a Ministry of Healing with Jesus Christ (Brad Long)

As you seek to actually move from the theory and theology of healing into its practice. The following observations may be helpful preparation.

A. Recognize and honor the different callings and giftings for different kinds of healing ministry.

9 *to another faith by the same Spirit, to another gifts of healing by that one Spirit,* (1 Corinthians 12:9, NIV)

Notice that Paul's word here about the gift of healing is plural. There are "gifts" of healing. In this manual, we have distinguished several different areas of brokenness and thus different forms of healing ministry.

Spiritual healing – Restoring a persons relationship with God

Inner healing – Restoring a person's emotional and psychological wholeness

Physical healing – Restoring the persons physical body.

Relational healing – Restoring a person's relationship starting first with Male/Female then expanding to include families, races, nations.

> **Environmental healing** – Healing of the relationships between human beings and the created order.

> **Deliverance** – Removing the obstructions to any or all of the above forms of healing caused by evil spirits.

While these different forms of healing are integrated into an interrelated whole they nonetheless present distinctive foci of Jesus' healing work. While there are some people who may be called gifted and empowered to move in all these different forms of healing, experience has demonstrated that God often calls and gifts people for specific forms of healing.

For example:

Dr. Billy Graham is immensely gifted as an evangelist who has been used greatly for spiritual healing. That is calling people to turn from their sins and be reconciled to God the Father through faith in Jesus Christ.

Others like Catherine Kuhlman demonstrated extraordinary gifts of physical healing.

William Seymour of the Azusa Street Revival and Martin Luther King Jr. were both called and gifted for relational healing especially between races. Dr. James Dobson of Focus on the Family has demonstrated an extraordinary calling to relational healing between male and female and of family systems.

Francis McNutt and Delores Winder have over the years demonstrated giftedness in both physical healing and inner healing.

As a child of God anointed by the Holy Spirit and called to follow Jesus, one may be called to enter any of these forms of healing. Nevertheless, it is often helpful to recognize that one may have a special gifting in a special area. Generally, we see the most results when we honor our areas of gifting. One must however avoid two forms of deception:

1. Thinking that one's own area of anointing and gifting is the only form of healing that is needed or that all people need what they have been empowered to offer. This is the sin of arrogance.

2. Being envious of someone else's' calling in an area of healing that one does not have. This is also a sin and a hindrance to one fully engaging Jesus in Healing ministry.

B. Develop a Ministry Team

Because of the above diversity of needs for healing and giftedness for healing the importance of developing a healing team is made clear.

As one starts to move into a healing ministry regardless of the type, a ministry prayer team becomes essential. Healing ministry is not for lone rangers and one-man or women shows. In the past, God has greatly anointed one man or women to move into gifts of healing. Often these were the great pioneers of this movement. Without in any way denying their giftedness we have found that God's normal way of operating in the church is through ministry teams.

The following reasons are given as to why it is helpful and even essential to develop a team.

1. To work in ministry teams is the method that Jesus used and instructed His disciples to use (Mark 1:16-20, Luke 10:1).

2. It is Jesus who does the healing, not us! A team approach helps one avoid the sin of pride when people are healed.

3. A team also lessens the danger of those who are blessed becoming dependent upon one person who is perceived as having brought the healing.

4. In all the forms of healing there is the need for the exercise of different gifts of the Holy Spirit for effective ministry. In a prayer team, many more gifts may be manifested. For instance, one person may have the gift of discernment; another may receive words of knowledge, etc.

5. The team guards against unwise intimacy developing between a solo counselor and a needy supplicant.

6. Often God's love and glory are more manifested in Christian teamwork than in one person.

We suggest the following for building a prayer ministry team:

A. Start with praying with and for one another. This will build a relationship of trust and openness with one another.

B. Practice listening to the Holy Spirit together in the group and learn how to corporately discern the leading of the Holy Spirit. This will require the discipline of debriefing and being willing to be open and vulnerable. Learn how to discern and act upon karious moments.

C. Practice receiving and using the manifestational gifts of the Holy Spirit. This may require receiving teaching together on the workings and gifts of the Holy Spirit. It will also demand a willingness to give freedom to the Holy Spirit to manifest the gifts in the group. Learn to appreciate the different ways that the Holy Spirit may manifest through different people.

D. Usually all forms of healing work best when the prayer team functions as an army platoon that is each persons gifting is used under the leadership of one person. In building a prayer team recognize that often one person will be the point person. This is especially important when working in deliverance ministry. Having one point person will avoid confusion and will help coordinate the expression of gifts. At the same time, it is helpful to have different members of the group in this position so that they may learn to provide leadership. Again this is especially helpful in deliverance where the point person may be taken out and need to be immediately replaced.

E. The best way to learn how to pray as a team is to pray as a team. Do healing ministry together and always debrief afterwards.

F. The team as a team should seek to deepen their understanding of healing misntry and cultivate their giftedness by being a part of practical but systemic training. This could be undertaken as individuals but is best if done as a team. This may include taking part in special equipping events such as the *Dunamis Project* as well as working out a course of study for the group. The Order of St. Luke materials is excellent for this. The group may also choose to read books on healing and then discuss them together.

G. Recognize that for some assignments the whole team may not be necessary. Usually for inner healing two people is enough. For deliverance ministry, the team may need to recruit more people. This requires great flexibility and a willingness to be a team that supports one another in prayer but recognizes that different configurations of people will be necessary at different times.

H. Healing ministry in all its forms is intended to take place as part of the advancement of the Kingdom of God. The vanguard of the Kingdom on earth is the Church. Healing ministry to stay balanced and biblical needs to take place in the context of a worshiping community where the marks of the true church of Jesus Christ are in evidence. According to John Calvin the marks of the true church of Jesus Christ are as follows:

From this the face of the church comes forth and becomes visible to our eyes. Wherever we see the Word of God purely preached and heard, and the sacraments administered according to Christ's institution, there, it is not to be doubted, a church of God exists [cf. Ephesians 2:20].For his promise cannot fail: "Wherever two or three are gathered in my name, there I am in the midst of them" [Matthew 18:20]. (Institutes Book 4, Ch. 1, Sec 9) Battles Translation

I. The healing prayer team and the individual members of the team must be active members of and accountable to the church as defined above. Otherwise, there is great room for deception. This is especially true today with the prevalence of new age healing.

J. The team should always work under the authority and covering of those placed in authority in the church. To work outside the authority structure is to invite trouble. In the Presbyterian and Reformed stream this means working under the authority of the pastor and the session/consistory in the local church. Or in the larger church working under the authority of the Presbytery or Classis. In the Catholic and Episcopal traditions, it means working under the direction of the priest or bishop. In all cases, if the pastor or priest is called and anointed for healing ministry he or she should be a part of the healing prayer team. This is the best way to insure connection to the whole church and its ministries.

IV. Let the Holy Spirit Lead You into Healing Ministry.

We may and must prepare to be in healing ministry. Nevertheless, it is not appropriate to demand to be in healing ministry. Jesus work of restoration of the image of God and advancing the Kingdom of God is to take place at the leadership and direction of the Holy Spirit. The Spirit will be the one to give you opportunities for healing ministry.

If you and your team are truly called by God to engage in this work then the doors will open and you will find opportunities coming to you. You will not have to force open doors or seek people to pray for. At the right time when the Spirit has prepared the person, they will open the door for you to minister.

Great damage has been done to individuals and the church when people eager to be in healing ministry seek to push open the doors of themselves. Usually such zealous healing minters are led neither by the Holy Spirit nor Christ's love but by their own personal needs.

The only appropriate motivation for being in healing ministry is a desire to follow Jesus Christ and a deep Christ-given love of people who are broken.

With all this in mind by way of preparation, let us now turn to a careful study of, how Jesus did healing ministry. He is our teacher in this work.

Teaching Charts

Part IV

Our Equipping for Sharing in Jesus' Healing Ministry Today

The Dunamis Project
Presbyterian-Reformed Ministries International

Our Call To Share With Jesus In Healing Ministry

Luke 9:1-6
Jesus calls and sends disciples and gives them authority
over all demons, to heal and to preach.

A. We are called and equipped to share in Jesus' ministry empowered by the Holy Spirit.

1. Jesus promised that those who believe will do the works that He did—in fact, greater works.
John 14:12-14

2. Jesus received the Holy Spirit's power, not just for Himself but also to equip us for power ministry.
John 1:33

B. The promise of Jesus' presence, power and authority always accompanies the commissioning.

John 20:21-23
Luke 24:48-49
Matthew 28:18

Ways To Be Equipped For Healing Ministry Today

A. Investigate

B. Listen

C. Study

D. Cultivate Expectancy

E. "Rekindle the Gift of God That is Within You"

F. Conquer Fear

G. Know Yourself

H. Keep Sacred an Unhurried Time with God Daily

1. Take the Time

2. Transforming Method of Scripture Meditation

3. Pray This Way-Matthew 6:9-13

I. Hearing the Voice of God

1. The Lord Promises to Guide Us – John 10:27, James 1:5

2. Seek an Attitude of Submission to the Will of God - John 7:17, Psalm 9

3. Cultivate an Inner Quietness that Listens for His Voice

4. The Sound of His Voice - 1 King 19:12

5. Obey What You Know To Do

6. Confirmation and Counsel - Psalm 112:4, 11:4

7. Remember: the Lord Leads Gently, Like a Shepherd

8. The Acid Test of Guidance - Isaiah 32:17, Colossians 3:15, Romans 14:17

Moving into a Ministry of Healing with Jesus Christ

Recognize and honor the different callings and giftings for different kinds of healing ministry.
(I Corinthians 12:9

Spiritual Healing -
Restoring a person's relationship with God.

Inner Healing -
Restoring a person's emotional and psychological wholeness.

Physical Healing -
Restoring the person's physical body.

Relational Healing -
Restoring a person's relationship starting first with male/female then expanding to include families, races and nations.

Environmental Healing -
Healing of the relationships between human beings and the created order.

Deliverance -
Removing the obstructions to any or all of the above forms of healing caused by evil spirits.

The two dangers to avoid - pride and envy

Building A Healing Prayer Ministry Team

A. Start with praying with and for one another.

B. Practice listening to the Holy Spirit together in the group and learn discernment.

C. Practice receiving and using the manifestational gifts of the Holy Spirit.

D. Usually all forms of healing work best when the prayer team functions as an army platoon - that is each person's gifting is used under the leadership of one person.

E. The best way to learn how to pray as a team is to pray as a team. Do healing ministry together and always debrief afterwards.

F. The team, as a team, should seek to deepen their understanding of healing ministry and cultivate their giftedness by being a part of practical but systemic training.

G. Recognize that for some assignments the whole team may not be necessary.

H. Healing ministry in all its forms is intended to take place as part of the advancement of the Kingdom of God - the team must not lose sight of this overarching purpose.

I. The healing prayer team and the individual members of the team must be active members of and accountable to the church.

J. The team should always work under the authority and covering of those placed in authority in the church.

Be Prepared!
But Let the Holy Spirit Lead You and your Team into Healing Prayer Ministry.

PART V

Jesus Ministry of Spiritual, Inner and Relational Healing

By Brad Long

The Dunamis Project
Presbyterian-Reformed Ministries International

I. JESUS' MINISTRY OF HEALING IS ROOTED FIRST IN THE NATURE OF GOD THE FATHER

Jesus' life and ministry can only be understood as we see His extraordinary relationship with God, the creator of the universe. Jesus calls this all-powerful God, Abba or Daddy.

> *36   "Abba, Father," he said, "everything is possible for you. Take this cup from me. Yet not what I will, but what you will." (Mark 14:36, NIV)*

This relationship with the Father has several dimensions to it that are directly related to Jesus' healing ministry and to ours. Actually we shall find that from Jesus' own perspective, His healing ministry as the redemption and restoration of a fallen humanity, flows from God the Father. As John Calvin says,

> "to the **Father** is attributed the beginning of activity, and fountain and wellspring of all things..."[1]

Jesus' relationship with God the Father has the following aspects that are important for healing ministry.

A. JESUS' RELATIONSHIP WITH THE FATHER IS REVELATORY

Jesus Christ, in His relationship with the Father, reveals the nature and intentions of the Father. According to Jesus' own admission, He has a direct personal knowledge of the creator of the universe that He may reveal to those human beings whom He chooses. If we know Jesus we will come to know the Father as well.

> *25   At that time Jesus said, "I praise you, Father, Lord of heaven and earth, because you have hidden these things from the wise and learned, and revealed them to little children.*
> *26   Yes, Father, for this was your good pleasure.*
> *27   "All things have been committed to me by my Father. No one knows the Son except the Father, and no one knows the Father except the Son and those to whom the Son chooses to reveal him. (Matthew 11:25-27, NIV)*

> *8   Philip said, "Lord, show us the Father and that will be enough for us."*
> *9   Jesus answered: "Don't you know me, Philip, even after I have been among you such a long time? Anyone who has seen me has seen the Father. How can you say, 'Show us the Father'? (John 14:8-9, NIV)*

Jesus shows us the following aspects of the Father's nature that relate directly to healing ministry.

---

[1] John Calvin, (Trans by F.L. Battles), *Institutes of the Christian Religion* (Philadelphia: Westminster, 1975) pp. 142-43.

1. God the Father's purposes include the redemption of the whole fallen cosmos

In the call of Abraham, we are given the first glimpse of the breadth of God the Father's plans for redemption.

> *1   The LORD had said to Abram, "Leave your country, your people and your father's household and go to the land I will show you.*
> *2   "I will make you into a great nation and I will bless you; I will make your name great, and you will be a blessing.*
> *3   I will bless those who bless you, and whoever curses you I will curse; and all peoples on earth will be blessed through you."* (Genesis 12:1-3, NIV)

It is not until the end of the story in the book of Revelations that we see the full staggering extent of God's redemptive purposes. They include not just the nations of the earth, but the whole cosmos. There shall be a new heaven and a new earth. Healing will be multidimensional and will be total. Further, this healing begins in the realm of the Spirit as we come to know Jesus Christ and are born again.

Meditate on the following visions. They may give us the hope to press forward with this work of healing in a painful and broken world.

> *1   Then I saw a new heaven and a new earth, for the first heaven and the first earth had passed away, and there was no longer any sea.*
> *2   I saw the Holy City, the new Jerusalem, coming down out of heaven from God, prepared as a bride beautifully dressed for her husband.*
> *3   And I heard a loud voice from the throne saying, "Now the dwelling of God is with men, and he will live with them. They will be his people, and God himself will be with them and be their God.*
> *4   He will wipe every tear from their eyes. There will be no more death or mourning or crying or pain, for the old order of things has passed away."*
> *5   He who was seated on the throne said, "I am making everything new!" Then he said, "Write this down, for these words are trustworthy and true."*
> *6   He said to me: "It is done. I am the Alpha and the Omega, the Beginning and the End. To him who is thirsty I will give to drink without cost from the spring of the water of life.*
> *7   He who overcomes will inherit all this, and I will be his God and he will be my son.*
> *8   But the cowardly, the unbelieving, the vile, the murderers, the sexually immoral, those who practice magic arts, the idolaters and all liars-- their place will be in the fiery lake of burning sulfur. This is the second death."* (Revelation 21:1-8, NIV)

> *1   Then the angel showed me the river of the water of life, as clear as crystal, flowing from the throne of God and of the Lamb*
> *2   down the middle of the great street of the city. On each side of the river stood the tree of life, bearing twelve crops of fruit, yielding its fruit every month. And the leaves of the tree are for the healing of the nations.*
> *3   No longer will there be any curse. The throne of God and of the Lamb will be in the city, and his servants will serve him.*
> *4   They will see his face, and his name will be on their foreheads.*

5   *There will be no more night. They will not need the light of a lamp or the light of the sun, for the Lord God will give them light. And they will reign for ever and ever.* (Revelation 22:1-5, NIV)

2.   God the Father's extraordinary love

In the dynamic relationship between the Father and the Son, the love of God the Father is clearly revealed. This love has the following dimensions:

The Father loves the Son

35   *The Father loves the Son and has placed everything in his hands.*
36   *Whoever believes in the Son has eternal life, but whoever rejects the Son will not see life, for God's wrath remains on him."* (John 3:35-36, NIV)

17   *For he received honor and glory from God the Father when the voice came to him from the Majestic Glory, saying, "This is my Son, whom I love; with him I am well pleased."* (2 Peter 1:17, NIV)

God loves the world

16   *"For God so loved the world that he gave his one and only Son, that whoever believes in him shall not perish but have eternal life.* (John 3:16, NIV)

God is love and loves us

7   *Dear friends, let us love one another, for love comes from God. Everyone who loves has been born of God and knows God.*
8   *Whoever does not love does not know God, because God is love.*
9   *This is how God showed his love among us: He sent his one and only Son into the world that we might live through him.*
10   *This is love: not that we loved God, but that he loved us and sent his Son as an atoning sacrifice for our sins.* (I John 4:7-10, NIV)

At the center of the universe is not some impersonal power. The creator of the universe has revealed His nature to us in Jesus Christ. It may come as a total surprise or a cosmic shock. This all-powerful creator God is love and He loves us. Jesus calls him Abba Father, and wonder of wonder, when we are born again the same Holy Spirit, who was at work in and upon Jesus, is at work in and upon us. We may know God's love and the Holy Spirit leads us with Jesus to pray, Abba Father.

6   *Because you are sons, God sent the Spirit of his Son into our hearts, the Spirit who calls out, "Abba, Father."* (Galatians 4:6, NIV)

The love of God the Father is vast and deep

God's power and love is so vast that He can create and name the stars. At the same time it is so deep and tender that He can heal our deepest, most personal, inner wounds.

> *3   He heals the brokenhearted and binds up their wounds.*
> *4   He determines the number of the stars and calls them each by name.*
> *5   Great is our Lord and mighty in power; his understanding has no limit.*
> *6   The LORD sustains the humble but casts the wicked to the ground.* (Psalm 147:3-6, NIV)

3.   God knows our inner being and the secrets of our heart

God the Father, the creator of all things, can heal us because He loves us. He can also heal us because He knows us. He sees into the depths of who we are. Nothing from a neuron in our brain to a lost thought in our subconscious is hidden from Him. The Father knew us before we were even conceived and will know us long after we have passed from this earth.

> *13   For you created my inmost being; you knit me together in my mother's womb.*
> *14   I praise you because I am fearfully and wonderfully made; your works are wonderful, I know that full well.*
> *15   My frame was not hidden from you when I was made in the secret place. When I was woven together in the depths of the earth,*
> *16   your eyes saw my unformed body. All the days ordained for me were written in your book before one of them came to be.*
> *17   How precious to me are your thoughts, O God! How vast is the sum of them!*
> *18   Were I to count them, they would outnumber the grains of sand. When I awake, I am still with you.* (Psalm 139:13-18, NIV)

B. JESUS' WORK IS SUBORDINATE TO THE FATHER

The relationship between Jesus Christ and the Father reveals the deep motivation behind Jesus' work. It also reveals the true source of Jesus' power and authority. Jesus is not working as some independent agent. Rather, in Jesus' life and ministry everything flows from the Father whom He loves and obeys.

> *17   Jesus said to them, "My Father is always at his work to this very day, and I, too, am working."*
> *18   For this reason the Jews tried all the harder to kill him; not only was he breaking the Sabbath, but he was even calling God his own Father, making himself equal with God.*
> *19   Jesus gave them this answer: "I tell you the truth, the Son can do nothing by himself; he can do only what he sees his Father doing, because whatever the Father does the Son also does.*
> *20   For the Father loves the Son and shows him all he does. Yes, to your amazement he will show him even greater things than these.*
> *21   For just as the Father raises the dead and gives them life, even so the Son gives life to whom he is pleased to give it.* (John 5:17-2, NIV)

This means that the healing ministry of Jesus is actually the healing ministry of God the Father. For those of us called to healing ministry the same principle of subordination also applies. It is not OUR ministry rather it is the ministry of God the Father, Son and Holy Spirit.

C. IT IS THE FATHER'S INTENTION THAT JESUS' MISSION INCLUDE HEALING OF THE WHOLE FALLEN PERSON

> *3   He was despised and rejected by men, a man of sorrows, and familiar with suffering. Like one from whom men hide their faces he was despised, and we esteemed him not.*
> *4   Surely he took up our infirmities and carried our sorrows, yet we considered him stricken by God, smitten by him, and afflicted.*
> *5   But he was pierced for our transgressions, he was crushed for our iniquities; the punishment that brought us peace was upon him, and by his wounds we are healed.*
> *6   We all, like sheep, have gone astray, each of us has turned to his own way; and the LORD has laid on him the iniquity of us all.*
> *7   He was oppressed and afflicted, yet he did not open his mouth; he was led like a lamb to the slaughter, and as a sheep before her shearers is silent, so he did not open his mouth.* (Isaiah 53:3-7, NIV)

This prophetic word from Isaiah has been fulfilled in Jesus Christ. He is the Father's remedy for the effects of the Fall.

II.   THE SCOPE OF JESUS' HEALING MINISTRY ON EARTH

Jesus states the purpose of His own mission as follows:

> *18   "The Spirit of the Lord is on me, because he has anointed me to preach good news to the poor. He has sent me to proclaim freedom for the prisoners and recovery of sight for the blind, to release the oppressed, to proclaim the year of the Lord's favor."* (Luke 4:18-19, NIV)

> *32   He replied, "Go tell that fox, 'I will drive out demons and heal people today and tomorrow, and on the third day I will reach my goal.'*
> *33   In any case, I must keep going today and tomorrow and the next day-- for surely no prophet can die outside Jerusalem!* (Luke 13:32-33, NIV)

From the above passages and from the Creation – Fall – Redemption framework for healing ministry we are strengthened in our thesis that there are the following foci of healing ministry.

Spiritual Healing - 2 Corinthians 5:17-19

Inner Healing - 2 Corinthians 3:17-18, Galatians 5:22-25

Relational Healing - Galatians 3:26-29

Physical Healing - John 11:25-26

Restoration of the Creation - Romans 8:18-25[2]

Jesus has been sent to restore and to transform into the Kingdom of God the whole fallen universe. The redemption that flows from the heart of the Father is both personal and cosmic.

III.   THE DYNAMIC OF JESUS' COOPERATION WITH THE HOLY SPIRIT IN HEALING MINISTRY

We must now turn to another question of great importance. How does Jesus actually do this healing ministry? The "how to" of Jesus ministry is directly relevant to us. According to Jesus' own promises and commands to us – we are sent just as He was sent and are to engage in the same type of ministries that He engaged in.

> *12   I tell you the truth, anyone who has faith in me will do what I have been doing. He will do even greater things than these, because I am going to the Father.*
> *13   And I will do whatever you ask in my name, so that the Son may bring glory to the Father.*
> *14   You may ask me for anything in my name, and I will do it.* (John 14:12-14, NIV)
>
> *21   Again Jesus said, "Peace be with you! As the Father has sent me, I am sending you."*
> *22   And with that he breathed on them and said, "Receive the Holy Spirit.*
> *23   If you forgive anyone his sins, they are forgiven; if you do not forgive them, they are not forgiven."* (John 20:21-23, NIV)

In the rest of this section we shall carefully examine how Jesus practically did spiritual, inner and relational healing. In a later section we shall focus on how Jesus did physical healing. This division is somewhat artificial to the biblical vision that is holistic and all-inclusive. However, separating out these different forms of healing will help us come to greater clarity about this work we are called to do. It also fits our actual practice of prayer ministry. Jesus' healing is ultimately all inclusive of all dimensions of brokenness. Nevertheless, here on earth before the fulfillment of the Kingdom of God, it is a process in which spiritual and inner healing is often the first priority.

From this study, we shall discover that there are certain fundamental principles or dynamics that are involved in our restoration and redemption. It is essential that we understand these fundamental principles if we are to effectively share in Jesus' healing ministry through the Holy

---

[2] The Healing of the creation will not be covered extensively in this manual but is none the less an important dimension of God's redemptive purposes as revealed in Jesus Christ.

Spirit.

The principles of healing, we shall find, are consistent in Jesus' age as well as our own. This is because God's heart for us is the same and so is fallen human nature. A fundamental connector between Jesus' healing work 2000 years ago and our participation in this work today is the Holy Spirit. It is the same Holy Spirit who was leading and empowering Jesus who leads and empowers us today.

A. THE AGENCY AT WORK IN AND THROUGH JESUS FOR HEALING WAS THE HOLY SPIRIT

> *14   Jesus returned to Galilee in the power of the Spirit*, *and news about him spread through the whole countryside.*
> *15   He taught in their synagogues, and everyone praised him.*
> *16   He went to Nazareth, where he had been brought up, and on the Sabbath day he went into the synagogue, as was his custom. And he stood up to read.*
> *17   The scroll of the prophet Isaiah was handed to him. Unrolling it, he found the place where it is written:*
> *18   "The Spirit of the Lord is on me, because he has anointed me to preach good news to the poor. He has sent me to proclaim freedom for the prisoners and recovery of sight for the blind, to release the oppressed,*
> *19   to proclaim the year of the Lord's favor."*
> *20   Then he rolled up the scroll, gave it back to the attendant and sat down. The eyes of everyone in the synagogue were fastened on him,*
> *21   and he began by saying to them, "Today this scripture is fulfilled in your hearing."*
> (Luke 4:14-21, NIV)

This is a critical passage for understanding the secret of how Jesus did His healing ministry. Jesus' position is as Son of God and as Messiah. He has authority to do the work the Father has sent Him to do. At the same time, the power that is flowing through Him to accomplish these works comes from the Holy Spirit who is working with Him. The work of healing, is the result of Jesus' cooperation with the Father and the Holy Spirit.

This dynamic cooperative relationship between Jesus and the Spirit that as revealed in the Luke 4 passage above is summarized as follows:[3]

> Jesus believed himself to be the one in whom Isaiah 61.1 found fulfillment; his sense of being inspired was such that he could believe himself to be the end-time prophet of Isaiah 61.1: He had been anointed with the Spirit of the Lord.
>
> Luke is quite justified therefore when he depicts Jesus as opening his public ministry in the full conviction and inspiration of the Spirit upon him. The power which he experienced in himself, the power which became evident in his healings (in his exorcisms in particular) and especially in his proclamation of the good

---

[3] Amazingly this observation is made by the liberal theological Rudolf Bultmann.

news to the poor, was in Jesus' view the eschatological Spirit operating in and through him – the power which brought God's forgiveness and acceptance effectively to his hearers. This power was the rule of God; to experience it in the ministry of Jesus was already to share in the kingdom of God (Luke 6:20). [4]

I would go further and affirm that Jesus not only believed Himself to be the one in whom Isaiah 61.1 found fulfillment - He IS the one who fulfilled the prophet's words!

We have already established a fundamental principle in the Gateways *Dunamis Project* manual: Jesus is fully God but also fully man. While on earth, however, His power for healing flowed not from His divinity but from the Holy Spirit. Jesus is a human being just like us who had the Holy Spirit upon Him for gifts and power

> 19   *and the people all tried to touch him, because power was coming from him and healing them all.* (Luke 6:19, NIV)

This means that the source of the power that people experienced for healing was the Holy Spirit who is dynamically making operative the Kingdom of God on earth.

Please see the Gateways Manual pages 173 – 175 for teaching on this concept. If you do not understand this Holy Spirit basis of Jesus' ministry, you will find it impossible to cooperate with the same Holy Spirit in Jesus' present day work of healing.

B. JESUS' APPROACH TO ALL HEALING CONFORMED TO THE BASIC PRINCIPLES OF POWER MINISTRY

1.   The dynamics of the Holy Spirit in power ministry

The Holy Spirit is free to work in any way that He wishes. In Scripture, however, we find that cooperation between the Holy Spirit and human beings has certain dynamics. A knowledge of these dynamics may better equip us to discern what the Holy Spirit is doing and, thus, open the way for us to more effectively participate in His vital work of healing. Jesus as second person of the Trinity understood perfectly this principle of cooperation with the third person of the Trinity. From Scripture this may be summarized as follows:

a. The Holy Spirit moves over a situation, person, or place in preparation to accomplish God's purposes. This may be called a "kairos moment."

b. The Word of God, embodying the intentions of God, is spoken or acted into the situation in which the Holy Spirit is moving.

c. God may speak this word directly, as in Genesis at the creation of the universe.

---

[4] James D.G. Dunn, *Jesus and the Spirit: A Study of the Religious and Charismatic Experience of Jesus and the First Christians as Reflected in the New Testament* p. 61.

Often, however, He chooses to speak it first to a human being who in turn obeys the leading of the Spirit and, either verbally or in actions, projects the Word of God into the context where the Holy Spirit is moving.
d. When this word of God is spoken or acted upon, it provides the raw material that the Holy Spirit will use to accomplish God's purpose.

e. Human faith is a necessary ingredient to God's actions. For the word of God to be the raw material of the Holy Spirit's action, it must fall upon the fertile seed-bed of faith.

In the life of the great prophets, the ministry of Jesus and in the ministry of the disciples divine-human cooperation is evident.

This dynamic of cooperation between Jesus and the Holy Spirit given above assumes two fundamental conditions that will also be preconditions of our cooperation as well:

The first principle is Jesus walking in submission to the will and intentions of the Father.

> *19   Jesus gave them this answer: "I tell you the truth, the Son can do nothing by himself; he can do only what he sees his Father doing, because whatever the Father does the Son also does. (John 5:19)*

The second principle is that of loving relationship between the Father and the Son.

> *20   For the Father loves the Son and shows him all he does. Yes, to your amazement he will show him even greater things than these.*
> *21   For just as the Father raises the dead and gives them life, even so the Son gives life to whom he is pleased to give it. (John 5:20-21 NIV)*

For us: When we are in the context of love and submission to the Father, Son and Holy Spirit the dynamics of cooperation with the Holy Spirit become operative for us and we may share in Jesus' healing ministry.

See the following chart that shows this dynamic.

The Dynamic of Cooperating with the Holy Spirit in Power Ministry
(For Jesus Christ and for us His Disciples)

Flow of Human History: Space and Time Continuum

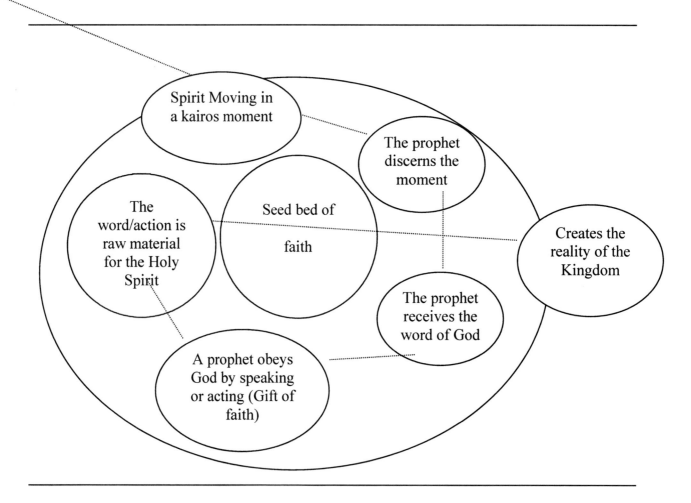

Kairos Moments in Chronos Time

As we look at the way Jesus did healing ministry, we shall see that He acted in a certain manner in order to cooperate with the moving of the Holy Spirit. Around this presupposition we shall organize these practical teachings of Jesus' ministry.

(For more detailed discussion of this human-divine cooperation dynamic of the Holy Spirit's work, see The Dunamis Project manual, "*In the Spirit's Power: Growing in the Gifts of the Holy Spirit*" Section III, Basic Principles of Power Ministry.)

2.   Jesus moved in the kairos moments of the Holy Spirit

The period following Jesus' baptism was a kairos moment in which the Holy Spirit was moving to heal. The multitudes of people who were healed and the two references to the nature of the power coming forth from Jesus confirm that this was a special time in which the Holy Spirit was moving.

> "*...and the power of the Lord was with him to heal.*" (Luke 5:17)

> "*...and all the crowd sought to touch him, for power came forth from him and healed them all.*" (Luke 6:19)

The whole of Jesus' ministry was characterized by healing, even to the restoration of the ear of the high priest's servant at the time of His arrest (Luke 22:50). Nevertheless there were periods when healing was especially prominent.

All these times of healing work were motivated and empowered by the Holy Spirit. Likewise, in our ministry of healing there may be special periods of the Holy Spirit's healing activity, or a time when He especially reveals His presence and power in this way. This is in accord with the episodic manner in which the power of the Holy Spirit is often manifested.

In the course of a worship service or prayer meeting there may be times when the Holy Spirit is especially moving in healing ministry. These times generally follow periods of worship and the proclamation of the word of God.

> For example, at PRMI Prayer Mountains and Dunamis Project retreats, there are almost always periods when it seems as if a window opens and the fresh breeze of the Holy Spirit's presence blows through. The result is effective healing ministry. These are kairos moments and we must act or speak as led by the Holy Spirit. If we fail to discern and to obey the inspiring presence of the Holy Spirit, signs and wonders will not occur. We must also discern whether the Holy Spirit is moving in a particular person or situation. This discernment will guide us in how we are to pray and to act.

There follows a discussion of the fundamental principles pertaining to how Jesus practically ministered in spiritual, inner and relational healing. (Physical healing will be dealt with in a later section of this manual.)

We believe Jesus has called us to follow Him and as we do we will do the same works that He did.[5] Our purpose is to understand how Jesus did these works and learn to cooperate with the Holy Spirit according to the same principles.

IV.   THE THREE PHASES OF JESUS' HEALING WORK WITH AN INDIVIDUAL

A study of the many stories in the Bible of how Jesus brought spiritual, inner, relational physical healing in individuals reveals a clear pattern of how the Jesus was working with the Holy Spirit and with the person. This pattern of engagement with people may be described as having the following three phases.

- **Phase 1** - Jesus first establishes the context for the Holy Spirit to work in a person by bringing the person into a relationship with Himself.

- **Phase 2** - In this relationship Jesus, led by the Holy Spirit, may do any number of things that overcome the effects of the Fall. These various actions, connecting with the Holy Spirit in kairos moments, all have to do with making real in the person's life the Kingdom of God and are all part of the process of their redemption. The result will be spiritual, inner, relational and physical healing.

- **Phase 3** - Jesus invites/commands the person to follow Him in faith and obedience as a disciple. The person is commanded to follow Jesus in an appropriate form of discipleship. This obedience of following Jesus is a vital part of the healing process and confirms that healing is not and end unto itself.

As a flow chart, Jesus' engagement with an individual that resulted in their healing may look like this:

Establishing the context for work by enabling relationship

Jesus' actions as led by the Holy Spirit bring healing and express the Kingdom of God in the person and their relationships.

Jesus calls the person in process of healing to follow Him as a disciple

---

[5] John 14:12-14

A. PHASE 1 –

Jesus establishes the context in which the Holy Spirit will work by bringing the person into a relationship with himself.

Establishment of relationship is the vital first step in healing ministry. This is the first and most important thing. The healing ministry of Jesus Christ takes place in the context of our relationship with Jesus. Jesus actively works to bring us into this relationship with Himself. We could also just as well affirm the Holy Spirit is at work establishing the context in which Jesus can work. The cooperation between Jesus and the Holy Spirit is so interwoven that it is truly difficult at times to sort out which person of the Trinity is doing what. This is especially true after Jesus' ascension into heaven.

1.   JESUS IS FILLED WITH THE HOLY SPIRIT: THIS IS THE SOURCE OF HIS POWER FOR MINISTRY AND SETS THE CONTEXT IN WHICH HE WORKS

When John baptized Jesus in the River Jordan the Holy Spirit fell upon Him. This began the empowering and gift giving operation of the Holy Spirit equipping Jesus for public ministry that would lead to fulfillment of His mission.

The Holy Spirit had previously been at work within Jesus brining knowledge of the Father and shaping His character.

> *21   When all the people were being baptized, Jesus was baptized too. And as he was praying, heaven was opened*
> *22   and the Holy Spirit descended on him in bodily form like a dove. And a voice came from heaven: "You are my Son, whom I love; with you I am well pleased." (Luke 3:21-22, NIV)*

> *14   Jesus returned to Galilee in the power of the Spirit, and news about him spread through the whole countryside.*
> *15   He taught in their synagogues, and everyone praised him.*
> *16   He went to Nazareth, where he had been brought up, and on the Sabbath day he went into the synagogue, as was his custom. And he stood up to read.*
> *17   The scroll of the prophet Isaiah was handed to him. Unrolling it, he found the place where it is written:*
> *18   "The Spirit of the Lord is on me, because he has anointed me to preach good news to the poor. He has sent me to proclaim freedom for the prisoners and recovery of sight for the blind, to release the oppressed,*
> *19   to proclaim the year of the Lord's favor."*
> *20   Then he rolled up the scroll, gave it back to the attendant and sat down. The eyes of everyone in the synagogue were fastened on him,*
> *21   and he began by saying to them, "Today this scripture is fulfilled in your hearing."*
> (Luke 4:14-21, NIV)

The Spirit upon Him sets the stage for moving in a ministry of signs and wonders that included spiritual, inner, relational and physical healing. These are all taking place in the context of the

Holy Spirit dynamically and powerfully working through Jesus.

> *36   All the people were amazed and said to each other, "What is this teaching? With authority and power he gives orders to evil spirits and they come out!"* (Luke 4:36, NIV)

> *17   One day as he was teaching, Pharisees and teachers of the law, who had come from every village of Galilee and from Judea and Jerusalem, were sitting there. And the power of the Lord was present for him to heal the sick.* (Luke 5:17, NIV)

For the first disciples and for us as well, the stage is also set for our healing ministry by the outpouring of the Holy Spirit. Healing ministry takes place as we are filled with the Holy Spirit - this is the filled meaning "upon for power" and as we work "in the name of Jesus." The power comes of the Holy Spirit the authority and grace from Jesus Christ. Our role is to cooperate with these two persons of the trinity so that God the Father may be glorified.

> *7   They had Peter and John brought before them and began to question them: "By what power or what name did you do this?"*
> *8   Then Peter, filled with the Holy Spirit, said to them: "Rulers and elders of the people!*
> *9   If we are being called to account today for an act of kindness shown to a cripple and are asked how he was healed,*
> *10   then know this, you and all the people of Israel: It is by the name of Jesus Christ of Nazareth, whom you crucified but whom God raised from the dead, that this man stands before you healed.*
> *11   He is "'the stone you builders rejected, which has become the capstone.'*
> *12   Salvation is found in no one else, for there is no other name under heaven given to men by which we must be saved."* (Acts 4:7-12, NIV)

2.   JESUS OBEYS THE FATHER: THIS IS THE SOURCE OF HIS DIRECTION AND PURPOSE FOR MINISTRY.

Jesus' relationship with the Father also set the stage for Jesus' healing ministry. The following passages from the Gospel of John clearly demonstrate the extraordinary relationship between Jesus and the Father.

> *17   Jesus said to them, "My Father is always at his work to this very day, and I, too, am working."*
> *18   For this reason the Jews tried all the harder to kill him; not only was he breaking the Sabbath, but he was even calling God his own Father, making himself equal with God.*
> *19   Jesus gave them this answer: "I tell you the truth, the Son can do nothing by himself; he can do only what he sees his Father doing, because whatever the Father does the Son also does.*
> *20   For the Father loves the Son and shows him all he does. Yes, to your amazement he will show him even greater things than these.*
> *21   For just as the Father raises the dead and gives them life, even so the Son gives life to whom he is pleased to give it.* (John 5:17-21, NIV)

28 I give them eternal life, and they shall never perish; no one can snatch them out of my hand.
29 My Father, who has given them to me, is greater than all; no one can snatch them out of my Father's hand.
30 I and the Father are one." (John 10:28-30, NIV)

49 For I did not speak of my own accord, but the Father who sent me commanded me what to say and how to say it.
50 I know that his command leads to eternal life. So whatever I say is just what the Father has told me to say." (John 12:49-50, NIV)

10 Don't you believe that I am in the Father, and that the Father is in me? The words I say to you are not just my own. Rather, it is the Father, living in me, who is doing his work.
11 Believe me when I say that I am in the Father and the Father is in me; or at least believe on the evidence of the miracles themselves. (John 14:10-11, NIV)

The ultimate source of Jesus' healing is God the Father to whom Jesus is subordinate. The healing ministry of Jesus Christ is thus ministry that takes place in the larger context of the other person's of the Trinity. Jesus is not a "one man show" rather He is doing ministry.

For human beings who are called to share in the healing ministry of Jesus Christ, the over arching context that is ministry to takes place in is the dynamic working of the three persons of the trinity.

3. WHILE ON EARTH JESUS ESTABLISHES THE BASIS FOR COOPERATING WITH PEOPLE BY ENGAGING THEM IN CONVERSATION

Often we find a curious habit that Jesus has of first engaging people in conversation. He does this by intentionally asking people questions.

Most of the cases of the Bible in which Jesus engages in conversation have to do with physical healing. But they seem to relate to spiritual and inner healing as well. For example:

a) Nicodemus and a Samaritan woman

Jesus draws both Nicodemus and the women at the well and into conversation with a provocative statement.

Nicodemus

3 In reply Jesus declared, "I tell you the truth, no one can see the kingdom of God unless he is born again."
4 "How can a man be born when he is old?" Nicodemus asked. "Surely he cannot enter a second time into his mother's womb to be born!" (John 3:4, NIV)

The Samaritan Woman

> *7   When a Samaritan woman came to draw water, Jesus said to her, "Will you give me a drink?"*
> *8   (His disciples had gone into the town to buy food.)*
> *9   The Samaritan woman said to him, "You are a Jew and I am a Samaritan woman. How can you ask me for a drink?" (For Jews do not associate with Samaritans.)*
> *10   Jesus answered her, "If you knew the gift of God and who it is that asks you for a drink, you would have asked him and he would have given you living water."* (John 4:7-10, NIV)

In both of these cases these conversations with Jesus led to the person's salvation.

b)   The man at the pool and blind Bartimaeus

Jesus asks an astonishing question of the invalid who waited 38 years beside the pool of at Bethesda.

> *6   When Jesus saw him lying there and learned that he had been in this condition for a long time, he asked him, "Do you want to get well?"* (John 5:6, NIV)

Jesus asks what seems to have been an obvious question of the blind Bartimaeus.

> *51   "What do you want me to do for you?" Jesus asked him. The blind man said, "Rabbi, I want to see."* (Mark 10:51, NIV)

c)   Zacchaeus the tax collector

Jesus engages the tax collector Zacchaeus in conversation with the command:

> *5   When Jesus reached the spot, he looked up and said to him, "Zacchaeus, come down immediately. I must stay at your house today."* (Luke 19:5, NIV)

It was in the context of a meal with Jesus that Zacchaeus certainly experienced relational and spiritual healing. This was evidenced first by the fact that Zacchaeus was willing to give to the poor and to restore fourfold what he had stolen. Second, Jesus declares:

> *9   Jesus said to him, "Today salvation has come to this house, because this man, too, is a son of Abraham.*
> *10   For the Son of Man came to seek and to save what was lost."* (Luke 19:9-10, NIV)

We may also conclude that this brief encounter with Jesus resulted in inner healing of wounds in Zacchaeus' heart. Without this inner healing it is doubtful that he could have made such a bold reformation of his life. We are not told what happened sitting around the table eating with Jesus but we may guess that it must have penetrated to the core of Zacchaeus' being. No one can share a meal with Jesus and remain the same.

d)   Simon the Pharisee

For Simon the Pharisee it was while eating when the sinful women started to wash Jesus' feet that Jesus suddenly engaged Simon in an in-depth conversation with the parable of the servants who owed money. Luke 7:36-50 We do not know what the result of this interaction with Jesus upon Simon was. For the woman, clearly it was spiritual and inner healing. She left forgiven of her sins.

e)   Application to our engagement in healing prayer ministry

Such conversations with Jesus, evoked by Jesus' own engaging statements and questions, may have several functions:

1. They engage the person in the process of healing. Jesus does not act upon people to heal and to save them. Rather, He acts with them. This honors human beings as made in the image of God with freedom and responsibility.

2. The questions that Jesus asks serves to evoke faith, which is the basis for Jesus being able to act in our lives. Indeed, He may directly ask, "Do you believe this?" This is how Jesus directly questioned Martha at the tomb of Lazarus.

3. Jesus has given us a promise, *"Whatever you ask in my name I will do it that the Father may be glorified."* When Jesus asks us, "What may I do for you?" He is giving us the opportunity to express the desires of our heart so that He may keep this promise.

Such questions seem to be comparable to our asking, "How may I pray for you?" or "What is it you seek from God?" These questions invite the person's participation in the healing process. They enable the prayer counselor to discern what the Holy Spirit is doing in the person. In the clinical model, this would be called the interview.

4.   JESUS ESTABLISHES THE CONTEXT FOR HIS WORK BY DEMONSTRATING HIS LOVE FOR US

As a part of spiritual healing, there is knowing and experiencing God's love. In the healing ministry of Jesus we see him loving people. We also see people responding to Jesus in love which is a reflection of Jesus having first loved them.

a)   The rich young ruler

> *21   Jesus looked at him and loved him. "One thing you lack," he said. "Go, sell everything you have and give to the poor, and you will have treasure in heaven. Then come, follow me."* (Mark 10:21, NIV)

b)   Lazarus who died

34   "Where have you laid him?" he asked. "Come and see, Lord," they replied.
35   Jesus wept.
36   Then the Jews said, "See how he loved him!" (John 11:34-36, NIV)

c)   The sinful women who shows her love for Jesus by washing His feet with her tears

37   When a woman who had lived a sinful life in that town learned that Jesus was eating at the Pharisee's house, she brought an alabaster jar of perfume,
38   and as she stood behind him at his feet weeping, she began to wet his feet with her tears. Then she wiped them with her hair, kissed them and poured perfume on them.
39   When the Pharisee who had invited him saw this, he said to himself, "If this man were a prophet, he would know who is touching him and what kind of woman she is-- that she is a sinner."
40   Jesus answered him, "Simon, I have something to tell you." "Tell me, teacher," he said.
41   "Two men owed money to a certain moneylender. One owed him five hundred denarii, and the other fifty.
42   Neither of them had the money to pay him back, so he canceled the debts of both. Now which of them will love him more?" (Luke 7:37-42, NIV)

d)   The ultimate expression of God's love and Jesus' love for us is the cross

8   But God demonstrates his own love for us in this: While we were still sinners, Christ died for us. (Romans 5:8, NIV)

35   Who shall separate us from the love of Christ? Shall trouble or hardship or persecution or famine or nakedness or danger or sword?
36   As it is written: "For your sake we face death all day long; we are considered as sheep to be slaughtered."
37   No, in all these things we are more than conquerors through him who loved us.
38   For I am convinced that neither death nor life, neither angels nor demons, neither the present nor the future, nor any powers,
39   neither height nor depth, nor anything else in all creation, will be able to separate us from the love of God that is in Christ Jesus our Lord. (Romans 8:35-39, NIV)

God the Father, while we were yet sinners, sent His only Son to die for us on the cross. This provides the whole possibility for us to even enter into a relationship with God. As the foundation for our relationship with God, the cross thus provides the context for our even being able to enter into a context where Jesus' healing work can begin. The cross provides the bridge across the gulf caused by our sin. Over it may come the extraordinary grace and love of God.

Love from Jesus, which is the love of the Father and the Spirit as well, is profoundly healing. Since God is love, we were made to love and to be loved when we were created in the image of God. One of the most disastrous effects of the Fall is that human beings have been cut off from the love that nourishes us and determines our identity. This loss of love begins first with our Father in Heaven but then extends to us and to all of our relationships.

Jesus' love brought spiritual, inner, relational, and physical healing to those whom he touched. While we do not often find this love named as in the cases above we see it again and again in Jesus' attitudes and effects upon people. This expression of love is the underlying dynamic in all the cases of Jesus' healing ministry that shall follow.

e)   Application to our sharing in healing ministry

The foundation, initiative and context for all Christian healing is this love of God. In inner healing we begin by assuring the person that God loves them unconditionally. We, who are called to healing ministry, must take the risk of loving those for whom we pray. Otherwise we are inadequate vessels for the healing power of God.

Mike Flynn offers the profound insight that Jesus loves us as much as the Father loves Him (John 15:9, 17:23). The corollary is that the Father loves us as much as He loves Jesus (I John 3:1). To contemplate and reflect on this as we study the New Testament is the most healing thing in the world. [6]

B. PHASE 2 –

Jesus and the Holy Spirit engage the person in various ways to bring the reality of the Kingdom of God which results in healing.

In all of these actions that follow, the dynamics of Jesus cooperating with the Holy Spirit are assumed to be operative. Jesus is speaking and acting in such a way that He is giving the Holy Spirit what He needs in order to work in the person. This is why when Jesus calls a person to repent or tells them that they are forgiven, the intent of His word is actually accomplished.

1.   JESUS BRINGS PEOPLE TO BE BORN AGAIN - THIS IS SPIRITUAL HEALING AND THE FIRST STEP INTO THE REST OF HIS HEALING WORK

In the midst of this fallen, sin-filled universe, with our human race bound over to the powers of death, God has established a way of life. This is through faith in Jesus Christ. Jesus is the King and the way into the Kingdom.

> *14   After John was put in prison, Jesus went into Galilee, proclaiming the good news of God.*
> *15   "The time has come," he said. "The kingdom of God is near. Repent and believe the*

---

[6] The Rev. Mike Flynn has for many years been the pastor of St. Jude Episcopal Church in Burbank, California. He has been a pioneer in the healing ministry.

good news!" (Mark 1:14-15, NIV)

12   Yet to all who received him, to those who believed in his name, he gave the right to become children of God--
13   children born not of natural descent, nor of human decision or a husband's will, but born of God. (John 1:12-13, NIV)
34   For the one whom God has sent speaks the words of God, for God gives the Spirit without limit.
35   The Father loves the Son and has placed everything in his hands.
Whoever believes in the Son has eternal life, but whoever rejects the Son will not see life, for God's wrath remains on him." (John 3:34-35, NIV)

The following verses reveal to us that Jesus' primary work is to make a way for us to enter into the Kingdom of God. It is in this Kingdom that all the processes of healing begin for us and may reach their completion. We find that while on earth after Jesus engaged the person in relationship, often a next step was to lead them into this spiritual healing of the broken relationship with the Father.

We see this clearly in the nighttime conversation with Nicodemus. After the provocative statements that elicited Nicodemus' response of how can this be, Jesus proceeds to tell him that the only way to see the Kingdom is to be born again.

The same thing happens to the woman at the well. An intellectual discussion on the nature of truth and true worship becomes an invitation to get living water from Jesus.

This spiritual healing of our broken relationship with God the Father, through faith in Jesus Christ, is the way into all healing that Jesus wants to offer us as we become part of His plans to redeem the fallen creation.

a)   What about those who have not been born again?

Does this mean that non-Christians my not experience healing and wholeness? No, they certainly may. Confession as making hidden wrongs known, forgiveness, and some of the other principles of healing that Jesus' ministry reveals to us are consistent with the spiritual and natural laws built into the fabric of the universe. For instance, the dynamic of confession brings at least some measure of healing whether it is in the context of psychotherapy or inner healing prayer. That these principles of healing and restoration are built into human nature is a sign of God's love and grace for all of creation.

Nevertheless, full healing, full restoration of the image of God, and reversing the damage of the Fall can only take place for those who, through Jesus Christ, are born again into the Kingdom. It is only in the Kingdom of God that full healing and restoration is possible. The river of life runs only through God's Kingdom, and on its banks alone grow the trees whose leaves are for the healing of the nations.

b)   Spiritual healing as the gateway into God's process of complete healing

The fundamental healing that takes place in God's Kingdom is "spiritual healing." That is, our relationship with God the Father is restored. While general principles of health and wholeness may be discovered by common sense, psychology and medical science there is only one way to restore this fundamental relationship with the Father.

> 6   Jesus answered, "I am the way and the truth and the life. No one comes to the Father except through me. (John 14:6, NIV)

It is through Jesus Christ alone that this fundamental relationship is restored. Being born into the kingdom of God initiates one into an extraordinary journey of experiencing the full extent of Jesus' healing ministry. This ministry will not cease until brought to completion with the fulfillment of the Kingdom of God.

c)   Application: Our sharing in healing ministry

Thus, for the Christian, the first step in healing ministry, is spiritual healing in which people are brought to faith in Jesus Christ and are born again. This was Jesus' priority and the priority of the Holy Spirit. If we are to cooperate with Jesus it must be our priority as well.

2.   CONFESSION, REPENTANCE AND WALKING IN THE LIGHT

There is built into the universe a fundamental spiritual principle. "Things that are willfully hidden from God, God will not heal."

One of the ways that human beings express their freedom of the will is to hide things. This was the first expression of Adam and Eve's will having been corrupted by their rebellion against God. They hid from God and they tried to hide from each other the fact that they were naked. (Genesis 3:7-10)

God, with a broken heart, sought out Adam and Eve in hiding, and out of immense love He will also seek us out of our hiding places. Nevertheless, God honors this perverse expression of our freedom: if we willfully insist upon staying hidden, He leaves us unhealed. Yet this is not His gracious intent for us.

The Holy Spirit, through the words of John, begs us to "walk in the light" so that the grace of God may have its full healing effect within us.

> 5   This is the message we have heard from him and declare to you: God is light; in him there is no darkness at all.
> 6   If we claim to have fellowship with him yet walk in the darkness, we lie and do not live by the truth.
> 7   But if we walk in the light, as he is in the light, we have fellowship with one another, and the blood of Jesus, his Son, purifies us from all sin.

8   If we claim to be without sin, we deceive ourselves and the truth is not in us.
9   If we confess our sins, he is faithful and just and will forgive us our sins and purify us from all unrighteousness.
10   If we claim we have not sinned, we make him out to be a liar and his word has no place in our lives. (I John 1:5-10, NIV)

This is a fundamental principle of wholeness and healing: We must walk in the light. This applies to individuals, families and nations. As a law of the universe, this principle of walking in the light applies regardless of whether people honor Jesus Christ or not.

For example:

In Taiwan there is seared in the consciousness of every Taiwanese Presbyterian the date, 2/28. This is the day in 1947 that the military governor, who had come from the Nationalist party in Mainland China, massacred thousands of the educated class of Taiwan. Many of those killed were Presbyterians. For this crime, the Nationalist Government later executed the governor. Nevertheless, for years the Nationalist Government that was set up in Taiwan by Chang Kai Chek denied that this atrocity ever happened. Hidden in the darkness this hurt festered like a cancer and poisoned the relationships between the native Chinese people of Taiwan and their Nationalist government. It was not until the 1990's when President Lee, a Presbyterian (and native born Taiwanese), came to office that this atrocity was openly confessed. Now there has been healing and, while it is still not perfect, the relationship between government and people is far better after this confession then it had been since 1947.

This same principle applies to an individual's sins and to hurts that we may receive: until they are brought out into the light through confession, even a loving and sovereign God will not heal them.

Often in Jesus' healing ministry, an important step is to bring into the light that which is hidden.

a)   The father of the demon possessed boy

In the case of the father of the demon possessed boy, the presence of Jesus and the shocking manifestations of the demons forced him to make a public confession of his lack of faith.

23   "'If you can'?" said Jesus. "Everything is possible for him who believes."
24   Immediately the boy's father exclaimed, "I do believe; help me overcome my unbelief!" (Mark 9:23-24, NIV)

This "walking in the light", through honest confession of unbelief, was the open door for Jesus' healing both the boy and also the father's hurt and doubt.

b)   The woman at Jacob's well

The woman whom Jesus met at Jacob's well had much in her life that was broken and sinful. Most likely there were layers of hurt going back to her childhood. In addition, she also carried in her heart the racial hurt of having been born a Samaritan who, as a people, were hated and despised by God's true chosen people the Jews. From the questions she asked Jesus we may surmise that she is seeking the truth, yet is hindered by personal and corporate hurt.

Early in the conversation, through a word of knowledge given by the Holy Spirit, Jesus exposes the woman's life of sin and hurt.

> 16   He told her, "Go, call your husband and come back."
> 17   "I have no husband," she replied. Jesus said to her, "You are right when you say you have no husband.
> 18   The fact is, you have had five husbands, and the man you now have is not your husband. What you have just said is quite true."
> 19   "Sir," the woman said, "I can see that you are a prophet. (John 4:16-19, NIV)

The woman does not deny her past nor does she hide. Instead she runs back to the town and tells everyone,

> "Come, see a man who told me everything I ever did. Could this be the Christ?" (John 4:29, NIV)

The result of this open confession is that the woman found her way into the river of life and brought many other people in her village with her.

c)   The women caught in adultery (John 8:1-11)

This woman's sin is brought out into the terrible light of day. It is exposed before the judging, unloving eyes of the Pharisees and before Jesus Christ the Son of God who is perfect. From Jesus she receives not well-deserved condemnation, but forgiveness and restoration.

> 10   Jesus straightened up and asked her, "Woman, where are they? Has no one condemned you?"
> 11   "No one, sir," she said. "Then neither do I condemn you," Jesus declared. "Go now and leave your life of sin." (John 8:10-11, NIV)

d)   Application to our sharing in healing ministry

The application to our sharing in healing ministry with Jesus is obvious. Part of the healing process will be bringing hidden hurts into the light so that they may be forgiven.

The role of much psychotherapy is bringing hurts buried in the unconscious into consciousness. In the light of conscious awareness these hidden hurts and feelings lose their power over us. This process is healing in itself because of the way God has constructed the human psyche.

As we cooperate with Jesus in healing prayer He does, through the Holy Spirit, exactly what we saw Him doing while walking on earth. Hidden things are exposed. In ministry, we find that the Holy Spirit may supernaturally bring a person's hurts and wounds into the light so that they may be healed.

The Holy Spirit, however, goes beyond confession into bringing Jesus' forgiveness. This is the source of spiritual, inner and relational healing in the Kingdom of God. This is a region of wholeness that is inaccessible to secular therapy. [7]

3.   JESUS OFFERS FORGIVENESS OF SINS THAT BRINGS HEALING AND RESTORATION

Repeatedly we see Jesus' offering forgiveness for sins. Sin is the fundamental source of inner hurt and of broken relationships. When sin is forgiven, people are not only restored to a right relationship with God, but they also experience healing of the effects of sin within themselves and in their relationships. Forgiveness is the key to most spiritual, inner and relational healing.

Jesus Christ as the Son of God who died on the cross for us has the authority to forgive sins. This is often His greatest ministry to us.

> 1   *Jesus stepped into a boat, crossed over and came to his own town.*
> 2   *Some men brought to him a paralytic, lying on a mat. When Jesus saw their faith, he said to the paralytic, "Take heart, son; your sins are forgiven."*
> 3   *At this, some of the teachers of the law said to themselves, "This fellow is blaspheming!"*
> 4   *Knowing their thoughts, Jesus said, "Why do you entertain evil thoughts in your hearts?*
> 5   *Which is easier: to say, 'Your sins are forgiven,' or to say, 'Get up and walk'?*
> 6   *But so that you may know that the Son of Man has authority on earth to forgive sins...." Then he said to the paralytic, "Get up, take your mat and go home."*
> 7   *And the man got up and went home.*
> 8   *When the crowd saw this, they were filled with awe; and they praised God, who had given such authority to men.* (Matthew 9:1-8, NIV)

[handwritten annotations: Jesus – give us authority They must 1st Repent & Confess We can declare in Jesus NAME You are forgiven!]

---

[7] Offering true, life transforming forgiveness from Jesus goes beyond what secular therapy and counseling can offer. The Catholic author, Morris West in his novel about Carl Jung entitled, *The World is Made of Glass*, brutally exposes this limit and reveals the incredible possibility of Christianity. The story is based on the reference by Jung in his book, *Memories Dreams and Reflections* to a woman that he failed to help in therapy. Morris' book is a brilliant presentation of Jung's therapeutic approach. This woman who Jung could not heal was brought to Jesus and His absolution and healing by a Catholic celibate homosexual doctor. This man of God is working among the city's prostitutes and invites this fallen, guilt-torn woman to join him. The final pages have these extraordinary lines: "I read Jung's notes on you very carefully. I understand you better than he does. I'm an odd one, like you. I'm also an old-fashioned absolutist – and so, God damn it, are you! You want to kill yourself. And you will one day; because you're a defaulting debtor and you don't want to face the accounting.... Jung wrote something about you that hit me like a hammer. 'She expects too much. She demands a God I can't reveal to her and absolution she hasn't earned and probably never will!' " ...What are you dong to me?" "Just what you asked Jung to do – except he didn't know how. This is a breech presentation, maximum risk, and high-forceps delivery. You're being born again – into Angel Lane!" (New York: Avon Books, 1983).

a)   In the house of Simon the Pharisee Jesus forgives the woman with many sins who washed His feet with her tears

We have already seen the love of Jesus displayed in this story. Now we see Jesus' forgiveness.

> *44   Then he turned toward the woman and said to Simon, "Do you see this woman? I came into your house. You did not give me any water for my feet, but she wet my feet with her tears and wiped them with her hair.*
> *45   You did not give me a kiss, but this woman, from the time I entered, has not stopped kissing my feet.*
> *46   You did not put oil on my head, but she has poured perfume on my feet.*
> *47   Therefore, I tell you, her many sins have been forgiven-- for she loved much. But he who has been forgiven little loves little."*
> *48   Then Jesus said to her, "Your sins are forgiven."*
> *49   The other guests began to say among themselves, "Who is this who even forgives sins?"*
> *50   Jesus said to the woman, "Your faith has saved you; go in peace." (Luke 7:36-50, NIV)*

b)   Jesus forgives and restores Peter Luke 22:60-62, John 21:15-19

The Bible gives us an unusually clear picture of Peter's fall into sin. Three times Peter denied that he knew Jesus. On the third occasion we see Peter's heart pierced by the look of Jesus whom he had just denied.

> *54   Then seizing him, they led him away and took him into the house of the high priest. Peter followed at a distance.*
> *55   But when they had kindled a fire in the middle of the courtyard and had sat down together, Peter sat down with them.*
> *56   A servant girl saw him seated there in the firelight. She looked closely at him and said, "This man was with him."*
> *57   But he denied it. "Woman, I don't know him," he said.*
> *58   A little later someone else saw him and said, "You also are one of them." "Man, I am not!" Peter replied.*
> *59   About an hour later another asserted, "Certainly this fellow was with him, for he is a Galilean."*
> *60   Peter replied, "Man, I don't know what you're talking about!" Just as he was speaking, the rooster crowed.*
> *61   The Lord turned and looked straight at Peter. Then Peter remembered the word the Lord had spoken to him: "Before the rooster crows today, you will disown me three times."*
> *62   And he went outside and wept bitterly. (Luke 22:54-62, NIV)*

Jesus' forgives and restores Peter after the resurrection.

> *7   Then the disciple whom Jesus loved said to Peter, "It is the Lord!" As soon as Simon Peter heard him say, "It is the Lord," he wrapped his outer garment around him (for he*

had taken it off) and jumped into the water.

8   The other disciples followed in the boat, towing the net full of fish, for they were not far from shore, about a hundred yards.

9   When they landed, they saw a fire of burning coals there with fish on it, and some bread.

10   Jesus said to them, "Bring some of the fish you have just caught."

11   Simon Peter climbed aboard and dragged the net ashore. It was full of large fish, 153, but even with so many the net was not torn.

12   Jesus said to them, "Come and have breakfast." None of the disciples dared ask him, "Who are you?" They knew it was the Lord.

13   Jesus came, took the bread and gave it to them, and did the same with the fish.

14   This was now the third time Jesus appeared to his disciples after he was raised from the dead.

15   When they had finished eating, Jesus said to Simon Peter, "Simon son of John, do you truly love me more than these?" "Yes, Lord," he said, "you know that I love you." Jesus said, "Feed my lambs."

16   Again Jesus said, "Simon son of John, do you truly love me?" He answered, "Yes, Lord, you know that I love you." Jesus said, "Take care of my sheep."

17   The third time he said to him, "Simon son of John, do you love me?" Peter was hurt because Jesus asked him the third time, "Do you love me?" He said, "Lord, you know all things; you know that I love you." Jesus said, "Feed my sheep.

18   I tell you the truth, when you were younger you dressed yourself and went where you wanted; but when you are old you will stretch out your hands, and someone else will dress you and lead you where you do not want to go."

19   Jesus said this to indicate the kind of death by which Peter would glorify God. Then he said to him, "Follow me!" (John 21:7-19, NIV)

Notice the way that with the building of the fire of coals Jesus invites Peter to recall and to relive the terrible night of his denial. I imagine that when Peter arrived dripping on the shore, he was shocked to see the fire of burning coals.[8] Most likely, all the images and emotions of that terrible night came flooding back to him. He heard again his own words denying Jesus whom he had sworn to follow even to death. The sound of the cock's crow rang again in his ears. Jesus' look that had pierced his heart rose in his mind's eye. He fought back the tears and battled with the lump of despair that was in his chest as he tried his best to eat breakfast. He did not know what to say nor did he have anything to say until Jesus spoke and offered absolution.

c)   Application in our sharing in healing ministry

Central to Christian teaching is God's forgiveness in Christ and the call to forgive others from the heart. In spiritual, inner and relational healing we pray that the Lord will so touch persons with His forgiving and healing love that their hearts will be melted and they will be released to forgive.

---

[8] The Greek word is "anthrakia", which means "a fire of coals". Some have suggested that this may have been a charcoal fire. The only other time what this word is used in the New Testament is in John 18:18. This was when Peter joined the people around the "fire of coals" the night Jesus was arrested. Thus when the resurrected Jesus built the "fire of coals" and invited Peter to join him and the other disciples around it for breakfast, it was an exact recollection of the context in which Peter had denied Jesus.

Jesus has granted to us the authority to forgive sins in His name.

> 21   *Again Jesus said, "Peace be with you! As the Father has sent me, I am sending you."*
> 22   *And with that he breathed on them and said, "Receive the Holy Spirit.*
> 23   *If you forgive anyone his sins, they are forgiven; if you do not forgive them, they are not forgiven."* (John 20:21-23, NIV)

This primary way that the prayer counselor actually brings healing to those who are broken is by offering forgiveness and absolution in the name of Jesus Christ. When this line is crossed, Holy Spirit-led healing prayer passes into a realm where psychotherapy cannot enter.

Example: My best friend offering forgiveness after my time of confessing sins committed while in Vietnam.

While in seminary, I had a heavy burden of sin from some things I had done while working in Vietnam the summer before entering seminary. I was tormented with guilt and the knowledge that I had greatly hindered the work of the Kingdom of God in that nation. Each night I went alone to the seminary chapel to pray, crying out to God to forgive me and lift the oppressive guilt.

I knew that on the cross Jesus had forgiven me. But in my heart I had no peace. Each morning after I prayed, I awoke with the same burden blotting out the sunshine. And day after day as I carried this guilt, I began to doubt my calling into ministry, and even to question my salvation.

Finally I had had enough. I sought out my best friend, Harris Ricks, who later would stand with me during my battle to accept the call to renewal ministry, and with whom I would meet Jesus. At this point he was neither minister nor priest, simply a Christian friend whom I loved and trusted. Late one evening I said to him, "Harris, let's take a walk. There are things that happened while I was in Vietnam that I must tell you about."

We walked along the wooded cross-country course in North Carolina as I poured out all my sin.

The only response I heard was the sound of my friend's feet plodding down the wooded path alongside me. Finally I sat down on an embankment, exhausted and ready to cry. The whole story had been told. It was a relief just to divulge my secrets.

Harris sat silently. I waited, filled with fear and embarrassment. Had I told him too much? Maybe he would laugh at me or reject me. Perhaps I had just lost my best friend.

After a long time, his voice revealing tears hidden by the darkness, he said, "Yes, you really have sinned against God. You've hindered the work of His Kingdom."

These words penetrated my soul. I began to weep.

Then he reached out and put his arm around me. "But I love you as a brother, and the good news of the Gospel is that Jesus Christ loves and forgives you."

As he said these words, a strange and wonderful thing happened. Jesus was there with us. It was He who, through my friend, had put His arm around me. I could feel the Holy Spirit, like clear, cool water flowing through me, washing away the guilt and healing the hurt. My friend had been my priest and mediator, and through him God had touched me, healed me and let me know His forgiveness. [9]

---

[9] Zeb Bradford Long, *Passage Through the Wilderness: A Journey of the Soul* (Grand Rapids: Chosen Books, 1998) p. 142-143.

4. JESUS OVERTURNS LIES SPOKEN BY SATAN, OTHERS OR OURSELVES WITH TRUTH ABOUT HIMSELF, OURSELVES AND REALITY

Repeatedly in the Gospels, there is the expression of Jesus; "I tell you the truth"

> *41   **I tell you the truth**, anyone who gives you a cup of water in my name because you belong to Christ will certainly not lose his reward.*
> (Mark 9:41, NIV)

> *23   "**I tell you the truth**, if anyone says to this mountain, 'Go, throw yourself into the sea,' and does not doubt in his heart but believes that what he says will happen, it will be done for him.* (Mark 9:41, NIV)

> *17   **I tell you the truth**, anyone who will not receive the kingdom of God like a little child will never enter it."* (Luke 18:17, NIV)

> *29   "**I tell you the truth**," Jesus said to them, "no one who has left home or wife or brothers or parents or children for the sake of the kingdom of God*
> *30   will fail to receive many times as much in this age and, in the age to come, eternal life."* (Luke 18:29-30, NIV)

More than just speaking the truth, Jesus is the truth.

> *6   Jesus answered, "I am the way and the truth and the life. No one comes to the Father except through me.* (John 14:6, NIV)

This is in contrast to Satan who is a liar and sows lies that deceive and keep people in bondage.

> *44   You belong to your father, the devil, and you want to carry out your father's desire. He was a murderer from the beginning, not holding to the truth, for there is no truth in him. When he lies, he speaks his native language, for he is a liar and the father of lies.*
> (John 8:44, NIV)

An encounter with Jesus is an encounter with the truth. In this encounter any lies, whether spoken to us by Satan or by our own depraved hearts, will be overturned and replaced with truth. As Jesus has confirmed this will result in freedom which is a critical step on the way to spiritual, inner and relational healing.

> *31   To the Jews who had believed him, Jesus said, "If you hold to my teaching, you are really my disciples.*
> *32   Then you will know the truth, and the truth will set you free."* (John 8:31-32, NIV)

We see the dynamic of Jesus' truth overcoming lies and deception at nearly every encounter He has with human beings. Jesus' presence is almost like a force field of truth that adjusts the warping effect of lies.

For instance –
   When Peter was busy denying Jesus - Jesus looked at Peter and the truth shattered

all of Peter's lies and pretence. (Luke 22:61-62, NIV)

When the men were ready to stone the woman caught in adultery a simple word
of Jesus "let he who has no sin throw the first stone" overcame their own lies with
the truth that their condition was actually no better than the sinful woman's.
(John 8)

In our own ministry of healing, we will find that lies play a role in holding people in bondage. It
is as these lies are replaced by Jesus' truth that healing and restoration begins to take place. [10]

5. JESUS CAST OUT DEMONS IN ORDER TO CLEAR THE WAY FOR A PERSON'S RESTORATION

This is a prominent part of Jesus' ministry. Casting out demons is an expression of compassion
for those who are afflicted. It is also a sign of the advancing Kingdom of God that overthrows
Satan's empire. By driving away demons Jesus enables people to first enter and then live in the
Kingdom of God where the redemptive processes of restoration are talking place. Fallen angels
under Satan's command have a major agenda of keeping human beings in bondage to their hurt.
They try to either keep people out of the Kingdom by blinding them to the truth, or, if they are
already born again, then they work very hard to keep them from experiencing the full restoration
of being a child of God. There follow two examples.

a) The man possessed by evil spirits set free to witness to Jesus

A great number of evil spirits who go under the name of Legion had driven this tormented man
among the tombs. In this haunted place of the dead he is beyond the boundaries of both human
and divine community. Jesus drives away the spirits and liberates the man for new life in the
Kingdom of God. He is sent back clothed and in his right mind into the human community as a
witness to Jesus Christ.

> *1   They went across the lake to the region of the Gerasenes.*
> *2   When Jesus got out of the boat, a man with an evil spirit came from the tombs to*
> *meet him.*
> *3   This man lived in the tombs, and no one could bind him any more, not even with a*
> *chain.*
> *4   For he had often been chained hand and foot, but he tore the chains apart and broke*
> *the irons on his feet. No one was strong enough to subdue him.*
> *5   Night and day among the tombs and in the hills he would cry out and cut himself*
> *with stones.*
> *6   When he saw Jesus from a distance, he ran and fell on his knees in front of him.*
> *7   He shouted at the top of his voice, "What do you want with me, Jesus, Son of the*
> *Most High God? Swear to God that you won't torture me!"*
> *8   For Jesus had said to him, "Come out of this man, you evil spirit!"*
> *9   Then Jesus asked him, "What is your name?" "My name is Legion," he replied, "for*

---

[10] I am indebted to Ed Smith and his Theophostic approach to healing ministry for this insight of Jesus' work of
overcoming lies with the truth.

we are many."

10   And he begged Jesus again and again not to send them out of the area.

11   A large herd of pigs was feeding on the nearby hillside.

12   The demons begged Jesus, "Send us among the pigs; allow us to go into them."

13   He gave them permission, and the evil spirits came out and went into the pigs. The herd, about two thousand in number, rushed down the steep bank into the lake and were drowned. ...

18   As Jesus was getting into the boat, the man who had been demon-possessed begged to go with him.

19   Jesus did not let him, but said, "Go home to your family and tell them how much the Lord has done for you, and how he has had mercy on you."

20   So the man went away and began to tell in the Decapolis how much Jesus had done for him. And all the people were amazed. (Mark 5, 1-20, NIV)

b)   A daughter of Abraham set free

In this story we have a faithful woman of God who for 18 years has been bound by an evil spirit. When the spirit is cast out she is set free and restored to health.

10   On a Sabbath Jesus was teaching in one of the synagogues,

11   and a woman was there who had been crippled by a spirit for eighteen years. She was bent over and could not straighten up at all.

12   When Jesus saw her, he called her forward and said to her, "Woman, you are set free from your infirmity."

13   Then he put his hands on her, and immediately she straightened up and praised God.

14   Indignant because Jesus had healed on the Sabbath, the synagogue ruler said to the people, "There are six days for work. So come and be healed on those days, not on the Sabbath."

15   The Lord answered him, "You hypocrites! Doesn't each of you on the Sabbath untie his ox or donkey from the stall and lead it out to give it water?

16   Then should not this woman, a daughter of Abraham, whom Satan has kept bound for eighteen long years, be set free on the Sabbath day from what bound her?" (Luke 13:10-16, NIV)

In our ministry of healing prayer, we may also meet blocks to the healing process. It is at this point that we must go deeper into an understanding of how the Holy Spirit works in the unconscious mind. This will be covered in Part 7. On the other hand, we may also be led into engaging evil spirits just as Jesus Christ did. These enemies of our God are working just as hard today as in the Bible times to hold human beings in bondage and to block them from receiving healing and wholeness. We will cover this dimension healing briefly in Part 9 and more completely in the following Dunamis Project Manual on Spiritual Warfare.

C. PHASE 3 –

Jesus invites/commands the person to follow Him in faith and obedience as a disciple.

1.   JESUS CALLS US TO FORGIVE OTHERS SO THAT HIS HEALING GRACE WILL NOT BE BLOCKED

On the cross Jesus won for us forgiveness of sins. God the Father, through Jesus, is ready and eager to forgive us. While His forgiveness is a free gift and powerful to cover any sin no matter how serious, there are nonetheless two actions on our part that may block our receiving this forgiveness.

a)   Our refusal to forgive others will block God's being able to forgive us

Jesus commands us to forgive others just as we have been forgiven.

> *21   Then Peter came to Jesus and asked, "Lord, how many times shall I forgive my brother when he sins against me? Up to seven times?"*
> *22   Jesus answered, "I tell you, not seven times, but seventy-seven times.* (Matthew 18:21-22, NIV)

If we do not forgive, we will not ourselves be forgiven.

> *12   Forgive us our debts, as we also have forgiven our debtors.*
> *13   And lead us not into temptation, but deliver us from the evil one.'*
> *14   For if you forgive men when they sin against you, your heavenly Father will also forgive you.*
> *15   But if you do not forgive men their sins, your Father will not forgive your sins.* (Matthew 6:12-15, NIV)

Why does our lack of forgiveness block God's forgiveness?

> "God's love is like sunshine. It will light up not only our spirit but also our mind and body as well. It is constantly available, but if we block it out by excluding anyone from our love, we should not complain if we soon begin to feel the effects mentally and physically."
>
> George Montague

2.   JESUS CALLS US TO RECEIVE THE WORKING OF THE HOLY SPIRIT AS FROM HIMSELF

There is another action that we may take that blocks God's grace operating within us. This is blasphemy against the Holy Spirit. This has been called the unforgivable sin.

This is so severe a warning that we need to view all three contexts where it appears if we are to gain an understanding of its meaning.

> *31   And so I tell you, every sin and blasphemy will be forgiven men, but the blasphemy against the Spirit will not be forgiven.*
> *32   Anyone who speaks a word against the Son of Man will be forgiven, but anyone who speaks against the Holy Spirit will not be forgiven, either in this age or in the age to come.* (Matthew 12:31-32, NIV)

> *28   I tell you the truth, all the sins and blasphemies of men will be forgiven them.*
> *29   But whoever blasphemes against the Holy Spirit will never be forgiven; he is guilty*
> *of an eternal sin."*
> *30   He said this because they were saying, "He has an evil spirit."* (Mark 3:28-30, NIV)

> *8   "I tell you, whoever acknowledges me before men, the Son of Man will also*
> *acknowledge him before the angels of God.*
> *9   But he who disowns me before men will be disowned before the angels of God.*
> *10   And everyone who speaks a word against the Son of Man will be forgiven, but*
> *anyone who blasphemes against the Holy Spirit will not be forgiven.* (Luke 12:8-10,
> NIV)

There have been many interpretations of these harsh verses. My understanding is that the sin that cannot be forgiven is when we attribute the gracious workings of the Holy Spirit to demons and attribute the work of demons to the Holy Spirit.

The reason it will not be forgiven is that we have in either case rejected the Holy Spirit who is the one who brings Jesus to us. This rejection is a sign of a lack of faith. And without faith there is no bridge to the grace of God. When we reject God reaching out to us in truth and grace through the Holy Spirit, by naming it the work of demons, we block the bridge that God is attempting to build to us.

These two requirements – forgiving others and receiving the Holy Spirit's work as His work are not limitations of the grace of God. Rather, they are cornerstones of our responsible participation in our relationship with God.

We may put the warning not to blaspheme the Holy Spirit into a positive principle of cooperation by rephrasing it to be - we are to welcome the working of the Holy Spirit with us as from Jesus. This welcoming of the Holy Spirit clears the way for spiritual, inner, relational and physical healing to take place within us to the glory of God the Father.

3.   JESUS INVITES/COMMANDS FAITH AND OBEDIENCE

In nearly every case of healing, Jesus invites or commands some type of human response. This is an integral part of the healings becoming active in the person. On some occasions this may be the requirement to have faith. At other times it is the requirement to go do something which is faith in action and a practical way of following Jesus.

Some examples:

Before the extraordinary miracle of the healing/raising of Lazarus, the dead man, Jesus required the action of Martha's confession of faith.

> *25   Jesus said to her, "I am the resurrection and the life. He who believes in me will live,*
> *even though he dies;*
> *26   and whoever lives and believes in me will never die. Do you believe this?"*
> *27   "Yes, Lord," she told him, "I believe that you are the Christ, the Son of God, who*
> *was to come into the world."* (John 11:25-27, NIV)

The man among the tombs who was demon possessed was commanded to go and tell people what God had done for him.

18 As Jesus was getting into the boat, the man who had been demon-possessed begged to go with him.
19 Jesus did not let him, but said, "Go home to your family and tell them how much the Lord has done for you, and how he has had mercy on you."
20 So the man went away and began to tell in the Decapolis how much Jesus had done for him. And all the people were amazed. (Mark 5:18-20, NIV)

For the woman at the well, the call to obedience was the open door for the whole extraordinary word of knowledge and discourse that followed. This resulted in Jesus touching her heart and bringing her into the river of living water.

15 The woman said to him, "Sir, give me this water so that I won't get thirsty and have to keep coming here to draw water."
16 He told her, "Go, call your husband and come back." (John 4:15-16, NIV)

When she finally did obey the command to "go call her husband" she went and called the whole village!

a) Application in our sharing in healing ministry

This call to faith and action connects the person and the healing taking place to the ultimate purpose of Jesus' healing. It is to send us out as His witnesses and living agents of the Kingdom of God.

In our prayer ministry, the Holy Spirit will often call a person to faith and to active obedience. This will be a part of the healing process itself.

Exactly how the person will be called to "get up" and follow Jesus into witness and service will depend upon the person's circumstances and the sovereignty of God. What is for sure is that each person Jesus touches with healing; He will also give to them the extraordinary invitation to "Follow Me!" As one acts in obedience even though one may still be emotionally wounded or physically scarred, the Holy Spirit will give the power and authority to do the impossible.

In this life the healing process may not be completed but that does not exempt us from having a role in the Kingdom of God. Generally it is "wounded healers" whom God has used most in this broken world.

Example: My personal struggle with dyslexia.

I have a learning disability that made it difficult for me to learn to read and to write. School was largely one long dismal failure. The result of these struggles and many failures left me filled with bitterness, and despair that I would have a useless life. Most strange was an insatiable, and given my disability, inexplicable desire to write. I knew I was called by God to be a writer but I was filled with explosive frustration because God had so ill equipped me to fulfill this call.

While missionaries in Korea at the 1975 Pentecost Conference, my wife, Laura, gathered a group to pray for me for healing for my dyslexia. As they prayed I experienced dramatic inner and relational healing. As I was able to forgive the students who had mocked me, teachers who failed me and God who made me, I was healed from my bitterness. Yet, in my brain nothing changed! I was just as dyslexic as ever and found writing even a few sentences an ordeal. Getting ideas from my mind to paper was like jumping an abyss. Even when I got to the other side, the grammar was terrible and most of the words were misspelled. Yet the command persisted. "Come follow me and even with your unhealed disability, write as I tell you to write! Write for my glory!"

Astonishingly I as I have obeyed, God has not only given the content but also the grace and power to write. He has also raised up co-authors, and editors to enable the process. That this manual has been written is a testimony to the healing power of Jesus Christ and also to the fact that He commands us to follow Him even when we are not completely healed.

4. JESUS PROMISES US THE HOLY SPIRIT TO GUIDE, GIFT AND EMPOWER US AS WE WALK AS HIS DISCIPLE.

7 But I tell you the truth: It is for your good that I am going away. Unless I go away, the Counselor will not come to you; but if I go, I will send him to you.
8 When he comes, he will convict the world of guilt in regard to sin and righteousness and judgment:
9 in regard to sin, because men do not believe in me;
10 in regard to righteousness, because I am going to the Father, where you can see me no longer;
11 and in regard to judgment, because the prince of this world now stands condemned.
12 "I have much more to say to you, more than you can now bear.
13 But when he, the Spirit of truth, comes, he will guide you into all truth. He will not speak on his own; he will speak only what he hears, and he will tell you what is yet to come.
14 He will bring glory to me by taking from what is mine and making it known to you.
15 All that belongs to the Father is mine. That is why I said the Spirit will take from what is mine and make it known to you. (John 16:7-15, NIV)

46 He told them, "This is what is written: The Christ will suffer and rise from the dead on the third day,
47 and repentance and forgiveness of sins will be preached in his name to all nations, beginning at Jerusalem.
48 You are witnesses of these things.
49 I am going to send you what my Father has promised; but stay in the city until you have been clothed with power from on high." (Luke 24:46-49, NIV)

4 On one occasion, while he was eating with them, he gave them this command: "Do not leave Jerusalem, but wait for the gift my Father promised, which you have heard me speak about.

5   For John baptized with water, but in a few days you will be baptized with the Holy Spirit."
6   So when they met together, they asked him, "Lord, are you at this time going to restore the kingdom to Israel?"
7   He said to them: "It is not for you to know the times or dates the Father has set by his own authority.
8   But you will receive power when the Holy Spirit comes on you; and you will be my witnesses in Jerusalem, and in all Judea and Samaria, and to the ends of the earth."
(Acts 1:4-8, NIV)

The Holy Spirit is promised us as we follow Jesus Christ.

Jesus calls us to forgive those who hurt us.	Matthew 6:12-16, 18:21-35
Jesus calls us to receive the working of the Holy Spirit as from Him.	Matthew 12:31-32
Jesus calls us to follow Him in faith and obedience.	John 4:15-16, 11:25-27, Mark 5:18-20,
Jesus promises us the Holy Spirit to guide, gift and empower us as we walk as His disciple.	Luke 11:13, John 20:21-23, Luke 24:46-49, Acts 1:4-5, 8

V.   SUMMARY CONCLUSION – HOW JESUS DID SPIRITUAL, INNER AND RELATIONAL HEALING

This simple three-phased dynamic with their basic components may be summarized in the chart below. In actual practice there will be great variations and immense creativity but this seems to be the essence of how Jesus worked with the Holy Spirit to bring spiritual, inner, and relational healing. A later chapter will focus on this same dynamic in regards to physical healing.

In Part Six we will make the transition from Jesus' ministry of healing to how we are called to share with the Holy Spirit in the same ministry. We shall find that according to the same principles Jesus Christ will continue His healing ministry on earth through us.

The Three Phases
of Jesus' Engagement with Human Beings
in Healing Ministry

- **Phase 1** - Jesus first establishes the context for the Holy Spirit to work in a person by bringing the person into a relationship with Himself.

- **Phase 2** - In this relationship Jesus, led by the Holy Spirit, may do any number of things that overcome the effects of the Fall. These various actions, connecting with the Holy Spirit in kairos moments, all have to do with making real in the person's life the Kingdom of God and are all part of the process of their redemption. The result will be spiritual, inner, relational and physical healing.

- **Phase 3** - Jesus invites/commands the person to follow Him in faith and obedience as a disciple. The person is commanded to follow Jesus in an appropriate form of discipleship. This obedience of following Jesus is a vital part of the healing process and confirms that healing is not an end unto itself.

The Basic Ingredients of Jesus' Spiritual, Inner, and Relational Healing Ministry

THE INGREDIENT	BIBLICAL EXAMPLES	HEALING OF...
	Phase 1 Jesus first establishes the context for the Holy Spirit to work by bringing the person into a relationship with Himself	
Jesus is filled with the Holy Spirit.	Luke 3:21-22, 4:14-21. 4:36, 5:17, Acts 4:7-12	This is the source of His power for ministry and sets the overall context for the Spirit working.
Jesus obeys the Father.	John 5:17-21, 8:28-29, 9:4-7, 12:49-50, 14:10-11,	This is the source of His direction and purpose for ministry .
Jesus drew people into conversations with himself	Mark 10:51, John 3:3, 4:7-10, 5:6, Luke 19:5-10, Luke 7:36-50	Establishes a relationship between the person and Jesus Christ – an essential for all forms of healing.
Jesus demonstrates His love for the people He is reaching out to.	Mark 10:21, John 11:34-36, Luke 7:37-42, Romans 5:8, 8:35-39	Essential in all forms of healing – Spiritual, Inner, Relational and Physical
	Phase 2 Jesus and the Holy Spirit engage the person in various ways to bring the reality of the Kingdom of God which results in	

	healing.	
Jesus leads people to be born again into the Kingdom of God	I John 1:5-10, Mark 1:15, Mark 9:23-24, John 1:12-13, 3:34-36, 4:16-19, 8:1-11, II Corinthians 5:17-21	Restoring our fundamental relationship with God. Bringing us into the healing process of the Kingdom of God.
Jesus enables and calls for confession, repentance, and walking in the light	I John 1:5-10, Mark 9:23-24, John 4:16-19, 29, 8:10-11	Brings hidden things into the light where they may be healed and forgiven thus removing the blocks to the Holy Spirit working in spiritual, inner, relational and physical healing.
Jesus forgives sins	Matthew 9:1-8, Luke 7:36-50, 22:60-62, John 21:15-19	The key to spiritual, inner and relational healing. May clear the way for physical healing.
Jesus overturns lies spoken by Satan, others or ourselves with truth about Himself, ourselves and reality.	Mark 9:41, John 14:6, John 8:44, John 8:31-32, Luke 22:61-62, John 8	Sets people free to be able to experience Jesus as the truth and to walk in the truth. Effects all forms of healing.
Jesus cast out demons to clear the way for healing, restoration and obedience.	Mark 5:1-20, Luke 13:10-16	Removes demonic interference to the Holy Spirit's work of healing and restoration. May affect all forms of healing.
	PHASE 3 Jesus invites/commands the person to follow Him in faith and obedience as a disciple.	

Jesus calls us to forgive those who hurt us.	Matthew 6:12-16, 18:21-35, John 20:23	We must forgive others; otherwise we block God's grace and forgiveness in ourselves.
Jesus calls us to receive the working of the Holy Spirit as from Himself.	Matthew 12:31-32	We must welcome and allow the working of the Holy Spirit in and with us as Jesus working with us. If we reject the working of the Holy Spirit by saying it is demon, then we will cut ourselves off from the possibility of Jesus working in us.
Jesus calls us to follow Him in faith and to obedience	John 4:15-16, 11:25-27, Mark 5:18-20,	Our faith and obedience is a part of the process of our experiencing healing in all of its forms. This is also the first step into the purpose of our healing: It is so we may be witnesses to Jesus Christ. This is part of our restoration.
Jesus promises us the Holy Spirit to guide, gift and empower us as we walk as His disciple.	Luke 11:13, John 20:21-23, Luke 24:46-49, Acts 1:4-5, 8	We are broken and wounded. We are also powerless to follow Jesus Christ. The Holy Spirit is promised to us to enable us to follow Jesus as His disciples.

Teaching Charts

Part V

Spiritual, Inner and Relational Healing

The Dunamis Project
Presbyterian-Reformed Ministries International

JESUS' MINISTRY OF HEALING IS ROOTED FIRST IN THE NATURE OF GOD THE FATHER

36   "Abba, Father," he said, "everything is possible for you. Take this cup from me. Yet not what I will, but what you will." (Mark 14:36, NIV)

"to the **Father** is attributed the beginning of activity, and fountain and wellspring of all things..." John Calvin

A. JESUS' RELATIONSHIP WITH THE FATHER IS REVELATORY -

Matthew 11:27-27, John 14:8-9

1. God the Father's purposes include the redemption of the whole fallen cosmos.

Genesis 12:1-3

Revelation 22

2. God the Father's extraordinary love

- ○ The Father loves the Son - (John 3:35-36, 2 Peter 1:17)

- ○ God loves the world - (2 Peter 1:17)

- ○ God is love and loves us - (I John 4:7-10, Galatians 4:6)

- ○ The Love of God the Father is vast and deep-(Psalm 147:3-6)

3. God knows our inner being and the secrets of our heart

Psalm 139:13-18

B. JESUS' WORK IS SUBORDINATE TO THE FATHER

John 5:17-21

This means that the healing ministry of Jesus
is actually the healing ministry of God
the Father.

For us called to healing ministry the same
principle of subordination also applies.

It is not our ministry, rather it is the ministry of
God the Father, Son and Holy Spirit.

C. IT IS THE FATHER'S WILL THAT JESUS' MISSION INCLUDE ALL FORMS OF HEALING - ISAIAH 53:3-7

Spiritual Healing -
2 Corinthians 5:17-19

Inner Healing -

2 Corinthians 3:17-18, Galatians 5:22-25

Relational Healing -
Galatians 3:26-29

Physical Healing -
John 11:25-26

Restoration of the Creation -
Romans 8:18-25

THE DYNAMIC OF JESUS' COOPERATION WITH THE HOLY SPIRIT IN HEALING MINISTRY

Why is the "How to" of Jesus' healing ministry
relevant to us?

We are called to the same form of engagement with the Holy
Spirit as Jesus is in order to share in His on-going healing
ministry!

John 14:12-14   John 20:21 -23

A. The agency at work in and through Jesus for healing was the Holy Spirit.

Luke 4:14-21

Luke 6:19

B. Jesus' approach to all healing conformed to the basic principles of power ministry.

The Dynamic of Cooperating With The Holy Spirit in Power Ministry
(For Jesus Christ and for Us, His Disciples)

Flow of Human History: Space and Time Continuum

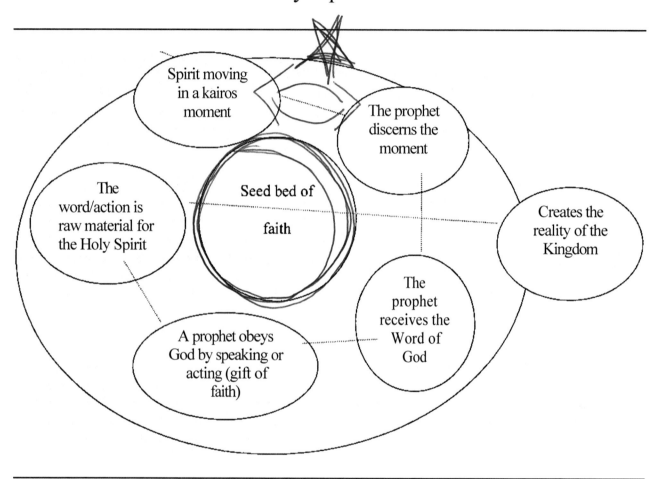

Kairos Moments in Chronos Time

THE PRMI *DUNAMIS PROJECT*
THE HEALING MINISTRY OF JESUS
PART 5 CHART3

Bible is Established Source Code

THE THREE PHASES OF JESUS' ENGAGEMENT WITH HUMAN BEINGS IN HEALING MINISTRY

PHASE 1

Jesus establishes the context in which the Holy Spirit will work by bringing the person into a relationship with himself.

PHASE 2

Jesus and the Holy Spirit engage the person in various ways to bring the reality of the Kingdom of God, which results in healing.

PHASE 3

Jesus invites/commands the person to follow Him in faith and obedience as a disciple.

The Basic Ingredients of Jesus' Spiritual, Inner, and Relational Healing Ministry

	Phase 1 Jesus first establishes the context for the Holy Spirit to work by bringing the person into a relationship with Himself.	
Jesus is filled with the Holy Spirit.	Luke 3:21-22,4:14-21. *4:36,5:17,* Acts 4:7-12	This is the source of His power for ministry and sets the overall context for the Spirit working.
Jesus obeys the Father	John 5:17-21,8:28-29, 9:4-7, 12:49-50, 14:10-11,	This is the source of His direction and purpose for ministry.
Jesus drew people into conversations with Himself.	Mark 10:51, John 3:3, 4:7-10, 5:6, Luke 19:5-10, Luke 7:36-50	Establishes a relationship between the person and Jesus Christ - an essential for all forms of healing.
Jesus demonstrates His love for the people He is reaching out to.	Mark 10:21, John 11:34-36, Luke 7:37-42, Romans 5:8, 8:35-39	Essential in all forms of healing - spiritual, inner, relational and physical.

	Phase 2 Jesus and the Holy Spirit engage the person in various ways to bring the reality of the Kingdom of God which results in healing.	
Jesus leads people to be born again into the Kingdom of God	I John 1:5-10, Mark 1:15, Mark 9:23-24, John 1:12-13,3:34-36,4:16-19,8:1-11, II Corinthians 5:17-21	Restoring our fundamental relationship with God. Bringing us into the healing process of the Kingdom of God.
Jesus enables and calls for confession, repentance, and walking in the light	I John 1:5-10, Mark 9:23-24, John 4:16-19, 29, 8:10-11	Brings hidden things into the light where they may be healed and forgiven thus removing the blocks to the Holy Spirit working in spiritual, inner, relational and physical healing.
Jesus forgives sins.	Matthew 9:1-8, Luke 7:36-50, 22:60-62, John 21:15-19	The key to spiritual, inner and relational healing. May clear the way for physical healing.
Jesus overturns lies spoken by Satan, others or ourselves with truth about Himself, ourselves and reality.	Mark 9:41, John 14:6,John 8:44, John 8:31-32, Luke 22:61-62, John 8	Sets people free to be able to experience Jesus as the truth and to walk in the truth. Affects all forms of healing.
Jesus cast out demons to clear the way for healing, restoration and obedience.	Mark 5:1 -20, Luke 13:10-16	Removes demonic interference to the Holy Spirit's work of healing and restoration. May affect all forms of healing

	Phase 3 Jesus invites/commands the person to follow Him in faith and obedience as a disciple	
Jesus calls us to forgive those who hurt us.	Matthew 6:12-16, 18:21-35, John 20:23	We must forgive others; otherwise we block God's grace and forgiveness in ourselves.
Jesus calls us to receive the working of the Holy Spirit as from Himself	Matthew 12:31-32	We must welcome and allow the working of the Holy Spirit in and with us as Jesus working with us. If we reject the working of the Holy Spirit by saying it is demon, then we will cut ourselves off from the possibility of Jesus working in us.
Jesus promises us the Holy Spirit to guide, gift and empower us as we walk as His disciple.	Luke 11:13, John 20:21-23, Luke 24:46-49, Acts 1:4-5,8	We are broken and wounded. We are also powerless to follow Jesus Christ. The Holy Spirit is promised to us to enable us to follow Jesus as His disciples.

PART VI

The Holy Spirit Continues Jesus' Healing Work

By Brad Long

The Dunamis Project
Presbyterian-Reformed Ministries International

I. THE HOLY SPIRIT CONTINUES JESUS' HEALING MINISTRY ON EARTH

A. JESUS CONTINUES TO WORK IN HUMAN LIVES TODAY THROUGH THE HOLY SPIRIT

Today the Holy Spirit continues Jesus' healing ministry. He does this by applying, in us and in our relationships, the same dynamic principles that we have observed in the life and ministry of Jesus. The radical good news of the gospel is that healing ministry takes place through Jesus Christ, who works through the Holy Spirit to do the same things He did when He walked on the earth in human flesh.

B. THE ROLE OF THE PRAYER MINISTER

Jesus Christ, as sovereign Lord of the universe, can work through the Holy Spirit in people's lives without the mediation of other human beings. Indeed this has often happened.

On the frontiers of the church, stories abound of the gospel being introduced to unbelievers through dreams or miracles without the mediation of missionaries or even the Bible. Further, nearly every mature believer has experienced the direct guidance and working of the Holy Spirit telling him or her how to follow Jesus and how to do His works.

At the same time, we do find that God's works among human beings are often mediated through other human beings. We see this pattern from the beginning of Jesus' ministry in which he called and sent out his disciples with authority to do the same work that He was doing.

We find that God also works in us the same way to advance His Kingdom.

As Paul says,

> *14   How, then, can they call on the one they have not believed in? And how can they believe in the one of whom they have not heard? And how can they hear without someone preaching to them?*
> *15   And how can they preach unless they are sent? As it is written, "How beautiful are the feet of those who bring good news!"* (Romans 10:14-15, NIV)

We may ask the same of healing ministry, "How will others know the healing power of Jesus Christ unless those who are born again are filled with the Holy Spirit and sent out into ministry?" We must become Jesus' hands, feet and heart.

In this section of the manual there will be presented the dynamic of how the Holy Spirit may work to bring Jesus' healing to us now. In this process Jesus Christ will be seen to be the chief actor and source of healing power, nevertheless the prayer counselor will be seen to have a vital role as a "co-worker" with Jesus and the Holy Spirit.

C. THE PREPARATION OF THE PRAYER COUNSELOR FOR WORKING WITH JESUS IN HEALING

It must be established that for this dynamic of Jesus' healing to function through a prayer counselor that person must have gone through the preparation already explored in Part 4. This preparation is as follows:

1. They have been born again.

2. They are abiding in Jesus Christ.

3. They are being filled with the Holy Spirit.

4. They have learned how to cooperate in the dynamic of the Holy Spirit's work through receiving gifts, discernment of kairos moments, and walking in obedience.

5. They are growing mature in the fruit of the Spirit, especially the fruit of love.

Without this preparation the person lacks that which Jesus uses to work through them to do His work in another person. This is Jesus' "special" healing work[1] that is obviously linked to Himself and the Kingdom of God. This is not just working for Jesus, but rather working with Jesus and the Holy Spirit for the glory of God the Father.

Skillful non-Christian doctors, counselors, and therapists may participate in the general work of healing based on the use of reason and coherence with God's laws built into the structure of the universe. Often Christian counseling is not done in the power of the Holy Spirit. It may be in the name of Jesus but it is actually, in method and in fruit, little different from the non-Christian's participation in general natural healing.

These two forms of healing are not at all contradictory. Indeed, they should be complimentary. The focus however of the *Dunamis Project* is on working with Jesus in the power of the Holy Spirit.

There follows a description of the process by which the Holy Spirit works to engage both the wounded person and the prayer counselor in the dynamic of Jesus' healing.

---

[1] We need a better term as we make the distinction between Jesus' direct supernatural healing work done through human beings filled with the Holy Spirit and the general healing work that is based on reason and natural systems. The terms "general" and "special" are based on special revelation through scripture and general revelation through creation.

II.   PHASES IN HOLY SPIRIT-DIRECTED PRAYER MINISTRY

A simple model or rubric for our cooperation with the Holy Spirit in Jesus' ministry of healing may be derived from a study of Jesus' ministry of healing. As we established in Part 5 Jesus' interaction with human beings has the following dynamic phases:

THE DYNAMIC OF JESUS' ENGAGEMENT WITH HUMAN BEINGS IN HEALING MINISTRY

PHASE 1 –

Jesus establishes the context in which the Holy Spirit will work by bringing the person into a relationship with himself.

PHASE 2 –

Jesus and the Holy Spirit engage the person in various ways to bring the reality of the Kingdom of God, which results in healing.

PHASE 3 –

Jesus invites/commands the person to follow Him in faith and obedience as a disciple.

The same framework that is found in Jesus' ministry will also apply to our own cooperation with the Holy Spirit. Within it may take place all the different forms of healing. In this and the next chapter we will apply it to spiritual, inner, and relational healing. In a later chapter we shall deal with this same dynamic as it relates to physical healing.

Inner healing is more an art than a science. Fundamentally it is a dynamic relationship with Jesus rather than a technique. These steps are actually the different phases of engagement and dialogue with Jesus Christ as He is working through the Holy Spirit to bring a person into the full reality of the Kingdom of God.

We have found in our experience of healing prayer that Jesus would often work in the following simple dynamic and people were always blessed. Around this engagement, there is ample room for the insights of psychotherapy, psychology and other human disciplines. Yet it should be recognized that Jesus Christ is the ultimate source of a person's healing and their restoration in the Kingdom of God.

There follows an adaptation of the phases of Jesus' healing ministry to our own cooperating with the Holy Spirit.

A. PHASE 1 –

PHASE 1

Jesus establishes the context in which the Holy Spirit will work by bringing the person into a relationship with Himself.

Jesus is filled with the Holy Spirit: this is the source of His power for ministry.	Luke 3:21-22, 4:14-21. 4:36, 5:17, Acts 4:7-12
Jesus obeys the Father: this is the source of His direction and purpose for ministry.	John 5:17-21, 8:28-29, 9:4-7, 12:49-50, 14:10-11
Jesus drew people into conversations with himself.	Mark 10:51, John 3:3, 4:7-10, 5:6, Luke 19:5-10, Luke 7:36-50
Jesus demonstrates His love for the people He is reaching out to.	Mark 10:21, John 11:34-36, Luke 7:37-42, Romans 5:8, 8:35-39

We work according to biblical principles to establish the context that welcomes the Holy Spirit to work.

In all forms of healing there is the setting of the context or the stage in which it takes place. A hospital with its staff of doctors, nurses, special equipment and atmosphere is a special context for enabling the natural laws of healing and health to work with maximum effectiveness.

The secular counseling or psychological practice with its specially trained people, atmosphere and established therapeutic techniques all set the stage for inner and relational transformations to take place.

1.   Healing ministry is to take place in the overall context of the Church as the Body of Christ

In Christian prayer ministry there must also be the establishment of a context in which the Holy Spirit may work to bring Jesus' healing. In the Bible, Jesus has revealed to us what type of context He and the Holy Spirit prefer to work in. God can work anywhere, but the following are the optimum conditions that have been mandated to us in Scripture. The Church as the body of Jesus Christ in which there is Holy Spirit-led worship, the faithful preaching of the gospel, living according to the truth and the ongoing work of prayer.

- A community of people who have faith in Jesus and the expectancy that the Holy Spirit is working. This includes nurturing the active processes of discerning the working of the Holy Spirit from that of other spirits and the cultivation of the spiritual discipline of cooperating with the Holy Spirit in ministry.

- A community in which the Bible is the authoritative word of God. The community is one that is actually experiencing the work of the Holy Spirit and moving in the spiritual gifts, but is also grounded in the Word of God which is God's objective truth revealed for all times and places.

- Prayer teams formed within this fellowship composed of people who are being filled with the Holy Spirit expressing diverse gifts. They are called and equipped to work in healing ministry together.

This Christ-centered, worshipping, ministering community in which the Word is truly preached and the gifts of the Holy Spirit welcomed provides the overall context for healing ministry.

2.   Preparation of the prayer counselor (or healing prayer team):

A further aspect of the creation of the context is the preparation of those who will be involved in prayer ministry. This all reflects an ongoing life style of being connected to Jesus Christ. This may be

- Abiding in Jesus Christ.

- Praying to be filled with the Holy Spirit.

- Being motivated by love of Jesus and of the person they are praying for.

- Walking in the light and being in the body of Christ that provides accountability and balance.

- Loving, attentive listening to the person.

- Active listening to the Holy Spirit.

- A heart set on obeying the guidance received from the Holy Spirit.

3.   Setting the context in the actual prayer session

We now move to the specific context when the actual prayer session takes place. This may be an agreed upon time or place requested by the person asking for prayer. It may happen after or during the worship hour at church. Whatever the actual time and place, the overall context has been identified above. There follows some ways that the actual prayer may take place.

a)   Initial conversation with the person to be prayed for and their personal preparation to welcome the Holy Spirit to work

Before going into prayer, it is important for those praying to engage the person to be prayed for in conversation.

The purpose of this initial conversation is to:

1.) Establish understanding and rapport.

2.) To discern the person's spiritual condition and their relationship with Jesus Christ.

3.) To determine what it is the person needs to be prayed for.

4.) To understand the person's background and history.

To help prepare the person spiritually for an encounter with Jesus Christ, the prayer counselor may be led by the Holy Spirit to lead the person in the following spiritual excersies:

- Surrendering to the lordship of Jesus Christ. (The submission of one's will to God's will.)

- Examination of life, with confession, for the removal of any obstacles that may be blocking one's relationship with Christ.

- Renunciation of any evil spirits, involvement in the occult or persistent sin.

- Acceptance of one's own responsibility and an identification of others who are responsible.

b) Shift from conversation into prayer for healing

After discussion with the person, the articulation of the need and the above spiritual exercises, the prayer counselor would then lead into prayer for healing. The Holy Spirit may lead these opening prayers in the following ways:

- Thanksgiving for Jesus' grace.
- Praise for Jesus' love for the person.
- An invitation for the Holy Spirit to come and work.
- Laying out before Jesus Christ the person's situation and their prayer request.

Often the prayer counselor may facilitate this final step by saying something like, "You have told me your situation, now tell Jesus." This is part of "confession" as one lays before Jesus a summary of one's need for healing.

Jesus tells us to specifically ask, so it is important to proceed and explicitly state what one is asking for.

4. Summary chart for Jesus Work and Our Work with Jesus in Phase 1

Summary of some things that the Holy Spirit may lead you to do in Phase 1:

Jesus' Work	Our work with Jesus
Jesus is filled with the Holy Spirit and obeys the Father.	We pray to be filled with the Holy Spirit and ask that the Holy Spirit come upon the person being prayed for in power. We invite the Holy Spirit to work.
Jesus obeys the Father: this is the source of His direction and purpose for ministry.	We surrender ourselves to walking in obedience to Jesus Christ.
Jesus drew people into conversations with himself.	We engage the person being prayed for in conversation through directly asking them questions and intentionally listening to them.
Jesus demonstrates His love for the people He is reaching out to.	We show forth both by word and actions the love that we have been given by Jesus for the person being prayed for.

B. PHASE 2

> ### PHASE 2 –
>
> Jesus and the Holy Spirit engage the person in various ways to bring the reality of the Kingdom of God, which results in healing.

Jesus leads people to be born again into the Kingdom of God	I John 1:5-10, Mark 1:15, Mark 9:23-24, John 1:12-13, 3:34-36, 4:16-19, 8:1-11, II Corinthians 5:17-21
Jesus enables and calls for confession, repentance, and walking in the light	I John 1:5-10, Mark 9:23-24, John 4:16-19, 29, 8:10-11
Jesus forgives sins	Matthew 9:1-8, Luke 7:36-50, 22:60-62, John 21:15-19
Jesus overturns lies spoken by Satan, others, or oneself with truth about Himself, reality and oneself.	Mark 9:41, John 14:6, John 8:44, John 8:31-32, Luke 22:61-62, John 8
Jesus cast out demons to clear the way for healing, restoration and obedience.	Mark 5:1-20, Luke 13:10-16

Jesus works through us and in the person being prayed for, as we are led and empowered by the Holy Spirit, to do those things He did while in the flesh that will make real the Kingdom of God.

---

1.   Invitation for Jesus to work

This is a continuation of the opening prayer. It is prayed either by the person asking for prayer or by the prayer counselor. This is a cry for help inviting Jesus to enter the situation. It is based on the faith that if we call, Jesus will indeed hear us and answer.

Along with this prayer for help there may be affirmations of faith and expressions that we are willing to do whatever Jesus asks us to do or wants to work in us. (John 7:17)

2. Conversation with Jesus Christ - getting direction about what He is doing and wants us to do with Him

Both the prayer counselor and the person being prayed for listen to the leading of the Holy Spirit. Jesus Christ may speak or act in some of the ways that are consistent with His speaking and acting in scripture. The various things He may do and call us to be involved in are listed above. However, Jesus and the Holy Spirit are both enormously creative, and each person's situation is unique. Therefore, these biblical examples are to serve as a menu of what Jesus may do rather than as a law of what He will always do in all cases.

Jesus may speak to the person being prayed for and to the prayer counselor and team.

A key to this whole process is the reality of Jesus actually speaking to both the prayer counselor and to the person being prayed for.

Jesus may speak in a variety of ways. A word whispered in the heart, verses of scripture, images and pictures.

As one enters this type of prayer Jesus will often speak through the gifts of the Holy Spirit especially the word of knowledge, the word of prophecy, the word of wisdom, and tongues with interpretation. See the next section that follows on the role of the gifts of the Holy Spirit in healing prayer.

In all these diverse ways that God will speak, three fundamental assumptions are being made:

- God does speak to us and we may actually hear His voice.

- God may actually speak to our unique situations giving direct clear guidance that is not word-by-word or verse-by-verse from scripture BUT this personal word will be consistent with the revealed word of Scripture.

- The prayer counselor and the one being prayed for hearing and obeying God's word or experiencing the operation of the gifts of the Holy Spirit must take place in a context in which there are in place processes of discernment. This guards against both deception as well as presumption.

For more on the process of discernment and how God speaks see the Dunamis Project Manual *In the Spirit's Power*.

a)   The role of the person being prayed for

The person being prayed for is both an active as well as passive participate in the process. They are to receive God's grace and love and to trust Jesus to work. The active part comes as they listen to the Spirit and participate with the prayer counselor(s) in what He is doing.

This may take the form of:

- Sharing with the prayer counselor what is going on in side of them in terms of memories, feelings, and thoughts.

- Reporting whatever God may be saying or doing.

b)   The role of the prayer counselor

The prayer counselor must also be engaged in active listening both to what is going on inside the person and to the Holy Spirit. This is the critical point where the gifts of the Holy Spirit may come into operation. They provide the supernatural tools for the prayer counselor to participate in Jesus' work.

See the next section on the gifts of the Holy Spirit by Bob Whitaker for specific examples of the gifts in operation in healing ministry.

At this phase the role of the prayer counselor is to help discern what the Holy Spirit is doing and saying. A part of this will be affirming when a word really is from Jesus and then encouraging the person to act upon it in obedience.

Knowing how Jesus worked in scripture gives the prayer counselor a "repertoire" of possible ways of cooperating with the Holy Spirit when in healing prayer. They must cultivate the spiritual discipline of being open to the creative leading of the Holy Spirit. This requires intentionally resisting the temptation to fall into set techniques or assuming that God will work the same way in each case. (See my book, *Passage Through The Wilderness* chapters 9 and 18 about the process of dying to spiritual technique and learning "to face the emptiness" as a way of giving space for God to work.)

3.   Summary chart of Jesus' work and our work with Jesus in Phase 2

Jesus' Work	Our work with Jesus
Jesus leads people to be born again into the Kingdom of God.	We present the gospel and invite the person to accept Jesus Christ as Lord and Savior, and then pray with them to be born again.
Jesus enables and calls for confession, repentance, and walking in the light.	Assure the person of Jesus' love and acceptance of those who turn to Him in confession and forgiveness. Read the Bible passages that reveal sin and its consequences. As revealed by the Holy Spirit, expose and name any sins and present them to the person for discernment. Invite the person to confess their sins and to walk in the light.
Jesus forgives sins.	After true confession from the heart, as led by the Holy Spirit, offer forgiveness in the name of Jesus Christ. This may be communicated by words spoken as well as by whatever sacramental or symbolic actions the Holy Spirit may direct.
Jesus overturns lies spoken by Satan, ourselves or others with truth about Himself, reality and us.	We discern and help the person discern those lies that have been received which are contrary to reality in the light of Jesus as the truth. As led by the Holy Spirit we expose the lies and in love and authority speak the truth into the person's life.
Jesus cast out demons to clear the way for healing, restoration and obedience.	Through rational analysis and the gifts of the Holy Spirit we discern the presence of any evil spirits in or around the person, close the "gateways" that gave them ground for attack and in the authority of Jesus Christ bind them and remove them from interfering with the person.

C. PHASE - 3

PHASE 3 –

Jesus invites/commands the person to follow Him in faith and obedience as a disciple.

Jesus calls us to forgive those who hurt us.	Matthew 6:12-16, 18:21-35, John 20:23
Jesus calls us to receive the working of the Holy Spirit as from Him.	Matthew 12:31-32
Jesus calls us to follow Him in faith and obedience.	John 4:15-16, 11:25-27, Mark 5:18-20,
Jesus promises us the Holy Spirit to guide, gift and empower us as we walk as His disciple.	Luke 11:13, John 20:21-23, Luke 24:46-49, Acts 1:4-5, 8

We are to help the person hear and discern how Jesus Christ is calling them to walk in obedience that will result in discipleship.

---

1.   Following in obedience – doing what Jesus wants us to do as His disciples

The Holy Spirit does not speak idly or for our entertainment. He expects us to obey. We are called then to do what Jesus commands us to do. Both the prayer counselor, as well as the person being prayed for, are called to walk in obedience.

At this stage the role of the prayer counselor may be as follows:

- Encourage obedience.

- Help work out a follow-up plan.

- Enter the process and by letting the Holy Spirit speak and act through them. The prayer counselor may become the means through whom Jesus mediates His response back to the person.

For example, if Jesus has called the person to forgive someone who has hurt him or her, the role of the counselor will be to encourage him or her to take that action. Here, again, the gifts of the Holy Spirit find their full and proper expression as the way that the prayer counselor would be able to cooperate with what Jesus is doing as He calls the person to follow Him.

Following Jesus is neither an abstraction nor an inspirational concept; rather it is a life style of obedience in specific actions that creates God's reality in our lives and the lives of others.

The exact from of obedience Jesus will require will be appropriate to the person and their circumstances and will enable them to be an effective witness to the Gospel.

2.   The critical importance of forgiveness

It often seems that the essence of Jesus' healing is found in his willingness to forgive us. Likewise for those who are hurt, healing can only take place when they actually follow Jesus by forgiving the person who has hurt them.

3.   For the person praying for healing, moving out in discipleship is part of the healing process

From our study of the Bible we must affirm that Jesus' healing ministry has three fundamental purposes:

- To show forth the love of God the Father, Son and Holy Spirit's to wounded and hurt people.

- To enable those called by God to go forth as His witnesses.

- To advance the Kingdom of God.

The command to follow Jesus Christ and be His witness may take place at any time during the healing process. Often this call comes before one is completely healed. There are some times when the healing process is completed only as one obeys. Like the ten lepers who are healed as they went on their way to show themselves to the high priest. (Luke 17:14)

At other times the call to follow Jesus by being a witness comes only after the healing has brought the person sufficient wholeness to be able to obey. This was the case with the man who was possessed by a legion of demons. It was only after he was set free "dressed and in his right mind" that Jesus gave the command.

18 As Jesus was getting into the boat, the man who had been demon-possessed begged to go with him.
19 Jesus did not let him, but said, "Go home to your family and tell them how much the Lord has done for you, and how he has had mercy on you."
20 So the man went away and began to tell in the Decapolis how much Jesus had done for him. And all the people were amazed. (Mark 5:18-20, NIV)

The call to discipleship places our participation in healing ministry in its overall context. The purpose is to advance the Kingdom of God.

4. Praying for the infilling with the Holy Spirit, for the gifts and power to follow Jesus and be His witness, and to continue following Jesus

Usually out of this type of prayer session there will have come clear directions for a life of following Jesus. Now, more than ever before, the person needs the power and guidance of the Holy Spirit to follow through and to continue in the healing process.

The role of the prayer counselor now shifts again to that of leading the person in prayer for the infilling with the Holy Spirit. This may require some teaching preparation.

5. Debriefing, reflection, plan for follow-up, discernment of what Jesus is calling you to do next

In order to verify what Jesus has done, there should follow a time of conversation and reflection. This is an opportunity to reflect rationally on what has been happening and to make specific plans for follow-up. At this phase the prayer counselor may need to step into the teaching mode to explain what has been happening from the biblical perspective. There will need to be the building of a biblical foundation for continued growing in Christian maturity.

At the end of this section we will offer several case studies that demonstrate this three phase dynamic of our participating in Jesus' work of spiritual, inner, and relational healing. Before doing so, we must first explore the role of the gifts of the Holy Spirit in healing ministry.

The practical way that the Holy Spirit brings these three phases of Jesus' healing into reality is through manifesting the spiritual gifts in the team, the prayer counselor and the person being prayed for. These gifts are the supernatural power tools that the Holy Spirit expresses through us, to advance the Kingdom of God on earth. These gifts may be manifested at all three phases of Jesus' healing process.

There follows a description of each of the manifestation gifts as listed in I Corinthians 12-14 and how they directly relate to healing. Keep in mind that this includes all the forms of healing but with a focus on spiritual, inner and relational healing.

6.   Summary Chart of Jesus' work and our work with Jesus in Phase 3

Jesus' Work	Our work with Jesus
Jesus calls us to forgive those who hurt us.	We pray that the person being prayed for may have the grace to forgive those who are responsible for their hurt.
Jesus calls us to receive the working of the Holy Spirit as from Him.	We help the person being prayed for to first discern and then to receive what the Holy Spirit is doing in them as from Jesus.
Jesus calls us to follow Him in faith and obedience.	In love and wisdom we walk with the person as they in faith and obedience seek to follow Jesus Christ.
Jesus promises us the Holy Spirit to guide, gift and empower us as we walk as His disciple.	We pray that the person who is in process of healing will be filled with the Holy Spirit to be an effective disciple of Jesus Christ.

III. THE ROLE OF THE GIFTS OF THE HOLY SPIRIT (BY BOB WHITAKER)

In this whole process of sharing with Jesus Christ in healing ministry, the gifts of the Holy Spirit pray a vital role. They are the power tools given to us for actually cooperating with Jesus Christ. Without them this becomes merely a human work. The gifts of the Spirit distinguish this process of sharing with Jesus in healing, from human therapeutic approaches. When the gifts of the Holy Spirit are active, we have a secondary role to Jesus who is the therapist.

(The observations and examples that follow come largely from the long experience in Holy Spirit empowered healing ministry of Bob Whitaker.)

It is not surprising that the ministry of emotional healing, herein described, grew out of the charismatic renewal in the 1960s. In my view participating with Jesus in His healing work really cannot be done effectively without a total reliance on the power and gifts of the Holy Spirit. In our life preparation and in our prayers in anticipation of times of ministry and in our invocations we are asking to be filled and equipped with the Holy Spirit and His gifts listed in 1 Corinthians 12:1-11. We will mention each gift and illustrate ways in which it is invaluable.

A. THE GIFT OF KNOWLEDGE (I CORINTHIANS 1:8)

The Greek word means a "deep knowing." In the Gospels it is translated "perceiving" in relationship to Jesus' knowing what was in the hearts and minds of those to whom He ministered. He was always on target because God gave Him this extraordinary sensitivity and penetrating gaze. When people cannot remember the sources of their hurt, we are continually amazed how the Lord will show it to us.

> A while ago I prayed for a woman elder; she was very bothered by the feeling that no one ever noticed her or paid any attention to her, especially when she really had something important to say. We talked about her family and wondered if she was taken seriously and listened to at home, but that seemed to be a dead end.
>
> Finally, I prayed for the Lord to reveal the root. A brief, gentle image came into my mind; it was a small square swimming pool with mostly white tile and some faded turquoise tiles. I prayed to know what it meant. Nothing came. So I asked the woman, "What does this picture mean to you?" Immediately she caught her breath as she flashed back to a time when as a small child she was in that pool drowning. There were people all around, but they were preoccupied. As she began to flounder, she was so scared she was speechless, and couldn't yell. Finally, in the nick of time, someone noticed and she was rescued. Naturally it was a traumatic memory, which had been repressed, but the word of knowledge brought it to the surface and then we prayed for the healing of the trauma and the fear she would not be noticed or heard.

Usually the word of knowledge comes as an inner prompting of what to say or pray as we guide or interact with people in the inner healing process.

B. WORD OF WISDOM (I CORINTHIANS 1:8)

While "knowledge" is an intuition concerning what is really going on behind the scenes humanly speaking, or a revelation of God's will in the situation, wisdom is the divine quick wittedness to know what to do with the knowledge imparted.

> One day, before a man even opened up with me; the Lord impressed upon me that he was homosexual. I thought to myself, "Why is this being revealed to me?" It seemed that the Lord was saying, "Figure it out." So I pondered why He might have revealed it. The thought came, "So that you can call him to healing and repentance." The man was seeking to keep the conversation centered on superficial needs. After rapport had been established, the Spirit checked me about telling him what had been revealed. Instead, I felt guided to gently ask him if he was a homosexual. He smiled in relief and said, "Something told me you were going to ask that." So we got into the real issue easily. I am happy to say that eventually he was healed and is happily married.

1.   When Nothing Seems to Work and Everything Seems to be Going Wrong

We should especially pray for the gift of wisdom when we are faced with knotty questions or are getting no where in the healing process. Repeatedly the word of wisdom comes as the divine solution that hits the nail on the head.

> Like the time that one of our young single women was devastated emotionally by an inner healing session with one of our leaders. As we struggled for a solution to this problem that was quickly getting out of hand one of the team members suddenly suggested, "Just get those two people together to talk." We then set up an interview where she was encouraged to confront him in our presence and talk it out. She was scared to death, and he made it difficult, but it was a big key in her emotional healing, and a major milestone in his own further healing. We received this guidance as the gift of wisdom that brought a solution to a potentially destructive situation.

2.   The Interpretation of Dreams

Dreams often play an important role in the process of spiritual, inner and relational healing. Dreams have several sources and different functions:

a)   A revelation from God

There is no doubt from scripture that God may reveal things to us through dreams. For instance, God spoke to Pharaoh King of Egypt through the strange dream of the seven lean cows eating up the seven fat cows. (Genesis 41:17-24) In dreams, such as these that are full of symbols their source may be the Spirit of God working in our subconscious minds. When the words spoken to us by God enters the conscious, they become clothed in the images and feelings gathered from the unconscious. This will often necessitate an interpretation from the same Holy Spirit who spoke in the first place.

This is what happened in the case of the King of Egypt. His own magicians were baffled by the dream, but Joseph who had the Spirit of God in him was given the interpretation. (Gen. 41:38-39) When Joseph interpreted the dream he was moving some combination of the revelatory gifts of the word of knowledge, prophecy as well as wisdom.

In the process of healing, God may well speak to a person telling them what the source of pain may be or giving some word that enables them to grow in faith.

For instance:

> A sister I was praying for had to go into surgery to have a lump in her breast removed. A needle biopsy showed some signs of cancer. This caused a great deal of fear and anxiety in this person. As the day of surgery drew near, she had a dream in which she had come downstairs one morning to find a cute little puppy swimming around in her aquarium. She awoke from the dream with the thought, "it is harmless, but it still must come out."
>
> Upon further reflection and prayer she realized that God was telling her that she did not have cancer and thus do not be afraid to face the surgery. This gave her great peace and assurance as she faced the surgery. The pathology report later revealed that there was no cancer or pre-cancer.

In this case, the Holy Spirit's revelatory gifts helped provide the interpretation for the dream which later proved to be an authentic word from the Lord.

At other times, the revelation may be more direct as when an angel appears to the person in a dream. For instance, an angel of the Lord appeared to Joseph warning him to take the baby Jesus and flee to Egypt. (Matthew 2:13)

Guidance that comes through dreams must, like all revelations from the Holy Spirit, be carefully discerned. One's own mind as well as evil spirits may also be the source of revelations in dreams.

b)   Dreams as revealing forgotten memories and hidden processes of the heart.

Part of the process of inner healing is to bring to conscious awareness those hurtful memories that we have pushed down into unconscious. In the light of confession, they may be released of their emotional power, forgiven and healed.

The Holy Spirit searches the depths of the human heart and may bring such memories to recollection. The content of these revelations are not directly from God, they are from ourselves. Nevertheless, the gift of wisdom as well as the revelatory gifts of word of knowledge and prophecy may be needed to understand the meaning of these memories that surface in the dream.

One may be intentional about this process of seeking guidance through dreams. When a person does not have a clue about root causes, we will suggest they ask God to give them meaningful dreams. Then we ask them to keep pencil and note pad on their nightstand and jot down the outline of dreams that come. They bring these in and we pray for the gift of interpretation. We find that much insight, understanding, self-acceptance and redemptive love comes through in this way.

C. FAITH[2]

There is faith for salvation and the daily walk, but then there is the gift of faith. This faith is an inner certainty that God wills something and He is going to do it. Although the outward evidence seems to deny it, we boldly act in accordance with that inner certainty.

This is the mountain-moving faith of Matthew 21:21, Mark 11:24 and Hebrews 11, and the faith of the Centurion in Matthew 8:10 and of the Canaanite woman in Matthew 15:28.

This is the faith that dares to call for total commitment and believes that people will respond. This is the faith that sees what God wants the church to do next, announces it, and calls for obedient response.

This is the gift that sees the wounded made whole and says, "Rise and be healed in the name of Jesus." This is the gift of being able to entirely trust God's provision, as when Jesus broke the bread and fish and distributed them to over five thousand people.

This kind of faith is sovereignly given by God; it is not a constant ordinary thing, but is given for special needs and circumstances chosen by God. In spiritual, inner and relational healing this is

---

[2] Faith in regards to healing is an area of considerable controversy and misunderstanding. Thus, we are going to take this opportunity to give a more extended treatment of this gift than the others. Part of what follows is from Bob Whitaker and Brad Long's section "In The Spirit's Power" Dunamis Project Manual. We shall also return to the issue of faith in the section on Physical Healing of this manual.

faith that discerns a kairos moment in the life of the person being prayed for and then acts in obedience to the leading of the Holy Spirit, and expects God to work.

1. The gift of faith in the ministry of Jesus

Most of the healings and miracles of Jesus' ministry are wrought through "the prayer of faith." Strictly speaking, He does not pray. He commands the healing to happen, as when He commands Lazarus to come forth from the grave.[3] He speaks authoritatively, and it happens, because He already has the supernatural conviction that it will happen. We see the same gift of faith at work first in Jesus and in other people when He announces that a person's sins are forgiven and He is confident that they actually are. (Mathew 9:2-6, Luke 7:48-50)

Where this gift of faith is not present, even Jesus is unable to move in power ministry. In his own country for instance, where they knew his family and took offense to Him, He was not able to move in the power of the Holy Spirit.

> *"And he could do no mighty work there, except that he laid his hands upon a few sick people and healed them. And he marveled because of their unbelief." Mark 6:1-6*

2. Faith in the ministry of the apostles

The apostles repeat the ministry of Jesus all through Acts. Chapter 3 is a good example. Peter commanded the lame man to walk, not on his own initiative, but because, as he explains in 3:16, a surge of faith came to him from the Lord. In the grip of that conviction, he dared to do what was beyond him - he grabbed the man, lifted him up, and commanded him to walk.

In Acts 27:24-25, during the shipwreck, St. Paul received this gift of faith. He announced with certainty that no harm would come to anyone on the ship.

James 5:15 speaks of the gift of faith in terms of the prayer of faith. It is clearly a miraculous thing because it is illustrated with a reference to Elijah making the rain stop and start through prayer.

3. The gift of faith and the working of God

The story of the Centurion's servant healed is essential to understanding the relationship between faith and God's activity. Matthew 8:5-13, Luke 7:2

> *"...But the centurion answered him, 'Lord, I am not worthy to have you come under my roof; but only say the word, and my servant will be healed. For I am a man under authority, with soldiers under me; and I say to one, "Go," and he*

---

[3] John 11:41

*goes, and to another, "come," and he comes, and to my slave, "Do this," and he
does it.' When Jesus heard him, he marveled, and said to those who followed
him, 'Truly, I say to you, not even in Israel have I found such faith...' And to the
centurion Jesus said, 'Go; be it done for you as you have believed.' And the
servant was healed at that very moment."* Matthew 8:5-13

In this account we find that the healing power of Jesus was not bound by time nor space. He did not have to actually lay hands on the servant but just spoke the word and, even though He was some distance away, the servant was healed, "that very moment."

The faith that is involved in this healing, and in many others in the life of Jesus, is not some worked up mental attitude of expectation that something will happen. Rather, it is an expression of trust that Jesus is able to work. The Centurion has a deep trust that Jesus has the authority to accomplish the healing.

Faith, then, is the ground of a relationship with Jesus. This is the type of faith that Jesus requires. He is not calling us to "faith healing," rather, He is calling us to trust Him who is the healer.

The final word of Jesus to the Centurion, *"Go; be it done for you as you believed"* is repeated to others. For instance, to the two blind men Jesus said, *"...According to your faith be it done to you."* Matthew 9:27-31

Does this reveal a fundamental principle of God's dealing with human beings? Does the shape of our belief determine the shape of God's relationship with us? God, in His sovereignty, does seem to act in accord with the largeness or smallness of our trust (faith) in what He can do. To those who trust Jesus, as the Centurion did, Jesus is able to do great things. But those with no trust, or who discount Jesus all together, Jesus is able to do little, indeed, may prove not even to exist.

What then is this strange thing called faith? It is, I believe, the medium connecting the spiritual with the material, and enables the spiritual realm to shape the physical realm. Without it, the spiritual is unable to connect with and work in the material realm. The gift of faith is essential if God is to work. By His sovereignty in the affairs of human beings He has chosen to make this the medium of working in the human sphere.

## 4.	The role of the gift of faith in spiritual, inner and relational healing

### a)	The faith to trust God to work in kairos moments

The gift of faith is often given with other manifestations of the Holy Spirit. This gift opens the way for the other gifts to be expressed and to be effective.

For instance:

I (Brad Long) was praying for people at the Dunamis on healing in Michigan. A man brought his wife up for prayer. As I laid hands on her, there suddenly popped into my mind the Wordsworth poem about fields of dancing daffodils. I then saw a picture of a little girl running and laughing through a field of daffodils. I did not know what to make of the image. Nevertheless, there was within me the faith that it had actually come from God and if I spoke it out, then the Holy Spirit would use the image to do His work in this sister. Therefore, in faith, I simply presented the picture to the couple. As I did the power of the Holy Spirit surged through me and she went down on the floor.

After the ministry time was over the couple gave this extraordinary testimony. She had had a childhood made miserable with abuse. She said, "I was never able just to run free and play like other children. Just before you prayed for me, I had told my husband that I wished that I could be made whole and regain my childhood and be able to run freely through fields of wild flowers. When you gave me that image, it was not you talking but Jesus. His love surrounded me, the past hurts were healed and I saw myself as a little girl running through fields of wildflowers."

In this case, it was the gift of faith that enabled me to receive and speak out the word of knowledge into the kairos moment. There was also the gift of faith on the part of the couple who received the image and let the Holy Spirit use it to bring Jesus' healing love.

b) The gift of faith as trusting God to work to redeem our hurtful past

In a general way the gift of faith is a trust that God can capitalize on a wretched life where there are painful memories of monstrous rejection, abuse, abandonment, terror and misery, and turn it into a testimony of His grace.

It is the gift of resurrection faith that causes us to believe that a blasted and ravaged past is an **opportunity** and a **proving ground** for God to show and demonstrate resurrection glory. He doesn't change what happens, but He changes the perspective and feelings of the person and His radiant healing love shines all the brighter in proportion to the blackness of the background. Release and transport to freedom is enjoyed most by the ones from concentration camps.

D. GIFTS OF HEALING (LITERAL TRANSLATION OF 1:9)

God has many and various ways of healing hurting people. Every Christian can be used in unique ways to communicate healing love. Sometimes it is through touch; sometimes it is the sound of one's voice, or the twinkle in their eye, or a smile, or spontaneous laughter and warmth. We've seen people healed through one well-chosen scripture, or through a sermon or teaching series or testimony. Sacramental actions like lying on of hands, anointing, communion, and renewal of baptismal or marriage vows can be very healing. Confession and assurance of pardon in the Spirit are powerful. Prayer for the healing of memory, when led by the Spirit, is powerful. The healing Lord is in His people and present where two or three are gathered in His name to obey His healing purpose. We are His hands and eyes and lips and He will always use us with more or less healing effect on those we minister to. Some are especially gifted in healing; we call them healers. That is why, when we make up healing teams, we try to be prayerfully guided so that we bring the strongest gifts to bear on the toughest cases, and the right combination of gifts to help each particular case.

E. MIRACLES

Most healings are not demonstrably apparent to everyone, but some are mighty "workings of power" and we call them miracles.

> For almost eleven years, our adopted son was shattered with epilepsy. Despite the use of every known appropriate drug and combination of drugs he was having thirty to forty major motor seizures a day, plus one knockout grand mal seizure per week that would waste him for a day or two. His Presbyterian Sunday School teachers, a young married couple, were gifted by the Spirit to help him.

> They were given *wisdom* (1) to know how to approach him, gain his confidence, and persuade him to let them pray for him. Since he loved dogs they invited him over to play with theirs' and their boys; he was so restless that to settle him down they had him hold their little dog on his lap while they talked to him and prayed.

> Through the *word of knowledge* (2) they were given a series of visions that showed that the roots of his epilepsy went back to a trauma suffered in the womb.

> Then, through *wisdom* (1) the Lord led them in how to pray for the healing of that trauma. They prayed with strong *faith* (3) and assurance. As they prayed, warmth and love, signs of the *gift of healing* (4) poured into his fearful mind and heart. After prayer the husband said, "He will never have grand mal seizures again." It proved to be a true *prophetic* (5) word!

> After that, through inner *knowledge* (2), they knew that they were called to intercede for him regularly and continue weekly prayers with us for his full healing. Within three or four months all the other seizures disappeared. Meanwhile, we were directed, through the gift of *discerning of spirits* (6), to pray for deliverance and protection from oppressing spirits.

> After his eleventh birthday in January 1978, we had to pinch ourselves every day to believe what we were seeing. Our son could run and play, bike and swim normally and go to school on his own like other children. Within one year he was out of grade school special education classes and could go to Junior High with his own age group. Everyone could see the wondrous work of God.

F. PROPHECY (12:10)

To speak words God inspires is the gift of prophecy, our marvelous privilege as Christians. In sharing in Jesus' healing it is an essential instrument for speaking words of "edification, encouragement and comfort" (1 Corinthians 14:3) *"For the word of God is living and active, sharper than any two-edged sword, piercing to the division of soul and spirit, of joints and marrow, and discerning the thoughts and intentions of the heart."* (Hebrews 4:12)

> Most of the persons we pray for are down on themselves; self-hate and depression are common. One bad-tempered person had been repeatedly criticized for being like a snorting bull on a rampage. He felt thoroughly condemned, and saw his "bullishness" with negative and self-defeating feelings.

> A prophetically gifted person singled him out after a worship service and asked if he could pray for him. As he sat down to be prayed for, the prophet said, I see a bull. The person felt, "Oh, no! The guy has seen right through me!" He almost fled, but then he thought, "Well, I guess the game is up; I've been found out, and I need to be chastened so I'll submit to ministry."

> To his astonishment, as the prophet began to pray for him he heard words like, "Thank you, Lord, that You've made this man strong as a bull; you've given him the endurance to pull a heavy load through tough places, and to overcome hard opposition, etc." The image of a bull in positive terms began to transform the person's self-image. He began to put off the old garment of self-hate, and to feel the affirmation of the Lord. This enabled him to make the most of his strengths for God's glory, and experience increasing deliverance from angry behavior.

G. DISCERNING OF SPIRITS (1 CORINTHIANS 12:10)

"The ability to distinguish between spirits." (1 Corinthians 12:10)

Most of the symptoms of spiritual, inner and relational brokenness can also be symptoms of demonic oppression. There are persons who are psychologically sick who need emotional healing and would be harmed by a deliverance ministry. There are others whose psychological problem may have begun through occult involvement or terror that requires deliverance.

How do you tell the difference? There are signs that indicate demonic oppression. (See Dunamis teaching on Discerning of Spirits and the section of Deliverance in this manual.) But even then there is no strong certainty without the gift of discerning of spirits. Persons with the gift see the spirits in mental pictures or visions. They show up often like the ugly imps we've seen in comic strip depictions of the devil. I like to have a person teaming with me who has this gift because usually I don't get the discernment, although sometimes I do.

> Recently I stayed with a fine Christian family; husband and wife were very well educated and dedicated evangelical Christians. But the wife had been having

severe pains in one breast for several months and an awful fear that she had cancer. It was hard for her to sleep at night. Extensive medical tests during the same period had been unable to discover any physical basis for the pain.

As I talked with her and her husband, I learned that this sort of thing had tormented her recurringly throughout her life. Also, through questions, I learned that in early childhood she had been through a fair amount of insecurity and debilitating fear. The hunch grew in me that a spirit of fear had gained a foothold in her emotions at an early age and was oppressing her with this recurring torment. But I had no certainty, just a growing conviction. So I suggested to her and her husband that we consider my hunch. Though it was novel and seemingly bizarre to them, they agreed when I proposed that we act on the hypothesis that it was demonic. I basically said, "I'll pray a deliverance prayer, and let's see what happens."

First, I outlined what I would do; then I took her hand and prayed, "You spirit of fear, I take authority over you in the name of Jesus Christ, and by the power of His blood, His resurrection, and the gift of His Spirit, I command you to stop oppressing her and to leave her immediately and cease to torment her; go to the place assigned to you by the Lord." After the prayer she expressed her feeling that she felt "something go" and felt considerably relieved and hopeful. I then instructed her and her husband about putting on the whole armor of God before going to bed, and how to pray their own prayers of deliverance, if she had any recurring night phantoms or fear or any further debilitating pain. The first night required some spiritual warfare by the two of them, but by the second night they slept peacefully and were buoyantly testifying to the Lord's deliverance. They are both serving the Lord, "rejoicing in the power of His Spirit."

H. TONGUES (1 CORINTHIANS 12:10)

This is a prayer gift; it is praying to God in a language that we do not normally understand. (1 Corinthians 14:2) It is praying in the Spirit as God leads us to pray. (Romans 8:26-27) It was the first spiritual gift manifested on the day of Pentecost (Acts 2), and the first to appear in many subsequent outpourings. (Acts 8:18, 10:44-47, 19:6)

There are those who contend that the gift of tongues is the "least of the gifts." Perhaps, but any gift of God is valuable, and only a mustard seed of faith can move mountains. In the same way, tongues "triggers" and is a stimulus for all the gifts. It is a door opener and a facilitator for the other gifts needed for ministry.

I (Bob Whitaker) believe this. I've found that if I pray in tongues fifteen to thirty minutes a day it is spiritually edifying, as Paul says (1 Corinthians 14:4). The nice thing about it is that while you are counseling and praying for a person for inner healing, you can be praying silently in your mind and/or throat at the same time you give the "person" your individual attention. My conviction is that the more we pray in tongues in these sessions the more something happens.

1. Facilitator of healing

The greatest healers of our generation all pray in tongues. Take for instance Agnes Sanford. God gave her a gift of healing. She used it to minister to people primarily in individual counseling. She was effective in that ministry and contributed to books as well. Then she received the gift of tongues. She became even more effective with better perception, insight, and power in ministry than before. She shared this truth with those of us whom she taught.

Francis MacNutt is one of the greatest healers of our day. I know him and have been privileged to minister with him. He prays for large numbers of persons in healing services. There just is not enough time to pray more than a few seconds with each. He has learned through experience that much more healing will come through to people if he prays for them, "in the Spirit" (a scriptural expression that may mean praying in tongues). Like many others he has discovered that as he prays in tongues, the persons prayed for will often "rest in the Spirit" and during that time, remarkable inner-healings often take place.[4]

2. Facilitator of revelation gifts

Sometimes in counseling, you may need wisdom, knowledge and discernment in order to get to the root of a problem, help the person face a certain truth, and motivate them to repent or to receive ministry. Praying in the Spirit again and again brings things to the surface and enables us to know what and how to pray.

3. Facilitator of deliverance

As we counsel and pray we find sometimes that a person is being oppressed or harassed by an evil spirit. As we pray for them to be delivered, quite often nothing happens until we pray for them out loud in tongues. Often people have said things like, "When you started to pray in tongues the thing started to loosen its grip and then it just went away." I've been in some desperate situations where praying in tongues saved me from being overwhelmed by evil temptations, fearful oppression, and ominous darkness.

4. Ministers Peace

Sometimes when a person is deeply troubled and upset I will be prompted to pray aloud in a tongue (it sounds like an Indian praying). Invariably the person will tell me later that it brought peace and comfort to them. There are times in public meetings when a person asks for, or has great need of, emotional healing, but we don't have time to hear them out and pray as usual. At

---

[4] See the book, *Resting in the Spirit* by Francis MacNutt.

such times we may pray a half-minute or so in tongues, and sometimes they rest in the Spirit. When they do, deep inner healings often take place.[5]

I. INTERPRETATION OF TONGUES

This gift is rarely operative in emotional healing in my experience.

> I remember one time, however, when I prayed for a woman who was later so happy and relieved that she started to give thanks to God in tongues. Intuitively I knew in my heart what she was saying, and I told her. She responded by saying, "I know that's what I prayed." She had received the interpretation also, as she prayed. It was a wonderful double confirmation to her of what God had done in healing grace in her life. It was strong encouragement to live it out.

Another way that the interpretation of tongues may function in the healing prayer setting is by giving the prayer counselor an awareness of what the Holy Spirit is praying through them for the person.

> I (Brad Long) was asked to pray for a situation in which I had no clue how or even what to pray for. So I prayed in tongues.   As I did, I became aware that the Spirit was praying through me for the person to know the love of Jesus Christ in the midst of their pain.

> When this awareness came to me, I started to speak them out in English and the found that the person was deeply moved for that was indeed what the Spirit of God was doing with in them.

Usually the gift of interpretation is manifested when a message in tongues is given in a public worship. In this context, the gift functions like a word of prophecy.   Since the private ministry session is a different context from public worship, we may expect this gift of interpretation to function differently. None the less, the purpose of the gift is to make known what the Holy Spirit may be praying. The reason for revealing the prayers of the Spirit is so that we may be able to pray with Him for the things on His mind.

IV.   EXAMPLES DEMONSTRATING THIS THREE PHASE DYNAMIC OF PARTICIPATION

First a summary of this whole dynamic. The gifts of the Holy Spirit may be manifested at all three phases of this dynamic.

---

[5] See Francis MacNutt's book, *Resting in the Spirit.*

Cooperating with the Holy Spirit and Jesus Christ to do Healing Ministry

---

PHASE 1

Jesus establishes the context in which the Holy Spirit will work by bringing the person into a relationship with Himself.

We work according to biblical principles to establish the context that welcomes the Holy Spirit to work.

Jesus' Work	Our work with Jesus
Jesus is filled with the Holy Spirit and obeys the Father.	We pray to be filled with the Holy Spirit and ask that the Holy Spirit come upon the person being prayed for in power. We invite the Holy Spirit to work.
Jesus obeys the Father: this is the source of His direction and purpose for ministry.	We surrender ourselves to walking in obedience to Jesus Christ.
Jesus drew people into conversations with himself.	We engage the person being prayed for in conversation through directly asking them questions and intentionally listening to them.
Jesus demonstrates His love for the people He is reaching out to.	We show forth both by word and actions the love that we have been given by Jesus for the person being prayed for.

PHASE 2 –

Jesus and the Holy Spirit engage the person in various ways to bring the reality of the Kingdom of God that results in healing.

Jesus works through us and in the person being prayed for, as we are led and empowered by the Holy Spirit, to do those things He did while in the flesh that will make real the Kingdom of God.

PRMI *DUNAMIS PROJECT*
THE HEALING MINISTRY OF JESUS

Jesus' Work	Our work with Jesus
Jesus leads people to be born again into the Kingdom of God.	We present the Gospel and invite the person to accept Jesus Christ as Lord and Savior, and then pray with them to be born again.
Jesus enables and calls for confession, repentance, and walking in the light.	Assure the person of Jesus' love and acceptance of those who turn to Him in confession and forgiveness. Read the Bible passages that reveal sin and its consequences. As revealed by the Holy Spirit, expose and name any sins and present them to the person for discernment. Invite the person to confess their sins and to walk in the light
Jesus forgives sins.	After true confession from the heart, as led by the Holy Spirit, offer forgiveness in the name of Jesus Christ. This may be communicated by words spoken, as well as by whatever sacramental or symbolic actions the Holy Spirit may direct.
Jesus overturns lies spoken by Satan, ourselves or others with truth about Himself, reality and us.	We discern and help the person discern those lies that have been received which are contrary to reality in the light of Jesus as the truth. As led by the Holy Spirit, we expose the lies and in love and authority speak the truth into the person's life.
Jesus cast out demons to clear the way for healing, restoration and obedience.	Through rational analysis and the gifts of the Holy Spirit we discern the presence of any evil spirits in or around the person, close the "gateways" that gave them ground for attack and in the authority of Jesus Christ bind them and remove them from interfering with the person.

PHASE 3 –

Jesus invites/commands the person to follow Him in faith and obedience as a disciple.

We are to help the person hear and discern how Jesus Christ is calling them to walk in obedience that will result in discipleship.

Jesus' Work	Our work with Jesus
Jesus calls us to forgive those who hurt us.	We pray that the person being prayed for may have the grace to forgive those who are responsible for their hurt.
Jesus calls us to receive the working of the Holy Spirit as from Him.	We help the person being prayed for to first discern and then to receive what the Holy Spirit is doing in them as from Jesus.
Jesus calls us to follow Him in faith and obedience.	In love and wisdom we walk with the person as they in faith and obedience seek to follow Jesus Christ.
Jesus promises us the Holy Spirit to guide, gift and empower us as we walk as His disciple.	We pray that the person who is in process of healing will be filled with the Holy Spirit to be an effective disciple of Jesus Christ.

There follow two cases that demonstrate this dynamic.

A. CASE 1: A WOMAN AND HER MALE PASTOR BOTH FALLING INTO ADULTERY

At a PRMI event a woman about the age of 35 approached me after hearing the teaching on the nature of spiritual wilderness. She was obviously disturbed and said, "I know I am in the wilderness and I think you will understand. Will you please pray for me?"

I invited another female member of the teaching team to join me and we went to a private place to pray.

Phase 1 – We work according to biblical principles to establish the context that welcomes the Holy Spirit to work.

The overall context

This request for prayer took place at a PRMI renewal event at a church in which there was already in place a worshiping, praying community. Jesus was being exalted and the Holy Spirit welcomed. This person was a deeply committed Christian who was the chairperson of the women's work at the church. The prayer team and I had already prayed to be filled with the Holy Spirit and were growing in Jesus Christ.

Entering into Conversation

We asked her, "Please tell us your situation and how specifically we may pray for you."

With this question there tumbled out a story of spiritual and moral struggle with all the signs of a major mid-life crisis. She said, "I am happily married to a wonderful man. My husband is an engineer in a large successful company. We share everything together including four happy children. There is however a problem, as I have grown in this work of the Holy Spirit through PRMI's ministry, I find that my husband is extremely supportive, but with his scientific mind and rational temperament he just does not experience life in the Spirit the way I do. My struggle is that I am overwhelmed by an emotional attraction to the pastor of my church. He is happily married too! His wife is beautiful and just right for his personality but she is very busy in a demanding career. I love their three children who are about the same age as my own. He is 38 and is restless with his present calling because the church is not growing in the gifts of the Holy Spirit as much as he had hoped. I am often in church meetings with him. I think I see more of him than his wife does. Best of all, we can really pray together and the Holy Spirit seems to work through us in ministry. I know he is wrestling with feelings toward me. I can just feel the energy between us. God! I did not invite this, nor did I want it. It just sort of grew as we grew in walking with Jesus." ("I feel really stupid and vulnerable telling you this.")

As we discussed further, it turned out that there had been some inappropriate touching. Both were terrified and both were resisting but felt themselves being drawn into adultery.

Demonstrating Jesus' love

By the time we got to this part of the story the person was in tears and obviously in great torment of mind and soul. My prayer partner and I both put our arms around her and just held her as she sobbed like a little child. At this point we were led to pray that Jesus would wrap her in His love. As she cried we prayed quietly in tongues and I was aware of the presence and reality of the Holy Spirit moving through me into her. When she recovered a little my co-worker read the passage from Romans 8:35-39 about how nothing can separate us from the love of God in Christ.

Phase 2 – Jesus works through us and in the person being prayed for as we are led and empowered by the Holy Spirit to do those things He did while in the flesh that will make real the Kingdom of God.

Confirming her faith in Jesus Christ and her willingness to follow Him

This person was already a Christian so there was no need to lead her to be born again. We did ask her however to confirm her faith in Jesus and recommit herself to following Him even in this deeply personal and terrible struggle she was having.

Shifting from conversation into prayer

When asked what her specific request was she said, "I don't know. I just need help. I just know I am helpless to help myself and to control the feelings in my own heart. I am afraid!"

After listening for a while, we moved into prayer. We invited the Holy Spirit to come and to lead us. We affirmed the Lordship of Jesus Christ.

When she had settled down, one of the prayer counselors said, "You have told us your struggle and your request. Now in your own words just tell Jesus and we will stand by you as witnesses." As the woman started to tell her story again the atmosphere changed completely. The communication was no longer directed toward us, but toward God.

Invitation for Jesus his work

We did not have to prompt this phase of the prayer. The person started to cry out to Jesus asking Him to enter into this situation and to help her. "Oh Jesus! I do not want to hurt the wonderful family that you have given me. I know this is wrong. But Jesus, please, help me. I am powerless to stop my emotions. Please show me what to do." We joined in this prayer with her and asked Jesus Christ to come, to speak and to act.

Moving into confession of sin

I knew that she needed to move into some confession both from scripture and from her story. So I just suggested, "Is Jesus saying anything to you? Is there any sin that you need to confess?" Immediately she said "yes" and confessed the inappropriate sexual contact. She also confessed that the feelings she was having were not consistent with her marriage covenant with her husband. This was done with tears and convulsions of grief. She felt terrible and sick about betraying her husband whom she truly loved.

I stated the obvious fact, "Yes, this is a sin against your husband as well as God."

Forgiveness

We just let her cry and experience the terrible weight of her sin. Then after all her confession seemed to have finished and her soul had plunged into despair, the Holy Spirit told me to offer some words of forgiveness. I said, "Hear the good news of the gospel. Jesus Christ who died for you, who forgave the woman caught in adultery and about to be stoned, also forgives you." As we prayed we could see her whole countenance change. There was a look of joy on her face as a huge burden lifted.

Dealing with lies

There may have been some lies involved in this situation, but they were not brought out to be dealt with at this time.

Dealing with demons

After we celebrated the forgiveness the woman asked, "this whole thing has been so strong and irrational, do you think evil spirits have gotten into me and are causing this?" Sexual sin may open doors to demonic oppression so we took this question seriously. Also, it is not at all uncommon for a person like the pastor, as well as this woman who are growing in power ministry, to be targeted by Satan in their area of weakness.

Just to make sure we explored any gateways and did a, "knock, knock whose there?"[6] No demons manifested. So we concluded that this was most likely an attack from without that was being aggravated by both of them being in mid-life crisis and both having spouses who were emotionally and spiritually not with them.

---

[6] This is a way of directly testing for the presence of evil spirits. It will be described in detail in Dunamis Six on Spiritual Warfare.

Phase 3 - We are to help the person hear and discern how Jesus Christ is calling them to walk in obedience that will result in discipleship.

The call to forgive

At this point I asked, "Is there anyone you need to forgive?" She said, "yes!" Who? "Myself!" We then led her into some prayers of forgiveness of herself for letting her heart cross the boundaries. (At this stage in the healing process she felt no need to forgive either her husband or the pastor nor anyone else.)

Discerning what Jesus was calling her to do

After this we asked again, "Is Jesus telling you anything else?" In a whisper about to break with emotion, she said, "Yes, I know what He is saying. Jesus is calling me to follow him and to love Him more than this man. I must break off the relationship." At this point she started to weep again.

The confession was the first act of obedience. Now, came the hard part.

My co-worker and I were praying, "Lord help us. We need your guidance." I felt led to then break the soul tie between her and the pastor. As we prayed we were all aware of God actually working in her.

Discerning how Jesus was calling her to follow Him as a disciple

After this we then entered into a heart-to-heart conversation about the concrete steps she would need to take to walk out of this dangerous place. We agreed to some measures of accountability and some other decisive actions to reverse the slide into adultery.

In the midst of this time of conversation the Holy Spirit gave a word of prophecy in the form of an image. I saw this person holding hands with her husband. I saw the pastor holding hands with his wife. Then suddenly, there was Jesus in the midst of these couples. He pointed forward and said, "Follow me and you will know my love and power. Follow me and I will heal your marriages. Follow me and you will be co-workers together in the kingdom of God." As I shared this word the Holy Spirit fell on the sister for whom we had been praying. It touched her deeply and came as a word of promise and hope that God was going to bring her through this situation.

Receiving the working of the Holy Spirit

During the whole prayer session there was not just guidance given by the Holy Spirit, but also the manifestation of several gifts of the Holy Spirit. These were all carefully discerned but also gladly received and acted upon by the team and by the person being prayed for as from Jesus Christ.

Prayer for the empowerment of the Holy Spirit

After giving thanks we laid hands on her and asked the Holy Spirit to come upon her in power to give the strength and gifts to follow Jesus on the painful road that was ahead.

It was a wonderful prayer session in which Jesus moved in grace and power. He actually spoke to the person and gave the grace to turn and walk out of a dangerous situation.

Notice that this prayer time did not flow exactly as the order suggested above. It rarely does. These are not exact steps. Rather, they are ways in which the Holy Spirit may move to enable us to experience Jesus' healing work.

I did not have the opportunity to pray with the pastor. Nevertheless, I later learned that after the sexual encounter took place he also "woke up" to what was happening and he had desperately sought out help. He also confessed his sin and out of commitment to follow Jesus, worked hard at turning away from the relationship.

I know this case does not fit the stereotype of the pastor abusing his power and position and the woman being the victim. I saw no evidence of those dynamics at all. Rather this was a case of two people, who loved Jesus and genuinely loved each other, but their love grew to be romantic and sexual and that was inappropriate to their circumstances and to them faithfully following Jesus Christ.

Both have taken responsibility for their actions, both have made themselves accountable, both are working on the weaknesses in their marriages, and both have backed away from a relationship that would have destroyed everything they held dear.

B. CASE 2: BRAD LONG DEALING WITH THE NEED FOR FORGIVENESS

This is a time when I needed prayer. I had been extremely hurt by someone I had trusted with responsibility in ministry. I went in to see Richard White, my pastor. I had a long list of all the reasons why I had every right to be angry with this person.

Richard did not have a special method for dealing with me in mind. Rather, he had a deep faith that Jesus Christ was the one who could deal with me in my anger and hurt. In the prayer session he spent most of the time listening to me as well as to the Holy Spirit.

The phases of the prayer conversation did not conform neatly to the guidelines (prayer with a living person rarely ever does), but the following highlights were consistent with the model of engagement.

1. Phase one – Establishing the context for the Spirit to work

I went into Richard's office at the end of my rope. I was intensely angry and very hurt. When I arrived he just listened to me blow off steam.

There was no formal setting of the context, other than the fact that I had gone to my pastor who I knew loved Jesus and would hold me accountable to my relationship with Him.

I also knew that Richard was filled with the Holy Spirit. (I had prayed for him and later seen indisputable evidence in his life and ministry that the power of the Holy Spirit was indeed upon him.) So I trusted that he could hear the Holy Spirit's guidance even when I was too hurt and angry to even want to listen.

Phase 2 – Jesus works through us and in the person being prayed for as we are led and empowered by the Holy Spirit, to do those things He did while in the flesh that will make real the Kingdom of God.

After I had settled down a little bit, Richard said, "Ok, I think we have talked enough. Let's go into prayer." I was too angry to pray so I said, "Why don't you pray for me, I can't!" Richard led in a prayer offering up the situation to the Lord.

Invitation for Jesus to do his work

Richard continued to pray asking Jesus to come and help me. I really could not pray at all. All I could think of was all the ways I would like to get revenge. Richard persisted in asking the Holy Spirit to come and to guide us.

The call to confession

It seemed that our prayers were not getting anywhere. Then Richard stopped and asked, "In this whole situation do you have any sin or anything to confess?" I told him that I had searched my heart and knew that I was not in the wrong in this situation. He, led by the Holy Spirit and just knowing me, said, "I know the situation and I believe you are right, but your desire for revenge for what was done is a sin. Is Jesus asking you to do anything about that?"

I knew he was right because along with his word came the convicting light of the Holy Spirit.

When Richard asked me to confess this desire for revenge. I knew I had to and so, with great struggle, I confessed my own sin of wanting revenge.

Phase 3 – We are to help the person hear and discern how Jesus Christ is calling them to walk in obedience that will result in discipleship.

Next Richard said, "Is Jesus asking you to do anything else?" We sat for a moment in silence. In my heart I knew exactly what Jesus was asking me to do. It was to forgive this person. I told Richard that I knew Jesus was asking me to forgive this person. But I told him that I had no idea how to since I had been so badly hurt. I could not make my heart quit being angry with this person.

I was by this time overwhelmed by the pain of the situation and my anger had given way to tears.

Richard then continued in prayer asking Jesus to give me the grace to forgive. He also prayed for healing for the hurt that I had received. As he prayed he led me to say what I had no power to say by myself, "I forgive _____ and I give up my right to revenge." As I prayed this after him as an act of obedience rather than out of feeling or conviction, I was aware of the Holy Spirit moving upon me. I suddenly was aware that the sword of revenge had been taken out of my hand. I was able to affirm that with Christ's love I could love this person who had hurt me so badly.

By this time Richard was already laying his hands on me. He prayed for blessing on me and gave thanks that I was able to forgive.

We then moved into a time of prayer for the person. He also asked for guidance about what to do next.

After a time of conversation Richard then prayed for the Holy Spirit to continue to change my heart from one of hatred to one of love and forgiveness. We also prayed for wisdom to know how to act in this situation in such a way that Jesus Christ would be pleased and glorified.

This was just one prayer time that we had. This did not fix the situation immediately. It persisted for about two years. During this period I had to go again and again for prayer. Each time it was a matter of obedience in letting go of the hurt, giving up my right for revenge and forgiving. Finally the healing was completed as the situation resolved itself. There was never any formal reconciliation but the forgiveness seemed to take place in my heart and I was no longer filled with anger and hurt. I was free.

V. SUMMARY AND CONCLUSION

This is a dynamic process of listening and obedience. It involves listening to the person and to the Holy Spirit. The steps are not often in neat order, but are rather a moving back and fourth as the Holy Spirit leads.

We have found that when the Holy Spirit leads this type of prayer engagement with Jesus there are often profound changes in the person. Spiritual, inner, relational and physical healing will take place.

In the two cases above the source of the hurt and the hurt itself is obvious and immediately before the person. The process of getting to the situation is straightforward. One was a case of a person falling into adultery, the other with my anger because I had been badly hurt by someone.

Many times, however the roots of one's hurts are hidden in the past. One is dealing with the results of past hurts that are no longer obvious and immediately accessible. In the next section we shall explore how this same threefold, dynamic of healing takes place in hurts that are no longer obvious and accessible to this approach to healing.

Teaching Charts

Part VI

The Holy Spirit Continues
Jesus' Healing Work

The Dunamis Project
Presbyterian-Reformed Ministries International201

The Holy Spirit Continues Jesus' Healing Ministry on Earth

A. Jesus continues to work in human lives today through the Holy Spirit. John 16:12-15

B. The role of the prayer minister. Romans 10:14-15, Acts 1:8

C. The preparation of the prayer counselor for working with Jesus in healing.

  1. They have been born again.

  2. They are abiding in Jesus Christ.

  3. They are being filled with the Holy Spirit.

  4. They have learned how to cooperate in the dynamic of the Holy Spirit's work through receiving gifts, discernment of kairos moments, and walking in obedience.

  5. They are growing mature in the fruit of the Spirit, especially the fruit of love.

Summary -
Cooperating with the Holy Spirit and Jesus Christ to do Healing Ministry

---

PHASE 1

Jesus establishes the context in which the Holy Spirit will work by bringing the person into a relationship with Himself.

We work according to biblical principles to establish the context that welcomes the Holy Spirit to work.

Jesus' Work	Our Work with Jesus
Jesus is filled with the Holy Spirit and obeys the Father.	We pray to be filled with the Holy Spirit and ask that the Holy Spirit come upon the person being prayed for in power. We invite the Holy Spirit to work.
Jesus obeys the Father: this is the source of His direction and purpose for ministry.	We surrender ourselves to walking in obedience to Jesus Christ.
Jesus drew people into conversations with himself.	We engage the person being prayed for in conversation through directly asking them questions and intentionally listening to them.

Jesus demonstrates His love for the people He is reaching out to.	We show forth both by word and actions the love that we have been given by Jesus for the person being prayed for.

PHASE 2

Jesus and the Holy Spirit engage the person in various ways to bring the reality of the Kingdom of God that results in healing.

Jesus works through us and in the person being prayed for, as we are led and empowered by the Holy Sprit, to do those things He did while in the flesh that will make real the Kingdom of God.

Jesus' Work	Our work with Jesus
Jesus leads people to be born again into the Kingdom of God.	We present the Gospel and invite the person to accept Jesus Christ as Lord and Savior, and then pray with them to be born again.
Jesus enables and calls for confession, repentance, and walking in the light.	Assure the person of Jesus' love and acceptance of those who turn to Him in confession and forgiveness. Read the Bible passages that reveal sin and its consequences. As revealed by the Holy Spirit, expose and name any sins and present them to the person for discernment. Invite the person to confess their sins and to walk in the light

Jesus forgives sins	After true confession from the heart, as led by the Holy Spirit, offer forgiveness in the name of Jesus Christ. This may be communicated by words spoken as well as by whatever sacramental or symbolic actions the Holy Spirit may direct
Jesus overturns lies spoken by Satan, ourselves or others with truth about Himself, reality and us.	We discern and help the person discern those lies that have been received which are contrary to reality in the light of Jesus as the truth. As led by the Holy Spirit we expose the lies and in love and authority speak the truth into the person's life.
Jesus cast out demons to clear the way for healing, restoration and obedience.	Through rational analysis and the gifts of the Holy Spirit we discern the presence of any evil spirits in or around the person, close the "gateways" that gave them ground for attack and in the authority of Jesus Christ bind them and remove them from interfering with the person.

PHASE 3

Jesus invites/commands the person to follow Him in faith and obedience as a disciple.

We are to help the person hear and discern how Jesus Christ is calling them to walk in obedience that will result in discipleship.

Jesus' Work	Our work with Jesus
Jesus calls us to forgive those who hurt us.	We pray that the person being prayed for may have the grace to forgive those who are responsible for their hurt.
Jesus calls us to receive the working of the Holy Spirit as from Him.	We help the person being prayed for to first discern and then to receive what the Holy Spirit is doing in them as from Jesus.
Jesus calls us to follow Him in faith and obedience.	In love and wisdom we walk with the person as they in faith and obedience seek to follow Jesus Christ.
Jesus promises us the Holy Spirit to guide, gift and empower us as we walk as His disciple	We pray that the person who is in process of healing will be filled with the Holy Spirit to be an effective disciple of Jesus Christ.

In Depth - Phase 1

PHASE 1

Jesus establishes the context in which the Holy Spirit will work by bringing the person into a relationship with Himself.

We work according to biblical principles to establish the context that welcomes the Holy Spirit to work.

1. Healing ministry is to take place in the overall context of the Church as the Body of Christ.

2. Preparation of the prayer counselor (or healing prayer team):

   • Abiding in Jesus Christ.

   • Praying to be filled with the Holy Spirit.

   • Being motivated by love of Jesus and of the person they are praying for.

- Walking in the light and being in the body of Christ that provides accountability and balance.

- Loving, attentive listening to the person.

- Active listening to the Holy Spirit.

- A heart set on obeying the guidance received from the Holy Spirit.

3. Setting the context in the actual prayer session

A) **Initial conversation** with the person to be prayed for and their personal preparation to welcome the Holy Spirit to work.

The purpose of the conversation -

1.) Establish understanding and rapport.

2.) To discern the person's spiritual condition and their relationship with Jesus Christ.

3.) To determine what it is the person needs to be prayed for.

4.) To understand the person's background and history.

<u>The prayer minister may be led by the Holy Spirit to lead the person in the following spiritual disciplines:</u>

• Surrendering to the lordship of Jesus Christ. (The submission of one's will to God's will.)

• Examination of life, with confession, for the removal of any obstacles that may be blocking one's relationship with Christ.

• Renunciation of any evil spirits, involvement in the occult or persistent sin.

• Acceptance of one's own responsibility and an identification of others who are responsible.

B) Shift from conversation into prayer for healing.

• Thanksgiving for Jesus' grace.

• Praise for Jesus' love for the person.

• An invitation for the Holy Spirit to come and work.

• Laying out before Jesus Christ the person's situation and their prayer request.

4. Summary chart for Jesus Work and Our Work with Jesus in Phase 1

Jesus' Work	Our work with Jesus
Jesus is filled with the Holy Spirit and obeys the Father.	We pray to be filled with the Holy Spirit and ask that the Holy Spirit come upon the person being prayed for in power. We invite the Holy Spirit to work.
Jesus obeys the Father: this is the source of His direction and purpose for ministry.	We surrender ourselves to walking in obedience to Jesus Christ.
Jesus drew people into conversations with himself	We engage the person being prayed for in conversation through directly asking them questions and intentionally listening to them.
Jesus demonstrates His love for the people He is reaching out to	We show forth both by word and actions the love that we have been given by Jesus for the person being prayed for.

In Depth - Phase 2

PHASE 2

Jesus and the Holy Spirit engage the person in various ways to bring the reality of the Kingdom of God that results in healing.

Jesus works through us and in the person being prayed for, as we are led and empowered by the Holy Spirit, to do those things He did while in the flesh that will make real the Kingdom of God.

---

1. In prayer giving the invitation for Jesus to work.

2. Conversation with Jesus Christ -getting direction about what He is doing and wants us to do with Him.

A) The role of the person being prayed for

• Sharing with the prayer counselor what is going on in side of them in terms of memories, feelings, and thoughts.

• Reporting whatever God may be saying or doing.

B) The role of the prayer counselor.

• Engage in active listening both to what is going on inside the person and to the Holy Spirit.

• Expect and welcome the gifts of the Holy Spirit to come into operation.

• Help discern what the Holy Spirit is doing and saying.

• Affirming when a word really is from Jesus and then encouraging the person to act upon it in obedience.

3. Summary chart of Jesus' work and our work with Jesus in Phase 2

Jesus' Work	Our work with Jesus
Jesus leads people to be born again into the Kingdom of God.	We present the Gospel and invite the person to accept Jesus Christ as Lord and Savior, and then pray with them to be born again.
Jesus enables and calls for confession, repentance, and walking in the light.	Assure the person of Jesus' love and acceptance of those who turn to Him in confession and forgiveness. Read the Bible passages that reveal sin and its consequences. As revealed by the Holy Spirit, expose and name any sins and present them to the person for discernment. Invite the person to confess their sins and to walk in the light
Jesus forgives sins.	After true confession from the heart, as led by the Holy Spirit, offer forgiveness in the name of Jesus Christ. This may be communicated by words spoken as well as by whatever sacramental or symbolic actions the Holy Spirit may direct.

Jesus overturns lies spoken by Satan, ourselves or others with truth about Himself, reality and us.	**We discern and help the person discern those lies that have been received which are contrary to reality in the light of Jesus as the truth.** **As led by the Holy Spirit we expose the lies and in love and authority speak the truth into the person's life.**
Jesus cast out demons to clear the way for healing, restoration and obedience.	**Through rational analysis and the gifts of the Holy Spirit we discern the presence of any evil spirits in or around the person, close the "gateways" that gave them ground for attack and in the authority of Jesus Christ bind them and remove them from interfering with the person.**

In Depth - Phase 3

PHASE 3

Jesus invites/commands the person to follow Him in faith and obedience as a disciple.

We are to help the person hear and discern how Jesus Christ is calling them to walk in obedience that will result in discipleship.

---

1. Following in obedience - doing what Jesus wants us to do as His disciples.

At this stage the role of the prayer minister may be as follows:

• Encourage obedience.

• Help work out a follow-up plan.

• Enter the process and let the Holy Spirit speak and act through them. The prayer minister may become the means through whom Jesus mediates His response back to the person.

2. The critical importance of forgiveness.

3. For the person praying for healing, moving out in discipleship is part of the healing process.

- Discipleship connects with the fundamental purpose of healing:

- To show forth the love of God the Father, Son and Holy Spirit's to wounded and hurt people.

- To enable those called by God to go forth as His witnesses.

- To advance the Kingdom of God.

4. Praying for the infilling with the Holy Spirit for the gifts and power to follow Jesus and be His witness.

5. Debriefing, reflection, plan for follow-up, discernment of what Jesus is calling you to do next

6. Summary Chart of Jesus' work and our work with Jesus in Phase 3

Jesus' Work	Our work with Jesus
Jesus calls us to forgive those who hurt us.	We pray that the person being prayed for may have the grace to forgive those who are responsible for their hurt.
Jesus calls us to receive the working of the Holy Spirit as from Him.	**We help the person being prayed for to first discern and then to receive what the Holy Spirit is doing in them as from Jesus.**
Jesus calls us to follow Him in faith and obedience.	**In love and wisdom we walk with the person as they in faith and obedience seek to follow Jesus Christ.**
Jesus promises us the Holy Spirit to guide, gift and empower us as we walk as His disciple.	**We pray that the person who is in process of healing will be filled with the Holy Spirit to be an effective disciple of Jesus Christ.**

PART VII

Inner Healing

By Brad Long

The Dunamis Project
Presbyterian-Reformed Ministries International

I. WHY WE NEED THE FOLLOWING PROCESS OF INNER HEALING

A. THE FUNDAMENTAL DYNAMIC OF JESUS' SPIRITUAL, INNER AND RELATIONAL HEALING

From the last chapter, we saw that while Jesus brought healing to a huge diversity of people with different problems, He consistently applied the same set of dynamic principles.

We also found that there is a basic dynamic of how we may cooperate with the Holy Spirit in praying for someone in need of spiritual, inner or relational healing. In this form of engagement between Jesus and the person in need of prayer the Holy Spirit may well apply the same dynamic principles as found in the ministry of Jesus.

The assumption is that the Holy Spirit will lead and empower us to do the same things that Jesus did. This is based on the following promises:

> *12   I tell you the truth, anyone who has faith in me will do what I have been doing. He will do even greater things than these, because I am going to the Father.*
> *13   And I will do whatever you ask in my name, so that the Son may bring glory to the Father.*   (John 14:12-13, NIV)
>
> *8   But you will receive power when the Holy Spirit comes on you; and you will be my witnesses in Jerusalem, and in all Judea and Samaria, and to the ends of the earth."*
> (Acts 1:8, NIV)

There follows a summary chart of Jesus' ministry

THE DYNAMIC OF JESUS' ENGAGEMENT WITH HUMAN BEINGS IN HEALING MINISTRY

PHASE 1 –
Jesus establishes the context in which the Holy Spirit will work by bringing the person into a relationship with himself.

Jesus is filled with the Holy Spirit and obeys the Father.
Jesus obeys the Father: this is the source of His direction and purpose for ministry.
Jesus drew people into conversations with himself.
Jesus demonstrates His love for the people He is reaching out to.

PHASE 2 –
Jesus and the Holy Spirit engage the person in various ways to bring the reality of the Kingdom of God, which results in healing.

Jesus leads people to be born again into the Kingdom of God.
Jesus enables and calls for confession, repentance, and walking in the light.
Jesus forgives sins.
Jesus overturns lies spoken by Satan, others, or oneself with truth about Himself, reality and oneself.
Jesus cast out demons to clear the way for healing, restoration and obedience.

PHASE 3 –
Jesus invites/commands the person to follow Him in faith and obedience as a disciple.

Jesus calls us to forgive those who hurt us.
Jesus calls us to receive the working of the Holy Spirit as from Him.
Jesus calls us to follow Him in faith and obedience.
Jesus promises us the Holy Spirit to guide, gift and empower us as we walk as His disciples.

Our cooperation with the Holy Spirit in the Healing Ministry of Jesus Christ

PHASE 1
We work according to biblical principles to establish the context that welcomes the Holy Spirit to work

We pray to be filled with the Holy Spirit and ask that the Holy Spirit come upon the person being prayed for in power. We invite the Holy Spirit to work.
We surrender ourselves to walking in obedience to Jesus Christ.
We engage the person being prayed for in conversation through directly asking them questions and intentionally listening to them.
We show forth both by word and actions the love that we have been given by Jesus for the person being prayed for.

PHASE 2 –
Jesus works through us and in the person being prayed for, as we are led and empowered by the Holy Spirit, to do those things He did while in the flesh that will make real the Kingdom of God.

We present the Gospel and invite the person to accept Jesus Christ as Lord and Savior, and then pray with them to be born again.
Assure the person of Jesus' love and acceptance of those who turn to Him in confession and forgiveness.
Read the Bible passages that reveal sin and its consequences. As revealed by the Holy Spirit, expose and name any sins and present them to the person for discernment. Invite the person to confess their sins and to walk in the light
After true confession from the heart, as led by the Holy Spirit offer forgiveness in the name of Jesus Christ. This may be communicated by words spoken as well as by whatever sacramental or symbolic actions the Holy Spirit may direct.
We discern and help the person discern those lies that have been received which are contrary to reality in the light of Jesus as the truth. As led by the Holy Spirit, we expose the lies and in love and authority speak the truth into the person's life.

PHASE 3 –
We are to help the person hear and discern how Jesus Christ is calling them to walk in obedience that will result in discipleship.

We pray that the person being prayed for may have the grace to forgive those who are responsible for their hurt.
We help the person being prayed for to first discern and then to receive what the Holy Spirit is doing in them as from Jesus.
In love and wisdom we walk with the person as they in faith and obedience seek to follow Jesus Christ.
We pray that the person who is in process of healing will be filled with the Holy Spirit to be an effective disciple of Jesus Christ.

B. THE PROBLEM – WHEN THESE PRINCIPLES DO NOT SEEM TO WORK

From the clear witness of scripture we may be certain that these fundamental principles are sound. Further, from what we know of human nature and the authority of Jesus Christ, when applied by the Holy Spirit, we may be assured that they will work. They must work because they are based on the word of God and the way God has structured reality.

1.   The persistence of hurt in the church and the world.

Yet we are often faced with a troubling problem: people in the churches are still hurting. They may be strong believers, have come into a personal relationship with Jesus, have been filled with the Spirit, and are active in the church's ministries, but may also be overwhelmed by unhappy feelings and behavior that is very contradictory to their confession of faith.

Despite diligent use of the means of grace (including the above principles), despite tearful apologies and repeated surrender to the Lord, fear, anger, self-hatred and compulsiveness seem to come out of nowhere to take joy and peace from them and from their relationships. Such people are found abundantly even in churches that stress sanctification, death to self, deeper life truths, and victory in Christ.

Examples: Three cases demonstrating the failure of healing prayer ministry

> Once an evangelical friend of mine was struggling with deep anger in her life. This anger was destroying her relationship not only with God, but also with her husband. Her husband's response was to tell her to do a word study on anger and forgiveness in the Bible. She faithfully did this and emerged just as angry as before. Why had the "Word" not been effective?

> A seminary student committed his life to following Jesus Christ when at a Billy Graham revival. He earnestly wants to serve God but he finds himself tormented with a mixture of love and lust for an older professor who has become like a father to him. He finds this attraction growing despite repeated desperate prayer for God's help. A female student is very attractive and obviously interested in him. Nevertheless, to his horror he feels nothing for her even though he sincerely wants to. During summer vacation he goes to a pastor and confesses his same sex attractions. The older man lovingly listens and then prays for forgiveness and healing. The student returns to seminary, but still finds that he is not cured. Why not? Why does his battle continue? Why does Jesus not heal him of these inappropriate desires? Why does Jesus not help this man who is trying so hard to live according to the law of God so clearly given in scripture that homosexual sex is wrong?

A 16-year-old girl was tormented by feelings of worthlessness. She was withdrawing into a shell of indifference convinced that no one would ever love her or ever could love her. She was brought to several prayer meetings where Christians earnestly prayed that she would know God's love. They sent her home with Bible verses to learn. Nevertheless this was all to no avail she continued to withdraw to such an extent that she had to be taken out of school and brought into an institution. Why did the love not get through?

A myriad of cases could be presented that pointedly pose the question: why do people not experience the healing power of Jesus Christ even when they seek Him?

2. Where is the problem?

The problem is not that the means of grace given to us are ineffective or that principles like forgiveness and knowing God's love are devoid of power. Rather, the nature of human beings requires that these be applied in certain defined ways in order to be effective.

There is power in the Word of God for healing. The problem is not with the Word but with our being able to hear the Word and have it penetrate to where our hurt is. These principles of healing are not magic formulas nor do they work automatically because they are backed by the sovereignty of God. The stern warning of Jesus that if we do not forgive neither will our Father in Heaven forgive us, strongly suggests that there is a cooperative role that we play in the healing process. (Matthew 6:14-15)

To cooperate with the Holy Spirit in situations when these principles do not seem to be readily effective requires us to understand the following:

- The nature of the human psyche

- The anatomy of inner hurts and the complication of evil spirits

- The process of our cooperating with the Holy Spirit to bring Jesus' healing into the hidden recesses of the human heart

As a way of going deeper into engagement with Jesus in His healing ministry we turn to these issues in this chapter.

This section proposes a theory of how the unconscious mind functions and how the Holy Spirit may work to bring healing of hurts in the unconscious.

The purpose of this chapter is to equip us to cooperate with the Holy Spirit as He works in the depths of the human soul.

II.   A MODEL OF THE HUMAN PSYCHE

Human beings, having been made in the image of God that was distorted by sin through the Fall, are extremely complicated. This complexity requires that we have some model or hypotheses to bring meaning and organization to the subject.

What follows is an attempt at a model that we believe is necessary if we are to have some grasp of how the Holy Spirit works to bring inner healing. No model is perfect or complete so use this model as it is helpful to you as you follow the Holy Spirit into the depths of the human heart. It may serve as a useful guide, but not as a detailed map.

One disclaimer: If you are coming to this chapter with a neat system of mind, body and spirit or soul, spirit and body you will be disappointed. While such systems are popular and useful to a degree, they really are not consistent with the holistic view of human nature that is found in the Bible. They are also not particularly consistent with our actual lived experience of ourselves.

A. COMBINATION OF BIBLICAL UNDERSTANDING OF THE HEART WITH DEPTH PSYCHOLOGY

This model grows out of our having been created in the image of God for relationship with God and others and for dominion over the earth. As John Calvin has already noted, every part has been tainted by sin. Nevertheless, the remnants of God's original construction still remains intact even in diminished form. To this biblical "heart model" we have added some of the insights from depth psychology[1].

The depth psychology model draws from the insights of the Swiss psychologist, Carl Jung. I recognize that many evangelical Christians have objections to the work of Jung. I share many of these same objections and believe that aspects of his system may indeed open a person up to the demonic. Jung's hypothesis of the human psyche, however, is extremely helpful for understanding how inner hurts are formed and how the Holy Spirit may work to heal them. I believe that Jung's insights included here may be safely used without contradiction to the biblical model. For instance in the following verses, the Bible speaks of the mysterious depths of the human heart.

> The heart is deceitful above all things and beyond cure. Who can understand it? "I the LORD search the heart and examine the mind, to reward a man according to his conduct, according to what his deeds deserve." (Jeremiah 17:9-10, NIV)

This mysterious depth of the heart out of which may come evil Jung has named the "unconscious." Our task is to understand the inner depths that God is searching and bring the operation of the principles of spiritual, inner and relational healing.

---

[1] **depth psy·chol·o·gy** *noun* **1. study of unconscious:** the study and psychology of the unconscious mind. (MS Encarta World English Dictionary) The primary founders of this school of psychology were Sigmond Freud and Carl Jung.

Figure 1

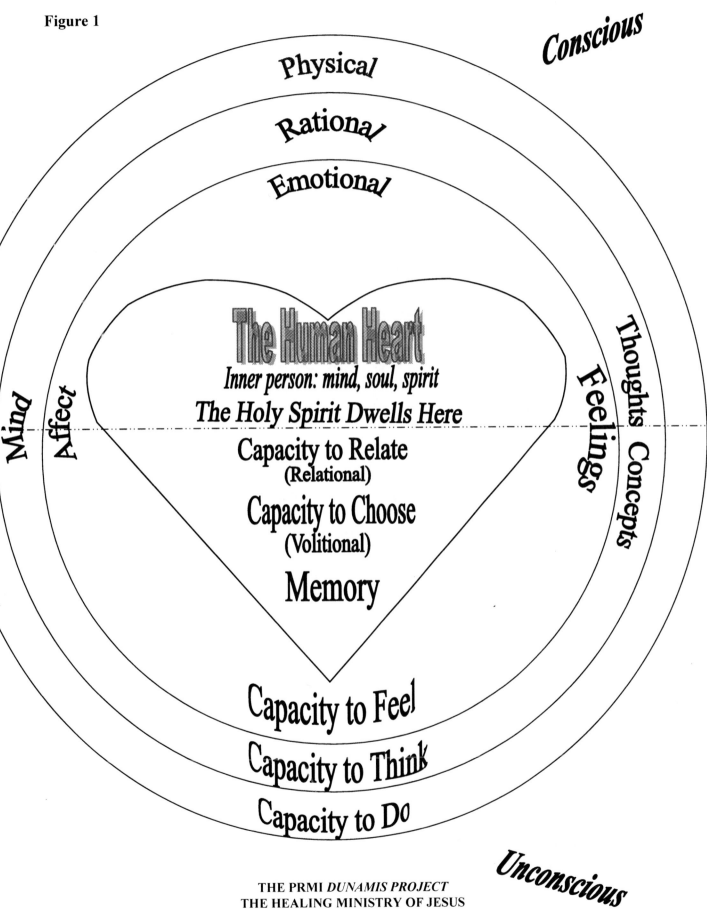

1. The Human Heart as the Center of the Human Being

In the biblical vision, the center of a human being is the human heart. By "heart" what is meant is not the physical organ, but rather the psyche at its deepest level. The word heart (hearts) is found 938 times in the Bible.

In Hebrew the word for "heart" is "lebab" and has the following wide range of meanings:

1) the midst (of things)
2) the heart (of man)
3) the soul, the heart (of man)
4) the mind, knowledge, the thinking, reflection, the memory
5) inclination, resolution, determination (of will)
6) the conscience
7) the heart (of moral character)
8) as the seat of the appetites
9) as the seat of the emotions and the passions
10) as the seat of the courage [2]

The word for "heart" is "Kardia," in Greek and has a range of meanings similar to the Hebrew:

a) that organ in the animal body which is the center of the circulation of the blood, and, hence, was regarded as the seat of physical life
b) denotes the center of all physical and spiritual life
c) the vigor and sense of physical life
d) the center and seat of spiritual life
e) the soul or mind, as it is the fountain and seat of the thoughts, passions, desires, appetites, affections, purposes, endeavors
f) used of the understanding, the faculty and seat of the intelligence
g) used of the will and character
h) used of the soul so far as it is affected and stirred in a bad way or good, or of the soul as the seat of the sensibilities, affections, emotions, desires, appetites, passions
i) used of the middle or central or inmost part of anything, even though inanimate [3]

The heart includes and is, at times, equivalent to the human spirit.

> Psalm 51:10 *"Create in me a clean heart, O God, and put a new and right spirit within me."*

This parallelism so common in Hebrew poetry confirms that the terms heart and spirit are equivalent. This interplay of meanings of the heart forces us to a complex holistic vision of the human psyche.

---

[2] From Brown-Driver-Briggs definition for word # 3824 PC Study Bible, Bible Soft.
[3] Thayer's definition for word # 2588 PC Study Bible, Bible Soft.

The heart is the center of the totality of who we are. The heart is the deepest me, which stands behind and is the ultimate source of my thoughts and all the vicissitudes of my emotions. It is my heart that provides the dwelling place for the Holy Spirit and is able to have faith in Jesus. My heart is clothed in my physical body and in the age to come will be recreated in a resurrection body. The biblical concept of "heart" is inclusive of all the forces and functions of "spirit" and "soul." Often, however, it is used to emphasize different aspects of the inner life and the source of the various aspects of ourselves.

The following observations come from Bob Whitaker's exhaustive study of the "human heart" and from the *The Interpreter's Dictionary of the Bible*, Vol. 2, 549-550.

a)   The heart is the seat of emotions

It is from the heart that our emotions like joy, discouragement, love, and sadness spring. It is the source of both good and bad appetites and desires.

Luke 24:32; *"Did not our hearts burn within us while He talked to us on the way?"* John 14:1;- *"Let not your hearts be troubled."* II Corinthians 7:3; *"you are in our hearts to die together and to live together."* (See also Matthew 5:28, 6:21, 12:34, 22:27, Acts 7:54, 21:13, 2 Corinthians 6:11-12, Ephesians 6:22, Colossians 4:8, Romans 10:1, Philippians 1:3-7.)

b)   The heart is the seat of the intellect

The heart is what directs the course of our thoughts and is the "me" within our mental processes that is doing the thinking, meditating and reflecting. The heart seeks understanding and wisdom.

Where we would speak of the illumination of the mind, the Bible often uses the word "heart" as in 2 Corinthians 4:6, Ephesians 1:18 and 2 Peter 1:19. *"Jesus, knowing their thoughts said, `Why do you think evil in your hearts?'"* Romans 1:21 in the RSV reads, *"their senseless minds were darkened."* The literal Greek is, "their undiscerning heart was darkened."

c)   The heart is the seat of the will and the moral life

The heart is the center of the will, which directs the course of our actions and is thus the wellspring of the moral life. The heart is ultimately the chief executive officer that directs our emotions and thoughts towards the ends that it has chosen. In general, the human heart is seen as perverse, capable of willing only that which is evil until made new through the indwelling of the Holy Spirit. (Jeremiah 17:9)

2 Corinthians 9:7, RSV, says, *"Each one must do as he has made up his mind."* The literal translation is, *"Every man as he purposes in his heart."* Luke 21:14, RSV, Jesus says, *"Settle it therefore in your minds."* Actually He uses the word "hearts." (See also Nehemiah 7:5, John 13:2, Acts 5:4, 8:20, 11:23.)

Matthew 5:8 says, *"Blessed are the pure in heart for they shall see God."* (See also Psalm 24:4.) I Thessalonians 3:13 speaks of *"hearts blameless in holiness."* (See also Hebrews 10:22.)

d)   The heart is the interface point between the human being and spiritual beings

In Psalm 51:10 and 51:17 "heart" refers to the "spirit" of a person. This is where God meets us and makes Himself known to us. *"Create in me a clean heart, O God; and renew a right spirit within me."* *"The sacrifice acceptable to God is a broken spirit; a broken and a contrite heart, O God, thou wilt not despise;"* *"I will put my law within them, and I will write it upon their hearts; and I will be their God and they shall be my people...they shall all know me;"* (Jeremiah 31:33-34) *"A new heart I will give you, and a new spirit I will put within you; and I will take out of your flesh the heart of stone."* (Ezekiel 36:26) (See also Jeremiah 17:9-10, Proverbs 4:23, Ezekiel 11:19, Romans 2:29 & 10:8-10, 1 Timothy 1:5, Hebrews 3:8 and 15, etc.)

The heart may be influenced by God. (Exodus 4:21, Revelation 17:17) The heart is the place of deep communion and communication with God. (Psalm 27:8) For the Christian the human heart is the dwelling place of Christ. (Ephesians 3:17) At the new birth we become a new creation with a new heart that knows God and knows His will.

The heart may also be influenced by Satan. (John 13:2) "And during supper, the devil having already put into the heart of Judas Iscariot, {the son} of Simon, to betray Him," (NAS)

e)   The heart has the capacity for creative imagination

Most important for our understanding of emotional healing and the use of active imagination (visualization) in its healing is to appreciate anew that the heart is the imagination center of our life. The rabbis taught this in olden times, and it is scripturally based. *"God saw that every imagination of the thoughts of his heart was only evil continually."* (Genesis 6:5) *"The imagination of man's heart is evil from his youth."* (Genesis 8:21)

This word for "imagination" is used in Deuteronomy 31:21, 1 Chronicles 28:9 and 29:18. In Hebrew, it is "yetser-" with the meanings of :

> a form, framing, purpose, framework
>   a) form
>   1) pottery
>   2) a graven image
>   3) a man (as formed from the dust)
>   b) purpose, imagination, device (intellectual framework) [4]

Generally, in the Old Testament the imagination is seen to produce bad things. As for instance being the source of false prophecies:

> *17   "Now, son of man, set your face against the daughters of your people who prophesy*

---

[4] From Brown-Driver-Briggs definition for word #   3336 PC Study Bible, Bible Soft.

out of their own imagination. Prophesy against them. (Ezekiel 13:17, NIV)[5]

Imagination is also seen as being able to conceive and to create things such as an idol.

> *18 "Of what value is an idol, since a man has carved it? Or an image that teaches lies? For he who makes it trusts in his own creation; he makes idols that cannot speak.* (Hab 2:18, NIV)

In the New Testament the Greek term often translated "imagination" is "dialogismos." It may be defined as follows:

> 1) the thinking of a man deliberating with himself
> a) a thought, inward reasoning
> b) purpose, design
> 2) a deliberating, questioning about what is true
> a) hesitation, doubting
> b) disputing, arguing[6]

In the New Testament, like the Old Testament, the ability of the fallen human heart to imagine evil is emphasized.

> *21 Because that, when they knew God, they glorified him not as God, neither were thankful; but became vain in their imaginations, and their foolish heart was darkened.* (Romans 1:21, KJV)

f) Memory

The "heart" includes memory.

> Luke 2:19 *"Mary kept all these things, pondering them in her heart."* (See also Luke 2:51)

In the Hebrew the term is "zakar" and has the following definition:

> to remember, to recall, to call to mind
> a) (Qal)[7] to remember, to recall
> b) (Niphal) to be brought to remembrance, to be remembered, to be thought of, to be brought to mind
> c) (Hiphil)
> 1) to cause to remember, to remind
> 2) to cause to be remembered, to keep in remembrance
> 3) to mention

---

[5] Here and in Ezekiel 13:2 the Hebrew word is actually the word "leb" for heart but translated in English as "imagination."
[6] Thayer's definition for word # 1261 PC Study Bible, Bible Soft.
[7] The "Qal", "Hiphal" and etc. are the different forms of the Hebrew Verb.

4) to record

5) to make a memorial, to make remembrance[8]

2.   Physiological systems

The human heart or spirit is a spiritual entity unto itself, transcendent to the physical body, but is interconnected with the human body, especially the brain which provides the "machinery" for its expression in the material realm.

The body and what happens to us in the body also affects the heart. According to the biblical vision of humankind we are a spiritual, bodily, mental, and emotional whole.

The functions of the heart are mediated through the mind and body. These functions are also experienced at different levels of our awareness, some are conscious, others are unconscious.

3.   Conscious awareness

Our conscious mind has both an inward and outward dimension.

To the outward dimension belongs empirically observable sensory experience. This also includes other aspects of the heart that are outwardly expressed, such as our verbal and emotional expressions, relationship with God and others, and our actions. We may consciously reflect critically upon who we are, our relationships, feelings and our actions.

Consciousness also has an inward direction. This includes our rational thought processes, the emotions of which we are aware and accessible memories. One may reflect not only upon what is happening in the outside world, but through introspection, the eye of conscious awareness is turned inward. In contemplative prayer the eye of conscious awareness is turned toward God.

The thought processes and structure of our awareness are under the direction of the heart, but they are also influenced by the unconscious mind, our relationships with others, the sensory world, and our internal physiological processes. In addition, spiritual beings from outside time and space may also impinge upon the heart.

The heart influences what one consciously thinks and perceives. But the heart may also be corrupted or ennobled by the character of what is thought and perceived. St. Paul recognizing this malleable nature of the heart. St. Paul urges us to carefully direct our thoughts to that which is good.

> 8   *Finally, brothers, whatever is true, whatever is noble, whatever is right, whatever is pure, whatever is lovely, whatever is admirable-- if anything is excellent or praiseworthy-- think about such things.* (Philippians 4:8, NIV)

For instance, if one chooses to direct one's thoughts toward that which is evil or hateful, such a

---

[8] From Brown-Driver-Briggs definition for word # 2142 PC Study Bible, Bible Soft.

decision may have arisen from an evil heart. But the choices will fill one's mind with evil and will deepen the heart's bondage to evil of the heart.

4.   Subconscious mind (unconscious)[9]

This is the realm beneath the conscious awareness. [10]

This realm is filled with different entities, some of which are entirely within us. Other emotions and thoughts, while objectively real, are invisible and impinge upon our unconscious self.

The unconscious mind, like the conscious mind, is subject to the heart but it also affects the heart.

5.   Emotional system

Our emotions are connected to the glandular system and to the automatic nervous system.

Our emotions have an inward dimension, which we experience as feelings. They also have an outward dimension in that they also find outward expression. There are also perceptions that elicit emotional responses.

Emotions connect with the conscious mind insofar as we are aware of them. There are other emotions that are beyond the scope of our awareness or are associated with repressed memories and interface with the unconscious mind. The heart is the ultimate source and director of our emotions.

6.   The genius of Jesus who understood the human heart

The prophets had perceived that, *"the heart is deceitful above all things and desperately wicked (sick)."* (Jeremiah 17:9) Jesus saw even more deeply that the heart was the source and fountain of all pollution and that what was needed was a radical transformation. In the passage on defilement (Matthew 15:1-20 and Mark 7:1-23) He said, *"For from within, out of the heart of man, come evil thoughts..."* The word translated "thoughts" is just as well translated "imaginations." (The Greek word is so translated in the key passage of Romans 1:21 KJV) I believe Jesus headed the list of sins pouring out of the heart with the word "imaginations" because He knew that the image-making faculty is the author of the evil deed. This comes out

---

[9] Carl Jung used the term; "unconscious". Freud on the other hand used the term "subconscious." While Jung and Freud understood the region beneath the conscious mind to contain very different entities and processes for our purposes the terms will be used interchangeably.

[10] The MS Encarta Dictionary defines this simply as - **mind's hidden part:** the part of the mind containing memories, thoughts, feelings, and ideas that the person is not generally aware of but that manifest themselves in dreams and dissociated acts.

forcefully in His teaching on adultery in Matthew 5:27-30 where the lustful thought/imagination is attacked as the root of the deed.

a)   Jesus' appeal to the imagination – using the imagination for good

Beyond perceiving that the root problem of human evil is the imagination; Jesus perceived the cure. Since the imagination was the trigger of any heart response, He sought to change hearts by appealing to the imagination. He vividly portrayed the Kingdom of God with word-pictures, parables, and picturesque sayings. In Matthew 13 He called His listeners to picture a sower. (In the KJV the parable is preceded by the word, "Behold." This can justifiably be translated, "Picture a sower going to sow.")

Then He explained why He spoke in parables (word-pictures); *"This is why I speak to them in parables, because seeing they do not see, and hearing they do not hear, nor do they understand."* (Matthew 15:13) Jesus wanted to captivate their hearts with a whole new vision that would displace the old evil imaginations. In this He was the fulfillment of the patriarchs and prophets -- they had all spoken in pictures because they were inspired by God who knows the secrets of hearts and knows that the eye-gate is the way to heart change. He himself spoke to them in dreams, visions, and vivid speech.

We shall be following Jesus in making use of images and pictures to reach the depths of the human heart in this process of spiritual, inner and relational healing.

B. DEPTH PSYCHOLOGY MODEL

To continue this description of the parts of the human psyche we need to step back from the heart and bring into view the unconscious. This has been the unique contribution of the Depth Psychologists such as Carl Jung. Here we do not depart from the Bible's model so much as to add further insights from modern psychology.

As has already been stated, Jung himself strayed far from orthodox Christianity. I do not recommend him or his thought as a model of the Christian life. He did, however, travel deep into regions of the human soul, into the realm of myth, and into the nether world of the demonic. From these journeys that led him so far astray from a center in Jesus Christ he returned with some useful insights and revealing maps. These may aid us as we follow the Holy Spirit into the unconscious realms for healing and restoration. They may also warn us not to trespass into regions where we may be in serious danger of being deceived.

Depth Psychology Model

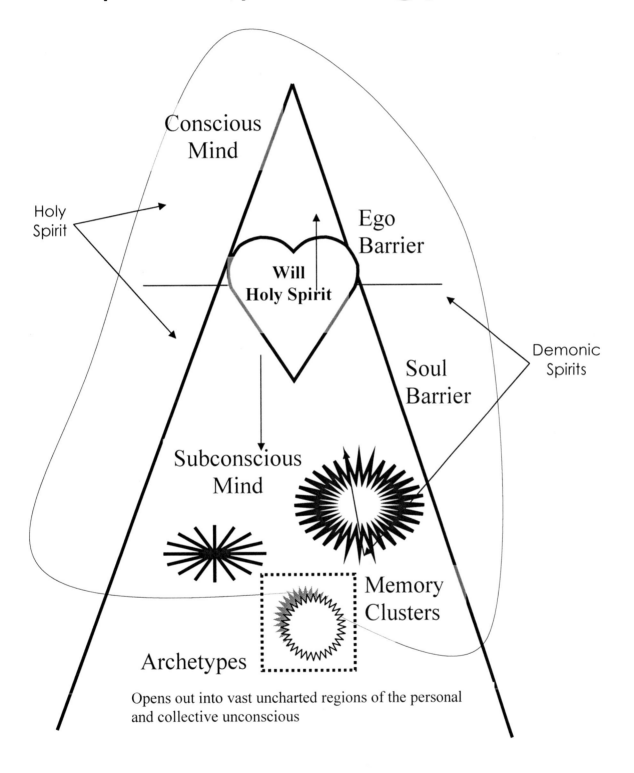

Conscious
Mind

Holy
Spirit

Ego
Barrier

**Will
Holy Spirit**

Soul
Barrier

Demonic
Spirits

Subconscious
Mind

Memory
Clusters

Archetypes

Opens out into vast uncharted regions of the personal
and collective unconscious

1.   The ego barrier

Between the conscious mind and the unconscious mind is the ego barrier. This barrier is like a porous membrane that contains a cell but allows for the inward and outward flow into and from the outside world.

To continue the image of the cell, the porousness of this membrane is controlled by the cell to allow in different types of solutions at different rates. There are times when the membrane breaks down and the cell is overwhelmed by the outside. Likewise, the heart exercises control of the barriers between the conscious and unconscious determining its permeability. This barrier is permeable as seen during sleep when dreams, which are unconscious contents, bubble up into our consciousness. Often nudges, insights, and intuitions are unconscious contents that have been allowed to pass the ego barrier and to enter consciousness.

While the heart may control the ego, there are, nevertheless, physiological and mental processes that may also influence the ego or may cause it to cease to function altogether. Various forms of mental illness result when the ego barrier breaks down and allows an uncontrollable invasion of unconscious contents into the conscious.

2.   Contents of the subconscious (unconscious)[11]

Some of the contents that may be found in the subconscious mind may be:

a. Memories of the past that are no longer readily available to the conscious mind. Some of these memories may have just sunk into the unconscious from lack of use. Others may have been actively suppressed because of their painful contents and associations.

b. Memories that have adhered around an intense emotional experience. These form into memory clusters. (Jung called these "complexes.")

c. Archetypes are inherited mental structures that allow us to give shape to our experience of reality.

d. Processes at the unconscious level that work to bring meaning and coherence to the psyche.

3.   The Holy Spirit

The Holy Spirit dwells in the inner sanctum of the heart. This is the interface between the human and divine. This is also the location of the new creature born of the Holy Spirit. Since the Holy Spirit transforms the heart, especially the will, in time the whole person will be

---

[11] Carl Jung called this region of the psyche the "unconscious", Freud called it the "subconscious". In this manual both terms will be used interchangeably as having the same meaning.

transformed.

The Holy Spirit may touch our unconscious mind and may speak to us through the language of visions, dreams, and intuitions. The Holy Spirit may at times directly address the conscious mind as well.

4.   The soul barrier

The soul and the human spirit seem connected and both seek expression through the human mind. While spatial relationships are difficult to discern, the soul does seem to surround the psyche and provide a barrier between the person and the surrounding spiritual world. This barrier may be penetrated to allow into the person demonic spirits as well as the human spirit.

5.   Angels

Most often in scripture angels seem to appear to people in the space/time realm. (Luke 24:4) That is, they are apprehended by the conscious mind. But they may also manifest their presence through the unconscious as when an angel appeared to Joseph in a dream. (Matthew 2:13) Angels, however, unlike the Holy Spirit, would not be able to reside in the person.

6.   Evil Spirits

These may afflict us at the unconscious as well as conscious level. Since they are spiritual entities like the Holy Spirit, they may also become attached at various places in the human body and psyche.

The human heart and psyche function as a complex system in which the various parts interface and interact. A person may have a heart that is redeemed and indwelt by the Holy Spirit. At the same time one may also know in his/her conscious mind what is right. But there is a vast in-between region in which there may be conscious and unconscious areas of resistance to doing what one knows in his/her mind and heart is right.

Paul notes that the spirit may be willing but the flesh is weak. He also calls us to take every thought captive to Christ. These statements suggest that there are parts of us that may, to some degree, be autonomous from the heart and must be brought into the lordship of Jesus Christ. It is also very possible to have one's heart inhabited by the Holy Spirit, be struggling to do what one knows is right and yet have evil spirits attached to some areas of the psyche.

In emotional healing we are often dealing with this inner space between the conscious mind and the inner most heart that is indwelt by the Holy Spirit.

We shall explore this further in reference, first, to the origins of emotional hurt and, second, to the process of healing.

7.   Other human spirits or souls

The soul or spirit of other human beings may impinge upon us and become connected to us. This makes possible for soul ties and soul connections. It is also possible for the soul or the spirit of another person to become entangled in our own.

III.   DIFFERENT SOURCES OF INNER HURTS

Return to Part One that established the "Creation-Fall-Redemption" framework for Jesus' healing ministry.

We have been created in the image of God with the potential for harmonious relationships with God, other human beings, and the created order. Because we are made in the image of God with a heart and spirit with their unconscious depths as demonstrated in the models of the human psychic given above, we may be wounded in some distinctive ways.

By living in a fallen world with its matrix of broken relationships, it is very easy for us to sin and be sinned against. Sin, as contrary to a harmonious relationship with God, always has hurtful consequences. When the Holy Spirit who brings to us the presence of Jesus Christ deals with these hurts quickly, usually they are healed and we continue forward in life. Things happen to us however at certain vulnerable stages in our lives that are not immediately healed. Rather, they become wounds in our hearts that adversely affect us in many ways.

There follows some of the things that may wound us.

A. GENEALOGICAL INFLUENCES

These influences are inherited from our parents and may go back many generations. They include personality types with certain emotional sensitivities. They may also include spiritual realities such as familiar spirits and curses.

Generally, these genealogical factors affect us at an unconscious level. They may also shape our emotional disposition.

> Example - A 35 year old man came for prayer with a deep debilitating fear that he would die before the age of 40. It turned out that his father had died young, as had his grandfather. There was in the family the saying, "the men of the family will not live past fifty." As he was being prayed for an evil spirit manifested itself. It responded to the name, "spirit of death." After it was driven out the fear of dying young ceased to torment him.

Unforgiven sin and unhealed hurt in families can create habits of relating that pass on the sin and hurt from generation to generation.

Examples abound:

> If parents are highly critical, then the children grow up with a destructive critical attitude. Families in which there is alcoholism tend to result in children who are more prone to having problems with alcoholism.

In this area, we are dealing with a complex combination of genetic predisposition and learned behavior. It is not always easy to tell the difference between "nature" and "nurture." Add to this the interference of evil spirits and one has a complicated situation indeed.

B. PRE-NATAL HURTS

If our mother experienced some great trauma while she was carrying us, this may affect us. On the other hand, if the mother from conception onward rejects the child, this also may have an effect.

The fetus, of course, cannot comprehend, let alone remember, what is going on but he or she can be affected by an atmosphere of hatred, tension, or fear. Such early impressions may be written within the unconscious of the child. These may surface years later in the form of irrational fears, insecurities, and, inappropriate behavior.

I am not at all sure of the exact mechanisms through which these pre-natal experiences are encoded into the child's unconscious mind, but there is ample empirical evidence that this is indeed the case.

Example –

> As mentioned in the section on the gifts of the Holy Spirit, healing for Bob Whitaker's epileptic son came only when a word of knowledge revealed that the roots of the problem were in pre-natal trauma.

> We also have dealt with many cases where a word of knowledge revealed that the emotional hurt took place because of an attempted abortion, the mother having been raped while pregnant, or during the pregnancy, the home was filled with strife.

> For example - A woman in China was being prayed for. At the evangelistic meeting when she accepted Christ a demon had manifested flinging her to the ground. The prayer that followed moved between inner healing for emotional hurts and deliverance of evil spirits. Finally at one in the morning, we were stumped. Through the manifestations of evil we knew that the deliverance was still not complete but we had no idea what the ground could be. As the evil spirit

would manifest the woman who was about 35 would involuntarily curl up in a fetal position. She would frail about as if seeking to resist blows by invisible fists.

As we prayed for guidance suddenly the Lord gave me an image of a baby in the mother's womb. The baby was being repeatedly struck by a long, tube-like object.

I had no idea what this meant – was it an attempted abortion? We silenced the demons who were tormenting the woman and asked her what the vision meant. She said, "I have no idea but why don't you ask my mother who is waiting outside. She is not a Christian and did not want to join in the prayer." So we called the mother in and shared the vision with her. Her first response was to say I don't know. The next moment however she was weeping. "You have just revealed my terrible secrete that I have carried for 35 years. My daughter does not know this, no one knows this, except your God! When I was seven months pregnant with this daughter I was brutally raped. I never really got over it and I could not help it but I hated my baby and the man who raped me.

Once this was revealed we prayed for healing of mother and the daughter. The demon gave one last convulsion and left. There was a tearful reconciliation between mother and daughter.

C. HURTS RECEIVED IN CHILDHOOD THAT ARE LEFT UNHEALED

Children are very vulnerable to inner hurt for the following reasons:

First, human beings require the context of love, security, and trust to develop the foundation for mental and spiritual health. Second, they are almost entirely dependent upon others who shape the reality in which they live. This reality in turn affects their own development. Their powers of understanding, as well as defense mechanisms, are not well developed.

A severe trauma or an emotionally charged event in early childhood may become an emotional hurt requiring inner healing in later life through the following process.

1. When things happen to children, unless the home is loving and understanding and can help the child "process" the events, the child has few options for dealing with the trauma except through suppression.

Painful memories and the associated emotions are pushed down into the unconscious mind. This allows the child to function normally at the conscious level.

2. The repressed memories of an event that is full of some intense emotion, such as fear or pain, will be like a vortex around which similar experiences are attracted. This configuration of associated memories and their emotions become a memory cluster.

We shall more fully describe this process of memory cluster formation in the next section.

D. HURTS THAT WOUND THE HEART

All of these hurts have an emotional or psychological dimension that may be described by such a term as psychological complexes or memory clusters. However, there is more to them than just these psychological mechanisms. There is also the heart or spirit dimension.

The emotional wounding is often reflective of a deeper wounding in our heart that scars the very source of our emotions, thoughts, and intentions. Thus, a child who has been rejected and abandoned will not only have some bad complexes to work through but will have had its heart so hurt that he or she will be unable to love. People deeply wounded by the abusive sins of others may have their heart so wounded that they are no longer able to will wholeness for themselves or others.

I believe that all hurts, since they arise either from our own sin or the sins of others, have impact upon the heart or spirit. There are however certain sins that more deeply wound the heart than others. For example:

- Sexual sin involves both the body and the soul and may penetrate not only the body, but also the ego and soul barrier.

- Engagement in the occult may wound the soul by inviting demonic spirits to enter into oneself or into others.

- Drug abuse (especially psychedelics) weakens the ego barrier and punches holes in the soul barrier.

The ultimate healing that we seek is not just emotional, but also spiritual and can come only from Jesus Christ.

The Holy Spirit often reveals this wounding of the soul in poetic images during the healing process.

Example –

> I was praying for an elderly Chinese man who had been taken as a POW in the Korean War. In the camp he had heard the gospel preached by a Presbyterian missionary and had accepted Jesus Christ. Despite his strong faith he had a major problem with boundaries - especially sexual boundaries. He had brought disgrace to his church when it was found that that he was sleeping with several of the pastor's wives and had attempted to seduce the pastor's wife. Women were afraid of him and felt intimidated as well as fascinated by his presence. These extramarital affairs finally had destroyed his marriage and alienated his children.

He confessed his near constant struggle with lust and inability not to violate women. He was a world class "dirty old man."

As we prayed and asked the Holy Spirit to reveal the source of his affliction, he spoke up and said, "We don't need to ask the Holy Spirit to help us on this one. I know exactly when this happened." It was when I raped several women during the war before being captured. Then in the camp I was gang raped myself. It was terrible and I think I know first hand what those women must have felt like. By this time he was weeping with bitter remorse. He started to relive these experiences. As we prayed, "suddenly I saw a piece of carefully woven cloth. Right in the middle of it was a jagged tear. I believe this was a glimpse of the tearing in his soul that had taken place when he raped those women and was himself violated.

We then were led in prayer in which he asked Jesus to take a needle and thread and sew up that hole in the cloth. There then came the command to give up the right to violate another person's soul through sex or any other way. He was able to forgive the men who violated him at the POW camp and, at the prompting of the Holy Spirit, gave names to each of the women he had raped and wrote a letter asking for forgiveness. This was then thrown into the river and washed out to sea as a sign of forgiveness. After this strange prayer of dealing with his wounded soul, this man was no longer tormented by the compulsive drive to violate boundaries.

E. SUMMARY: THE MOST COMMON HURT SYMPTOMS AND POSSIBLE ROOT CAUSES (AS DISCERNED BY BOB WHITAKER)

The way we know that we have been wounded in our heart is through the symptoms. These are often obvious in our every day behavior. Their causes however are usually hidden in the unconscious and thus are not immediately accessible to our conscious participation in Jesus' healing work.

1. Deep sense of inferiority

An inability to feel that I am lovable to God or others.

The person feels it's useless to pray because, "Why would God want to help me?" Low self-image and poor self-esteem dog most Americans.

Normally rooted in rejection, feeling unwanted as a child, being put down and lacking parental affirmation.

2. Anger, hostility, rebellion, judgementalism, self-hate

Rooted in verbal and/or physical abuse or sexual abuse, and/or lack of affection and demonstrable consistent love from parents, and compounded with guilt.

3. Unreasonable fear and anxiety

Fear of people and criticism, fear of situations, afraid to try, shy and withdrawn, nervous, suspicious, distrusting. Often rooted in trauma (can go back to the womb or birth), danger, insecure home life, abusive environments, guilt.

4. Perfectionist performance orientation

Striving, driving, stressful, restless workaholics tyrannized by "should" and "ought." Normally rooted in homes where children are pressured to perform, where love is conditioned by performance.

5. Unexplained obsessive or compulsive behavior

Fits of anger, periodic depression, perverted sex drives, addictions to drugs, alcohol, sex, spending, food, or pleasure. Rooted in outrage, rejection, condemnation, and compulsive families.

THE PRMI *DUNAMIS PROJECT*
THE HEALING MINISTRY OF JESUS

6.   Depression, sadness

Rooted in deprivation, loss, anger, oppression, and a broken heart.

7.   Supersensitive

Rooted in persecution, teasing, shaming.

These things kill the happy, creative, spontaneous, open, loving, caring, trusting, hopeful, delighted child in us. They take joy and peace from us, and they make stressful homes and uptight dysfunctional churches where a forced gaiety and superficial friendliness replaces **koinonia** joy in the Lord.

We need to explore how these things actually wound us. To do this we must return to the models already given and understand further how our memory functions.

How past events affect us and the dynamics of our psyche will be directly related to our being able to cooperate with the Holy Spirit in bringing healing.

IV.   THE ANATOMY OF INNER WOUNDS

There now follows a step by step development of the psychological process that are involved in the formation of inner wounds. It is of utmost importance for us to understand the nature of inner hurts if we are to fully cooperate with the Holy Sprit in healing ministry. He knows every cell of our bodies and also searches the secret recesses of our hearts.

A. THE DIFFERENT ASPECTS OF MEMORY

To understand how past hurtful events may wound us we must first understand how memory functions. Memory is an extraordinary aspect of our make up as well as our identity.

St. Augustine in the Confessions explores the wide spectrum of experience that may be contained in our memory.

> 13. All these things, each of which entered by its own avenue, are distinctly and under general heads there laid up: as, for example, light, and all colors and forms of bodies, by the eyes; sounds of all kinds by the ears; all smells by the passage of the nostrils; all flavors by that of the mouth; and by the sensation of the whole body is brought in what is hard or soft, hot or cold, smooth or rough, heavy or light, whether external or internal to the body. All these doth that great receptacle of memory, with its many and indescribable departments, receive, to be recalled and brought forth when required; each, entering by its own door, is hid up in it. And yet the things themselves do not enter it, but only the images of the things perceived are there ready at hand for thought to, recall. And who can

tell how these images formed, notwithstanding that it is evident which of the senses each has been fetched 'm and treasured up? For even while I live in darkness and silence, I can bring out colors in memory if I wish, and discern between black and white, and what others I wish; nor yet do sounds break in and disturb what is drawn in by mine eyes, and which I am considering, seeing that they also are there, and are concealed, laid up, as it were, apart. For these too I can summon if I please, and immediately they appear. And though my tongue be at rest, and my throat silent, yet can I sing as much as I will; and those images of colors, which notwithstanding are there, do not interpose themselves and interrupt when another treasure is under consideration which flowed in through the ears. So the remaining things carried in and heaped up by the other senses, I recall at my pleasure. And I discern the scent of lilies from that of violets while smelling nothing; and I prefer honey to grape-syrup, a smooth thing to a rough, though then I neither taste nor handle, but only remember. [12]

This multitude of content of our memory that Augustine so wonderfully describes is no doubt consistent with our own experience. It seems as if memory records all things that enter into us by the various senses as well as from our own mind and spirit. This astonishing diversity of memory contents may be reduced to the following four broad categories.

The Four Aspects of Memory

- Conceptual/ Cognitive

- Sensory: Visual, Auditory, Olfactory, Taste and Touch

- Emotional

- Body Memories and Kinesthetic

To illustrate, we move from Augustine's introspection to a case of inner healing ministry that demonstrates these four aspects of memory.

> While praying for a woman in her fifties I received a word of knowledge as follows: I saw a little girl running from room to room in a big house crying "Mommy, Mommy!" Finally not finding her mother anywhere she falls on her mother's bed sobbing. As I shared this word of knowledge, the woman I was praying for suddenly broke down sobbing. She said, "The Lord has just given you a picture of the most terrible day of my life. That was the day when I was ten years old when my parents had a horrible argument. My father hit my mother very hard, she ran into another room crying and screaming. My father stormed out of the house. I went running after him crying. Without looking back at me he walked down the long driveway of the house and disappeared over

---

[12] From Book 10, Chapter 8, sec 13 of the Confessions of St. Augustine.

the hill. I turned back to find my mother. I could hear her crying somewhere in the house. I searched through the house, when I did not find her in her bedroom my whole world was shattered and I fell on the bed crying. I never saw my father again.

As we prayed for this woman the memory of this terrible day all came back to her and she relived it. As she did, we could see that her memory of this event had four important components:

1. Conceptual/cognitive

This aspect of memory was the set of mental interpretations of what had happened that day. They included things like "daddy hit mommy, daddy walked out, he did not look at me. I have been abandoned. I have done something very bad to have daddy leave home. At last daddy is gone and will stop hurting mommy and etc."

2. Sensory: visual, auditory, olfactory, taste and touch

Within the memory too was the information from the five senses. She could actually hear, see and smell the way it was when this event happened. She could again see the bedroom, with its blue sun-faded curtains and could smell the sheets on the bed with the lingering sweaty odor of her father. She could see and hear her father slamming the door and walking out.

3. Emotional

Worse than the conceptual and sensory memory was that the emotions of that terrible day were all still engraved in her heart. She could feel the blinding terror that her mother would be hurt. She could feel again her heart breaking with the wave of rejection that had assaulted her as her father had left without even looking back. She could feel again the despair and fear when she could not find her mother. It was a deep pain in her chest as the precious and secure family relationships were shattered.

4. Body memories, kinesthetic

As she recalled this event, her body was aware again of the tight ball of pain she had felt in her chest and the sick feeling in her stomach. To give another illustration of body memory: when I was about 8 years old, I was playing in the stream. I jumped up on to a large flat rock, but slipped and fell. I landed hard on my knee. I am now 48. One day while walking by that stream I happened to notice the rock on which I fell. The moment I saw it, I felt a sharp pain in my knee.

Then I recalled that that was where I had fallen. An example of kinesthetic memory is your fingers being able to spell words on a typewriter without looking at the keys or even consciously thinking of the word.

In summary: The memory retains the entire texture of the experience in the various ways that we experienced it as well as the interpretations that we add to the experience to give it meaning.

B. THE PROCESS OF FORGETTING

Some memories are readily recalled while others slip into forgetfulness. Memories have different ways of being forgotten.

1.   Memories naturally sinking into the subconscious

One may imagine the mind as a pool and the memories of recent events as fallen leaves floating on the surface. As time passes there is the natural process of the leaves sinking into the water and slowly drifting out of sight into the murky depths. So too memories naturally sink into the depths of the unconscious with the passage of time. There they lie forgotten. This is the fate of most memories.

2.   Repression

If memories are painful or unpleasant the human heart often deals with them through repression. That is, they are willfully pushed down into the subconscious where they no longer actively torment the person's conscious awareness. Just because something is forgotten does not mean that it has ceased to exist. It does exist and continues in the subconscious mind.

There follows a psychoanalytic definition of this common defense mechanism.

> Repression consists in an activity of the ego that bars from consciousness the unwanted id impulse or any of its derivatives, whether memories, emotions, desires, or wish fulfilling fantasies. All are as though they did not exist as far as the individual's conscious life is concerned. A repressed memory is a forgotten one from the subjective point of view of the individual in whom repression has taken place.[13]

The important thing about repression of memories is that it takes place automatically without the person's conscious participation in the process.

> "… The entire process [of repression] goes on unconsciously. It is not only the repressed material that is unconscious. The activities of the ego which constitute repression are quite as unconscious. One is no more aware of "repressing" something than one is of forgetting something. The only thing one can be aware of is the end result.[14]

---

[13] Charles Brenner, M.D., *An Elementary Textbook of Psychoanalysis* (New York: Anchor Press/Doubleday, 1974), pp. 80-81.
[14] Ibid., p. 83.

Repression is a useful defense mechanism that is often employed by children to deal with traumatic or painful events. Children usually lack the capacity to analyze their experiences or to deal with painful emotions. Often without adult love and direction they do not know how to seek out healing in Jesus. So these memories of painful experiences are suppressed and pushed out of sight so that the mind can continue functioning. This process however requires constant effort of the mind to hold down the memory. It is like the effort required to hold a beach ball under water. Repression often robs the mind of energy and creativity.

Remember that what is repressed is not just the thought connected with a bad experience, but the emotions and bodily sensations as well.

For instance if a child is unjustly punished not only will there be locked in the memory the concept of the injustice, but the emotions of fear and pain of the actual spanking. All will be retained in the subconscious.

Repression of bad memories may be a useful defense mechanism for allowing the person to cope. It however does not actually solve anything. The memory still contains the pain. The unconscious nature of the process of repression means that the fundamental spiritual principle of "walking in the light" has also been violated. Memories that are repressed cannot be healed. We do not even know we have them so they are not actively brought into the presence of Jesus Christ.

3.   Suppression of memories

Suppression is another way of dealing with painful memories.

> However, there is a conscious activity that is somewhat analogous to repression. This activity is usually referred to as suppression in the psychoanalytic literature. It is the familiar decision to forget about something and to think no more about it. It is more than likely that there are intermediates between suppression and repression and it may even be that there is no truly sharp line of demarcation between the two[15].

The end result of both suppression and repression is the same. The memory is forgotten and beyond our ability to consciously bring it into the context where the dynamic of Jesus' healing ministry may be operative. For instance, it is impossible to follow Jesus' command to forgive someone if the memory of the person hurting you has been forgotten.

---

[15] Ibid., p. 83

4.   Dissociation

Dissociation is the opposite of association.[16] Dissociation takes place when the heart separates a part of itself off from the rest of itself. Between isolated part and the rest of the self there is erected a wall of amnesia. Usually dissociation takes place as the mind's defense against trauma.

> Dissociation is the most wonderful protection against pain that any child could ever develop. There could be no more effective defense – the child pretends the traumatic event happened to somebody else, and then…Poof! … COMPLETELY forgets about it. It is gone.[17]

This separation of the part of the psychic that contains the painful memory protects the core person for wounding and allows them to function normally.

All people dissociate to some degree as a way of dealing with painful experiences. The complexity of the dissociative process is that this may take place with different aspects of memory and at different levels of the physic.

For instance, a person may be able to recall the traumatic experience and rationally reflect upon it but will have dissociated the emotional component of the memory. Therefore, they feel nothing, as they are able to describe in vivid detail a terrible experience.

In some cases when there is a persistent trauma and the right personality attributes of high intelligence and creativity the dissociation may proceed to such a degree that the physic fragments into separate personalities. When this takes place the dissociation includes not just the components of memory but also the conscious, unconscious and the will.

A full development of dissociation and the formation and healing of alternate personalities is beyond the scope of this manual. What is important for us is to know that we may well come across this phenomenon in inner healing ministry. For further study and for learning how to discern the presence of alter personalities I strongly recommend the book by James Friesen, *Uncovering the Mystery of MPD: Its Shocking Origins…Its Surprising Cure.*

---

[16] **dissociation** is defined in the MS Encarta World Dictionary as follows:

1. **treatment of something as unconnected:** the treatment of somebody or something as distinct or unconnected, or the fact of being regarded in this way
4. CHEMISTRY **division of molecule:** a breaking up of a molecule into simpler components
5. PSYCHIATRY **separation of emotions:** the separation of a group of normally connected mental processes, for example, emotion and understanding, from the rest of the mind as a defense mechanism

[17] James Friesen, *Uncovering the Mystery of MPD* (San Bernardino, CA: Life Publishers, Inc., 1991), p.114.

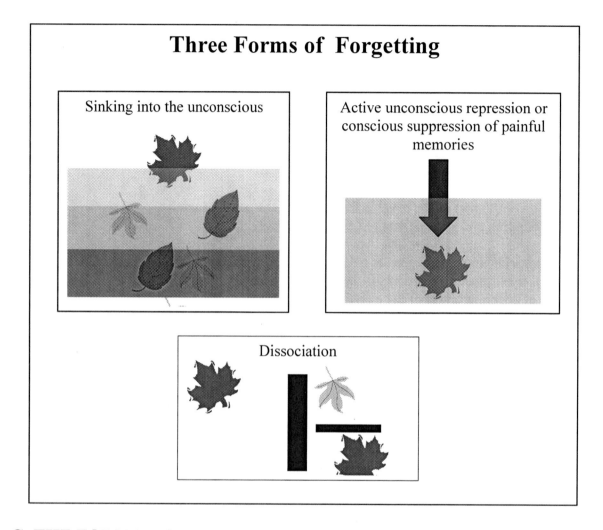

C. THE FORMATION OF VORTEX MEMORIES

The picture of leaves drifting to the bottom of the lake or actively being pushed down is helpful only for understanding the process of forgetting. Memories with their four components are active and alive. In addition, dynamic processes in the unconscious are working to bring meaning and coherence to these memories.

Memories come from experiences that have different levels of intensity. Memories with great emotional intensity or meaning have the potential to form in the unconscious what may be called a "vortex" memory.

Webster's gives the following definition for vortex:

> A whirling mass of water forming a vacuum at its center, into which anything caught in the motion is drawn; a whirlpool. A whirl or powerful eddy of air; a whirlwind. Any activity, situation, or state of affairs that resembles a whirl or

eddy in its rush, absorbing effect, irresistible and catastrophic power, etc.

A memory with certain qualities will have the same effect in the psyche as described above of water, wind or activity. We shall see that a vortex is a good descriptive name for this type of powerful memory.

The following observations may be made about how vortexes form and function in the unconscious.

1. **Caused by a profound, emotionally-charged event whose memory lives on in the present and will influence our future. May be positive or negative.**

As I have explored my mind there are some memories that have great power. Most happened when I was young. They are forgotten but when brought to light still sparkle with all the radiance of fresh cut jewels.

Example: Brad Long's encounter with God in nature.

> Once when I was ten or eleven years old on a summer Saturday morning I headed down to the stream to play. I had thoroughly explored the stream and woods near our house, but that day I suddenly stepped into a glade I had never been to before. It was filled with ferns and wild flowers; high over head like a green cathedral were the arching boughs of trees.
>
> The whole place was infused with a brilliant soft light. Every fern sparkled with morning due. I sat down and just took in the beauty. I imagined that I had stumbled on the gathering place for fairies. Then I became aware that God was there like in the Garden of Eden. I did not see Him but knew that He was there by the love and beauty that enveloped me. Suddenly with a start, I realized that it was getting dark. I jumped up and ran home bewildered by where the time had gone but overjoyed at the secret place I had found. The next day and for many days afterwards I sought this magical meeting place. I could never find it.

This experience formed a vortex memory of great power within me. This vortex is entirely positive and has drawn me into a quest for God. It has also left its mark by instilling in me a deep love of nature.

Other vortex memories have their roots in not so positive experiences. The example already given to illustrate the four components of memory in IV A of the "day daddy left" formed a powerful vortex in the little girl. This was a center of fear and rejection.

What is it that gives an experience and its memory vortex potential? The answer to this question really has two parts. The person him or herself and the nature of the experience itself.

Why does the same experience form a vortex in some people and not in others? Why for example does the same traumatic event have such different long-term effects upon the different children of the same household?

Some factors in the person:

```
┌─────────────────────────────────────────────────────────────┐
│             THE CHARACTERISTICS OF THE PERSON                │
│                                                              │
│                       Sensitivity                           │
│                                                              │
│   Low -----------------------------------------------High    │
│                                                              │
│                  Personality Orientation                    │
│                                                              │
│   Optimism --------------------------------------- Pessimism │
│                                                              │
│                      Environment                            │
│                                                              │
│   Healthy/loving --------------------------Unhealthy/unloving│
└─────────────────────────────────────────────────────────────┘
```

In addition to the above characteristics, there is also the person's preferred method of coping with painful or hurtful experiences. Most of these tactics result in the person not processing traumatic or painful experiences. They are the cleaver ways that the mind may devise to not "walk in the light" which is one of the essential principles of inner healing. By not dealing directly with experience the use of these Defense mechanisms contribute toward the formation of memory vortexes that will have a negative influence in the psyche. A further negative consequence is that because they are driven into the unconscious they become less assessable to the Healing work of Jesus Christ.

DEFENSE MECHANISM	WHAT IT DOES
DISSOCIATION	Keeps apart ideas that emotionally belong together or severs ideas from their appropriate emotion.
RATIONALIZATION	Offers apparently plausible explanation for behavior to conceal the true nature of the underlying impulse.
DENIAL	Refuses to face painful thoughts or feelings.
PROJECTION	Unrealistically attributes an objectionable tendency or his own to another person instead of recognizing it as part of himself.
REGRESSION	Resorts to age – inappropriate behavior to avoid responsibility or demands from others and to allow self-indulgence.
DISPLACEMENT	Temporarily and unsuccessfully represses unacceptable impulses or

	memories by attaching them to something else that is unrelated or inappropriate.
REPRESSION	Totally inhibits feelings or ideals, or memories. Repressed material revealed only symbolically as in dreams or expressed in inappropriate responses to situations.

In addition to the characteristics of the person, the experience may also have the following characteristics that effect its potential to create a vortex memory.

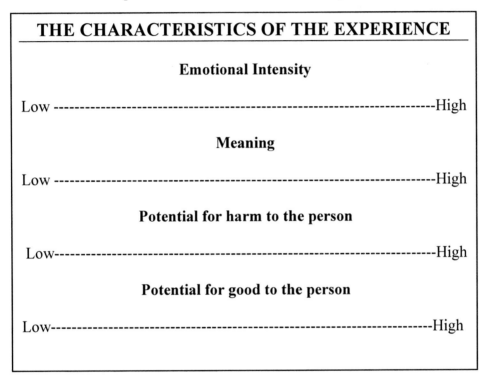

THE CHARACTERISTICS OF THE EXPERIENCE

Emotional Intensity

Low ---High

Meaning

Low ---High

Potential for harm to the person

Low---High

Potential for good to the person

Low---High

2.   Contains the four aspects of memory

Regardless of whether a vortex memory is buried in the unconscious or vivid in the conscious awareness it will contain the four aspects of memory. This means that the memory may be reentered and relived in all the rich texture of the original experience.

3.   The vortex will include truths or lies that interpret and give meaning to the original experience that produced the memory.

Human beings are not passive receivers of sensory data. Rather, the human heart always brings structure to the experience that gives it meaning. Further, the heart actively seeks to interpret the experience and place it in the context of a larger structure that becomes one's personality and worldview. (For further in-depth discussion of this process of interpreting and organizing experiences please see, *The Collapse of the Brass Heaven: Rebuilding you Worldview to*

Embrace the Power of God.)

For the work of inner healing, it is important for us to understand the following about this process of interpretation:

A. The process of interpreting and organizing experience comes from within the person but also from without. The outward sources of interpretation may be from our culture, other human beings, or from the Holy Spirit or from evil spirits.

B. These interpretations, if from the Holy Spirit and from other people who are speaking the truth, may be true. Alternatively, they may be lies given to us by evil spirits or by evil or deceived people. The heart may also bring to the interpretation of experience its own truth or lies. The Bible tells us that the unredeemed human heart, if left to itself, is full of deceit and will either create its own lies or readily accept the one's spoken to it from with out.[18]

C. These lies or truths imbed themselves in the memory of the experience and become a part of the vortex. Most likely they will become part of the conceptual part of the memory but not exclusively so. A lie or truth will usually have an emotional component to it.

To demonstrate the development of a truth or a lie that takes root in the heart there follows two examples:

a) An example of truth spoken into the heart: The encounter with God in the woods:

Return to my example of the mystical moment of meeting God in the woods. This powerful experience dominated my thoughts as I struggled to understand what had happened. I knew the experience had meaning for me personally. I also knew but could not articulate it – especially as an eleven-year-old – that a divine someone had revealed Himself to me.

Around this time, my mother was reading to us the Narnia books by C. S. Lewis. She read a description about how all the forest had come alive when Aslan appeared. As she read suddenly, I understood what had happened to me. God had walked in the forest and it had all become alive with His life and glory. The truths embedded in that memory vortex were:

> God is real.
> God is the creator and all nature reflects His glory.

18

Jeremiah 17:9
The heart is deceitful above all things and beyond cure. Who can understand it? (NIV)

Ephesians 4:22-25
You were taught, with regard to your former way of life, to put off your old self, which is being corrupted by its deceitful desires; to be made new in the attitude of your minds; and to put on the new self, created to be like God in true righteousness and holiness. Therefore each of you must put off falsehood and speak truthfully to his neighbor, for we are all members of one body. (NIV)

God loves me so much that He showed me His glory.
God wanted me to keep searching for Him.

It was C. S. Lewis with the inner working of the Holy Spirit who spoke these truths into my heart about this experience. This experience was so deep, strange and private that for years I did not speak of it to anyone. Indeed I could not for it sunk into my unconscious and only recently came back as I was in a time of prayer.

This experience and its memory holding these truths have had a profound influence on my personality. This vortex was used by the Holy Spirit to form in my personality a yearning for God and a boldness to seek Him.

b) An example of lies spoken into a memory: The little boy left to fish alone

Once I was praying for an elderly pastor. He was deeply depressed. He felt himself to be a failure in ministry. He felt abandoned by God. We could not get to the root of the problem and were not even sure how to pray for him.

Suddenly there came into my mind the picture of a little boy sitting on the bank of a wide river holding a fishing poll. Beside him, lying on the ground was another fishing poll. The boy's face was engulfed in sadness and his eyes had a lonely far away look. [19]

When I shared this image the man looked up in amazement. Then he started to cry and to shake all over. Finally when we could get him to talk he said, "that little boy is me. My father was a busy pastor but on Mondays we would just get away after school and go fishing together at the river. That was about the only time we ever had together. When I was fifteen during the Sunday service, he died suddenly of a heart attack. On Monday, my mother was distraught. The whole community was taken up with the arrangements. No one spoke so much as a word to my older sister or to me. I took my father's fishing rod and went to the river. I knew it was crazy but I thought somehow he would be there and everything would be ok again. When I got to our favorite place, of course, he was not there. I sat by the river alone and cried. I found myself thinking dreadful things. God does not exist. If my father had really loved me, he would have come fishing with me. God must not love me or have any use for me, otherwise he would not have taken my father at the Sunday service.

The man became a pastor like his father. But as we prayed for him, he confessed that those lies sown the day at the river that God did not exist or did not love him

---

[19] I often move in words of knowledge that bring forgotten vortex memories to conscious awareness. First, please do not come to the conclusion all vortex memories are inaccessible in the unconscious. They are not. Some may be vividly recalled indeed the person may never be able to forget them. Secondly, if they are buried, in the unconscious the most common way that they are brought to awareness is by the Holy Spirit working within the person bringing important but forgotten memories to awareness.

had hung like a dark cloud over his whole life and ministry. Then he wept again as he said, "But I know God does exist and that He does love me because He just gave you, a complete stranger, a vivid picture of the memory of that day at the river that has been seared in my soul for over fifty years. This marked the healing of his depression and a recovery of usefulness in ministry. (There is much more to this story: at the guidance of the Holy Spirit, he was able to forgive both God and his father. Through this experience of healing he also was opened up to the power and gifts of the Holy Spirit. The end result: The last years of this pastors ministry were more rewarding and fruitful then all the others put together.)

The devastating lies that God did not exist or did not love him may have come from Satan who seized upon this moment of weakness. It may also have come from the boy's own heart. In this case the lie may also have been spoken by the behavior of the church people and mother who were so devastated by the loss of their pastor and husband that they had no time for a little boy and girl who had just lost their father.

If someone had just taken time to give them a hug perhaps the children would not have felt so abandoned. On the other hand, if one of the other men had gone out fishing perhaps the truth of God's love would have been planted instead of these lies of Satan.

c)   More about truths and lies: Their ultimate source is God or Satan

One of the greatest contributions of Ed Smith's Theophostic approach to healing prayer is the insight about the role of lies. I recommend that those called into healing ministry study the Theophostic manual and/or take the video course.

Here let us establish as a fundamental principle that lies come from Satan and from the fallen human heart. This was certainly the understanding of Jesus.

> *44   You belong to your father, the devil, and you want to carry out your father's desire. He was a murderer from the beginning, not holding to the truth, for there is no truth in him. When he lies, he speaks his native language, for he is a liar and the father of lies.* (John 8:44, NIV)

> *18   But the things that come out of the mouth come from the heart, and these make a man 'unclean.'*
> *19   For out of the heart come evil thoughts, murder, adultery, sexual immorality, theft, false testimony, slander.* (Matthew 15:18-19, NIV)

> *45   The good man brings good things out of the good stored up in his heart, and the evil man brings evil things out of the evil stored up in his heart. For out of the overflow of his heart his mouth speaks.* (Luke 6:45, NIV)

On the other hand the truth is Jesus Christ. The truth as Jesus, truth about Jesus, and about our identity in the light of Jesus Christ all comes from the Holy Spirit.

> *13   But when he, the Spirit of truth, comes, he will guide you into all truth. He will not speak on his own; he will speak only what he hears, and he will tell you what is yet to*

come. (John 16:13, NIV)

Both lies and truths may be mediated to us through other people who impart their interpretations to our experiences. For instance, a parent, because of their authority and the vulnerability of children, may implant either a lie or a truth into a child's memory as they interpret their life experiences. In any case, the ultimate source of lies in the world is Satan. The source of truth is God.

d) Truths or lies are not passive facts but active principles working within us.

These truths or lies are not passive within us, rather they actively work in the psyche to produce our personality and to lead us into further experiences that support them.

For instance in the case of the girl that was sexually molested, the lies that she was dirty and worthless led her into a time of being sexually promiscuous which gave her a number of bad experiences that simply confirmed the lies.

The truths that were spoken to me through the encounter with God in the woods and interpreted by the words of C. S. Lewis opened me up to other experiences of God.

4. Vortexes, depending on their contents, may open a person to the Holy Spirit or to interference by evil spirits. They may also be spiritually neutral.

Some experiences form vortex memories that open us to God. This was the case of my mystical experience in the woods. There follows another experience with the supernatural that did form a powerful vortex memory that has opened the person to the spiritual realm. This could have had extremely evil consequences if it had not been immediately followed by ministry.

Example – The 18-year-old Brenda being hit by an evil spirit at a Dunamis in Brazil.

The whole story of what happened at the Healing Dunamis in central Brazil is recorded in my book *Prayer that Shapes the Future*.[20] In the midst of the teaching on Jesus' healing, a high level demon manifested and attacked first my translator and me. It then swooped down on the group of about 80 young people who were having a meeting about two hundred yards away. This direct encounter with the supernatural was a terrifying experience for all of us, especially for those who were directly hit by the spirit.

Brenda Pina is the daughter of the directors of the Central Brazil Dunamis Project. She was helping with the young people when she saw, in the Spirit, something black swiftly coming toward the group. The next moment she said that it was like the black evil thing was choking her with an awful deathlike presence. At the same time several other of the young people had fallen on the ground and were having what appeared to be convulsions. As the whole group prayed

---

[20]Brad Long and Doug McMurry, *Prayer that Shapes the Future: How to Pray With Power and Authority* (Grand Rapids , MI: Zondervan, 1999), pp. 158-161.

together and called out in the name of Jesus the evil thing left. Edie Lowe (a member of the American team) describes what happened to Brenda:

> While Brenda was on the ground, she was thrashing about rolling on the floor and others witnessed that she was trying to push something back with her hands. She spoke at times in Portuguese and at times in English. In English, she asked for those around her to pray for the angels. Allison prayed for the angels to surround her and that whatever was afflicting her would leave her. Then Brenda spoke of the darkness and said that it wasn't inside of her but around her. Doris was praying for Brenda and told Brenda to repeat these words, "In the name of Jesus, I command the darkness to be gone." When Brenda spoke these words, she immediately saw the light breaking forth through the darkness. She then started to laugh.

Surely this terrible experience had the potential to create vortex that could have blocked Brenda from growing in her faith. This may well have been the intention of the demon in assaulting this young woman with great potential for Christian leadership but it back fired!

> That night in the meeting the Holy Spirit fell in tremendous power, especially upon the young people. Brenda started to writhe and twist in her mother's arms. She had been opened up to the realm of the demonic, shattering her innocence of the true depth of evil in the world. It was like she had been spiritually raped with the demonic contamination of her soul. As we prayed, the Holy Spirit did a cleansing work in her and filled her with the love of Jesus Christ. The reality of darkness was not denied only overshadowed by the reality of Father, Son and Holy Spirit. That night she was baptized in the Holy Spirit to receive power to witness.

This experience, both of the demonic and of the power and reality of God, has formed a vortex memory that profoundly shaped Brenda's life. The Holy Spirit has continued to use it to lead her in greater openness to following Jesus Christ.

Brenda's was an experience of evil that was healed, so it ended up being positive. If on the other hand, the vortex contains unhealed hurt and unconfessed sins, then they may give ground to evil spirits to attack from without or actually become attached within us. In this case, the vortex becomes like a stronghold that is inhabited by an evil spirit.

A demon getting attached in the vortex may happen in many ways.

As for example a case of being terrified by some traumatic experience like in Brenda's case but it not healed. Another frequent cause is being sexually molested by another person who is demonized and the hurt is not dealt with. Further emotional hurts that are intentionally inflicted upon a child during occult practices are almost certain to be an open door for an evil spirit to attach in the vortex.

Here is one horrible illustration: A five-year-old girl is sexually abused.

Her husband and pastor brought this woman to me for prayer. She had been in therapy for 12 years for depression and an overall dysfunctional life. The persistent ineffectiveness of the therapy had led the pastor to the conclusion that there may be demonization. Through both words of knowledge and the Holy Spirit working in the person's own heart, a terrible memory was admitted to consciousness; one that had been impervious to 12 years of therapy.

The girl was five years old. Some older boys dragged her out into the woods. They tore off all her cloths and tied her spread eagle between some trees. They sexually molested her. They had shot a rabbit and then chopped it up in front of her as a warning that the same thing would happen to her if she told anyone what had happened. There also seemed to be some satanic ritual overtones.

That day lies were spoken to her that Satan used to weave a powerful vortex memory. Lies like you are dirty, you deserve to be used. No one loves you. If God loved you, He would not have let this happen to you. You belong to the devil not to God.

Through the abuse itself, the lies spoken, and the fact that those who did this horrible thing were themselves most likely demonized, an evil spirit attached itself in this memory vortex.

The girl was too terrified to tell anyone what had happened to her. The only way to deal with the memory was to suppress it. Left unhealed and the demon undisturbed, the memory formed a powerful vortex in the unconscious that for years shaped her personality.

The following chart provides a summary of the nature of a vortex memory.

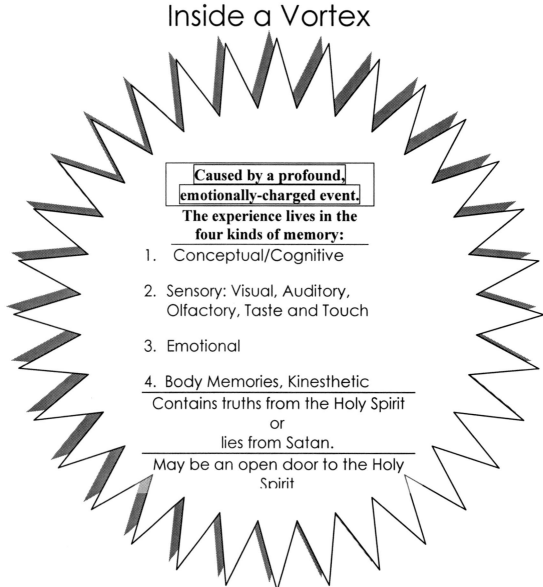

Inside a Vortex

Caused by a profound, emotionally-charged event.
The experience lives in the four kinds of memory:

1. Conceptual/Cognitive

2. Sensory: Visual, Auditory, Olfactory, Taste and Touch

3. Emotional

4. Body Memories, Kinesthetic

Contains truths from the Holy Spirit
or
lies from Satan.

May be an open door to the Holy Spirit

D. VORTEX MEMORIES FORM MEMORY CLUSTERS

Vortex memories will, like gravity, attract other memories to themselves and bind them together in clusters. Regardless of whether they are conscious or residing in the unconscious, memory clusters will exert influence on our feelings, reactions, worldview and behavior. In summary, these memory clusters have a significant role in shaping the person's personality.

Memories will be connected to the VORTEX MEMORY to form clusters according to the following well-established psychological principles.

1.   Similarity

Memories that are similar or that have aspects that are the same may be connected together. For instance, in the case of the girl who was sexually molested there were a large number of other memories associated with the vortex memory having to do with hurtful experiences with men.

For the boy who lost his father, there were other memories that had the common thread of abandonment, rejection and loneliness.

2.   Association/coinhereance[21]

There are occasions when memories themselves have nothing in common themselves. What connects them is a common experience in which different aspects are put together.

For instance:

> Laura and I were walking in a sculpture garden in South Carolina. As we passed a bed of white flowers, the fragrance came over me. Suddenly the memory came back to both of us of taking a walk together in a park on a balmy night in Taiwan in 1980. With it there also came the emotions of eager anticipation, as well as confusion, of having arrived in a strange country and given what then felt like an impossible task of learning Chinese. Upon examination, we realized that the white flowers were the same as the ones that we had often seen and smelled in Taiwan. The fragrance had touched the fringes of a memory cluster buried in our unconsciousness'.

The memories of walking together, the emotions of having just arrived in a strange country, the fragrance of the flower are not in themselves similar yet they were associated together by having arisen out of the same experience.

3.   Same lie or truth

The same lie or truth embedded in different memories may help to connect them together. The same truth or lie will also help connect memories to the vortex by giving them place in a larger framework of meaning. For instance, the truth "you are loved by God" will be the connector with other memories containing the same truth, "you are loved by God."

4.   Drive for meaning

Within the psyche there are dynamic processes that are working to put our memories into some sort of coherent order and structure that has meaning and that results in our being able to effectively function in the world.

These internal processes work to put memories together in clusters and then to associate various

---

[21] "Coinhere" is defined as to inhere or exist together; to be included in the same thing or substance.

clusters.[22]

5.   Demonic or Holy Spirit bonding

The Holy Spirit, as well as evil spirits, may also be at work within the psyche actively connecting memories together in ways that will serve their diverse purposes.

For instance, the Holy Spirit will be working to put together memories that further His purposes of bringing us into wholeness as children of God.

The Dynamic of forming a memory Cluster around a Vortex

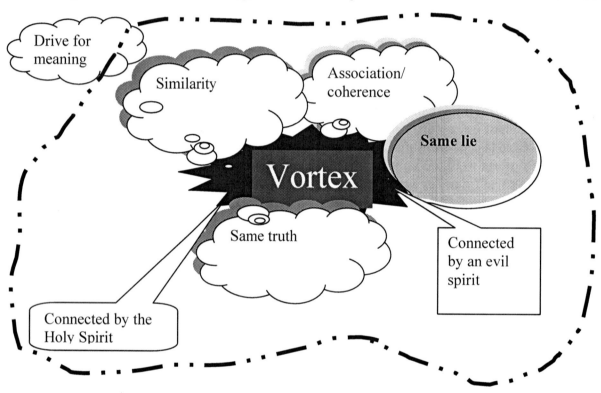

_____

[22] My term "drive for meaning" is very similar to Jung's "transcendent function" which he describes as follows: This is a complex function made up of other functions, and "transcendent" not as denoting a metaphysical quality but merely the fact that this function facilitates a transition from one attitude to another. The raw material shaped by thesis and antithesis, and in the shaping of which the opposites are united, is the living symbol. It s profundity of meaning is inherent in time and dissolution; and its configuration by the opposites ensures its sovereign power over all the psychic functions. Carl Jung, *Psychological Types* (Princeton, NJ: Princeton University Press, 1971), p. 480.

E. MEMORY CLUSTERS MAY BE CONNECTED TO OTHER MEMORY CLUSTERS

Memory clusters themselves may be connected according to the same four principles that memories were attracted to the vortex.

1.   **Similarity**

2.   **Association/coinhereance**

3.   **Same lie or truth**

4.   **Drive for meaning**

5.   **Demonic or Holy Spirit bonding**

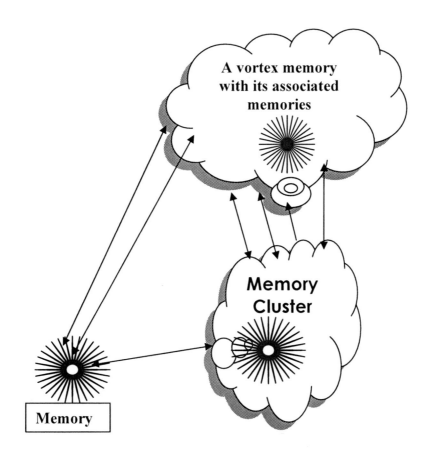

The memory clusters connecting together like linking molecules will help shape a person's personality.

These connections may serve as bridges to go to the formative but forgotten memories in the person's unconscious. In this way, they are extremely important in the process of uncovering deep hurts from the past. Later we shall see that these connections will be the bridges the Holy Spirit will use to bring forgotten hurts in the healing light of Jesus.

F. CONNECTED MEMORY CLUSTERS SHAPE A PERSON'S PERSONALITY, BEHAVIOR AND RELATIONSHIPS

Connected memory clusters in the subconscious will have a powerful influence on the person's personality. They will also effect a person's behavior and relationships in their present.

1.   The results of unhealed hurt-filled memory clusters

If memory clusters contain painful memories, lies or have attached demonic beings then there may take place the following negative consequences.

a) We may be blocked from loving and serving God fully with a whole heart.

b) We may be unable to enter into a loving relationship with someone else.

c) We may be hindered by irrational fears or have an inferiority complex.

d) We may be driven by insecurity to cling to others, to use them or hurt them.

e) We may cause mental problems such as depression or emotional breakdown.

f) We may be opened up to demonic attack or possession.

g) We may become physically ill with ulcers, cancer, high blood pressure, or some other emotionally-related disease.

They may create the specific symptoms of inner hurts that have already been listed in section III, E.

2.   The inner child of the past

A poetic and often helpful way of describing the effect of painful vortex memories in the unconscious is to name them the "inner child of the past."

When a serious wound has been experienced at a certain age, if the trauma is unhealed, it will form a vortex and memory cluster with feelings and reactions characteristic of a person of the age at which the trauma took place. Another way to speak of this is to say that the part of the personality embodied in the vortex and cluster of memories is fixated at that age. The person will act and think in a way appropriate to their age until something triggers the memory cluster containing the trauma. Then their thoughts, feelings and reactions may become that of the age at which the trauma took place.

For instance:

> Return to the case of the girl who was sexually abused at the age of five. When I started to pray for her she was 37 years old. When she walked into my office with her husband and pastor she could hardly speak and was carrying a large teddy bear. During our initial interview in which she demonstrated extreme nervousness she clung tightly to her teddy bear. Her thoughts and actions were that of a young, frightened child. While the vortex memory, with its terrible pain, was deeply repressed, there were many things in the counseling situation that were apparently triggering the four aspects of the memory that went back to when she was five years old.

> As we proceeded with the interview it turned out that there were many other age inappropriate behaviors that were disrupting the normal functioning of this 37-year-old woman. As for instance, even through she was married to a wonderful Christian man, sexual intimacy was not a pleasant experience. It triggered the fears and behaviors of the five-year old who was sexually abused.

The "inner child of the past" is an extremely useful facilitator of inner healing ministry. Often when the Holy Spirit begins to penetrate a hidden vortex memory and bring it into the light for healing, He does so by giving a picture of a child at the age the trauma took place.

Here is another example from my own life of how the "inner child of the past" was helpful in my own healing.

> I have dyslexia and had a dismal experience in school. My son Stephen also has dyslexia and ADD. One day I was working with him to learn some spelling words. As I called the words out to him and watched him struggle with not only getting the spelling right, but also with reversing letters. I suddenly found myself getting extremely angry and choked up. I even started to get dizzy. Even though these were simple words I could not spell them either and had no idea whether Stephen was getting them right or not. The next thing I knew my stomach was feeling nauseous and I felt like I was going to throw up. I wanted to throw the spelling book at Stephen and run out of the room. I was astonished at my reactions as I found myself not reacting to Stephen like his father, but as a little boy.

> Then there flashed into my mind an image of a boy Stephen's age sitting in the classroom taking a spelling test. He had chewed up his pencil and had written nothing. I knew that I had touched a vortex memory of my Fridays when in elementary school. For me Friday was hell day! It was the day that we not only had a spelling test, which I always failed but had a spelling bee, in which the other students always jeered at me. The vortex memory still contained the little boy

with all the feelings of failure. All of this was forgotten, hidden away in my unconscious, but with the right trigger events the little boy would come out of hiding and dominate my feelings and reactions.

Shortly after this I was at a Dunamis event in Alaska where there were some wonderful Spirit-filled teachers of children with learning disabilities. They prayed for me and that little boy was healed of the hurt.

In both my case and the case of the woman who was abused at age five the image of the child was the key to entering into the memory cluster of hurt and seeing the principles of Jesus' healing work actually become effective. For the woman, after several prayer sessions she no longer had to carry her teddy bear. For me, I was able to work with Stephen on his homework without all my own hurt feelings coming back.

The Inner Child of the Past

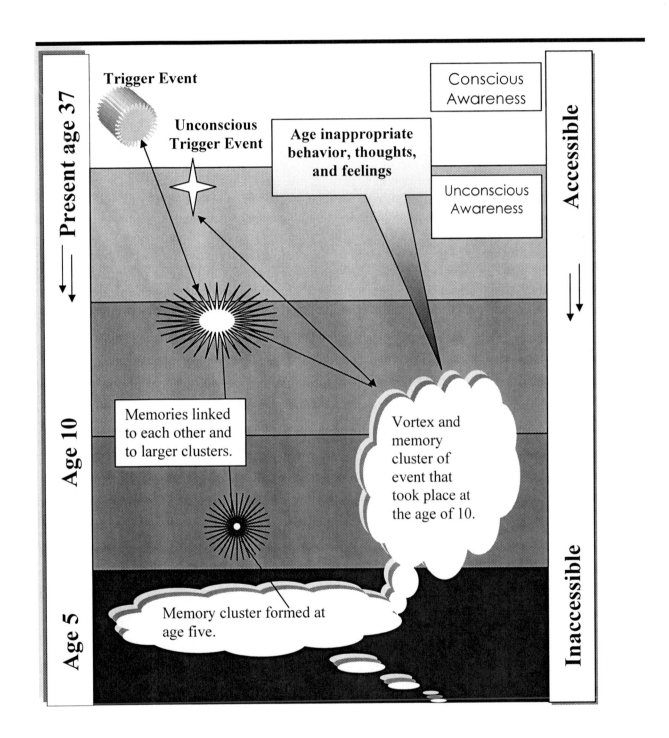

In cases of extreme and persistent trauma, the vortex with its memory cluster and other clusters associated with it may actually form itself into an alternate personality. We have already observed that the psychological mechanism at work is dissociation. This happens as a defense mechanism for isolating a set of traumatic memories and keeping them from affecting the whole personality. The personality functions like having several different hard drives in a computer each with its own operating system, programs and saved files. In extreme cases the will forms walls of amnesia between the alternate personalities and the dominant normally functioning personality will not know of the existence of the alternative personalities.

The dynamic of inner healing ministry with a personality that is fragmented into alternate personalities requires some special skills and gifts and is beyond the scope of this manual. For more detailed teaching on the formation of alternate personalities and the process of applying the principles of Jesus' healing, we recommend Charles Kraft's book on <u>Deep Wounds Deep Healing</u> by Regal Books. The important thing for us to be aware of is that MPD or Dissociative Identify Disorder is something that one may indeed come across as one deals with broken and hurting people. It represents an extreme case of the processes that have already been observed to be operative in the formation of the "inner child of the past." The dynamic of seeing the healing work of Jesus take place in them is basically the same as for cases with just one personality, it is just more complex. Also the hurt is often extreme, intentional and persistent over an extended period of time. All this means that the wounds to the psyche are very deep. They often require healing prayer, deliverance as well as psychotherapy.

This is definitely not the preview of well-intended amateurs. If you think you are running up against a case in which there is DID, then seek out those experienced in this type of ministry.

V. HOW THE HOLY SPIRIT WORKS TO BRING INNER HEALING

Now that we have gained some understanding of how inner wounds are formed in the unconscious we may turn to the good news of how the Holy Spirit works to bring into them the healing reality of Jesus Christ. The following is an extension into the mysterious regions of the human heart of the dynamic of cooperating with the Holy Spirit. There we will find the same dynamics of how Jesus did healing in operation as has already been presented in Chapters five and six. The three-fold dynamic of Jesus' healing work has been summarized at the beginning of this chapter. Keep this in mind as we move into the details of how the Holy Spirit works to bring deep inner healing.

A. THE HOLY SPIRIT PENETRATES INTO THE VORTEX OF THE MEMORY CLUSTER

If a person is born again the Holy Spirit already dwells in the inner sanctum of their heart. From that center, the Holy Spirit knows the person's inner-most being. He is able to enter into vortex memories that are hidden in the unconscious. At times when the gifts are manifested or there are expressions of the Holy Spirit's love and power then this work of entering memory vortexes may be a part of the "outward" operation of the Holy Spirit. (This may be the case when the Holy Spirit works in inner healing with those who are not yet Christians.)

Time and space do not bind the Holy Spirit. So He is able to deal with events in our past just as He can present events. Actually memory clusters are not past but are active and alive in the present. They are just hidden in the unconscious and thus not accessible to our present rational understanding. Nor are we able to bring them into the light for Jesus' healing.

The Holy Spirit enters into the vortex from the inside and sets in motion the following healing processes.

B. BRINGS TO CONSCIOUS AWARENESS THE MEMORIES IN THE MEMORY COMPLEX

Recall the fundamental spiritual principles demonstrated first in the Garden of Eden. **"Things that we intentionally hide from God, God will not heal."** One of the first things that the Holy Spirit does is to bring to our recollection the suppressed, repressed or dissociated memories.

The Holy Spirit enables us to recall and then to reenter the memory vortex that has preserved the four aspects of memory as listed below.

- Conceptual/Cognitive

- Visual, Auditory, Olfactory, Taste and Touch

- Emotional

- Body Memories, Kinesthetic

When this happens the person may actually relive the experience in all its rich texture.

How does this actually happen? There are deep mysteries of how the unconscious works. Indeed there are greater mysteries of how the Holy Spirit works. So what follows are just theories to account for what is an observed fact.

1.   The Holy Spirit leads us into the vortex and the memory cluster by following the rules of association.

Often the Holy Spirit will bring to conscious awareness some image, picture or word that will be the bridge into the vortex memory. Then the Holy Sprit will work according to the four principles already named for why memories and memory clusters may become attached together.

For instance:

> Tom White who is greatly gifted in deliverance ministry prayed for my wife Laura. He did a "knock, knock, whose there"[23] to determine if there were any evil spirits attached to her. In response to this prayer, something did manifest itself by a feeling of hatred of Tom and of Jesus within Laura. Tom then asked the Holy Spirit to reveal how the evil spirit got in.

> As they prayed, suddenly there popped into Laura's mind the image of the family piano and her as a little girl playing under it. Tom asked, "Well, what does that mean?" At first, Laura did not know. Then suddenly she remembered that the great grandmother who was into spiritualism had given that piano to her family. With this there came back a vortex memory of the great grandmother showing the little girl, Laura, fairies that she said were dancing in the trees.

In this way by bringing up the image of the piano, the Holy Spirit worked with the rules of association to get to the vortex memory as well as the gateway for how the evil spirit was able to get into the family line. The Holy Spirit could choose to use any of the other principles for connecting memories and memory clusters as bridges into the vortex

Knowing that the Holy Spirit works like this will enable the prayer counselor to be alert to the connections between memories that the Holy Spirit is wishing to make. This is what Tom did. When the piano image came, he suspected it was just a step on the way into the memory cluster where the evil spirit had found ground to hold onto. Tom assisted in this process by asking, "what does this mean?"

---

[23] This is a way of directly confronting evil spirits in the name of Jesus Christ to force them to manifest their presence so that they may be cast out. The process of discernment and casting out evil spirits will be elaborated in the Spiritual Warfare Dunamis Project manual.

2.   Bringing the love, presence, and reality of Jesus Christ that sets the person free to allow to consciousness the suppressed, repressed or dissociated memories.

To understand how the Holy Spirit works in this second way we must return for a moment to the diagram on how we forget and ponder why a person would suppress, repress or dissociate a memory in the first place.

Most of the time these processes of forgetting take place as a means of defending the person from a memory that if allowed to conscious awareness would be disruptive to normal functioning. The person simply cannot deal with the pain, rage, anger, fear, guilt, disorientation, etc. that may be contained in the memory. Most of the time this forgetting is the mind's own effective defense mechanism and allows the person to function normally in most areas of life. However, as we have seen, things that are hidden are not healed and from the unconscious may work havoc on the person's life.

At other times, the forgetting is imposed from without. As for instance when a person is not allowed to grieve the loss of a loved one. As often happens in sexual abuse they are forbidden to express their fear, hurt and shame.

The Holy Spirit will overcome this imposed forgetting by surrounding the person with the presence of Jesus Christ. In His presence there is love, grace and acceptance that enables the person to consciously and unconsciously relax their defense mechanisms and allow forgotten memories to bubble up into conscious awareness.

For example:

> Ken Shay and I were at a seminary in Mainland China. There were about four hundred church leaders present. I had just taught on the promise of the equipping of the Holy Spirit when suddenly He fell upon the whole group. I had an image of Jesus walking through the group just loving the people. As I shared this image, a strange thing started to happen. The people started to weep and to wail. The Holy Spirit fell on Ken Shay. He exuded the love of Jesus. About thirty people surrounded Ken and were clinging to him. They had drenched his clothes with their tears. The people almost in one voice were weeping and a number were on the floor in convulsions of grief. Others were praying for each other with bitter tears. I did not know what was happening and was actually a little frightened at this extraordinary outpouring of emotion.
>
> I rushed from group to group trying to hear what they were grieving about. As I did, I heard the people expressing the hurts of fifty years of communist oppression. Parents were grieving for children taken from them in the Cultural Revolution and never seen again. Wives were grieving for husbands they had been told to criticize until they were driven away during Mao's great plan to destroy the Chinese family system. Old men wept like babies over the land they had lost when they were forced to move to collective farms. Repeatedly there

were cries of anguish of those who had been lost through starvation, or prison. It was the most heart-rending thing I had ever experienced.

For fifty years, these hurts had been denied by the communist culture. People had not been allowed to grieve over those who were lost. Whole generations had not been allowed to take the risk of showing their true feelings. These memories of past oppression and hurt had all been pushed in the subconscious and forgotten so that the people could function in their society. Then that night Jesus manifested His presence. All the barriers came down, and that was the reason for the great release.

Later I led the group in prayers for forgiveness and asked Jesus to come and to heal their hearts. The joy that broke loose after that was more overwhelming than the grief.

For the prayer counselor it is extremely important for them to recognize that their role is often to mediate the presence and love of Jesus Christ. Their unconditional love and acceptance of the person in need, when empowered by the Holy Spirit, is experienced by the person as Jesus Christ Himself loving and accepting them. This is a critical aspect of the first step to healing prayer which is establishing the context for the Holy Spirit to work. This atmosphere of love and trust enables the person to risk letting down their defense mechanisms so that hidden memories may come to the surface.

It is also important for the prayer counselor to recognize that often when defenses are down, the four aspects of memory, like buckets of water may all be spilled out at once. The resulting emotional deluge may be disorientating. The counselor must be ready to be there with the person as this happens otherwise it may lead to hysteria or cause an emotional break down.

The following chart shows the various ways that the Holy Spirit may work to enter a memory vortex.

How the Holy Spirit Enters Vortex Memories

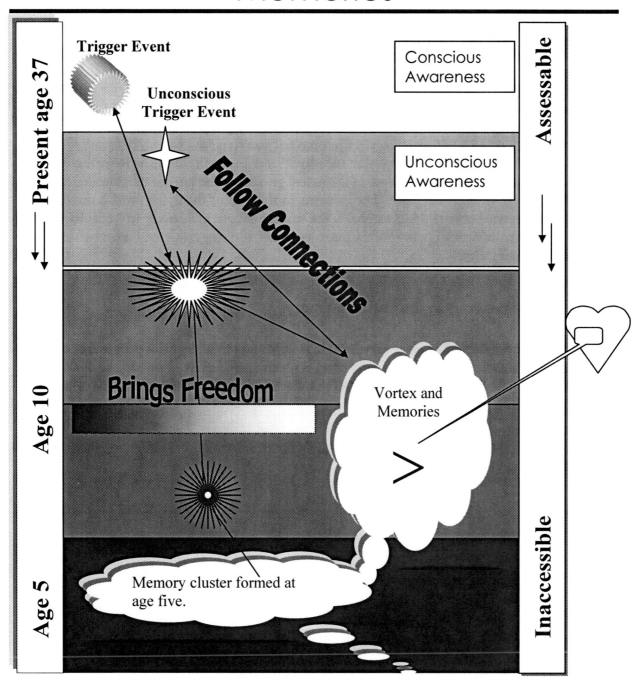

C. THE HOLY SPIRIT BRINGS THE PRESENCE AND WORKING OF JESUS CHRIST INTO THE MEMORY CLUSTERS

It is the character and work of the Holy Spirit to bring to wherever He may be the presence and reality of God the Father and God the Son.

As the Holy Sprit brings the vortex memory into the light, then the presence and reality of Jesus Christ may enter into the memory. We encounter a deep mystery here, for it seems that Jesus does not just enter the memory in our heart but enters the past experience itself. Or perhaps the person is just made aware that Jesus Christ was there all along but unrecognized. Whatever the case, our Lord who is not bound by time and space invites the person to go with him into healing the wounds of the past. It is like all barriers of time fall away and the person is actually with Jesus where he may do the same things that we saw Him doing in the Bible as He actually met people face to face. Whether in the now of the actual present or the now of an unhealed vortex the healing work of Jesus is the same. For instance, in the eyes of the Spirit there is no substantial difference between Jesus forgiving the women caught in adultery in Acts chapter 8, or Jesus forgiving the woman in the vortex memory of her adultery that could have twisted her personality 40 years later.

1.   What Jesus does in the vortex memory.

Is really no different than what He does when He is in healing ministry with people face to face. To refresh us of this three fold dynamic the chart is given again below. Further, the dynamic of our cooperating with the Holy Spirit is about the same as dealing with on the surface or in buried memory complexes.

THE DYNAMIC OF JESUS' ENGAGEMENT WITH HUMAN BEINGS IN HEALING MINISTRY

PHASE 1 –
Jesus establishes the context in which the Holy Spirit will work by bringing the person into a relationship with himself.

Jesus is filled with the Holy Spirit and obeys the Father.
Jesus obeys the Father: this is the source of His direction and purpose for ministry.
Jesus drew people into conversations with himself.
Jesus demonstrates His love for the people He is reaching out to.

PHASE 2 –
Jesus and the Holy Spirit engage the person in various ways to bring the reality of the Kingdom of God, which results in healing.

Jesus leads people to be born again into the Kingdom of God
Jesus enables and calls for confession, repentance, and walking in the light
Jesus forgives sins
Jesus overturns lies spoken by Satan, others, or oneself with truth about Himself, reality and oneself.
Jesus cast out demons to clear the way for healing, restoration and obedience.

PHASE 3 –
Jesus invites/commands the person to follow Him in faith and obedience as a disciple.

Jesus calls us to forgive those who hurt us.
Jesus calls us to receive the working of the Holy Spirit as from Him.
Jesus calls us to follow Him in faith and obedience.
Jesus promises us the Holy Spirit to guide, gift and empower us as we walk as His disciple.

2. How does Jesus actually do these things in a memory cluster?

This question leads us into the fluid, creative and dynamic working of the Holy Spirit within a person. The way this works is more easily described through poetic images and testimonies than through scientific principles. What we are sure about is that the results are profoundly life-giving and results in actual changes in behavior, feelings and attitudes.

We shall delay providing a case and making observations of the dynamics of the Spirit's work at this point, until we bring in the prayer minister as the other person involved in these dynamic processes. He or she will be joining with Jesus and the Holy Spirit to accomplish this extraordinary work.

Inside the Memory Vortex the Holy Spirit mediates Jesus Christ

Brings the presence and reality of Jesus Christ which is life and healing

PHASE 1 –
Jesus establishes the context in which the Holy Spirit will work by bringing the person into a relationship with himself.

PHASE 2 –
Jesus and the Holy Spirit engage the person in various ways to bring the reality of the Kingdom of God, which results in healing.

PHASE 3 –
Jesus invites/commands the person to follow Him in faith and obedience as a disciple.

D. THE RESULT OF JESUS' HEALING WORK IN THE VORTEX MEMORY

When the Holy Spirit enters a vortex memory to bring the presence and work of Jesus a number of things happen that actually change or reconfigure the internal structures that have built the person's personality. Some of these are as follows:

1.   When a vortex of hurt that is hidden in the subconscious is made conscious it begins to lose its power over the psyche.

There is something profoundly healing about just bringing things hidden into the light. They begin to lose their mystery. They may be subjected to rational analysis and understanding, enabling us to name the memory. To name what happens is one of the powerful ways that the Holy Spirit does this to us. When something is given a name, even though evil, we can begin to master it.

For example:

> A 50-year-old pastor asked for prayer because of paralyzing anxiety that was preventing him from saying yes to a new opportunity on the mission field. This opportunity came after years of praying to be used by God on the mission field. It looked like the open door of a lifetime but immediately there seemed to be a tight knot in his chest and a sense of panic. He even awoke one night with a terrible dream of an angelic figure hurling him off a cliff into an abyss. In prayer, the Holy Spirit started to bring back a vortex memory of a time in college when the pastor had taken a step of faith into a form of Christian service that proved to be the gateway into a terrible wilderness. Then the Holy Spirit gave the word, "Fear of not obeying God, and fear of obeying God." This was the core emotion locked in the vortex memory. Once named, the pastor was able to rationally understand his feelings. This naming of the present emotion was the gateway into healing the vortex caused by the previous experience. Once that was accomplished, he was able to wholeheartedly say yes to the new call.

2.   When Jesus Christ overcomes the lies in the vortex with His truths, the lies lose their power to define reality.

Lies that are embedded in the vortex memory have great power. They interpret the original hurtful event in such a way that the hurt is deepened, the person is kept in bondage, and set up for more hurt. In addition, the lies in a vortex help connect other memories to itself and give them the same interpretation.

When these are replaced by the truths brought by the Holy Spirit, the person's original experience is interpreted in the light of Jesus Christ. The other memories and memory clusters connected by the same lie begin to lose their "coinherance". This dissolves the power block of hurt in the personality and gives the freedom for new interpretations and connections to be formed.

It must be emphatically stated that this process does not deny or distort the actual vortex causing event. That is real and is not changed by the healing work of Jesus.

> For instance, the woman in John 8 really was caught in adultery. That is a fact. If she had not met Jesus and been healed, the lies spoken to her by the Pharisees who caught her would have been things like, "you are a sinner and can never be forgiven." "You are unclean and deserve to die." "You are a worthless whore with no place in the Kingdom." If she had not been stoned, those lies would surely have sunk into her unconscious and shaped her personality and identity. If forty years later, the Holy Spirit was to have brought the presence of Jesus into that suppressed vortex memory, He would have overcome the lies with the truths, "You are a sinner but I have forgiven you. You are now clean by my blood. You are my precious daughter." These truths do not change the fact that she did indeed commit adultery. What is gone are the lies planted in her heart through men by Satan that have held her in bondage to that sinful tragic event.

God's truth redefines the structures of meaning for the person's restoration.

3. Healing the hurt in the vortex causes it to lose its gravitational power to attract and configure other memories around itself.

This process of causing the vortex to lose its power to hold a set of negative memories together happens as the emotions of the hurt are expressed and the original hurt itself is healed.

For instance:

> I was praying for an older lady who all her life had been governed by an intense hatred of her father. She could name many things that had happened that had contributed to their bad relationship. The person could no longer recall exactly why she hated her father, she just did. She used these events that she could name as a way to justify her hatred. None of these things, most of them trivial, seemed to justify the intensity of the hatred. As we prayed the vortex memory came back with great power. It was a vivid picture of her father angrily waving her sister's report card in front of her. "See they are all "A's " all you get are "Cs. Why are you so stupid and lazy? Why can't you get good grades like your sister? I am ashamed of you." When this memory came back, the floodgates of rage, and despair poured out. Then came tears of rejection and hurt." Through the Spirit, Jesus spoke to her gently calling her to forgive her father, her sister and herself. Amid many tears she was able to do this. The result was that the vortex of hatred and anger toward her father was defused. Its power to shape her identity and personality was just gone. This now made room for a new ordering of the personality based on forgiveness and acceptance of herself. She never became a great scholar but she was a wonderful wife and mother with and a gift of gracious hospitality.

Here it needs to be added that when vortexes are healed, the healing is often immediate but the process of reconstructing the personality will often be a lengthy process. In addition, there will often be years of habitual ways of responding to things based on the vortex and its associated memories. For instance, the woman above had developed deeply ingrown, habitual ways of responding and thinking based on hatred of her father. Suddenly, when that was healed, it took her several years to change the habits.

4.   Ground is removed from evil spirits

As has already been noted, if the vortex memory contained unconfessed and unforgiven sin this may give ground to attacks by evil spirits.

a)   Driving out demons that are attached in the complex

Many times we have found that a vortex memory, because of its sinful contents, will give ground to a demon that will attach itself in the psyche. There it hides in our own thoughts and feelings and does everything possible to shut Jesus out of the vortex and prevent His healing work from talking place. The demon wants to keep the person from walking in the light. They want them to be angry, lustful, fearful, hurt and wounded. These are the building blocks of their home within the person.

Oftentimes in the healing process one will be met with internal resistance. For instance, despite the best efforts of psychotherapy, and healing prayer ministry, no progress is made at getting to the vortex memory. Then one may need to move from healing prayer ministry into deliverance ministry.

Often the healing processes described here will be stymied until the demon is cast out. For more on how to discern the presence of evil sprits and expelling them please see the section in this manual by Victor Matthews. Also, for more complete teaching see the *Spiritual Warfare Dunamis Project Manual.*

Later it may be important for you to go in much greater depth on the topic of deliverance ministry. At this point it is important to know that complete restoration of the person as brought by Jesus will include removing the ground of entry to evil spirits and removing the spirits themselves. This inner healing and deliverance are both part of this process.

b)   Closing the door to flaming darts from without

Before leaving this topic of the interfering role of evil spirits one other aspect must be noted. There are times when the evil spirits have not actually gotten attached within the person. Rather, the vortex, with its unhealed and unconfessed sin, provides an open door for flaming dart attacks from without. The healing of the vortex will close the doors to these attacks.

For instance:

A successful Holy Spirit empowered pastor secretly asked for prayer. I got some men together and asked how we could pray for him. He said that for years he had been tormented with sudden bouts of homosexual lust. "I know that I am not gay. I am passionately in love with my wife. We have a great sex life and, if anything, I often have to deal with attractions to other beautiful women. Therefore, I just do not understand where this other stuff comes from! Nevertheless, all of a sudden I will be hit with such fantasies of having sex with another man that I will get aroused. It is terribly embarrassing and to me inexplicable. I do not normally have such attractions to men as I do with women, so this feels like a flaming dart attack rather then any confusion with sexual orientation. Jesus I need help!"

We asked questions about whether there had been any homosexual encounters or indulgence in homosexual pornography. This brother thought deeply for a while and said, "No, nothing that I can recall. But I have a nudging that there is something there that has opened the door to this stuff. I just cannot let myself recall it".

We prayed Jesus' love and forgiveness and asked the Holy Spirit to show us whether there was any open door or ground that made these attacks possible. As we prayed there suddenly came into this man's mind the vivid memory of his church's youth pastor. We asked, "Well what about this man?" "Oh there was nothing wrong with him at all. He really loved us kids, he led me to Christ and discipled me throughout my high school years. I am deeply grateful to him." We kept praying. Then one of the team members saw an image of a log cabin. "This is crazy but I see this log cabin out in the woods does this mean anything?" "Oh yes, that is the summer camp…" Suddenly he was overcome with emotion. As it turned out, while at church camp, at the age of 15, in the middle of the night, this pastor had awakened with the youth minister lying beside him. The youth pastor was having oral sex with him. The 15 year old had found it delightful and terrible. Fully awake he had participated in the sex, then had gone back to sleep. In the morning, he was tormented with guilt and desire and drove the experience from his mind, telling himself it had only been a dream.

This never happened again. Nonetheless the experience went unconfessed and unhealed so it formed a vortex memory of guilt, confusion and desire within him. Apparently it formed a cluster of memories from years of lust attacks. We could find no demons actually attached in this memory cluster. However, this was a vulnerable point that Satan had found to be fertile ground for flaming dart attacks.

During the healing prayer all these suppressed emotions were expressed and confessed and the youth director forgiven. After this the pastor had no further flaming darts of homosexual lust.

E. BRINGS A CHRIST-CENTERED IDENTITY AND TRUE SELF UNDERSTANDING

This work of the Holy Sprit to penetrate vortexes, bringing them into the light and manifesting the presence of Jesus in them is all part of His "inward" sanctifying work of the believer. It is the work of restoring in us the shattered image of God and enabling us to more and more reflect the character of Jesus Christ. The outward behavior and attitudinal expressions of this process of character transformation are the fruit of the Spirit as listed in Galatians 5.

Within the personality a number of important transformations have taken place that yield the fruit of the Spirit.

Some of these are:

1. The memory of painful or hurtful experiences that are still in the heart. (These are the unalterable facts of our existence in a fallen world.) Nevertheless, they have been drained of their guilt, pain, fear, etc. so they no longer have the power of vortexes shaping the personality.

2. The lies have been overcome by the truth. This gives new interpretation to events and allows new memory associations to form.

3. The ground allowing evil spirits to hinder the process of sanctification would have been removed.

4. A new identity based on the truth revealed in Jesus Christ by the Holy Spirit now begins to form.

5. Those vortexes based on experiences of God's reality, love and truth are now able to become the primary organizing units in the personality. There is a new ordering of memories for a Christ-centered personality.

6. A person's actions, responses, attitudes and feelings, are no longer controlled by buried hurtful memory clusters that covertly exercise their power over their conscious life. Rather, reason and emotions appropriate to our experiences may rule our conscious life of following Jesus Christ.

Inside the Memory Vortex the Holy Spirit Mediates Jesus Christ

Brings the presence and reality of Jesus Christ which is life and healing.

Through the Holy Spirit Jesus then does His various healing works.

When The Vortex Based On Hurt Is Healed And
Christ's Truth Replaces The Lies –
Any demonic entities that may have been attached
leave.
Then the vortex loses its cohesive power - the
memories lose their power over us.

A new identity in the truth and reality of Jesus Christ
may begin to be constructed in our psyche.

Past memories are reinterpreted and reorganized.

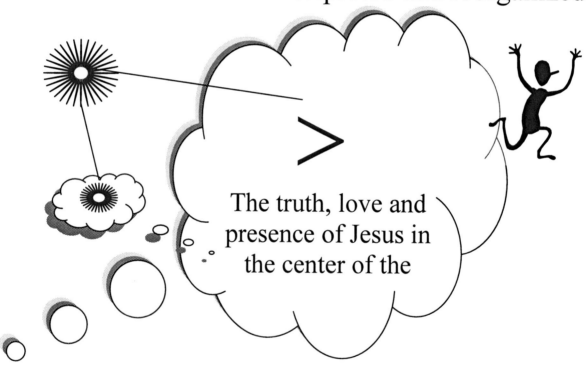

VI. OUR COOPERATION WITH THE HOLY SPIRIT IN PENETRATING AND HEALING VORTEX MEMORIES

Having established the process of how the Holy Spirit works to penetrate and bring healing to vortex memories, we are ready to explore our role of cooperation with the Spirit.

The following steps are ways that we have found helpful for cooperating with the Holy Spirit as He works in the depths of the human heart. These are not rules nor are they a technique for bringing healing. Rather, they are part of our dynamic engagement with the Holy Spirit, Jesus and the person we are praying for. Further these steps are placed with the threefold dynamic of how we are to cooperate with the Holy Spirit in healing ministry.

1.   Listen to the Holy Spirit who, through the reasoned observation, supernatural gifts and/or through the person, will reveal what Jesus is doing

The role of the prayer minister must be that of active listening to the person, to themselves, to the prayer team and above all to the Holy Spirit. The person being prayed for, often because of emotional or demonic interference, cannot hear what either the Holy Spirit or their own hearts are saying. That is why having others join in this process is so necessary.

The role of the prayer minister as listener is essentially that of discernment and director of the human responses to what the Holy Spirit is doing.

See the *"In the Spirit's Power"* Dunamis Project manual for a more complete description of how to listen to the Holy Spirit and cooperate with Him in power ministry.

2.   Invite the Holy Spirit to bring to recollection what happened in the experience that has formed into the vortex memory. (stirring up the darkness)

If the prayer counselor suspects that there is a vortex memory then they may specifically invite the Holy Spirit to reveal it. This process may be aided by asking specific questions.

For instance:

> You have told me that you had a bad relationship with your father, but does one event that symbolizes the relationship come to your mind that you could tell us about.

> If an image or thought does come to mind the prayer minister may ask questions that would expose memory connections.

If the prayer minister receives what may be a word of knowledge then it should be humbly offered to the person being prayed for discernment. In this way, the Holy Spirit may reveal the vortex memory or some important connection.

This seeking the vortex memory is an active process engaged in by both the prayer minister and the person as the Holy Spirit aids both. Often times this is a step-by-step process of following the trail of associations. One memory will lead to another deeper and deeper into the human heart until the vortex is hit.

When a vortex is hit usually there will be an immediate response from the person. They will often begin to vividly feel the emotions or see the images locked in the vortex.

The theophostic term for this is "stirring up the darkness". I find this an excellent description of this dynamic of unearthing the vortex with its four contents.

3. Invite the person to "relive" the memory or to "re-enter" the event

Oftentimes this just begins to happen spontaneously. If the original event was especially embarrassing or traumatic, the person may need to be encouraged to relive or to reenter the memory. This is usually impossible unless the atmosphere of Jesus' love and forgiveness has first been established.

The four components of memory make this reliving possible.

Two questions may arise at this point.

a) A. What is the role of images and imagination?

Oftentimes memory content will be presented to the person in the form of images. Or if the Holy Spirit gives a word of knowledge exposing the vortex this will often be in the form of an image or a picture.

This does not happen to everyone but does seem to be the way that many engage with the Holy Spirit in this process of inner healing.

This happens because much inner healing work deals with the unconscious. The language of the unconscious is not discursive reason and logic, but rather images and pictures. This is the language of the unconscious.

Jesus recognized this and spoke in parables (which are vivid word pictures) that speak to the reason and penetrate to the heart. If we are to share with the Holy Spirit in this inner healing work, we too must learn the language of the unconscious.

b)   Are these pictures of real events or just symbols?

As you move with the Holy Spirit in this process you need to be aware that memory is rarely an objective photograph or recording of what actually happened. The mind always interprets experience and thus will shape the memory to fit its interpretations. The mind may create memories that are entirely the product of its own imagination. The mind may also create memories of events that are symbolic of a situation rather than being actual facts.

For instance:

> Once I was praying for a man around the age of 45 who reported that he had been unloved by his father. As we were praying for guidance from the Holy Spirit suddenly I received a word of knowledge in the form of an image. I saw a little boy running into his father's study eager to show him a little crystal radio he had made. The little boy was saying "Daddy, Daddy look what I made!" But the father was busy reading a newspaper and did not look up. I saw the little boy's face fill with disappointment. Then he ran out of the room saying, "Mommy, Mommy look what I made!" When this was shared the man responded immediately. "Yes, that's it! He started to reenter the memory and had all the feelings of hurt of that little boy.

The question is, was that an actual event? We may never know. It may have simply been a symbol of many events in which the father had been too preoccupied to respond to his son. What is important is the door was opened into a vortex and a huge memory cluster of painful memories connected to this man's father.

In other cases other people's interpretation of a person's situation may find their way into the person's mind and create memories to justify this interpretation. This may lead to "false memory syndrome."

For example:

> A father came to me deeply distressed. His daughter had gone to counseling after the break up of her engagement. In the process of the therapy with the counselor's assistance, a hidden memory had come back to the girl of her father sexually abusing her and her older sister when they were five and eight. This was interpreted by the counselor to be related to the break up of the relationship with the girl's boy friend. At the urging of the counselor the daughter had confronted her father about this sexual abuse.
>
> The father was astonished. He had always been a good father and had never done anything inappropriate to his daughter. Where had this memory come from? We suspect it was created by the interpreted lenses brought to the girl's present pain of losing the love relationship with someone she thought she would marry. The counselor seemed to have a view of reality that assumed that all emotional problems were related to some form of sexual abuse.

After much turmoil and pain caused to the father and the family this charge was dropped. Mostly because the older sister had no such recollection of sexual abuse ever having taken place. It was also totally out of character of the father and his relationship with his children.

When one is cooperating with the Holy Spirit in going deep into the unconscious one must be very careful not to bring one's own interpretations to the other person's memories. One may actually create memories that have no basis in reality.

As with the use of any of the gifts of the Holy Spirit, the prayer counselor and those in the prayer group as well as the person being prayed for must maintain a process of discernment throughout the inner healing prayer. .

4. Ask the Holy Spirit to help the person to name the emotions and the lies that are contained in the vortex memory.

This is part of stirring up the complex and beginning to bring it into the light. Often the person will begin to feel within themselves the contents of the vortex but it is just confusing. Naming what is going on often is extremely helpful in enabling the person to bring some balance and understanding to the vortex contents as they bubble up into the conscious awareness.

5. Invite Jesus Christ, through the Holy Spirit, to act and to speak to the person in the recollected memory.

At this point it is important for the prayer minister to shift the focus away from the memory contents that may be overwhelming and intense into engagement with Jesus Christ.

Here the Holy Spirit may speak and act to show what Jesus is doing. Sometimes the person or the prayer minister may actually see Jesus doing something or hear him saying something to them. At other times the Holy Spirit may just give the prayer minister or the person guidance of what Jesus would have them do.

Once again this may come as a thought amid one's own thoughts, as a word of scripture, as a mental picture and so forth.

Expect Jesus to do any of the things that we see him doing in the Bible when he brought healing.

For instance:

> We were praying for a pastor who had had an affair when he was young. Even though he had broken off this relationship he was still tormented with guilt and remorse for what he had done. He also grieved the consequences of his indiscretion. His wife whom he deeply loved had discovered him. For over ten years he had left the ministry in order to get his life back together. He was now remarried and pastor of a thriving church but the guilt was still there.

In the prayer session the Holy Spirit led him back to the vortex memory of when his wife had discovered him making love to the other woman in the church office. It was terrible as the pastor relived the worst day of his life. We invited Jesus into the memory and prayed that He would do his healing work. Suddenly the pastor said, "Oh, my God, I see Jesus coming into the study. I see him taking my wife into his arms and comforting her. Now he is looking at me!" We asked is he saying anything to you? "No he is just looking at me with tears in His eyes." At this point the man fell on the floor overcome with grief. He wept and wept and all the while asked Jesus to forgive him for what he had done to his wife and to himself. The prayer team was praying for him in the Spirit. It seemed that there was no end to the man's grief and torment.

Then I saw a picture of Jesus now holding this man still with tears in his eyes. I shared the vision. And asked, "Do you see that or is it just my imagination." The pastor who had grown completely still said, "Yes, I do see that. Oh, yes! Jesus is carrying me now. I see him carrying me into a river of crystal clear water. Oh it's wonderful! It is like this is the river of life and it's all over me and in me." After a while the image ceased and we moved into prayers of thanksgiving for Jesus' cleansing and healing work.

The result: After years of torment the pastor was healed in his heart from the hurt of his sin and cleansed from the guilt that was poisoning his soul. After this acting on the guidance that he felt he had received from Jesus, he wrote his ex-wife a long letter asking her forgiveness for what he had done to her.

Often these images that come in prayer have a dream-like quality. They may be strange and not very logical. Nevertheless if they are given by the Holy Spirit and are consistent with the inner realities of the unconscious then they will have a profound impact on the person and will result in healing of the inner hurts.

6.   Follow up on what Jesus says and does as is reported by the person and discerned by the prayer team.

As before one will need to commit to obedience to Jesus Christ and carry out the guidance that one receives. This may be something to be done after the prayer session as for instance the pastor writing a letter asking forgiveness from his ex-wife.

Often times it will be some form of obedience called for in the recollected memory itself.

For instance:

A woman in an impossible family situation was harassed by thoughts of killing herself. We had worked through a lot of inner healing with her. At one point, while in prayer, she was given an image of a dark cave. On one side was death and on the other side was the cross with the resurrected Jesus standing beside it saying, "Choose life and come to me." As she reported this prayer vision to the team we prayed for her to choose life and go to Jesus. It took a great struggle and included expelling an evil spirit but finally she was able to say, "Lord I choose life!" Then the guidance came to lock the door of the cave and take the key to Jesus. While the prayer minister had given this part of the image, it immediately became her own and she knew that she was called to the act of obedience of shutting the door to killing herself as a way out. After much struggle she suddenly cried out in joy, "Yes, I see myself shutting a big iron door to that cave of death, now I have locked it, and I am walking toward Jesus and handing the key to Him. Then she started to cry with joy and said, "Now Jesus is giving me a hug and saying to me, 'I am the way of life forever and you are mine forever!"

After this foray into these pray symbols the women no longer dealt with thoughts of killing herself and some significant changes took place in her family situation.

Here the obedience was something that took place within the prayer work itself.

The end result is that we are called to follow Jesus in the depth of our hearts or in our outward behavior. To follow Him is the source of life and healing

Here is a summary of this process:

a) Listen to the Holy Spirit who, through the reasoned observation, supernatural gifts and/or through the person, will reveal what Jesus is doing

b) Invite the Holy Spirit to bring to recollection what happened in the experience that has formed into the vortex memory. (stirring up the darkness)

c) Invite the person to "relive" the memory or to "re-enter" the event.

d) Ask the Holy Spirit to help the person to name the emotions and the lies that are contained in the vortex memory.

e) Invite Jesus Christ, through the Holy Spirit, to act and to speak to the person in the recollected memory.

f) Follow up on what Jesus says and does as is reported by the person and discerned by the prayer team.

VII.   SUMMARY: PUTTING THE PROCESS OF SPIRITUAL AND INNER HEALING ALL TOGETHER

Cooperating with the Holy Spirit and Jesus Christ to do Healing Ministry

---

PHASE 1

Jesus establishes the context in which the Holy Spirit will work by bringing the person into a relationship with himself.

We work according to biblical principles to establish the context that welcomes the Holy Spirit to work.

Jesus' Work	Going deep with the Holy Spirit in Inner Healing	Our work with Jesus at all levels
Jesus is filled with the Holy Spirit and obeys the Father.	Listen to the Holy Spirit who, through the reasoned observation, supernatural gifts and/or through the person, will reveal what Jesus is doing	We pray to be filled with the Holy Spirit and ask that the Holy Spirit come upon the person being prayed for in power. We invite the Holy Spirit to work.
Jesus obeys the Father: this is the source of His direction and purpose for ministry.	Invite the Holy Spirit to bring to recollection what happened in the experience that has formed into the vortex memory. (stirring up the darkness)	We surrender ourselves to walking in obedience to Jesus Christ.
Jesus drew people into conversations with himself.	Invite the person to "relive" the memory or to "re-enter" the event.	We engage the person being prayed for in conversation through directly asking them questions and intentionally listening to them.
Jesus demonstrates His love for the people He is reaching out to.	Ask the Holy Spirit to help the person to name the emotions and the lies that are contained in the vortex memory.	We show forth both by word and actions the love that we have been given by Jesus for the person being prayed for.

> ## PHASE 2 –
>
> Jesus and the Holy Spirit engage the person in various ways to bring the reality of the Kingdom of God that results in healing.

Jesus works through us and in the person being prayed for, as we are led and empowered by the Holy Sprit, to do those things He did while in the flesh that will make real the Kingdom of God.

Jesus' Work	Going deep with the Holy Spirit in Inner Healing	Our work with Jesus at all levels
Jesus leads people to be born again into the Kingdom of God.	Invite Jesus Christ, through the Holy Spirit, to act and to speak to the person in the recollected memory. (May lead us to do any of the things in the right hand column.)	We present the Gospel and invite the person to accept Jesus Christ as Lord and Savior, and then pray with them to be born again.
Jesus enables and calls for confession, repentance, and walking in the light.		Assure the person of Jesus' love and acceptance of those who turn to Him in Confession and forgiveness. Read the Bible passages that reveal sin and its consequences. As revealed by the Holy Spirit, expose and name any sins and present them to the person for discernment. Invite the person to confess their sins and to walk in the light
Jesus forgives sins.		After true confession from the heart, as led by the Holy Spirit offer forgiveness in the name of Jesus Christ. This may be communicated by words spoken as well as well as by whatever sacramental or symbolic actions the Holy Spirit may direct.

Jesus overturns lies spoken by Satan, ourselves or others with truth about Himself, reality and us.		We discern and help the person discern those lies that have been received which are contrary to reality in the light of Jesus as the truth. As led by the Holy Spirit we expose the lies and in love and authority speak the Truth into the person's life.
Jesus cast out demons to clear the way for healing, restoration and obedience.		Through rational analysis and the gifts of the Holy Spirit we discern the presence of any evil spirits in or around the person, close the "gateways" that gave them ground for attack and in the authority of Jesus Christ bind them and remove them from interfering with the person.

PHASE 3 –

Jesus invites/commands the person to follow Him in faith and obedience as a disciple.

We are to help the person hear and discern how Jesus Christ is calling them to walk in obedience that will result in discipleship.

Jesus' Work	Going deep with the Holy Spirit in Inner Healing	Our work with Jesus at all levels
Jesus calls us to forgive those who hurt us.	Follow up on what Jesus says and does as is reported by the person and discerned by the prayer team. (May lead us to do any of the things in the right hand column.)	We pray that the person being prayed for may have the grace to forgive those who are responsible for their hurt.
Jesus calls us to receive the working of the Holy Spirit as from Him.		We help the person being prayed for to first discern and then to receive what the Holy Spirit is doing in them as from Jesus.
Jesus calls us to follow Him in faith and obedience.		In love and wisdom we walk with the person as they in faith and obedience seek to follow Jesus Christ.
Jesus promises us the Holy Spirit to guide, gift and empower us as we walk as His disciple.		We pray that the person who is in process of healing will be filled with the Holy Spirit to be an effective disciple of Jesus Christ.

Teaching Charts

Part VII

Inner Healing

The Dunamis Project
Presbyterian-Reformed Ministries International

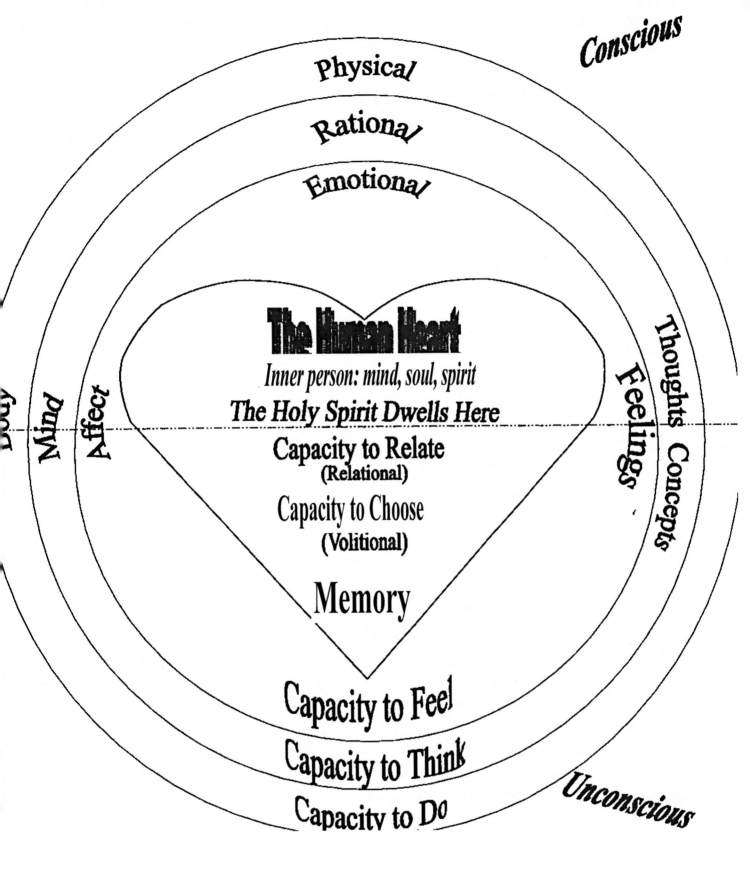

Conscious

Physical

Rational

Emotional

Body

Mind

Affect

Thoughts

Concepts

Feelings

The Human Heart

Inner person: mind, soul, spirit

The Holy Spirit Dwells Here

Capacity to Relate
(Relational)

Capacity to Choose
(Volitional)

Memory

Capacity to Feel

Capacity to Think

Capacity to Do

Unconscious

Depth Psychology Model

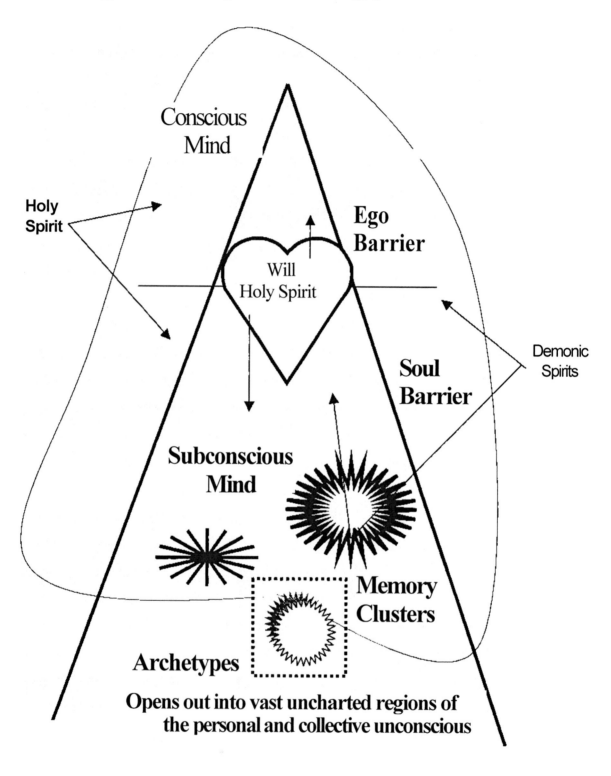

Conscious
Mind

**Holy
Spirit**

**Ego
Barrier**

Will
Holy Spirit

**Soul
Barrier**

Demonic
Spirits

**Subconscious
Mind**

**Memory
Clusters**

Archetypes

**Opens out into vast uncharted regions of
the personal and collective unconscious**

The Four Aspects of Memory

- Conceptual/Cognitive

- Sensory- Visual, Auditory, Olfactory, Taste and Touch

- Emotional

- Body Memories, Kinesthetic

Four Ways of Forgetting

Sinking into the unconscious

Active unconscious **repression** or conscious **suppression** of painful memories

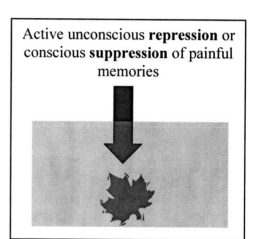

Dissociation

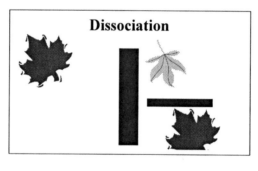

FACTORS THAT GIVE AN EXPERIENCE VORTEX FORMING POTENTIAL

THE CHARACTERISTICS OF THE PERSON

Sensitivity

Low --High

Personality Orientation

Optimism --- Pessimism

Environment

Healthy/loving ---------------------------------------Unhealthy/unloving

THE CHARACTERISTICS OF THE EXPERIENCE

Emotional Intensity

Low --High

Meaning

Low --High

Potential for harm to the person

Low--High

Inside a Vortex

Caused by a profound,
emotionally-charged event
The experience lives in the four
kinds of memory

1. Conceptual/Cognitive

2. Sensory: Visual, Auditory,
   Olfactory, Taste and Touch

3. Emotional

4. Body Memories, Kinesthetic

Contains truths from the Holy
Spirit or
lies from Satan.

May be an open door to the Holy
Spirit
or ground for attachment by evil
spirits.

THE FORMATION OF MEMORY CLUSTERS

Vortex

Memories Connected Around the Vortex

1. Similarity

2. Association/coinherance

3. Same lie or truth

4. Demonic or Holy Spirit bonding

5. Drive for meaning

The Dynamic of Forming a Memory Cluster around a Vortex
Showing Rules for Connections

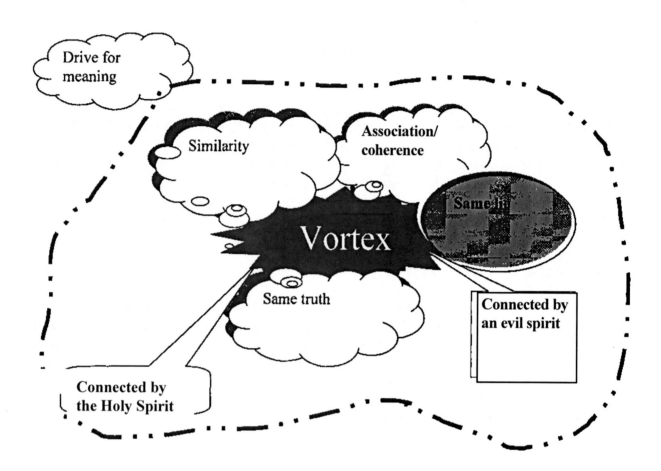

Memory clusters may be connected. These connections may serve to shape the personality and conscious behavior.

1. Similarity

2. Association/coinherance

3. Same lie or truth

4. Drive for meaning

5. Demonic or Holy Spirit bonding

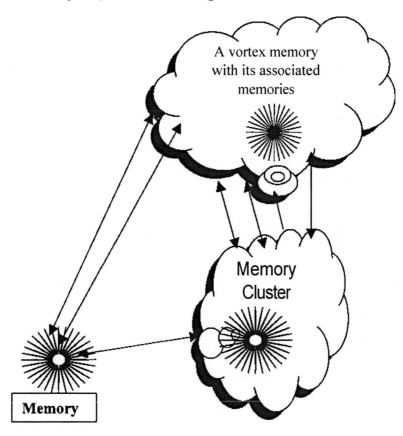

THE RESULTS OF UNHEALED HURT-FILLED MEMORY CLUSTERS

If memory clusters contain painful memories, lies or have attached demonic beings then there may take place the following negative consequences.

1. We may be blocked from loving and serving God fully with a whole heart.

2. We may be unable to enter into a loving relationship with someone else.

3. We may be hindered by irrational fears or have an inferiority complex.

4. We may be driven by insecurity to cling to others, to use them or hurt them.

5. We may cause mental problems such as depression or emotional breakdown.

6. We may be opened up to demonic attack or possession.

7. We may become physically ill with ulcers, cancer, high blood pressure, or some other emotionally-related disease.

The Inner Child of the Past

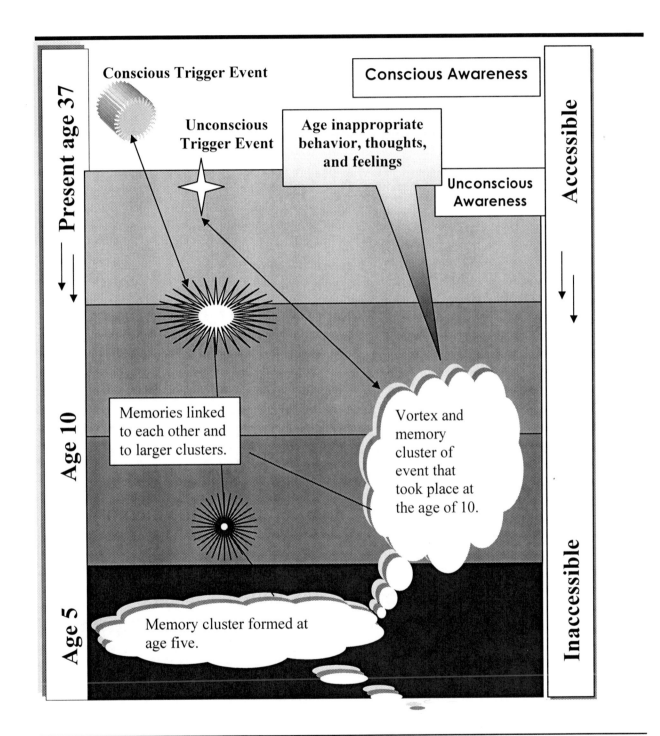

Conscious Trigger Event

Conscious Awareness

Unconscious Trigger Event

Age inappropriate behavior, thoughts, and feelings

Unconscious Awareness

Present age 37

Accessible

Memories linked to each other and to larger clusters.

Vortex and memory cluster of event that took place at the age of 10.

Age 10

Age 5

Memory cluster formed at age five.

Inaccessible

SUMMARY:
HOW THE HOLY SPIRIT WORKS
TO BRING INNER HEALING

A. THE HOLY SPIRIT PENETRATES INTO THE VORTEX OF THE MEMORY CLUSTER

B. BRINGS TO CONSCIOUS AWARENESS THE MEMORIES IN THE MEMORY CLUSTER

1. The Holy Spirit leads us into the vortex and the memory cluster by following the rules of association.

2. The Holy Spirit may reveal the contents of the memory vortex or cluster through supernatural gifts.

3. Bringing the love, presence, and reality of Jesus Christ that sets the person free to allow to consciousness the repressed or dissociated memories.

C. BRINGS THE PRESENCE AND WORKING OF JESUS CHRIST INTO THE MEMORY CLUSTERS

1. In the memory vortex Jesus may work according to the same principles of spiritual, inner, and relational healing as revealed in scripture.

2. The role of the prayer minister.

3. The role of the gifts of the Holy Spirit and the imagination.

D. THE RESULT OF JESUS' HEALING WORK IN THE VORTEX MEMORY

1. When a vortex of hurt that is hidden in the subconscious is made conscious it begins to lose its power over the psyche.

2. When Jesus Christ overcomes the lies in the vortex with His truths, the lies lose their power to define reality.

3. God's truth redefines the structures of meaning for the person's restoration.

4. Healing the hurt in the vortex causes it to lose its gravitational power to attract and configure other memories around itself.

5. Ground is removed from evil spirits so they may be expelled.

E. BRINGS A CHRIST-CENTERED IDENTITY AND TRUE SELF UNDERSTANDING

1. The memory of painful or hurtful experiences that are still in the heart. (These are the unalterable facts of our existence in a fallen world.) Nevertheless, they have been drained of their guilt, pain, fear and etc so they no longer have the power of vortexes shaping the personality.

2. The lies have been overcome by the truth. This gives new interpretation to events and allows new memory association to form.

3. The ground allowing evil spirits to hinder the process of sanctification would have been removed.

4. A new identity based on the truth revealed in Jesus Christ by the Holy Spirit now begins to form.

5. Those vortexes based on experiences of God's reality, love and truth are now able to become the primary organizing units in the personality. There is a new ordering of memories for a Christ-centered personality.

6. A person's actions, responses, attitudes and feelings, are no longer controlled by buried hurtful memory clusters that covertly exercise their power over their conscious life. Rather, reason and emotions appropriate to our experiences may rule our conscious life of following Jesus Christ.

How the Holy Spirit Enters Vortex Memories

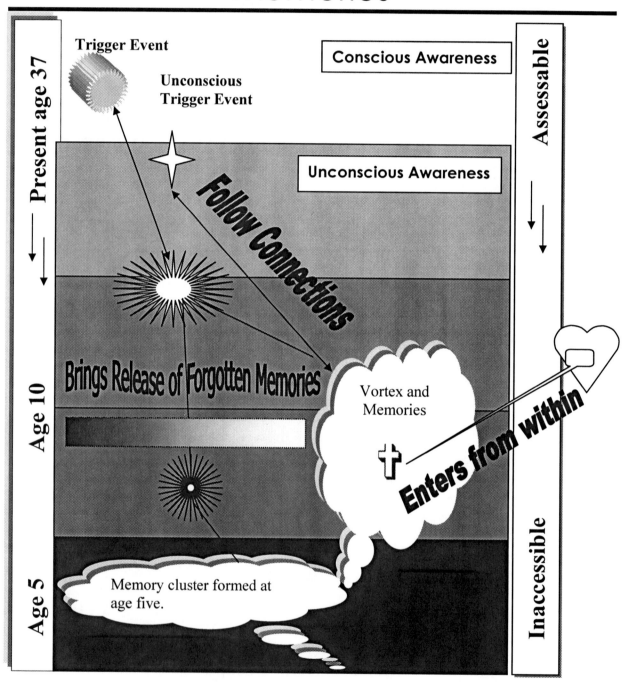

Inside the Memory Vortex the Holy Spirit Mediates Jesus Christ

Brings the presence and reality of Jesus Christ which is life and healing

PHASE 1 -

Jesus establishes the context in which the Holy Spirit will work by bringing the person into a

relationship with himself.

PHASE 2 -

Jesus and the Holy Spirit engage the person in various ways to bring the reality of

the Kingdom of God, which results in healing.

PHASE 3 -

Jesus invites/commands the person to follow Him in faith and obedience as a disciple.

The Results of Jesus' Healing

When the vortex based on hurt is healed and Christ's truth replaces the lies -demons are removed...

Then the vortex loses its cohesive power - the memories lose their power over us.

A new identity in the truth and reality of Jesus Christ may begin to be constructed in our psyche.

Past memories are reinterpreted and reorganized.

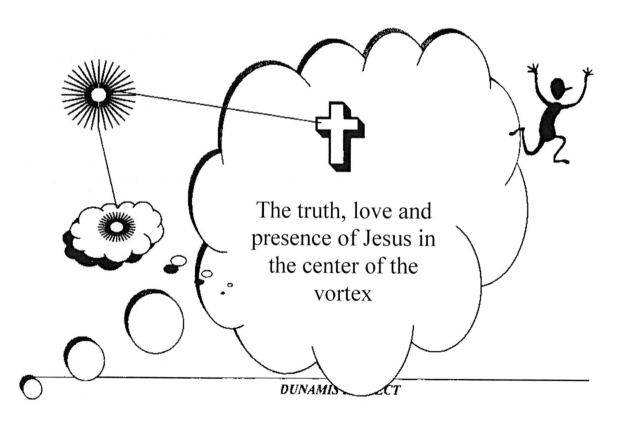

The truth, love and presence of Jesus in the center of the vortex

OUR COOPERATION WITH THE HOLY SPIRIT IN INNER HEALING

a) Listen to the Holy Spirit who, through the reasoned observation, supernatural gifts and/or through the person, will reveal what Jesus is doing.

b) Invite the Holy Spirit to bring to recollection what happened in the experience that has formed into the vortex memory. ("Stirring Up The Darkness")

c) Invite the person to "relive" the memory or to "re-enter" the event.

d) Ask the Holy Spirit to help the person to name the emotions and the lies that are contained in the vortex memory.

e) Invite Jesus Christ, through the Holy Spirit, to act and to speak to the person in the recollected memory.

f) Follow up on what Jesus says and does as reported by the person and discerned by the prayer team.

PUTTING IT ALL TOGETHER

Cooperating with the Holy Spirit and Jesus Christ to do Healing Ministry

PHASE 1
Jesus establishes the context in which the Holy Spirit will work by bringing the person into a relationship with Himself.

We work according to biblical principles to establish the context that welcomes the Holy Spirit to work.

Jesus' Work	Going deep with the Holy Spirit in Inner Healing	Our work with Jesus at all levels
Jesus is filled with the Holy Spirit and obeys the Father.	Listen to the Holy Spirit who, through the reasoned observation, supernatural gifts and/or through the person, will reveal what Jesus is doing	We pray to be filled with the Holy Spirit and ask that the Holy Spirit come upon the person being prayed for in power. We invite the Holy Spirit to work.
Jesus obeys the Father: this is the source of His direction and purpose for ministry.	Invite the Holy Spirit to bring to recollection what happened in the experience that has formed into the vortex memory, (stirring up the darkness)	We surrender ourselves to walking in obedience to Jesus Christ.
Jesus drew people into conversations with himself	Invite the person to "relive" the memory or to "re-enter" the event.	We engage the person being prayed for in conversation through directly asking them questions and intentionally listening to them.
Jesus demonstrates His love for the people He is reaching out to.	Ask the Holy Spirit to help the person to name the emotions and the lies that are contained in the vortex memory.	We show forth both by word and actions the love that we have been given by Jesus for the person being prayed for.

PHASE 2

Jesus and the Holy Spirit engage the person in various ways to bring the reality of the Kingdom of God that results in healing.

Jesus works through us and in the person being prayed for, as we are led and empowered by the Holy Sprit, to do those things He did while in the flesh that will make real the Kingdom of God.

Jesus' Work	Going deep with the Holy Spirit in Inner Healing	Our work with Jesus at all levels
Jesus leads people to be born again into the Kingdom of God	Invite Jesus Christ, through the Holy Spirit, to act and to speak to the person in the recollected memory	We present the Gospel and invite the person to accept Jesus Christ as Lord and Savior, and then pray with them to be born again.
Jesus enables and calls for confession, repentance, and walking in the light		Assure the person of Jesus' love and acceptance of those who turn to Him in confession and forgiveness
Jesus enables and calls for confession, repentance, and walking in the light		Assure the person of Jesus' love and acceptance of those who turn to Him in confession and forgiveness. Read the Bible passages that reveal sin and its consequences. As revealed by the Holy Spirit, expose and name any sins and present them to the person for discernment. Invite the person to confess their sins and to walk in the light.

Jesus overturns lies spoken by Satan, ourselves or others with truth about Himself, reality and us.		We discern and help the person discern those lies that have been received which are contrary to reality in the light of Jesus as the truth. As led by the Holy Spirit, we expose the lies and in love and authority speak the truth into the person's life.
Jesus cast out demons to clear the way for healing, restoration and obedience.		Through rational analysis and the gifts of the Holy Spirit we discern the presence of any evil spirits in or around the person, close the "gateways" that gave them ground for attack and in the authority of Jesus Christ bind them and remove them from interfering with the person.

PHASE 3

Jesus invites/commands the person to follow Him in faith and obedience as a disciple.

We are to help the person hear and discern how Jesus Christ is calling them to walk in obedience that will result in discipleship.

Jesus' Work	Going deep with the Holy Spirit in Inner Healing	Our work with Jesus at all levels
Jesus calls us to forgive those who hurt us.	Follow up on what Jesus says and does as is reported by the person and discerned by the prayer team.	We pray that the person being prayed for may have the grace to forgive those who are responsible for their hurt.
Jesus calls us to receive the working of the Holy Spirit as from Him.		We help the person being prayed for to first discern and then to receive what the Holy Spirit is doing in them as from Jesus.
Jesus calls us to follow Him in faith and obedience.		In love and wisdom we walk with the person as they in faith and obedience seek to follow Jesus Christ.
Jesus promises us the Holy Spirit to guide, gift and empower us as we walk as His disciple.		We pray that the person who is in process of healing will be filled with the Holy Spirit to be an effective disciple of Jesus Christ.

PTSD a Medical diagnosis

Both Award

PART VIII

Inner and Physical Healing and the Demonic: A Biblical Perspective

By Victor Matthews

The Dunamis Project
Presbyterian-Reformed Ministries International

This section dealing with the demonic is included because of the fact that one often encounters demonic entities in the process of spiritual, inner and relational healing. As has been suggested in Part 7 in the formation of some vortex memories and their resulting memory clusters it is very possible for evil spirits to become attached in them. This situation makes inner healing more difficult and necessitates the prayer minister moving from prayers for healing, into deliverance ministry.

The Rev. Victor Matthews has had extensive experience in both inner healing and deliverance ministry. He offers here a summary of the inter relationship between the spiritual, inner and relational healing with the process of discerning and expelling evil spirits.

A more detailed teaching on this topic is provided in the PRMI Spiritual Warfare Dunamis Project manual.

I. Introduction: The Continuing Role Of The Devil In Afflicting Human Beings

The Biblical record makes it clear that there may be a cause and effect relationship in our afflictions, in which the suffering (mental, emotional, volitional, spiritual, physical, social) is caused by demonic oppression.

In approaching this subject it is important to keep in mind the following truths.

- All effects of the Fall have not been removed from the redeemed in this world.

- While the Kingdom of God is powerfully present it is not fully present.

- We live in a fallen world that is largely controlled by the demonic.

- In our life of progress, stress and pressure we are often struggling not with "flesh and blood" but with "spiritual forces of evil."

- The devil seeks to humiliate the Lord Jesus through those who believe on Him.

- Our Father allows some demonic activity among us for discipline and instruction.

- Our Father wants us to live in wholeness and freedom. But His greater desire is that we would live in faith and love with hope. And through the exercise of His gifts, to glorify Him through ministering to others, in evangelism, healing, deliverance and discipleship. He may use afflictions, and even the devil—to teach and encourage us in such a life and ministry.

- While we should not jump to the conclusion that the devil is the cause of every affliction and sickness, the following passages make it clear that that may be true for some.

A. Scriptures that indicate a demonic source of sickness.

1. The healing of the demon-possessed man who was both blind and mute.

Then they brought him a demon-possessed man who was blind and mute, and Jesus healed him, so that he could both talk and see. Matthew 12:22 (See also 9:32,33)

Comments:

Notice that the word "healed" (therapeuo) is used to cover both the release from demon-possession as well as the inability to talk and see.

The presence of the enemy in the life of this man caused him to be <u>deprived</u> of two important functions that were his by creation.

2. The healing of the demon-possessed man who was mentally and emotionally unstable.

A man with an evil spirit came from the tombs to meet him (the Lord Jesus). *This man lived in the tombs, and no one could bind him any more, not even with a chain. For he had often been chained hand and foot, but he tore the chains apart and broke the irons on his feet. No one was strong enough to subdue him. Night and day among the tombs and in the hills he would cry out and cut himself with stones... When he saw Jesus from a distance, he ran and fell on his knees in front of him. He shouted at the top of his voice, "What do you want with me, Jesus, Son of the Most High God? Swear to God that you won't torture me!" For Jesus had said to him, "Come out of this man, you evil spirit!" Then Jesus asked him, "What is your name?" "My name is Legion," he replied, "for we are many." ... The demons begged Jesus, "Send us among the pigs; allow us to go into them." He gave them permission, and the evil spirits came out and went into the pigs. The herd, about two thousand in number, rushed down the steep bank into the lake and were drowned... The people went out to see what had happened. When they came to Jesus, they saw the man who had been possessed by the legion of demons, sitting there, dressed and in his right mind; and they were afraid... Then the people began to plead with Jesus to leave their region.* Mark 5:1-20 (See also Matt 8:28-34 and Luke 8:26-38)

Comments:

It is interesting that in the original "For Jesus had said," is "had been saying" (V8) and in V9 the words "then Jesus asked him" is "kept on asking him." It seemed necessary for the commands to be repeated over and over.

Through the presence of these demons the man was <u>deprived</u> of a normal life and was made a social outcast. Luke the physician points out his unusual strength, that he lived in a cemetery, how he would scream—perhaps in torment, and cut himself. The man was almost totally without self-control and tortured by the demons. The Lord Jesus brought spiritual, mental, emotional, volitional, physical, and social healing to him. He was a testimony to the powerful grace and mercy of God.

The people of the area were afraid when they saw the man clothed and in his "right mind." Such a deliverance, as well as the destruction of the pigs, caused them to plead with the Lord Jesus to leave their region. How strange are the effects of sin—these folk would rather have a demon-possessed man and pigs in their community—than the Lord Jesus! Notice: the Lord Jesus does not stay where He is not wanted.

3. The healing of the child who was mute and had seizures.

Teacher, I brought you my son, who is possessed by a spirit that has robbed him of speech. Whenever it seizes him, it throws him to the ground. He foams at the mouth, gnashes his teeth and becomes rigid. I asked your disciples to drive out the spirit, but they could not... When the spirit saw Jesus, it immediately threw the boy into a convulsion. He fell to the ground and rolled around, foaming at the mouth... Jesus ... rebuked the evil spirit. "You deaf and mute spirit," he said, "I command you, come out of him and never enter him again." The spirit shrieked, convulsed him violently and came out.... "This kind can come out only by prayer."
Mark 9:17-29 (See also Matt 17:14-19 and Luke 9:37-43)

Comments:

The boy's father spoke of loss of speech as the most prevalent characteristic of his son's possession. He said his boy had been "robbed." Perhaps the epileptic manifestations were only occasional.

When the Lord Jesus addressed the demon he called him a "deaf and mute spirit" indicating his main work in the boy. This child was also <u>deprived</u> of two of his divinely ordained functions.

Notice that the demon "convulsed (the boy) violently" as he came out of him.
Satan and his demons enjoy pain and when found out like to "show off" their power.

When the Lord Jesus asked the boy's father "How long has he been like this?" the answer "from childhood," may indicate the demon had access to the boy through the sins (ground) of his parents or/and ancestors.

4. The healing of Peter's mother-in-law of a fever.

Jesus left the synagogue and went to the home of Simon. Now Simon's mother-in-law was suffering from a high fever, and they asked Jesus to help her. So he bent over her and rebuked the fever, and it left her. She got up at once and began to wait on them. Luke 4:38,39 (See also Matt 8:14-17 and Mark 1:29,30)

Comments:

It is very significant that the Lord Jesus "rebuked (epitimao) the fever and it left her." Note that it is the same (Greek) word used in V 35 when He spoke directly to a wicked spirit.

This event teaches us that there are times, when led by the Holy Spirit, that we should take spiritual authority over sickness and rebuke the wicked spirits that are causing it. This passage indicates the enemy robbed her of her normal way of life by "adding" something to her—a high fever.

5. The healing of the woman with a curvature of the spine.

On a Sabbath Jesus was teaching in one of the synagogues, and a woman was there who had been crippled by a spirit for eighteen years. She was bent over and could not straighten up at all. When Jesus saw her, he called her forward and said to her, "Woman, you are set free from your infirmity." Then he put his hands on her, and immediately she straightened up and praised God. (Criticized by the Synagogue ruler, the Lord Jesus replied), ... *"Should not this woman, a daughter of Abraham, whom Satan has kept bound for eighteen long years, be set free on the Sabbath day from what bound her?"* Luke 13:10-17

Comments:

The oppression of the enemy had <u>deprived</u> this woman of her created ability to straighten her back and she had to live "bent over." As a result she is described by the Lord Jesus as "crippled," having an "infirmity," and "bound for eighteen long years."

What purpose could the enemy have in afflicting this woman as he did? Perhaps it was only that the demon enjoyed hurting her and demonstrating his power. Wicked spirits are proud, act like bullies, and are envious and hateful toward humans in that they are not created in the image of God. And we must never forget the basic reason is to bring hurt to the Lord Jesus, bring reproach against His character, and derail His Kingdom. We often hear, "Why did God do this to us?" "How can God be there and be love—when He either allows such things to happen, or does it Himself?" The initial source of such an attitude is clearly demonic.

B. An explanation of our Savior's ministry by the Apostle Peter.

Then Peter began to speak ... You know what has happened throughout Judea ... how God anointed Jesus of Nazareth with the Holy Spirit and power, and how he went around doing good and healing all who were under the power of the devil, because God was with him. Acts 10:34-38

Comments:

Peter's brief and clear-cut summary of the work of the Lord Jesus is fascinating in its explanation. And, we must keep in mind it is by an eyewitness who was a participant in these events. His message to Cornelius, his family and friends included a number of important truths.

The work of the Lord Jesus was historical—not some myth or legend.

The clear emphasis upon the Trinity and their cooperative relationship.

The work of the Lord Jesus is described as "good" and "powerful" and due to an anointing by His Heavenly Father in which He was given the Holy Spirit.
The anointing the Lord Jesus received resulted not only in the Holy Spirit being with the Savior but also His Father.

Because this explanation is in the Book of Acts—the ministry described by Peter is still going on today. And every believer stands, at least legally, in a spiritual position whereby he can personally receive the ministry of the Lord Jesus and cooperate with the Trinity in bringing it to others.

In regard to our theme—it is interesting to see how he describes <u>all healing</u> to be a release from "Being under the power of the devil." Peter is probably tracing all affliction and sickness back to the Fall and the devil's part in it. But there is no question that he is also giving a first-hand report of the many times he saw the Lord Jesus set a person free from some affliction or sickness by rebuking the demons who were causing it. .

Michael Brown, in commenting on this theme and Peter's explanation stated,

> Jesus' ministry of healing is inextricably lined with the ministry of deliverance from demons, and sickness is frequently associated with satanic power in the Gospels. This is in keeping with the OT view that sickness in and of itself is bad, often associated with the anger and curse of God, while healing is good, always associated with his favor and blessing... However, the NT revelation of the diabolical character of much sickness, disease, and infirmity goes beyond the general tenor of that which is disclosed in the OT... Yet, when understood properly, it does not *contradict* the foundations laid

in the Hebrew Scriptures; rather, it *builds* on that which has been e:
Thus it is important to stress that in healing the sick and delivering
Jesus was only doing the will of God.
According to Acts 10:38, those whom he healed (here *iaomai*) "wer
 under the power of the devil." In that sense, every healing is a
deliverance from an oppressive condition (and sometimes spirit),
 while every deliverance is a healing from a demonic bondage.
Likewise, both *therapeuo* and *iaomai* can be used with reference to exorcisms.
Israel's Divine Healer (Zondervan) 1995, p. 227

II. How Evil Spirits Get Attached To Human Beings (By Brad Long)[1]

Before turning to how to discern the presence of evil spirits and the then process of getting rid of them we must first deal with two important questions. First why do they get in and where do they attach themselves to us. Answering these two questions will lead us back to the teaching already given in Chapter 7 about the formation of inner wounds. The same factors that are at work in the formation of vortex memories also provide the ground for evil spirits to enter into us.

A. How do demons affect Christians?

One question must be dealt with first: What about Christians? Can evil spirits possess us? Is if possible for us who have been born again but who have inner hurts to have evil spirits afflict us?

The authors of this manual, through much first hand experience and also from our theological perspective have concluded that all forms of demonic attack and oppression, except possession, are possible for the Christian.

A Christian cannot be possessed by an evil spirit for the reason that the Holy Spirit occupies the inner sanctum of the Christian and therefore cannot be occupied by an evil spirit. Water baptism, which signifies our being born into Jesus Christ, serves as a shield against demonic attack or attachment at the deepest level of our being.

There is, however, a lot of room between the inner sanctum of the heart that is occupied by the Holy Spirit and the rest of the person in which ground may be given to Satan. The Christian may thus be oppressed by evil spirits and even have them attached to him or her in a vortex memory buried in their unconscious.

Tom White offers the analogy of our body being the temple of the Holy Spirit to further clarify how evil spirits can oppress a Christian.

"Paul indicated that the physical body of the Christian is a `temple of the Holy Spirit.' Let me offer an analogy to the Old Testament temple. The physical body corresponds to the outer court of the temple, accessible to both Jew and Gentile, a

---

[1] This is from the PRMI Dunamis Manual, Spiritual Warfare and Kingdom Advancement.

place subject to spiritual contamination. The soul corresponds to the holy place, accessible only to the sanctified Jew. And the spirit of a man is parallel to the holy of holies, accessible only to the priest. Unconfessed sin in the life of the priest brought death in the presence of God. Neither sin nor Satan can occupy the same space filled with the holiness of the Almighty. Within man, there is a separation of the spirit, sanctified and set apart for eternal redemption, from the corruptible aspects of the human soul and body. Thus, a Christian, saved but not yet fully sanctified, may experience bondage to besetting sins or the partial "demonization" of evil spirits."

B. Why Do Evil Spirits Attach Themselves to People?

Scripture does not directly deal with this question of why evil spirits attach themselves to human beings. It is just taken as a fact that they do. What follows is speculation that is based on inferences made from scripture as well as human experience with evil spirits.

1.   Demons are bodiless spirits that need some mode of working in the physical realm. They seek a place of rest.

"When the unclean spirit has gone out of a man, he passes through waterless places seeking rest; and finding none he says, `I will return to my house from which I came.' And when he comes he finds it swept and put in order. Then he goes and brings seven other spirits more evil than himself, and they enter and dwell there; and the last state of that man becomes worse than the first." (Luke 11:24-26)

The story of the Gadarenes demoniacs demonstrates the evil spirits' desperate desire to have a place. They begged to be allowed to enter the herd of swine. In Jewish eyes this clearly showed the unclean nature of these entities. It also revealed their desperate need for some living creatures to inhabit. Part of the torment that they dreaded was to be homeless.

Once in a person, evil spirits seek to shape the person's body, mind, emotions and spirit to conform to their perverse nature and to accomplish the objectives of the Kingdom of Satan.

Some options:

i.   Because evil spirits are afflicted and tortured, they afflict and torture the person.

ii. Satan's kingdom is an empire in which there is no freedom, only coercion and control. Likewise spirits control, manipulate, and hold in bondage.

iii. They may use the person as a means of attack against others.

iv. The person may be used as an entry point into this realm so that evil spirits may attack a group of people or a place.

v. They live out their vile nature that is opposed to everything that is good and of Gc
They cooperate with fallen human nature to express the works of the flesh as lisu
Galatians 5:19-21. Each of these sins reflect the nature of evil spirits.

2. **They are like parasites that sustain their own dead being by feeding upon those who are alive.**

George McDonald, in *Lilith,* explored the mysteries of evil. Lilith is a vampire who is dead in herself but lives by the life of others. In mythology and fantasy she is Adam's first wife, an angelic being who in her fallenness became the Queen of Hell.

"Vilest of God's creatures, she lives by the blood and lives and souls of men. She consumes and slays, but is powerless to destroy as to create."[2]

This is an apt description of evil spirits. They seem to live on those they are attached to. It is found consistently in praying for inner healing that demons work to obstruct the healing process. This is partly due to the fact that the unhealed hurt may provide the grounds of their entry, but also it seems that they get some "life" from the hurt and suffering itself.

Once, at Jesus Abbey during a deliverance, a very strong demon told Archer Torrey the following chilling reasons why it was afflicting a deeply wounded person. "We demons eat human misery like you humans eat bread." Whether literally or symbolically, demons do seem to thrive on human misery, bondage, and death.

3. <u>Generally Satan and demons express their power and presence in time-space reality through human beings.</u>

Human beings are both spirit and body. As such, we provide an interface or channel between the spiritual realm and material realm. We become the means by which not only the Holy Spirit but also evil spirits may express their intentions in the world.

M. Scott Peck summarized why evil spirits need human bodies.

"Satan cannot do evil except through a human body. Although `a murderer from the beginning,' it cannot murder except with human hands. It does not have the power to kill or even harm by itself. It must use human beings to do its devilry."[3]

I believer Scott Peck is right in affirming that demons may work through human beings.
However to say that they cannot attack directly simply does not hold up to the actual facts.
There have been many recorded experiences when evil spirits have indeed attacked people through the air.

What are the...

---

[2] George McDonald, *Lilith* (Grand Rapids: Eerdmans, 1981), p. 148.
[3] Scott Pack, *The People of the Lie* (New York: Simon and Schuster, 1983), p. 206.

...es given in the section on Night Terrors and also in the section on high level ...rfare.

C. How Do Evil Spirits Get Into People?

The bottom line continuum that determines the seriousness of the attachment and oppression is our sinfulness which brings a sympathy in our nature and the nature of the afflicting spirits.

Recorded in Jessie Penn-Lewis' classic, *War on the Saints*, is a summary of this aspect of sympathetic nature and the process of attachment.

> "They (demons) seek out those whose make-up and temperament is most congenial to themselves, and then seek to fasten themselves on to some part of the body, or brain, or some appetite, or some faculty of the mind, either the reason, or imagination, or perception; and when they get access, they bury themselves into the very structure of the person, so to identify themselves with the personality of the one they possess. In a great many instances they do not get possession of the individual, but obtain such a hold on some part of the mind as to torment the person with periodical attacks of something strange and abnormal, out of all proportion to the general character and make-up of the individual."[4]

Tom White said:

> **"Always in my observation, evil spirits are present for a reason. The bondage traces back to a particular cause, a point of entry, or a lapse in moral life."[5]**

This cause or point of entry is always connected to some expression of human sin. Both the nature of the sin and our response to it are determining factors. All sin opens us to the possibility of being afflicted by evil spirits. But if it is forgiven and cleansed in Jesus Christ, then the door is closed. All sin gives Satan an opportunity but some sin, such as sorcery and other occult practices clearly forbidden in scripture, especially open us up to demonic oppression.

It may be helpful at this point to think of demons as analogous to bacteria or virus. These microscopic entities are everywhere but they only invade the body and cause sickness when there is some breakdown in the body's defense mechanisms. Likewise evil spirits may be present but they only enter when our spiritual defenses are broken down.

D. Some Possible Open Doors To Oppression:

1. Ancestral Sin:

Unforgiven unhealed sin of past generations may open doors for evil spirits to enter a family line and be passed from one generation to the next.

---

[4] *War on the Saints* (Fort Washington: The Christian Literature Crusade, 1977), p. 150.
[5] Tom White, *Believer's Guide* (Ann Arbor: Servant, 1990), p. 30.)

"...you shall not bow down to them or serve them; for I the Lord your God am a jealous God, visiting the iniquity of the fathers upon the children to the third and the fourth generation of those who hate me, but showing steadfast love to thousands of those who love me and keep my commandments." (Exodus 20:5-6)

Evil spirits look for ground that is given to them. Here in the Ten Commandments there is the suggestion that sin may linger and have affect through the generations. The prophet Ezekiel in Chapter 18 makes it clear that this cannot be seen as an absolute law of retribution. That is, the children will automatically experience the consequences of the parent's sins. Ezekiel stated, *"Behold, all souls are mine; the soul of the father as well as the soul of the son is mine: the soul that sins shall die."* (Ezekiel 18:4)

While the fact that one's parents sinned does not automatically mean God's wrath upon the next generation, experience has taught that evil spirits who do not play fair may look for open doors and points of weakness left by past generation's sins.

Evil spirits, in looking for a home, may find a ready host in the next generation that has been weakened or adversely affected by the sins of the parents.

For instance, if parents were involved in spiritualism and were demonized because of this and raised their children in that atmosphere, demons may find a ready ground of entry in the children. Further, since demons are active, insidious beings they may actually take advantage of the situation and perpetuate behaviors, attitudes or hurts that prepare the next generation as a ready home. Tom White calls these generational cling-ons.

Further, it is a fact that dysfunctional families seem to perpetuate themselves from generation to generation unless the cycle is broken. Thus demons may find a continued ground of entry in this natural propensity of parents to nurture their sins and dysfunctions in their children.

Generational sins that may open doors to demons:

Involvement in spiritualism, the occult or some false religion. The generational curse is pointedly applied to those who do not worship and honor the one true God but give their allegiance and worship to things that are not of God (Exodus 20:3-6).

There is also the cause when parents do things that nearly insure that the child will be demonized. This occurs in satanic ritual abuse. In Taiwan parents will offer their children to a god in the temple, or a child is sold into prostitution.

Any number of other sins, such as, murder, sexual infidelity and so forth may open doors for generational attachment. The issue is not so much the nature of sin but rather as whether it has been dealt with through confession and forgiveness in Christ.

Usually, when the next generation surrenders to Christ, these generational cling-ons just fall away. At other times, because the person himself has given them ground, the demons may need to be dealt with intentionally.

Example: In Taiwan among two generations of Christian tribal people, we occasionally dealt with cases of demonization by spirits who had entered their ancestors through the practice of head hunting.

Many times we have had to deal with spirits allowed in because of a parent's or grandparent's involvement in the occult of spiritualism.

Ancestral sin and generational cling-ons must be dealt with by renouncing the generational sin and asking for forgiveness and cleansing for it. It is also helpful to break any spiritual ties that may exist. Then any evil spirits that have gotten in must be exposed and expelled.

2. One's own sin:

Pre-conversion sin: Sins that may have been committed before one was a Christian.

These may range from any number of things, however, the most serious are those in which one has intentionally opened the door for Satan through the occult or spiritualism.

Pre-conversion sin must be dealt with by forsaking it entirely, cleansing and forgiving, and expelling any evil spirits that may be clinging on.

Post-conversion: This is one's own present sin that if unconfessed and unforgiven may give ground for demonic oppression.

3. Being sinned against -

Demonization may occur by being victimized by another person who is demonized.

Sexual abuse, rape, or being offered up to an evil spirit all break down the defense mechanisms of the ego and make one vulnerable to demonization. It seems that an evil spirit may actually be transferred from one person to another by such invasive actions.

Further, being sinned against often leaves within the person deep anger, hatred and hurt that are often suppressed into the unconscious where they form powerful psychological complexes. Unless there is healing of these hurts, as well as confession and forgiveness, these sins now provide ground for the attachment by evil spirits. The resulting psychological complex provides a ready home for evil spirits.

4. Demonic attachment by being in a place or around a person infested with demons -

There are some places, like brothels, pornography shops, shamanist temples, New Age meditation centers, and other centers of sin that welcome evil spirits.

In or near such places evil spirits may not only attack from without as flaming darts but also actually get attached. Usually this is possible because there is some weakness or a chink in the armor that allows the evil spirit some ground of entry.

The following is a list by Tom White of the various ways that evil spirits may find open doors to oppress a believer.

Beel...

E. How Satan Gains A Hold On Believers By Tom White.

1 Samuel 16:14   DISOBEDIENCE: Saul was attacked by a spiritas a consequence of sin. His lack of repentance made him targetable.

Luke 22:31   UNBELIEF: a weakening or failure of faith. Peter, unknowingly, became a vessel for satanic influence by resisting revealed truth.

Acts 5:1-11   DECEIT: Ananias and Sapphira, through willful lying, fell prey to immediate satanic "invasion," and received immediate judgement.

2 Cor. 2:10,11   UNFORGIVENESS: the lack of reconciliation through forgiving love opens to door to satanic influence.

1 Cor. 5:4,5   IMMORALITY: the unrepentant sin of immorality carries the danger of direct affliction of the flesh by Satan. *whom*

Galatians 3:1   FALSE DOCTRINE: Paul describes the Galatians as having been "bewitched" ("demonized") by believing lies of false doctrine.

Ephesians 4:27   ANGER: failure to deal with and cleanse the sin of anger allows the devil to gain a "place," a "foothold."

I Timothy 1:20   BACKSLIDING: Hymaneaeus and Alexander were "handed over to Satan" by Paul for disciplinary instruction.

I Timothy 3:6,7   PRIDE: a word of warning that a new convert may fall prey to pride, and be subject to the "devil's trap."

James 3:13-16   ENVY/SELFISHNESS: a warning addressed to believers to be wary of selfish ambition that causes strife. This is "of the devil," and leads to "every evil practice."

2 Cor. 11:3   DECEPTION: by heeding false teaching, Paul fears the Corinthians would be led astray, through Satan's cunning, from the purity of the gospel.

make your own list
Being Snared again

A REASSURING WORD

The child of God who longs with sincerity of heart to follow Christ need not walk in a dreaded state of spiritual paranoia worrying that he will be jumped or invaded by an evil spirit when he stumbles. God's loving grace and keeping power shield me from Satan's onslaughts. When I sin, His Spirit works to convict me. If I respond to the conviction with confession (agreeing that He is right), I receive cleansing (1 John 1:9) and a covering of righteousness (Ephesians 6:14). If, however, I deny or dodge this conviction, or prolong it through willful rationalization or rebellion, I run the risk of coming under Satan's direct accusation/oppression. Note here the admonition to deal with anger before too much time elapses, so Satan will not gain a "foothold" (Greek "Topos," geographical location, place of influence). If one takes the easy way out of denying the memory or the feelings then they may form vortexes in the unconscious. There while hidden from our conscious awareness they will still contain the "foothold" for evil spirits to get attached afflict us.

The clear condition of divine protection is walking in obedience to truth
(2 Thessalonians 2:2,3 and 1 John 5:18,19).

F. Where Are Evil Spirits Attached To Us?

In this question, "Where do demons attach themselves to human beings?" we are dealing with the mystery of how something spiritual may interface with that which is material. The question of where and how demons may attach themselves in us is similar to how the Holy Spirit resides in us. We also confront the complexity of human nature in which we are one interconnected whole consisting of mind, body, and spirit.

1. In the body

It is difficult to tell whether demons actually become attached to a particular point in the body or whether they are simply manifesting their presence through a particular place in the body.

Often, when commanded to manifest, they will do so by a pain in the stomach, tightening of the chest, pressure in the head or some other somatic disturbance. This may indicate their actual location and point of attachment.

On the other hand, demons may not be attached to the body at all, rather as spiritual entities they may be attached to the mind, emotions or to the spirit. But they are manifested in our bodies just as emotional stress or guilt due to spiritual sin may find expression in our stomachs and cause ulcers.

2. In the mind and thoughts

Demons apparently attach themselves to our minds and thought processes. They occupy mental strongholds composed of false or sinful thoughts.

Francis Frangipane made the following observations about how thought structures provide a place for demons.

> "In speaking of spiritual warfare, the Apostle Paul enlists the word "stronghold" to define the spiritual fortresses wherein Satan and his legions hide and are protected. These fortresses exist in the thought-patterns and ideas that govern individuals and churches, as well as communities and nations.[6]

> "The Apostle Paul defines a stronghold as `...speculations, [a] lofty thing raised up against the knowledge of God' (2 Corinthians 3:5). A demonic stronghold is any type of thinking that exalts itself above the knowledge of God, thereby giving the devil a secure place of influence in an individual's thought-life.[7]

> "However, Christians can be oppressed by demons, which can occupy unregenerated thought-systems, especially if those thoughts are defended by self deception or false doctrines!"[8]

Left unanswered is the exact mechanism by which demons attach themselves to these thought structures while not simply being thoughts themselves. Experience shows that demons do nonetheless find room in these mental structures.

3. In hurtful vortex memories that form memory clusters.

Demons seem also to attach themselves in our emotions. Just as they find a home in our thought structures, they also find a home in the vortex memories and memory clusters buried in the heart.

The formation of inner wounds has already been covered in Chapter Seven. The important thing to note is that when one is hurt emotionally there is an emotional response of anger, fear and guilt. There is nothing wrong with these feelings in themselves; just as physical pain, they tell us that we are being hurt. But when the hurt is unhealed and unforgiven, they may become hatred, resentment, and unforgiveness. This becomes a matter of the human spirit. Whether justified or not these are themselves sins that may open doors or give ground to evil spirits. The evil spirits then, like parasites, attach themselves in the vortex memory that contains these sins.

4. Implications for the process of Discernment and Inner healing.

These observations about the location of attachment have significant implications for the process of discernment deliverance.

---

[6] Francis Frangipane, *The Three Battlegrounds* (Marion, Iowa: 1989), p. 14.)
[7] Ibid., p. 15
[8] Ibid., p. 16.

- Demons are imbedded in the body, thoughts or emotions of the person. They will seek to remain hidden simply as a thought or feeling among the person's own thoughts and feelings.

- The process of discernment is forcing them to separate to where they may be distinguished as alien entities that are not a part of the person. (How this is done will be dealt with in part 7.)

- Because demons find a home in thought strongholds and psychological complexes, part of the deliverance process will be dismantling and healing these structures.

- This implies that being set free from evil spirits will not just be a power encounter between the authority of Jesus and the evil spirits, but also a truth encounter as well as inner healing.

- Thought strongholds and psychological complexes are very powerful structures. They often function with a great deal of autonomy and are not fully under the control of the person. When they are dealt with there will be strong uncontrollable reactions by the person.

- In deliverance one must be careful to distinguish these autonomous expressions from evil spirits that are also autonomous.

- The amazing complexity and holistic nature of human beings means that healing and deliverance must be approached with great care and wisdom.

- Deliverance is not just a matter of chasing away a few demons. Rather, it is bringing healing and balance to a whole set of mutually interrelated systems of which a person is composed.

- This means that our healing from demonization often does not take place with one quick fix, rather it will be a process of removing the ground where demons have entered, healing of the hurt and restoration of the person.

III. How to tell if a sickness, affliction or inner hurt has a demonic source and what to do about it.

A. Preparation for discerning and dealing with demons

Keep in mind that all prayer and ministry is basically the work of the Holy Spirit. He is the One Who has given us gifts and He seeks to bring the grace and power into the lives of individuals so they will enter into freedom and glorify God.

It is very important to actively trust Him for help. Whether the opportunity for prayer is a spontaneous one, such as following a service at Church, or a planned session, ask Him to give you love and patience, the awareness to hear His voice and follow His leading, and to protect you. Without His help we are quite helpless.

It is always good to take spiritual authority over the situation. If possible do this before you pray for a person and in many situations do it again with the person, perhaps as a team, for the sake of all who are there. Something like the following is helpful.

> *In the name of the Lord Jesus Christ, we unite together and speak
> directly to any wicked spirits involved here. We bind open your ears,
> rebuke you, stop all your working and bind you back from us and in
> particular from* (name the person for whom you are praying).

In a planned prayer session make sure the one seeking prayer is a believer, an honest seeker, and has some knowledge of how to worship God and make decisions of faith, love and hope.

Treat the person with respect and ask God to help you to love and accept them.
Keep in mind you are only a servant and are serving under the direction of the Holy Spirit.
Do not pressure the individual, ask embarrassing questions, or manipulate them. Treat them as you would like to be treated. Work hard on making your relationship with them a safe and accepting one.

The individual may need some aspects of discipleship, counseling, reconciling of the past, encouragement and accountability.

It maybe very helpful to present to them the basic message of such important books as *Telling Yourself the Truth,* William Backus (Bethany House), *Healing for Damaged Emotions,* David Seamands (Victor Books), and *The Adversary,* Mark Bubeck (Moody).

B. Pointers to the Presence of wicked spirits

As you do this preliminary work watch for areas of the individual's life that would indicate tension, pressure, shame, lack of self-control, passivity, fantasy, hopelessness, obsessive behavior, controlling relationships, soul-ties, anger, bitterness, fear, pride, unforgiveness, addictions, defensiveness, pretending, and manipulation. Be very watchful for any inability to accept forgiveness or the love/approval of God. .

> Linda was a pretty girl who could not believe that God had forgiven
> her. She was very open about telling me she had been sexually abused
> by her brother until she was old enough to stop it.
>
> She was raised in a Christian home, was a believer, and was attending a
> fine evangelical Church in our area. In spite of her knowledge of the
> Bible, and the benefits of salvation, she often cried in a rather agonizing

way about how "dirty" she was and how she felt far from God.

One day I asked her permission to talk with her about the abuse. When she gave me the permission I asked her if she had come to enjoy the sexual encounters. After lots of tears she admitted that she did.

I explained how God had made us sexual beings and how, in the involvement with her brother, her body had started to respond to the sexual stimulation and her desire for those feelings naturally followed.

Her response surprised me. She said, "I understand, and while I'm ashamed of that, and have confessed it to God a number of times, I still cannot escape the fact that I'm just a "dirty" kind of person."

The word "dirty" seemed to be underlined by the Holy Spirit. I asked her if I could address any work of the enemy related to her problem. She said "Yes." I prayed with her briefly and then commanded "Dirty Linda" to come out of hiding and come to attention.

The girl's body jerked and I knew there was a wicked spirit there who had been counterfeiting Linda and telling her she was a "dirty girl." I led her in taking back ground for listening to him and we joined together in binding up his false teaching, conditioning, systems, and sent him where the Lord Jesus wanted to send him.

In the next few days Linda testified that she no longer felt dirty nor did she feel far from God.

When you see such areas keep them in mind and ask the Lord to give you wisdom as to their significance and when to pursue them. As you continue to talk and pray with the person you will probably see some of the above problem areas as important and others as unimportant. Some of them may be a "pointer" to the work of the enemy.

A woman came for help regarding her relationship to her immediate family. I'd known her and the family for a few years and often preached in the Church they attended. She had a fine husband and three teen-age boys who where believers.

She got right to the point when she said, "I'm an irritant to my husband and boys. I've got a problem with my mouth." She emphasized the word "mouth."

When I asked her to give me an illustration of what she did to irritate the family she told the story. She said her husband and boys were very close, and tried to do things together on Saturday, which caused her to feel a little left out. But, she said, "That's not my problem. It's what I say to them. For example, last Saturday they were looking at this football game, laughing together, eating popcorn, and rooting for their team. They were having a wonderful time. But in the middle of it all, I walked in and said, "Why don't you go out and paint the back of that garage!" I knew it was wrong, and I knew how it hurt, but I couldn't stop myself.

What happened then? I asked. She said "I went into the kitchen and said, 'Why don't you just shut-up.'" As she cried, she said, "I need help, I cannot control my tongue—no matter how I pray about it."

It was evident my friend needed healing but I knew she also had some demonic control behind that. If it were not demonic her prayers would have been answered in some way.

As we prayed together, I spoke to the real source of her problem, broke their control over her, sent the enemy and their work out, and then prayed for her healing and freedom. The healing she needed seemed to be as important as the deliverance.

When it was over I asked her how she was doing. She tried to smile, and then pointed to her mouth. After a few minutes she said, "It feels like my mouth and throat just received a big shot of novocaine. It's all numb." After a few minutes we laughed together and thanked the Lord. The next time I saw her she said it was OK.

While it may not seem appropriate at first, to talk or even pray with the person about basic problem issues, keep in mind the source of the affliction or sickness may be in a spiritual, mental, emotional, volitional, physical, social or relational area of the person's life. And behind that or those areas may be demonic control.

As you work with the person, explain and pray the truth of James 4:7. Trust the Lord to direct you and give you some guidance.

> *Heavenly Father, we unite together to ask that You would show us*
> *what we need to know about this problem. Whatever there may be*
> *of Your plan and purpose in these issues for _____ then we*
> *accept it and trust You to make it clear. But, if there is anything of*
> *sin or the world or the enemy in what is troubling _____*
> *then we reject it and ask You to show us what we need to do to*
> *honor You.*

C. What to do when you hit "Walls" that prevent in-depth prayer and healing

Many times you will sense that you have come against some kind of a "wall" when you are praying for a person. It will feel spiritually, as though you bump into something or you step into an area where it is hard to pray. When you do—then talk to the person about it, ask them if they know what it is, and use the James 4:7 principle.

If you, or they, know what the "wall" is—ask the person if you can get rid of it. If they give you permission then continue. If they refuse or are hesitant then stop and come to some agreement about further procedure. If it is something that would involve counsel then stop and do that.

> My engineer friend Ed is a case in point. He told me one day at lunch about his irrational belief that he would fail and end up on some skid row. We both laughed about how contradictory it seemed, in that he was a well-taught believer, had a good family, and was a very successful business man.
>
> Ed went on to explain what he thought was the origin of his problem. He said his father had deserted the family when he was about 5 years of age. It was during the Depression. Because his mother had no money, no source of income, and no relatives—she took Ed and his older sister to an orphanage and left them there for about three years. Ed said it was a terrible time for him and he missed his mother and sister a great deal. After lunch I asked him if I could pray for him. We went to my office and after some prayer, I addressed the wicked spirit who was telling my friend that he would end up on skid row.
>
> Ed started to cry. I led him in a statement of renunciation in which he took back ground form the enemy, and then we sent the wicked spirit to the pit. Ed wiped his face and said, "I'm glad that's over," and we had a good laugh together.
>
> I saw my friend two weeks later and he said he'd not had one thought about ending up on skid-row and felt very peaceful inside.

Explain how such walls or compulsions may be some stronghold (a hold that is strong) (2 Cor 10:4,5) of the enemy. You may need to lead the person in a confession to God and a statement of renunciation in which they take back any ground ("foothold," Eph 4:27) they have given to the enemy.

D. How to Pray to expose and to remove evil spirits.

As you pray for a person have them relax and close their eyes. Watch their face and look for indications of anger, irritation, restlessness, shaking or dropping of the head, trembling, and fluttering of the eyes. Ask the Lord to tell you what such indications mean and how to proceed. (For the full process of discerning and removing evil spirits, please see the PRMI Dunaius Project manual "Spiritual Warfare and Kingdom Advancement")

If the enemy is close to the surface the person's eyes may suddenly pop open and you realize a wicked spirit is looking at you. Stare right back, reject your fear, speak directly to the demon, rebuke him in the name of the Lord Jesus, and command he stand back from the person.

Explain to the person what happened and ask them if they were aware of it. They may be able to tell you the source of power the enemy has over them. If so then lead them in confession, renunciation of the enemy and taking back ground. It may be necessary for them to spend time in repentance and make some serious decisions, to make things right. The observations by Charles Kraft, that demons are like rats and feed on garbage is an appropriate one. Once you clean up the garbage you can easily get rid of the rats. See his *Christianity with Power* (Vine Books), *Defeating Dark Angels* (Vine Books), *Deep Wounds Deep Healing* (Vine Books), and *I Give You Authority* (Chosen Books).

If the enemy is causing some affliction or sickness then the problem may be worse the day before, or the day of the appointment. The person may be hindered in coming to Church, coming forward or coming for the appointment.

The problem may leave when the person comes to the service, or appointment or when you pray for them and then return when they leave. If the person is in pain then it may "travel around" their body as you pray for them.

Often the enemy will attack the person in some subtle or counterfeiting way when you get close to healing or deliverance. Many times after significant success and progress in setting a person free from the enemy they will come for a session and boldly say, "I'm sure my problem is not demonic." And, they may not give you permission to continue.

In such a situation, I silently address the demon who said that to the person, rebuke him, stop his work, and command he release the person. You may have to say this a couple times—forcefully and aggressively. Continue to smile, say something neutral, and then ask if they wish to continue to do Bible study pray. If they are willing, pray in a general way for them and eventually use the James 4:7 truth.

Pray a good deal for the person on your own. And then at some other session try to explain what happened and when you feel it is appropriate ask the person again if you can continue to do healing and delivering prayer. If so then address the wicked spirit who spoke such a lie to them.

It is very productive, when appropriate, to pray against and pull out fiery darts and the poison they produce (Eph 6:16), to break down strongholds (2 Cor 10:4,5) of gossip, criticism, unforgiveness, spiritual laziness, grudges, pornography, homosexuality, lust, obsessions, addictions all forms of self-centeredness, and sinful relationships of all kinds. God has given us these weapons and as the text states, He will work powerfully with us to clean up our own lives, and those for whom we pray. However, we have to use them before He can release His power.

In many of these cases the enemy may not be present but their work will be there. This is often confusing in a prayer or deliverance session. A person may have an affliction, sickness, compulsion or addiction that both of you know is of the enemy. However, as you address the <u>cause</u> of the problem—you get nothing (your words of rebuke suddenly "feel" like you are talking to a "dead phone").

In such a case the enemy has probably "built" something into the person (conditioning, programming, etc., that may be "triggered" by certain people, words, events, time sequences, sounds, odors, etc., or it may be constant—as in sickness). If this is the case, address the problem, demolish it (use strong words you may need to repeat a few times), pull it out and send it where the Lord Jesus sends it. You may need to work with some of these areas more than once. And, teach the person in question to do so, and to be aggressive in saying "I will not accept that pain, invitation, temptation etc., and I give it all to the Lord Jesus." Teach them to fight, to wear the armor, pray in the Spirit, and watch for any "triggers" that would indicate an area of the enemy's work. .

Many times you will be hindered in your progress with a person. As you continue to trust God to tell you what to do—make sure both you and the person have broken relationships with those close, socially and relationally (parents, relatives, people important to you and them, and anyone who has been hurtful. This may involve people in the past also) as well as with one another.

Use something like the following: *"In the name of the Lord Jesus Christ, I smash and break all relationships set up by Satan and wicked spirits between _____ and myself. I cancel all these relationships and command that all their effects upon me must leave me now."*

<u>Do not consider this suggestion to be unimportant.</u> There have been many times when people have called me on the telephone about a problem they are having in deliverance. Often they are in the midst of a session, the enemy is manifesting, laughing at them, and people are being hurt and attacked.

When I ask about breaking relationships I usually get the answer, "I don't know what you mean by that," or "I guess we forgot to do that." I find by a later 'phone call that doing so cause a dramatic change in the session and they were able to continue successfully.

Do not consider yourself as a counselor to be above such a suggestion. In more than one case I have found the hindrances I was having in praying for a person were found in the way the enemy was pouring power into my life, without me realizing it, through someone else I was working with.

If you keep running into confusion as you pray and work with a person, make sure the person is honest and cooperating with you in how they live. You may also find that the person you are working with has a Dissociative Identity Disorder (Multiple Personality Disorder) or a number of children within. You will find the latter to be very common.

It is important not to speak to an inner child or alter as a demon and try to send them to the pit. We all need a lot of wisdom, discernment, and the ministry of the Holy Spirit about this area.

The book recommended earlier by Charles Kraft is quite helpful, *Deep Wounds Deep Healing* (Vine Books). If the person is DID (MPD), and you do not have training and experience in such areas, then recommend they go to a Christian therapist who understands and is successful in helping people with such issues.

However, it may be very productive for the person for you to continue to meet with them for healing prayer and encouragement. And by being available they will know you are not abandoning them. But, be careful not to counsel them in the areas covered by their therapist. It may confuse them and may give the enemy an opportunity to pit you against the therapist.

One further note, the important thing is not the demon! The important thing is the healing and restoration of the person in the Kingdom of God to be witnesses to Jesus Christ. Do not get diverted into deliverance ministry. Its purpose has been to remove demonic blocks to the healing process. So once the wicked spirits have been removed return to the inner healing process as directed by the Holy Spirit.

PART IX

Relational Healing

By Rinda Dean

The Dunamis Project
Presbyterian-Reformed Ministries International

I. A Definition Of Relational Healing

"We know that we have passed from death to life because we love one another." *(I John 3:14)*

Relational healing is the process of the restoration of our ability to both give and receive love within our various relationships. We increase our capacity for fulfillment, as individuals, as members of the body of Christ, and as bearers of the Good News as we cooperate with God's original intent for relationships. Both the Old and New Testament Scriptures place a strong emphasis on maintaining relational integrity with the people that have been placed in our lives.

In order to "grow up into Christ who is our head," both individually and corporately, it is necessary to integrate all aspects of God's healing into our lives. The Biblical imperative to "be transformed" extends beyond our own inner growth into the larger context of our lives; it extends to each and every person to whom we relate.

The Scriptures indicate that Jesus deeply valued each exchange - every conversation and action- between himself and others. Jesus possessed the ability to transmit the healing love of his Father through word and action, to all who were willing to receive it. As we are open to receiving that same transforming love we, like Jesus, are also able to extend ourselves to others for healing. If we lack the knowledge and expertise required we have only to ask for the needed wisdom and resources and God's Spirit will show us the way.

Peary's Parable
The following excerpt is a "parable" illustrating the necessity of seeking relational wholeness in conjunction with other aspects of our growth in Christ. Here is a brief account of an experience of Admiral Peary's while exploring the arctic:

> "Peary relates that on his polar trip he traveled one whole day toward the north, making his sleigh dogs run briskly. At night he checked his bearings to determine his latitude and noticed with great surprise that he was much further south than in the morning. He had been toiling all day toward the north on an immense iceberg drawn southwards by an ocean current." (Families & Family Therapy- Minuchin,)

Peary's experience is much like ours when we attempt to progress in spiritual maturity apart from progressing in relational maturity. The Christian life invites us, not only to be transformed in character, but to be transformed in the broader scope of our existence as well. It is impossible to deepen our relationship with Christ without deepening our relationship with others. It is impossible to experience ongoing reconciliation in Christ, without experiencing ongoing reconciliation with others. If we seek only to grow intellectually or emotionally as Christians we jeopardize our own spiritual maturity and effectiveness for the Kingdom, much as Peary impeded his own goal of reaching the North Pole.

Relational healing, like spiritual and inner healing, is an ongoing process. Becoming more and more whole enables us to become more deeply grounded in reality; it provides us with the ability to see "the bigger picture" and not be confined to the limited view of our own individual "iceberg." Our temptation is often to minimize the importance of relational integrity and then wonder why a sense of fulfillment and joy eludes us.

II.   THE OLD TESTAMENT - Relational disintegration and God's plan for restoration

The restoration of our ability to give and receive love begins with the realization that each one of our relationships have been impacted by the effects of original sin, as was the case for our Biblical ancestors. As a result we have both caused and suffered hurts, within and without our families. The purpose of acknowledging our struggles, both as individuals and families, is not to assign blame, it is not to indulge in endless introspection, nor is it to bury us in despair. The point of facing our human shortcomings is to turn and be healed and released to grow together in God's love and his wonderful purposes for us.

A. Adam and Eve

In the Genesis account of the Garden of Eden God does a curious thing. He separates Eve out of Adam and then in the next breath directs them to be one again. Having just proclaimed that his creation of Adam was very good, he then states that "it is not good for man to be alone." God draws Eve from Adam's side, blesses them, commissions them, and instructs them as to their limitations. Adam, it seems, is to experience wholeness, not just within himself, but as he is joined to another human being, who is "bone of his bone and flesh of his flesh."

When Adam and Eve experienced spiritual death as a result of the Fall, they were not only separated from God; they experienced disintegration within their own personalities and the loss of the vital union between them. For the first time they experienced guilt and shame and immediately were thrown into conflict with each other. Their loss was monumental; no longer did they possess the ability to communicate effectively with God together, to walk and talk in the intimacy of the garden with their Creator, to be before each other naked and unashamed and to fully "become one".

B. Biblical Ancestors

The Genesis account shows that the relational separation that Adam and Eve experienced between themselves is born out in their son Cain's life as well. The effects of deception and disobedience then continued to be passed from generation to generation until the ninth generation when, as the sixth chapter of Genesis reports, violence and wickedness were pervasive upon earth. It was the preponderance of intense relational conflicts, spilling over into violent thoughts and behavior, which so grieved the Creator.

Genesis 6 states that:

"the earth was corrupt in God's sight and was full of violence...the Lord was grieved...and his heart was filled with pain" to the point where he decided to *"wipe humanity from the face of the earth...But Noah found favor in the eyes of the Lord."*

While the people of Noah's day are described as violent and corrupt, Noah himself is described as *"blameless among the people of his time, and he walked with God."* Even here, in this early Biblical account, behavior towards God and others is intricately bound up together. Noah's walk with God directly influenced his relationships with others.

Our early spiritual ancestors knew Yahweh, not through the written word, or a fellowship of believers, but through his loving revelation of himself to them personally. In spite of their many shortcomings and conflicts, God spoke over and over again to both husbands and wives, revealing his purposes to them, for their families, and for the coming generations.

Genesis 17:7 records but one instance of God's many conversations with Abraham conveying his desire to establish a generational covenant with him and his descendants. The relationship of parent to child was essential to the preservation and communication of the faith. The covenant was to be conveyed from one generation to the next and the successful continuation of the faith was dependent upon that generational bond remaining intact.

"I will establish my covenant as an everlasting covenant between me and you and your descendants after you for the generations to come, to be your God and the God of your descendants after you."

B. The Law and the Land

From his preservation of humanity through Noah, and his covenant with Abraham, to Moses' miraculous signs and wonders, to the giving of the Law and a Promised Land, God's overriding desire for spiritual and relational integrity is revealed. As Yahweh provides a place for his people wandering in the wilderness, the force with which Joshua and his men capture the Promised Land is sometimes startling. It was, however, in response to the pagan practices of idol worship (which is actually demon worship, I Cor.10: 20) which resulted in temple prostitution, and child sacrifice, that Yahweh rejected those earlier inhabitants of Canaan. God's loving justice would not tolerate a people's sinfulness which extended so far as to embrace idolatry, adultery, and murder; all of which were practiced in the name of religion.

The numerous Old Testament Levitical laws clearly outlined acceptable and unacceptable behavior, much of which was relational in nature. Of the Ten Commandments God gave to Moses on Mt. Sinai, the first five were directed towards our relationship with God, the last five towards others, beginning with our parents.

The following are some examples of Yahweh's careful attention to detail in the matter of human relations:

> *"If a person sins because he does not speak up when he hears a public charge to testify regarding something he has seen or learned about, he will be held responsible."* (Lev.5:1)

"No one is to approach any close relative to have sexual relations. I am the Lord." (Lev:18:6) (verses 7 through 18 elaborates on 'close relative')
"Do not give any of your children to be sacrificed to Molech, for you must not profane the name of your God. I am the Lord." (Lev:18:21)

"Do not lie with a man as one lies with a woman; that is detestable." (Lev.18:22)

"Do not go about spreading slander among your people." (Lev. 19:16)

"Do not endanger your neighbor's life." (Lev. 19:16)

"Do not hate your brother in your heart." (Lev. 19:17)

"Rebuke your neighbor frankly so you will not share in his guilt." (Lev. 19:17)

"Do not seek revenge or bear a grudge against one of your people, but love your neighbor as yourself." (Lev.19:16-18)

"Do not degrade your daughter by making her a prostitute, or the land will turn to prostitution and be filled with wickedness." (Lev.19:29)

"Rise in the presence of the aged, show respect for the elderly and revere your God. I am the Lord." (Lev.19:32)

"When an alien lives with you in your land, do not mistreat him. The alien living with you must be treated as one of your native-born. Love him as yourself, for you were aliens in Egypt. I am the Lord your God." (Lev.19:33)

When the Israelites sinned against one another detailed directives were provided concerning the appropriate sacrifices which were to be made. It is notable that sacrifices to God were required to repair damage done between people. The implication is that when one person sins against another person, God himself is offended as well. An example of God's close identification with his people is seen in Leviticus 2:6

"If anyone sins and is unfaithful to the Lord by deceiving his neighbor..."

And later in Proverbs

"He who oppresses the poor shows contempt for their Maker but whoever is kind to the needy honors God." (Prov.14:31)

C. The Prophets

Following miraculous signs and wonders, the giving of the Law and the Land, the Lord God next addresses Israel through the Prophets. Both the Major and Minor Prophets continue to reinforce

Yahweh's claim on his chosen people to put aside other gods and turn their allegiance to him alone. In the face of repeated rebellion on Israel's part God shows himself faithful over and over again. The straying of Israel's hearts and minds not only jeopardizes their relationship to Yahweh, but to each other as well.

Again, Yahweh does not settle for adherence to ceremonial law and the performance of religious duties, such as fasting, as the litmus test of Israel's faithfulness and obedience. Instead, he insists on fair and responsible treatment of one another as the real sacrifice acceptable to the Lord. God is apparently unimpressed with our religious disciplines such if they are severed from the everyday realities of our lives.

The 58th chapter of Isaiah records this exchange between Israel and Yahweh:

> *"Day after day they seek me out: they seem eager to know my ways…they ask me for just decisions and seem eager for God to come near them.*
>
> *Why have we humbled ourselves, and you have not noticed?*
>
> *Yet on the day of your fasting you do as you please and exploit all your workers. Your fasting ends in quarreling and strife, and in striking each other with wicked fists. You cannot fast as you do today and expect your voice to be heard on high.*
>
> *Is not this the kind of fasting I have chosen: to loose the chains of injustice and untie the cords of the yoke, to set the oppressed free and break every yoke? Is it not to share your food with the hungry and to provide the poor wanderer with shelter-when you see the naked, to clothe him, and not to turn away from your own flesh and blood?*
>
> *Then your light will break forth like the dawn, and your healing will quickly appear: then your righteousness will go before you, and the glory of the Lord will be your rear guard. Then you will call and the Lord will answer; you will cry for help, and he will say: Here am I.*
>
> *If you do away with the yoke of oppression, with the pointing finger and malicious talk, and if you spend yourselves in behalf of the hungry and satisfy the needs of the oppressed, then your light will rise in the darkness, and your night will become like the noonday."(Is.58:3-10)*

Blessing or Curse?
The prophet Malachi reemphasizes the prophetic theme of relational responsibility. As was the case with Abraham, Yahweh again insists that the generational bond be maintained, not only for the sake of the family, but the faith. The covenant must always be transferred from one generation to the next, which can only be accomplished through hearts turned to one another. The very last verse of the Old Testament clearly reveals this intent. The book closes with both a promise and a warning:

"See, I will send you the prophet Elijah before that great and dreadful day of the Lord comes. He will turn the hearts of the fathers to their children, and the hearts of the children to their fathers; or else I will come and strike the land with a curse." (Malachi 4:5-6)

After four hundred years of silence between the Old and New Testament, the opening chapter of Luke picks right up where Malachi left off. The prophecy of John the Baptist's birth and call, which was delivered to his father, Zechariah, by an angel, confirms Malachi's prediction and reaffirms his message.

"...he will be filled with the Holy Spirit even from birth. Many of the people of Israel will he bring back to the Lord their God. And he will go on before the Lord, in the spirit and power of Elijah, to turn the hearts of the fathers to their children and the disobedient to the wisdom of the righteous; to make ready a people prepared for the Lord." (Luke1:15-17)

John, the one baptizing with water, comes preaching the repentance of sins, insisting his followers "produce fruit in keeping with repentance." The "fruit" which he refers to is not to perform a particular religious duty, but to share clothing and food with those who have none. (Luke 3:11) John comes to prepare the way of the Lord and the primary evidence of this will be revealed through relational repentance – fathers and children will be turned to one another and the poor will be cared for.

John has been referred to as the last of the Old Testament prophets. He, like the Law and the Prophets, informed Israel that all was not well. Changes must be made in preparation for the one coming after him who would baptize, not with water, but with the fire of the Spirit.

"I baptize you with water for repentance. But after me will come one who is more powerful than I, whose sandals I am not fit to carry. He will baptize you with the Holy Spirit and with fire." (Matt.3:11)

III. The New Testament – Relational Healing - The restoration of our capacity to give and receive God's love

"Teacher, which is the greatest commandment in the Law? Jesus replied: 'Love the Lord your God with all your heart and with all your soul and with all your mind. This is the first and greatest commandment. And the second is like it: 'Love your neighbor as yourself'. All the Law and the Prophets depend on these two commandments."　(Matt.22:37,39)

This was the simple but profound response Jesus made in his reply to the Pharisee's question that day before the crowds. Jesus considered our relationships with others of utmost importance, secondary only to loving God himself. Just as the Old Testament taught consistency between expressions of love for God and relational integrity, so does the New Testament.

"Therefore, if you are offering your gift at the altar and there remember that your brother has something against you, leave your gift there in front of the altar. First go and be reconciled to your brother; then come and offer your gift."
(Matt.5:23)

While this passage in Matthew 5 addresses an instance in which someone else holds something against us, Matthew 18 provides directives for occasions in which we have been sinned against.

"If your brother sins against you, go and show him his fault, just between the two of you. If he listens to you, you have won your brother over. But if he will not listen, take one or two others along...if he refuses to listen tell it to the church...I tell you the truth, whatever you bind on earth will be bound in heaven, and whatever you loose on earth will be loosed in heaven." (vs.15-18)

It is within this context of relational restoration between believers that Jesus affirms his presence among us, for verse 19 states:

"...if two of you agree about anything you ask for, it will be done for you by my Father in heaven. For where two or three come together in my name, there am I with them."

The word "agree" as used here connotes more than simple intellectual assent among two or three people, instead it refers to a fundamental unity of heart and mind before God and each other, free from the obstacles of relational injury, which has just been addressed in verses 15 through 18. It is within this context of resolved conflicts and confirmed love that Jesus gives us authority to bind and loose and confidently ask our Father for "anything".

A. Jesus Last Hours

In Jesus' last hours with his disciples he speaks at length about love for his Father and his followers; and about our love for him and for each other. He reveals his desire for us in these concise statements:

"A new command I give you: Love one another. As I have loved you, so you must love one another. All men will know that you are my disciples if you love one another." (John 13:34-35)

"If you love me, you will obey what I command. And I will ask the Father, and he will give you another Counselor to be with you forever—the Spirit of truth." (John 14:15)

"If anyone loves me, he will obey my teaching. My Father will love him, and we will come to him and make our home with him." (John 14:23)

"If you obey my commands, you will remain in my love, just as I have obeyed my Father's commands and remain in his love. I have told you this so that my joy

*may be in you and that your joy may be complete. My command is this: Love
each other as I have loved you." (John 15:9-12)*

This imperative to love, Jesus says, actually originates with the Father himself.

> *"These words you hear are not my own: they belong to the Father who sent me."*
> *(John 14:24)*

B. Four Results of Obeying the Commandment to Love

Jesus promises four amazing things in these if we will but take his Father's words to heart:

1) He will send the Spirit of truth to us
2) He and his Father will come and make their home with us
3) He would put his joy within us and that it would be complete
4) The world will know that we are his disciples

The theme of love and obedience are interwoven continuously throughout chapters thirteen
through seventeen of John's gospel. Jesus speaks fervently of the love he and his Father share
and insists that if we are his disciples we will share in it as well. It is not coincidental that in the
midst of Jesus repetition of the commandment to "love one another" he includes the revelation
that he will be sending the Spirit of truth. He knows that what he is asking is impossible for us to
accomplish with our own limited resources.

As much as our human relationships are often a source of nurturing, strengthening, and rich
fulfillment there is also often a sense of deep disappointment which persists. It seems that,
especially within families, our deepest longings often go unmet, or even unvoiced; longings to be
heard and understood, to be respected and appreciated, to give and to receive. Too often we
remain unfulfilled in relationships, not because we want to, but because we lack the wisdom,
courage, or most importantly the power to effect a change.

IV. The Necessity of the Spirit's Empowerment for Fulfilling the Law of Love

The Old Testament Law and Prophets, and the baptism of John, were given to let us know what
God expects of us. They were also given to let us know, without a shadow of a doubt, that we
could not, in and of ourselves, fulfill the letter of the Law.

> *"For what the law was powerless to do in that it was weakened by the sinful
> nature, God did by sending his own Son..." (Rom.8: 3)*

Not only are we unable to fulfill the letter of the Law in our own strength, we are also not able to
fulfill the Law of Love on our own. Although we may accept our inability to satisfy the
demands of the Law on our own merit, we sometimes feel we just need to "try harder" to love

others. It is only as we acknowledge our weakness in this area and ask for supernatural help that we will be able to love as Jesus has asked us to. We cannot love and forgive others as Christ loved and forgave us apart from the power of the Spirit within us. Sometimes it is our very striving which hinders our healing with others. At other times it may be our unwillingness to admit that anything is wrong that keeps us from God's grace.

Jesus, having lived in perfect communion with his Father his whole life, experienced estrangement from him for the first and only time on the cross. He drops the intimate title of "Father" as he cries out "My God, my God, why have you forsaken me?" In embracing his sacrifice and accepting him as Lord and Savior all self-efforts to free our selves from sin can finally cease. At the same time all self-efforts to set ourselves right relationally can cease as well. As Jesus took on the sins of our hearts and minds, he also took on the sins of our broken relationships with others.

Spirit or Flesh?

It is imperative that we surrender the means and timing of relational restoration to the Lordship of Jesus Christ. Only the Spirit of God discerns the depths of the human heart and he alone is able to accomplish true healing. Suppose a little boy, having brought a broken toy to Daddy to fix, insists on continually yanking it back or grabbing the tools away from his father to fix it himself. His very efforts to "help" prolong or even prevent the job from getting done. So it is with our own self-generated efforts to either "fix" or "avoid" our own brokenness that we often get in the way of what God is attempting to do in our relationships with others.

In the third chapter of Galatians Paul asks "After beginning with the Spirit, are you now trying to attain your goal by human effort?" Paul upbraids the Galatians attempts to live out a life which is pleasing to God through their own resources and righteousness. We are often tempted to try to accomplish healing and reconciliation, which originate with the Spirit of God, in the strength of our own flesh. It will not be by proving that we are right (righteous) and the other person is wrong, that our relationships will be restored.

Does this mean that we sit idly by, knowing that misunderstandings or injuries persist? When the crowd asked Jesus "What must we do to do the works God requires?" Jesus replied, "The work of God is this: believe in the one he has sent." (John 6:28,29) This is the very first thing we must do; believe. Active, wholehearted dependence on the Lord is foundational to the healing process. We must believe that God desires wholeness for us in our relationships and trust that he knows the best way to go about accomplishing it. By relinquishing the "works" of fleshly strategies and relying instead on God's sufficiency we take a profound step towards transformation.

Seek Specific Guidance

As we bring our concerns about a particular relationship before the Lord the Spirit may direct us simply to wait on him. Some relationships are far more complicated than others and require more time and prayer. Sometimes, however, there will be specific things we are led to do. Referring back to the "broken toy" analogy, the Daddy in the workshop may, in fact, ask the little boy to turn on the light, or hand him a tool, or indicate some other helpful task. Likewise, the Holy Spirit may direct us to specific "tasks," along with exercising dependency on the Lord. Sometimes the task we're given feels too difficult, such as "if your brother sins against you, go and show him his fault". Once again we must acknowledge our own inadequacy, be driven back into prayers for wisdom and courage, and rely on the Spirit, not the flesh for empowerment.

Our heavenly Father understands our weaknesses better than we do ourselves and knows how hard it is for us to pursue healing. Although he may be asking us to do something difficult, he never requires anything without providing the power. If we can grasp, even in part, that his motive is that "our joy would be complete", then we can trust that whatever we're being asked to do will be well worth it. If, like a child, we ask for his help in the midst of our fears, disappointments, and broken trusts, he will gladly provide anything we need to take the next step. We have only to ask and obey.

V. Contexts for Relational Healing

A. Family

Just as a pebble tossed in a pond creates every widening concentric circles, emanating from the center outward, so our lives are comprised of "rings of relationships." Originally God was to inhabit the very center of our existence, with all other relationships being defined and determined by this initial one. Moving from that center outward, our first "ring" of relational experiences occurs within our families. These primary relationships which contain a tremendous potential for nurturing and instruction, for forming our identity and formulating our world view, also carry the potential for conflict, stress, and alienation.

B. Family of Faith

We often relate to people in our churches that we would not otherwise know outside of the church context. The wide diversity of those found within most congregations is a testimony to the fact that the body of Christ transcends human personalities, preferences and loyalties. As is the case with families, churches can provide a very positive context for worship, growth and service to others. However, due to our fallen humanity relational conflict is inevitable, whether it is within the leadership, member to member, or between leaders and members. Some of these conflicts are mild and short-lived, while others are intense and persist for years.

C. Friends and Acquaintances

From the center outward the ring of relationship widens to include friends and acquaintances. As can be true with family, and even church members, some of the people to whom we relate in our wider context of relationship may not know Christ. They may even be antagonistic to our faith. Regardless of another's relationship with God we are required to love them and to live at peace with them as much as we are able. Our intercession for others, asking that they would come to know and love Jesus, can effect great change in their relationship to God as well as others.

"Christ in You"

Whether in families, church, or community, the power of God can impact our relationships with one another, regardless of whether the others acknowledge Christ. If they are in relationship with you, and you have "Christ in you, the hope of glory", then they are coming in contact with Christ and his influence, whether they are consciously aware of it or not. In Christ, we need to take the authority that belongs to us and release the power of God into our relationships with family, friends, co-workers …everyone!

Sometimes the healing will occur quickly, sometimes it will take years, and sometimes we have to wait until we're with the Lord to experience the full results we long for. We can always ask for the gift of forgiveness from God when we have either injured or been injured, and with that we will experience great release and joy, but we may not always experience full reconciliation due to the circumstances involved. The essential thing is that our hearts are set toward healing, and that we are moving in that direction, not away from it, with our faith and obedience.

"Be Perfect"

"You have heard that it was said, "Love your neighbor and hate your enemy. But I tell you: Love your enemies and pray for those who persecute you that you may be children of your Father in heaven. If you love those who love you, what reward will you get? Are not even the tax collectors doing that? And if you greet only your brothers, what are you doing more than others? Do not even pagans do that? Be perfect, therefore, as your heavenly Father is perfect." (Matt.5:43-48)

It is interesting that Jesus makes this statement concerning perfection in the context of his directive to love others, even our enemies. This verse is sometimes interpreted in broad moralistic terms pointing to Jesus as the ideal to which we must somehow "strive to arrive." By so doing we slip back into the letter of the Law mindset in which we must somehow meet a certain set of exterior rules through the exercise of the will. Jesus is asking instead that we be perfected in love. The Sermon on the Mount, in which this passage is placed, is not a new set of religious laws to try to satisfy in our own strength, but a picture of what our love is to look like.

> *"For I tell you that unless your righteousness surpasses that of the Pharisees and the teachers of the law, you will certainly not enter the kingdom of heaven."*
> (Matt.5:20)

Pleasing God is not a matter of ceremonial sacrifice and religious duty. Each of our relationships, from the most intimate to the most casual, can now be submitted to the Lordship of Jesus and the empowerment of the Holy Spirit to glorify God the Father. This is what is truly pleasing to God.

D. Where are you?

If a relationship is troubled sometimes it is very difficult as human beings, and especially as Christians, to admit it. The Lord calls to us just as he did to Adam in the Garden, "Where are you?" And often our explanation resembles Adam's; "I was afraid…I hid." If our hiding is not as literal as Adam's, it is no less real. The simple reality is that there is no such thing as a perfect parent or a perfect child. There are no perfect single or married people. There are no perfect friends, pastors, or church members. In Christ we are extended the opportunity to admit to our failings and be freed, and yet we often choose, like Adam, to hide from God and each other rather than to heal.

At one point in my own life when I was struggling with a broken relationship I sensed the Lord telling me that "There is nothing I cannot heal as long as it is in the light." In our physical bodies, wounds that are left untended can fester and eventually spread disease to the whole body. In the same way relational wounds and unforgiveness will also fester and spread when left unattended.

In their book entitled <u>Beating Burnout</u>, authors Minority and Emir reveal an interesting outcome of a study they undertook to measure and assess the leading causes of burnout. They discovered that the leading cause of burnout in America, rather than being caused by stress related to overwork, was actually caused by bitterness. It seems it requires a large amount of energy to maintain an unforgiving heart and live with unresolved conflicts; so much so that we can actually impair our ability to function and weaken our immune systems through relational stress.

E. The Role of Satan in Relational Brokenness

Often our unwillingness to expose our wounds and sins is the very thing hindering us from closeness to Christ and others. Satan uses our human pride and fear of rejection to his advantage by feeding us lies that convince us that we can never be honest about who we really are and what hinders us.

Satan has manipulated our circumstances and us in order to wreak havoc on families, on churches, and society in general. His intent is to keep us from restoration with God and each other and one of his primary tools is shame. Mired in shame, either as a result of things we have done or of things done to us, we are reluctant to come out into the light of Christ. As long as misunderstandings and hurts remain unaddressed within a relationship, darkness has some degree of a hold upon us. The same principle that holds true in exposing Satan's lies in the process of inner healing also applies in relational healing.

The "lines" that we repeat continuously and the "scripts" that we act out day after day, originate within our fallen nature, are transmitted through relational wounds, and are used strategically by the evil one to keep us separated from each other. It is not that these "lines" do not contain some truth, the problem is that we often stay "stuck" repeating them, rather than experiencing change and growth.

"She doesn't understand me." "He won't listen to me." "All I get is criticism!" " They don't appreciate me and all I've done for them." "Why don't they trust me?" "My parents treat me like I'm still a child." "Why try? Things will never change." "That's just the way he is." "Why talk to them, they won't listen anyway."

These are frequent refrains from those who, having hoped for a meaningful relationship, have instead encountered difficulties resulting in discord or avoidance. The feeling of having something important to say, and not being able to adequately voice it, is not uncommon.

Satan is masterful at taking our God-given desires and concerns which are yet unmet, and twisting them into angry criticisms or silent withdrawal, which further separate rather than reconcile us.

VI. The Process of Relational healing

A. Jesus as Lord of Relationship

The Holy Spirit is referred to as Comforter, and Counselor. The first step to relational healing begins with an acknowledgement of Jesus' Lordship over our whole lives, inwardly and outwardly. We then need to invite the Holy Spirit to fill us and be released into every aspect of our lives, including every relationship. If we know Christ and are empowered by his Spirit, we can stand on the authority of God to destroy any Satanic strongholds that are hindering relational wholeness.

B. Steps to Relational Healing

1) Admit to yourself and to the Lord that your relationship with the other person needs healing and restoration; be specific about hurts you have inflicted or received.

2) Invite Jesus to become Lord of the relationship and ask the Spirit of God to release forgiveness and restoration to all involved.

3) Tell the Lord your longings and expectations for the relationship and surrender your own strategies.

4) Curb chronic complaining to others about the other person.

4) Seek intercession from trusted others, if needed.

5) Ask for specific guidance and direction from the Spirit, as confirmed by the Scriptures. If trusted others are able to provide godly support and counsel it may be helpful to seek their discernment regarding the direction you believe you have received.

6) Ask for any further resourcing you may need; prayer ministry, counseling, books, etc.

Speak the Truth in Love

Of any of the specific tasks we may be led to undertake, going to the other person to directly address your concerns is probably the most difficult. This step requires great wisdom and courage. Circumstances vary greatly from relationship to relationship. If the person you want to address is unstable in any way, but you believe the Lord is leading you to go to them, get help from a trusted, competent source. If the situation is safe, but you feel embarrassed or awkward, ask the Lord to give you everything you need to overcome your fear. You may want to ask a trusted friend to pray for you as well.

Often times a very important element of relational transformation lies in our willingness to speak and hear both sides. This is true whether we're attempting to resolve a conflict or simply increase our sense of fulfillment in the relationship. Each person has their own side to voice. Hearing the other person's perceptions and experience, as well as expressing our own, can increase our understanding of the other person significantly. Ask the Lord to provide a safe context in which to speak and listen to each other effectively.

Honest, responsible dialogue is an essential tool in the healing process. So often the old adage "It's not what you say, but how you say it…" is at least partially true. Although what we say is certainly important, it's also important how we say it. So often the "what" becomes lost in the "how", and our efforts at communication become unproductive and discouraging. For instance, it can be far more effective to simply state the fact that you're angry about something than to explode in an outburst.

Both the Old and New Testaments encourage us to "speak the truth". Often when faced with conflict we either communicate poorly or not at all. Sometimes it is fear or embarrassment that holds us back; sometimes pride or self-righteousness. Sometimes it is due to a lack of knowledge or modeling; we simply have never learned how to voice our side or listen to others.

So often I'll hear someone say they need to "confront" someone they're in conflict with. Confrontation seldom accomplishes anything except to throw the other person on the defensive to the point where they are unable to hear what it is you are trying to say. Paul instructs Timothy to "gently instruct" those he is called to work with; a word applicable to us as well. If we explain our concern to the other person gently, but firmly, we are more likely to attain positive results than if we approach them with either a cowering or confrontive attitude.

Whatever the obstacle may be it is essential to our overall wellbeing to grow and mature in the area of communication with others. The area of increasing effective communication skills has largely been given over to our educational system, to the therapy room, or the business setting, and yet the Scriptures historically have provided excellent guidelines for the people of God in this crucial area of human relations.

C. Hindrances to Healing

1) Sometimes people believe that relational healing is not possible because the others involved refuse to acknowledge any shortcomings. In the same way that it only takes one person to open the door to invite a guest into the house, it only takes one person to invite the Lord to release healing in a relationship.

2) We may wonder if it's God's will to heal a particular relationship. God's word asks us to love everyone, even our enemies, therefore we can pray in confidence, asking for healing in every one of our relationships. It may take months, or years, or not occur until we are with the Lord, but just by engaging in the process of prayer we allow the Holy Spirit, the Comforter and Counselor, to begin to do his work. This, in and of itself, brings us closer to the Lord and will bear fruit in our lives.

3) We may be reluctant to forgive because we feel this is minimizing or denying the hurt that was caused. We feel it is unfair to simply excuse someone's behavior, especially where severe abuse has occurred. In forgiving another the exact opposite actually occurs. Rather than minimizing the offense, as it is exposed to the perfect light of Christ and the unfathomable sacrifice that he offered in the other's place, we realize how hurtful the offense really was that it would cause Christ to have to suffer and die.

4) Another barrier to seeking relational healing stems from the misunderstanding that forgiveness equates with reconciliation. Another's unwillingness to change negative behavior, extenuating circumstances, or even death, can prevent us from enjoying the restoration of a relationship while here on earth. Regardless of these hindrances, we are still free to forgive and enjoy freedom from the bondage of bitterness and pain.

5) Sometimes we are frustrated and confused because we have sought to forgive someone and just seem unable to do it. Jesus knows how difficult it is for us to forgive. Ask him to meet you where you are and provide what you need to be able to embrace forgiveness. Then ask him to seal what he has done in your heart forever.

As we call upon God's strength in the midst of our weakness we are able to stand up to our adversaries of relational healing, both within us and without. God asks us to believe in his healing love for our lives and to release others from past hurts through receiving and extending forgiveness. It is only as we appropriate the work of the cross and the empowerment of the Holy Spirit that we are able to grow in our capacity to love and be loved by our Father and others.

The Cross is the Key

The key to relational healing is the cross of Jesus Christ, and the forgiveness extended to us there. Take some time regularly to be with the Lord. Ask him to take you to the cross with him. Linger there until you can grasp something of the supreme sacrifice of the Father surrendering his Son to separation and death, so that we could be with him and each other forever. Ask to hear Jesus speak the words deep within your own heart and mind "Father, forgive them, for they know not what they do". As we allow ourselves to enter into the mystery of the cross we will be transformed through an experiential knowledge of God's all consuming passion for his people.

VII. Summary Conclusion: The Ancient Paths

> *"Stand at the crossroads and look; ask for the ancient paths, ask where the good way is, and walk in it, and you will find rest for your souls." (Jer.6:16)*

> *"For this is the message you have heard from the beginning, that we should love one another." (I John 3:11)*

Though we can never be restored to perfect integrity here on earth, any more than we can enjoy perfect communion with our Creator, we can still commit ourselves to walking the "ancient path" of loving one another. If the lawlessness upon the earth at Noah's time grieved the heart of

God, surely our present lovelessness must sadden him as well. If the Lord is grieved by this lack of love, it is also reasonable to assume that he is pleased, perhaps even delighted, by our smallest steps of obedience in this area.

The eleventh chapter of Hebrews says that God responded to Noah's faith by sparing the human race and animals from extinction, and that because of Abraham's faith, God established a covenant to last throughout the generations. In the same way each of us are able to effect great change in the lives of those around us if we will engage our faith by listening to and obeying the Spirit of God. As we do this we will grow in our capacity to give and receive love and to spread the Good News of God's transforming power in human lives.

"For the love of God is this, that we obey his commandments. And his commandments are not burdensome, for whatever is born of God conquers the world."

(I John 5:3,4)

Addendum
Revised Chapter 10
The Healing Ministry of Jesus Christ

February 6, 2003

Jesus' Ministry of Physical Healing

By Brad Long and Cindy Strickler

The Dunamis Project
Presbyterian-Reformed Ministries International

I.   Jesus Is Our Model for Physical Healing

Moving in healing ministry rests upon the gifts and power of the Holy Spirit. Our task is to receive the provision that God gives us and to learn how to cooperate with the Holy Spirit in this work of Jesus Christ.

Healing ministry is divinely inspired and directed. But there is a learning process that includes study, sharing in ministry with those gifted in healing, and, as led by the Holy Spirit, putting into practice what one has learned.

This is the model of teaching that Jesus used with His disciples. They listened to Him teach and preach. He was available to answer questions. They also were with Him when He healed the sick, cast out demons and did other mighty works. Lastly, their education did not remain at the theoretical level; He sent them out two-by-two empowered to do what He had done.

I believe that we may receive the same process of instruction as we prepare for healing ministry. First, we must understand the theological and biblical basis of healing ministry. The second phase is to be an apprentice to those who are gifted in healing ministry. The third step is to actually set out and, as led by the Holy Spirit, begin to pray for those who need healing.

In regard to the second step, remember that while the Holy Spirit may raise up those who may serve as our mentors, Jesus Christ is to be our primary model. Observe the following chart which lists the ways that Jesus engaged in healing ministry.

II.   Chart Of Healings By Jesus Christ

Individual Healings by Jesus Christ

	Matthew	Mark	Luke	John
Nobleman' son				4 : 46-54
Unclean spirit		1 : 21-29	4 : 31-37	
Simon's mother in law	8 : 14-15	1 : 29-31	4 : 38-39	
A leper	8 : 1-4	1 : 40-45	5 : 12-16	
Paralytic carried by four	9 :1-9	2 : 1-12	5 : 17-26	
Sick man at the pool				5 : 2-18
Withered hand	12 : 9-14	3 : 1-6	6 : 6-11	
Centurion's servant	8 : 5-13		7 : 2-10	
Widow's son raised			7 : 11-17	
Demoniacs at Gadara	8 : 28-34	5 : 1-20	8 : 26-36	
Issue of blood	9 : 20-22	5 : 25-34	8 : 43-48	
Jairus' daughter raised	9 : 18-19 23-25	5 : 22-24 35-43	8 : 41-42 49-56	
Two blind men	9 : 27-31			
Dumb devil possessed	9 : 32-34			
Daughter of Canaan woman	15 : 21-28	7 : 25-30		
Deaf, speech impediment		7 : 32-37		
Blind man of Bethesaida		8 : 22-26		
Epileptic boy	17 : 14-21	9 : 14-29	9 : 37-42	
Man born blind				9 : 1-38
Man blind, dumb, possessed	12 : 22-30		11 : 14-26	
Woman bent double			13 : 10-17	
Man with dropsy			14 : 1-5	
Raising of Lazarus				11 : 1-44
Ten lepers			17 : 11-19	
Blind Bartimaeus	20 : 29-34	10 : 45-52	18 : 35-43	

Multiple Healings by Jesus

	Matthew	Mark	Luke	John
Crowd at Peter's door	8 : 16-17	1 : 32-24	4 : 41-41	
Crowds after leper healed			5 : 15	
Crowd near Capernaum	12 : 15-21	3 : 7-12	5 : 17-26	
Answering John	11 : 2-6		7 : 18-23	
Before feeding 5,000	14 : 13-14		9 : 11	
At Gennesaret	14 : 34-36	6 : 53-55		
Before feeding 4,000	15 : 29-31			
Crowds beyond the Jordan	19 : 1-2			
Blind, lame in temple	21 : 14			
Some sick of Nazareth	13 : 53-58	6 : 1-6		
All kinds of sickness	4 : 23	6 : 56		
Every sickness and disease	9 : 35			
All oppressed	(Acts 10:38)			

Don Bartow[1]

III. Observations On The Physical Healing Ministry Of Jesus

A. Jesus Healed a Great Variety of Disorders

When one looks at a serious case, such as a terminal cancer patient or a person with a mental illness that persists despite the best therapies available, one may be tempted to despair that he or she is beyond God's help.

However, in the Gospels we find a great variety of disorders that Jesus healed. His work included minor illnesses, such as healing Peter's mother of a fever, and medically impossible miracles, such as healing Lazarus from four days of death and decomposition.

This fact should build our faith and expand our expectation to understand that no disorder or condition is beyond the reach of Jesus' healing love and power.

---

[1] Don Bartow, Bartow's Healing Handbook (Canton, 1992), pp. 126-128, 134.

B. Jesus' Approach To Physical Healing Conformed To The Basic Principles Of Participation In What The Holy Spirit Was Doing

1. Jesus' physical healing and the dynamic of the Holy Spirit in power ministry

The Holy Spirit moved through Jesus in power to bring about physical healing. This dynamic has been described throughout this manual as well as in other Dunamis manuals. The dynamic is summarized in Teaching Chart #3 at the end of this section.

2. Jesus Moved in the Kairos Moments of the Holy Spirit

The period following Jesus' baptism was a kairos moment in which the Holy Spirit was moving to heal. The multitudes of people who were healed and the two references to the nature of the power coming forth from Jesus suggests that this was a special time in which the Holy Spirit was moving.

> "...and the power of the Lord was with him to heal." (Luke 5:17)

> "...and all the crowd sought to touch him, for power came forth from him and healed them all." (Luke 6:19)

The whole of Jesus' ministry was characterized by healing, even to the restoration of the ear of the high priest's servant at the time of His arrest (Luke 22:50). There were periods when healing was especially prominent, and all were motivated and empowered by the Holy Spirit.

Likewise, in our ministry of healing there may be special periods of the Holy Spirit's healing activity, or a time when He especially reveals His presence and power in this way. This is in accord with the episodic manner in which the power of the Holy Spirit is often manifested.

In the course of a meeting there may be times when the Holy Spirit is especially moving in healing ministry. These times generally follow periods of worship and the proclamation of the word of God. For example, at PRRMI Prayer Mountains and Dunamis Project retreats, there are almost always periods when it seems as if a window opens and the fresh breeze of the Holy Spirit's presence blows through. The result is effective healing ministry. These are kairos moments, and we must act or speak as led by the Holy Spirit. If we fail to discern and to obey the inspiring presence of the Holy Spirit, signs and wonders will not occur. We must also discern whether the Holy Spirit is moving in a particular person or situation. This discernment will guide us in how we are to pray.

3. The Compassion Of Jesus

Though participating with the Holy Spirit in power ministry as listed above may sound mechanical, it is really relational.

The heart attitude of the one through whom the Holy Spirit works is a basic ingredient. Jesus' ministry of healing is not a cold, technical, disinterested process of using the gifts of the Holy

Spirit like tools. No! The medium of the power of the Holy Spirit is Jesus' deep love and compassion for the people. The following examples illustrate this.

> a. Jesus had compassion on the crowds of people who followed Him. His compassion led Him to pray for them, as well as to work miracles of healing and provision on their behalf (Matthew 9:36 and 14:14).

> b. In Mark 1:41, when the leper came beseeching Him for healing, it was written of Jesus, "*Moved with pity, he stretched out his hand and touched him, and said to him, `I will; be clean.'*"

> c. Despite the crowd that tried to quiet them, two blind men cried out to Jesus, "*Have mercy on us, Son of David!*" and Jesus "*in pity touched their eyes, and immediately they received their sight and followed him.*" (Matthew 20:34)

> d. When Jesus saw the funeral procession of the widow's only son and the widow weeping behind the bier, moved by compassion, He touched the bier and commanded the young man to arise. This awesome display of the power of God over the finality of death sprang from Jesus' heart, which was broken at the sight of such suffering (Luke 7:11-17).

> e. This same deep compassion is evidenced when Jesus wept at the tomb of Lazarus.

If we are to move in the gifts and power of the Holy Spirit, we must have the Holy Spirit within us shaping our character and yielding, above all, the fruit of love. In 1 Corinthians 13, St. Paul made it clear that the only atmosphere consistent with the nature of the Holy Spirit's being and power is love.

Those who are most effective in healing ministry are often those who, like Jesus, have great compassion for the sick. They are willing to have their own hearts broken by exposure to human suffering. If unable or unwilling to experience the pain or the burdens of others, one should stay away from healing ministry.

Often one form of preparation for healing ministry is to have suffered deeply oneself. Usually it is those who have experienced healing themselves whom God uses most effectively for the healing of others.

It was not until I (Brad) found myself afflicted with a severe back problem that I had the empathy and compassion necessary to pray effectively for others with physical problems. Until this had happened, I did not have any idea what it was like to be seriously ill or rendered helpless by a physical problem.

4.   Jesus Worked in Accord with the Precondition of Faith

a. Jesus Discerned the Faith to be Healed

Jesus knew faith was a critical ingredient to moving in healing ministry. In His own country, He found that where people knew his family and took offense to Him, He was not able to move in the power of the Holy Spirit. His own obedience in providing the Holy Spirit with raw material was largely in vain.

"And he could do no mighty work there, except that he laid his hands upon a few sick people and healed them. And he marveled because of their unbelief." (Mark 6:1-6)

Often, before dealing with sickness, Jesus first dealt with the crucial element of faith.

Jesus discerned the presence of faith and proceeded with the healing.

Jesus saw peoples' faith and knew that if He obeyed the leading of the Holy Spirit, prayers for healing would be effective. Note that the faith could be that of the one seeking healing, or it could be of the one who brought someone to receive healing.

"And, behold, they brought to him a paralytic, lying on his bed; and when Jesus saw their faith he said to the paralytic, `Take heart, my son; your sins are forgiven.'" (Matthew 9:2)

What did Jesus see when He "saw their faith?" This is directly relevant to us for we also need to discern the existence of faith.

Some possibilities:

> * There are some definitive expressions of faith. In Mark 2:1-5, four friends, in order to get a man to Jesus, made a hole in the roof and lowered the man down. This visibly expressed their belief that Jesus could do something about the situation.
>
> Likewise, there may be little indications that the person has faith. For instance, they may have come forward to ask for prayer. If they did not believe that it would make a difference, they would not have come forward in the first place.
>
> * Faith may be intuitively discerned in the expressions of the person. His eyes will reveal awe, love, or trust toward Jesus.
>
> * The Holy Spirit may give the gift of discerning faith. This may be expressed through an intuitive awareness that faith is present.

Often there was a verbal expression of faith.

The text records that often those who received healing did so after verbally expressing their faith that Jesus was able to heal. At other times it was not the sick who expressed faith but, rather, someone who prayed on their behalf. When no one acknowledged the presence of faith, Jesus Himself did.

Examples:

1. **The leper cleansed:** Matt 8:2-4, Mark 1:40, Luke 5:12

Kneeling before Jesus the leper said, *"Lord, if you will, you can make me clean."*

This suggests an affirmation of faith that was born of reverence and awe of Jesus.

2. **The centurion's servant healed:** Matthew 8:5-13, Luke 7:2

The centurion expresses a faith in the power of Jesus so deep that even Jesus is amazed.

> "...But the centurion answered him, `Lord, I am not worthy to have you come under my roof; but only say the word, and my servant will be healed. For I am a man under authority, with soldiers under me; and I say to one, "Go," and he goes, and to another, "come," and he comes, and to my slave, "Do this," and he does it.' When Jesus heard him, he marveled, and said to those who followed him, `Truly, I say to you, not even in Israel have I found such faith...' And to the centurion Jesus said, `Go; be it done for you as you have believed.' And the servant was healed at that very moment."* (Matthew 8:5-13)

The healing power of Jesus was not bound by time or space. He did not actually have to lay hands on the servant. Rather, He simply spoke the word and, though some distance away, the servant was healed *"that very moment."*

3. The woman with the flow of blood: Matthew 9:20, Mark 5:24-34, Luke 8:42

This story shows the woman's tremendous faith and trust in Jesus through her own inner dialogue in which she said to herself, *"If I only touch his garment, I shall be made well."*

This matter of faith was so important that Jesus, discerning of its presence, did not let the healed woman slip away unnoticed. He called attention to her by acknowledging her faith. He said, *"Daughter, your faith has made you well; go in peace, and be healed of your disease."* (Mark 6:34)

The nature of faith

Part of the nature of faith is that it is to be acknowledged orally. It is not a worked up mental attitude of expectation that something will happen. Rather, it is an expression of trust that Jesus is able to work. It is the ground of a relationship with Jesus. It is faith of this nature that Jesus requires. He is not calling us to "faith healing." Rather, He is calling us to trust Him, the Healer.

Jesus' final word to the centurion, *"Go; be it done for you as you believed"* is repeated to others. To the two blind men Jesus said, " *...According to your faith be it done to you."* (Matthew 9:27-31)

"According to your faith." Does this reveal a fundamental principle of God's dealing with human beings? Does the shape of our belief determine the shape of God's relationship with us? God in His sovereignty does seem to act in accord with the largeness or smallness of our trust (faith) in what He can do. To those who trust Jesus as the centurion did, Jesus is able to do great things. But for those with no trust, or who discount Jesus all together, He is able to do little.

What then is this strange thing called faith? In some deep mysterious way it may be the medium connecting the spiritual with the material that enables the spiritual realm to shape the physical realm. Without it, the spiritual is unable to connect with and work in the material realm.

In healing ministry it is important that we give people the opportunity to express their faith in who Jesus is and what He can do. The oral expression of faith is often the first step in obedience of living by faith. It also may serve to build up the faith of others.

b. Jesus Challenged People to Have Faith

Often in Scripture, a person would not voluntarily proclaim his faith. Perhaps this was because his faith was weak, or perhaps it was because he did not know that the proclamation of faith was a part of the preparation for Jesus to work in healing. Jesus then would directly ask the individual about his faith.

In Matthew 9:27-31, Jesus asked the two blind men who sought healing, "*Do you believe that I am able to do this?*" When they said to him, "*Yes Lord,*" He touched their eyes and said, "*According to your faith be it done to you.*"

In the same way, at the tomb of Lazarus, Jesus first dealt with the faith of Martha before moving to raise Lazarus from the dead. Apparently Martha knew and trusted in Jesus' love and healing power for she had already confessed her confidence that if Jesus had been there, Lazarus would not have died. Jesus, however, pushed her faith even further.

> Jesus said to her, "*I am the resurrection and the life; he who believes in me, though he die, yet shall he live, and whoever lives and believes in me shall never die. Do you believe this?*"

> She said to him, "*Yes, Lord; I believe that you are the Christ, the Son of God, he who is coming into the world.*" (John 11:25)

Why did Jesus ask, "*Do you believe that I can do this?*" Why did He ask a person to confess his or her faith? There may be two reasons:

i. The question commands human participation.

There is a similar dynamic here as when God asked Ezekiel, standing before the valley of dry bones, "*Son of man, can these dry bones live?*" Or when God asked Cain, "*Where is Abel your brother?*" The question brought the person into participation with God acting in the world.

Healing is an act of God, but God has made us free and responsible. Thus, we are called to have a part in the healing work of Jesus Christ, regardless of whether the healing is our own or someone else's.

In healing ministry it is important not to encourage an unhealthy passivity. The person being healed is often called to take part in the healing. Thus, the question, "*Do you believe that Jesus can do this?*" Or as Jesus asked the blind beggar Bartimaeus, "*What do you want me to do for you?*" (Mark 10:51)

ii. The question imparts faith.

I suspect that there is another reason that Jesus asked, "*Do you believe that I can do this?*" Through the very act of asking, He enabled the person to discover that the Holy Spirit had already given the gift of faith within him, and he was unaware of this until directly asked. Also, in challenging the person to have faith, He also may have been imparting the gift of faith itself.

c. Jesus' Compassion When We Do Not Have Faith But Want It

For Jesus to work mightily, He promised that all we need is faith as small as a mustard seed (Matthew 17:20). Yet, for some, in the face of life's impossibilities, even faith this small is not present.

Faith in Jesus can not be worked up by an emotional effort nor can it be willed into existence. Rather, it comes by the inward working of the Holy Spirit. So what do we do if we do not believe? We fling ourselves upon the mercy of God.

Our paradigm for dealing with a lack of faith when we want to believe and cannot is Mark 9:14-29, the story of the father with the demonized boy. This is a powerful account which reveals our human condition as well as the mercy of God. One can see the agony of the father. One can see the demon manifest in the presence of Jesus Christ, tormenting the boy. Then Jesus told the father that all things were possible if he would just believe. And then the desperate father cried, "*I believe! Help my unbelief!*" (Mark 9:25) Then Jesus, in mercy, acted to deliver the boy.

Healing and deliverance rest upon the mercy and sovereignty of God. While faith is the medium of God's work in the world, faith itself is a gift from the One who chooses to work His good pleasure. While discerning the presence of faith is important in healing ministry, do not rely completely upon it. Rely on Jesus! Confess you unbelief and trust yourself to Jesus who loves us so much that He indeed may help our unbelief.

5.   Jesus Provided The Holy Spirit With The Raw Materials For Healing Ministry By Speaking Or Acting Out The Word Of God

Introduction

We do not have access to what was going on inside of Jesus as He discerned the leading of the Holy Spirit. All we have is the record of His obedience.

Time and time again Jesus acted, we assume at the leading of the Spirit, to provide the Spirit with the raw material with which to work. If Jesus had not been obedient and had not acted, then regardless of the moving of the Holy Spirit, nothing would have happened.

Likewise, the Holy Spirit may be moving in a place or may be eager to work in a person. There may be faith in Jesus Christ, and it may be the time for God to manifest His love and presence. But He is waiting for someone to listen and to obey and, in their obedience, to provide the materials with which the Holy Spirit may work. An awareness of how Jesus was called to move with the Spirit may guide us in discerning the ways that the Holy Spirit may call us to cooperate with Him in healing ministry.

We shall see that Jesus' obedience took a variety of forms such as laying on of hands or speaking a word. There was not, I believe, any "magic" about the words or actions of Jesus. Rather, at that time and place, they were the embodiment of the word of God, empowered by and used by the Holy Spirit.

While empty themselves of any power to heal, in some cases these forms do have a connection with the conditions that they are being used to heal. I do not believe the connection, however, is that of a medical remedy suited for a particular disorder. Rather, the connection is that of allusion and metaphor. A finger put in the ear or washing in the river are metaphors of the Holy Spirit's opening the eyes of the deaf or washing clean the skin of the leper.

a. Touch

In the majority of cases in Scripture, Jesus touched people. As summary of this aspect of His ministry:

> "*Now when the sun was setting all those who had any that were sick with various diseases brought them to him; and he **laid his hands on everyone** of them and healed them.*" (Luke 4:40)

Jesus' touch was tender and natural as when He healed Peter's mother-in-law:

> "*And when Jesus entered Peter's house, he saw his mother-in-law lying sick with a fever; **he touched her hand**, and the fever left her, and she rose and served him.*" (Matthew 8:14-15)

Sometimes Jesus radically departed from social convention in order to touch a person who was not only sick but also ritually unclean. This was the case with the leper:

> "*...and behold, a leper came to him and knelt before him, saying, "Lord, if you will, you can make me clean." **And he stretched out his hand and touched him**, saying, "I will; be clean.*" (Matthew 8:2-3)

In reaching out His hand toward this man, Jesus pierced though the man's socially constructed prison that had shut lepers out of human community as unclean.

At times Jesus touched people in the places where they were afflicted. Concerning the two blind men who called out to Jesus:

> "*And Jesus stopped and called them, saying, "What do you want me to do for you?" They said to him, "Lord, let our eyes be opened." And Jesus in pity **touched their eyes**, and immediately they received their sight and followed him.*" (Matthew 20: 32-34)

At the time of Jesus' arrest, one of the disciples drew a sword and struck the slave of the high priest cutting off his ear.

> "*But Jesus said, "No more of this!" And he **touched his ear** and healed him.*" (Luke 22:51)

Why did Jesus often touch people when the story of the Centurion reveals to us that His healing power worked even at a distance? Likewise, why may we be led at times to lay hands on the sick? Does God need us to do that for His divine power to work?

Reasons for the effectiveness of touch in healing ministry:

1. **Touch is a natural human way of communicating love and concern.**

Sickness is a time of social isolation when we hunger for inclusion in the human community. In Jesus' day some diseases, such as leprosy, carried with them the additional stigma of being unclean which automatically meant that one was an outcast from society. AIDS and other sexually transmitted diseases carry the same stigma.

By touching these outcasts, Jesus broke through the wall of isolation and communicated love and acceptance. This in itself was immensely healing.

Furthermore, I believe there is something basic to our nature that needs the touch of other human beings. When I was in Vietnam working for the Holt Adoption agency, I saw how orphaned children who were fed, but not touched, became listless and often died for no apparent medical reason.

2. The Holy Spirit may use touch as a "conductor" for healing power and blessing.

The Holy Spirit is not some kind of spiritual electricity, so not just any touch will serve this purpose. To serve as a "conductor" of His healing power and blessing, the hands must be extended in faith and obedience. Jesus' touch was received as healing and also as a blessing.

3. Laying on of hands may be a physical sign upon which faith in Jesus may be focused and made vivid.

Faith is to be in Jesus Christ alone. But in our weakness and humanness, faith in an invisible God often needs tangible visible expressions. We need hooks upon which to hang our belief that Jesus can heal. Jesus' touch or our touching Jesus is just such a hook.
In the story of the woman cured of the flow of blood, it was the hem of Jesus's garment that centered her faith. Peter was used so mightily in healing ministry that people even placed the sick in the street so that his shadow would fall upon them (Acts 5:15). There was not any intrinsic power in these things. Rather they were faith contacts that led people to focus faith in the true source of healing power, Jesus.

Lest we are overcome by our reformed revulsion at the idolatry and superstition that has often been associated with such practices, let me suggest that Jesus recognized better than the theologians our need for such contacts for faith beyond just the word in Scripture. For example, He gave the bread and wine of the Lord's Supper, the water of baptism, and the symbol of the cross.

The bread and wine are a special symbol that when received in faith and animated by the Holy Spirit become the presence of Jesus Christ. Likewise, the laying on of hands as Jesus laid on hands, when received in faith and directed by the Holy Spirit, may become the healing touch of Jesus Himself.

b. Word Spoken

the whole person

Jesus also provided the Holy Spirit with His inspired Word. The Word of God has power to accomplish the end for which it was spoken. This is the nature of God. There is not a gap between what He intends in His Word and the accomplishment of His Word. No shadow falls as in T.S. Eliot's poem:

> Between the idea
> And the reality
> Between the motion
> And the act
> Falls the Shadow
> (T.S. Eliot - *The Hollow Men*)

Not faith in person but because of faith

Through Isaiah the prophet, God said of His intentions expressed in His word:

THE PRMI *DUNAMIS PROJECT*
THE HEALING MINISTRY OF JESUS

(handwritten margin notes:) with no faith healed 70% / 10% within church

*"For as the rain and the snow come down from heaven,
and return not thither but water the earth,
making it bring forth and sprout,
giving seed to the sower and bread to the eater,
so shall my word be that goes forth from my mouth;
it shall not return to me empty,
but it shall accomplish that which I purpose,
and prosper in the thing for which I sent it."*
(Isaiah 55:10-11)

In the healing ministry of Jesus, there is the dynamic combination of the word of God spoken into the embrace of the Holy Spirit. Ways that the Word of God is spoken in the ministry of Jesus:

A word spoken to the whole person

(handwritten margin notes:) There is no technique / It's the Holy Spirit working / we must partner with H. Spirit

The man with the withered hand:

> *"Again he entered the synagogue, and a man was there who had a withered hand. And they watched him, to see whether he would heal him on the Sabbath, so that they might accuse him. And he said to the man who had the withered hand, "Come here." And he said to them, "Is it lawful on the Sabbath to do good or to do harm, to save life or to kill?" But they were silent. And he looked around at them with anger, grieved at their hardness of heart, and said to the man, "**Stretch out your hand.**" He stretched it out, and his hand was restored. The Pharisees went out, and immediately held counsel with the Herodians against him, how to destroy him."* (Mark 3:1-6)

The crippled man who was let down through the roof:

> *"And behold, men were bringing on a bed a man who was paralyzed, and they sought to bring in and lay him before Jesus;....Which is easier, to say, `Your sins are forgiven you,' or to say, `Rise and walk'? But that you may know that the Son of man has authority on earth to forgive sins" - **he said to the man who was paralyzed - `I say to you, rise, take up your bed and go home.'** And immediately he rose before them, and took up that on which he lay, and went home, glorifying God...."* (Luke 5:18-26)

When He dealt with the demonic, Jesus seemed to rely upon the power of the Word rather than on other means:

> *"That evening they brought to him many who were possessed with demons; and **he cast out the spirits with a word**, and healed all who were sick."* (Matthew 8:16)

In dealing with the boy who was epileptic and demonized:

> *"...And of the crowd answered him, "Teacher, I brought my son to you, for he has a dumb spirit; and wherever it seizes him, it dashes him down; and he foams and grinds his teeth and becomes rigid; and I asked your disciples to cast it out., and they were not able.*

"And he answered them, `O faithless generation, how long am I to be with you? How long am I to bear with you? Bring him to me.'

"And they brought the body to him; and immediately it convulsed the boy, and he fell on the ground and rolled about, foaming at the mouth.

"And Jesus asked his father, "How long has he had this?" And he said, `From childhood. And it has often cast him into the fire and into the water, to destroy him; but if you can do anything, have pity on us and help us.' And Jesus said to him, `If you can! All things are possible to him who believes.' Immediately the father of the child cried out and said, `I believe; help my unbelief!'

*"And when Jesus saw that a crowd came running together, **he rebuked the unclean spirit, saying to it, `You dumb and deaf spirit, I command you, come out of him, and never enter him again.'** And after crying out and convulsing him terribly, it came out, and the boy was like a corpse; so that most of them said, `He is dead.' But Jesus took him by the hand and lifted him up, and he arose. And when he had entered the house, his disciples asked him privately, `Why could we not cast it out?' And he said to them, `This kind cannot be driven out by anything but prayer (and fasting).'"*
(Mark 9:17- 29)

This is a detailed account of a major deliverance by Jesus. While there are many elements of this story, the emphasis here is that the breakthrough came by Jesus' directly commanding the spirit to leave. The spirit left! This clearly demonstrates the authority that Jesus had over spirits. It was His word of command, filled with authority and directed by the Holy Spirit, that brought freedom to this tormented family.

While often including healing, the episodes of casting out demons are in a little different category than that of healing physical or emotional problems. Demons must be dealt with through a direct word of command because they are intelligent, non-physical entities that recognize and must submit to the authority of Jesus. One does not cast out a sickness or a disorder as one does an evil spirit. There are times, however, when Jesus seems to speak to the condition.

Speaking to the condition in the case of the deaf and dumb man:

*"...he put his fingers into his ears, and he spat and touched his tongue; and looking up to heaven, **he sighed, and said to him, `Ephphatha,' that is, `Be opened.'** And his ears were opened, his tongue was released, and he spoke plainly."* (Mark 7:33-35)

Jesus spoke to the person a word of healing.

Healing also seems to have taken place during the preaching of Jesus:

"When the crowds learned it, they followed him; and he welcomed them and spoke to them of the Kingdom of God, and cured those who had need of healing."
(Luke 9:11)

"And Jesus went about all the cities and villages, teaching in their synagogues and preaching the gospel of the Kingdom, and healing every disease and every infirmity." (Matthew 9:35)

This clearly shows that a natural result of Jesus' preaching ministry was the healing of the sick. He did not merely talk about the Kingdom of God. It happened! In their midst as the Word went forth empowered by the Holy Spirit it immediately brought fruit.

Whether the healing took place while Jesus was preaching or whether He preached or taught and then healed is not clear, but the "and" suggests that both took place in the same context, though not necessarily simultaneously.

This is of vital importance. If we are to do the works that Jesus did, we need to change radically our understanding of the purpose and nature of preaching. Rather than modifying our preaching to fit our western worldview by turning it into a rational presentation of truth, we need to see preaching as a mode of God's activity. Jesus not only presented truth, but the people experienced the power of truth! As St. Paul affirms, *"...but to those who are called, both Jews and Greeks, Christ the power of God and the wisdom of God."* (1 Corinthians 1:24) In the preaching we see the wisdom, in the signs and wonders we see the power. In the ministry of Jesus where the Kingdom of God was present wisdom and power went together. Today, as the Holy Spirit moves and the Kingdom of God is present, Christ will also be present as the wisdom and power of God.

c. The People are Required to Perform Some Act of Obedience in order to Participate in their Healing.

Again and again, in obedience to the leading of the Holy Spirit, Jesus provided the Word with which the Spirit worked. It seems that the role of the person who received the healing was simply to receive Jesus in faith. He may have been asked to confirm his faith, but the rest was the work of Jesus.

In most of the healings one may see hints of a divine-human cooperation. For example, the man with the withered hand was commanded first to "stand over here" and then to, "stretch out his hand." These were actions requiring his participation and initiative, even though, of course, it was humanly impossible for him to stretch out his withered hand. Yet he acted in obedience, the power of the Holy Spirit became active, and he was healed.

Time and time again the power of the Holy Spirit is manifested when a step is taken in faith and obedience. Often it is Jesus' faith and obedience; other times it is that of the one being healed.

The following are occasions when Jesus called for the person to participate through a specific act of obedience in what the Holy Spirit was doing:

The man born blind was healed as he acted in obedience

> *"As he said this, he spat on the ground and made clay of the spittle and anointed the man's eyes with the clay, saying to him, `Go, wash in the pool of Siloam' (Which means Sent).* ***So he went and washed and came back seeing.***" (John 9:6-7)

The ten Lepers

> *"On the way to Jerusalem he was passing along between Samaria and Galilee. And as he entered a village, he was met by ten lepers, who stood at a distance and lifted up their voices and said, `Jesus, Master, have mercy on us.' When he saw them he said to them, `Go and show yourselves to the priests.'* ***And as they went***

they were cleansed. Then one of them, when she saw that he was healed, turned back, praising god with a loud voice; and he fell on his face at Jesus' feet, giving him thanks. Now he was a Samaritan. Then said Jesus, `Were not ten cleansed? Where are the nine? Was no one found to return and give praise to God except this foreigner?' And he said to him, `Rise and go your way; your faith has made you well.'" (Luke 17:11-19)

It was the obedience of the ten lepers that opened the doors to God's healing power. Notice that Jesus confirmed that it was the faith that went with and was expressed in the obedience that allowed the Holy Spirit to work.

Sometimes the Holy Spirit may lead us in a similar manner to ask for an expression of obedience as we pray for someone who is sick. We must be very careful here, however, that it is the Holy Spirit speaking and not us. For example, there have been those who have demanded that a person give up his medicine and later the person died.

This obedience is not a way of testing faith. Rather, when led by the Holy Spirit, it is faith in action, and it provides the Spirit with the Word with which to work His purposes.

d. A Combination of Words or Actions

Jesus not only used a variety of means, but He used the means in various combinations. Often an action such as the laying on of hands is done with the word spoken.

For example:

> *"...And there was a woman who had had a spirit of infirmity for eighteen years; she was bent over and could not fully straighten herself. And when Jesus saw her,* **he called her and said to her, `Woman, you are freed from your infirmity.'** *And* **he laid his hands upon her,** *and immediately she was made straight, and she praised God."* (Luke 13:11-13)

Actions often need the Word of God spoken to clarify their full meaning and import. The actions themselves have no power to heal. Rather they are the incarnations of the Word of God that the Holy Spirit uses.

e. Jesus Used a Diversity of Methods in Physical Healing

In healing ministry there is often the temptation to develop fixed routines or formulas that may have worked in the past and to apply them without discernment in all cases.

I once heard, "to the person who is good with a hammer most everything looks like a nail!" Likewise, in healing ministry it is easy to let one's area of giftedness become the filter through which all of the cases are perceived.

For example, some follow the example of Jesus' rebuking Peter's mother-in-law's fever, and they rebuke all ailments. Others approach everything as if it were a demon. Others always assume that legs need lengthening, whereas others always command some display of faith.

At a Prayer Mountain I once saw a Chinese evangelist treat every person exactly the same way. He always placed his hand on the person's head and shouted, "In the name of Jesus, be healed." Some were truly healed, but others left confused or had their faith badly shaken.

As we have clearly seen, Jesus used certain approaches that were means of expressing the Holy Spirit's power. He also used a tremendous diversity of means. We may use some of these same means by setting them up as formulas or techniques, but they may also become a very serious block to effective prayer for the following reasons.

1. Healing ministry rests upon the power and the guidance of the Holy Spirit, not upon some technique.

While Jesus used certain approaches to healing, the power to heal did not rest in the technique. Rather, Jesus was empowered by the Holy Spirit and "did what He saw the Father doing." The techniques were governed by the leading of the Holy Spirit.

When we get locked into one method of healing prayer that we apply to all people without careful discernment, it is often an indication that we have stopped listening to the guidance of the Holy Spirit and have started to rely upon ourselves.

Listening to the Holy Spirit is hard work. It requires that we maintain the discipline of prayer as well as walking in the light. It is much easier simply to develop a routine way of praying. While God may sometimes honor such prayers, in the long run, it is not the way to effectively participate with Jesus in healing ministry.

As we grow experienced in healing ministry, we will develop a large store of past experiences of approaches that have worked. We must also be familiar with the variety of ways that Jesus ministered to the sick. This background gives us a deeper awareness of the ways that the Holy Spirit may work.

As we begin to pray for someone, we may need to suspend judgment about the approach to use until we have listened deeply to the person and have sought guidance from the Holy Spirit.

In approaching healing prayer we need to be as flexible in method as Jesus was.

2. When we stop listening and depend upon a technique, there is a very good chance that we will seriously hurt those who have come to us for ministry.

When we apply technique without careful listening, we fail to fully participate in the unique things that the Lord may be doing in the individual's life.

Applying the wrong approach or assuming that one knows exactly what the person's problem is may add to his emotional hurt, weaken his faith, or altogether discredit the healing work of Jesus.

A book of horror stories could be written about how well-meaning, but undiscerning, Christians have wracked havoc in the lives of others. People have died because they were told to let go of their medication as a test of faith. Emotional damage has been inflicted by casting out demons that were not there. People have left feeling condemned because they did not have enough faith when the healer ordered them to get up and to walk, and so on. **Let this be fixed in your heart: When God calls you to healing ministry, He gives you an awesome responsibility. He places in your hands His hurt,** vulnerable children. **You are given power to minister to them, but that ministry must be wrapped in love and must be led by the Holy Spirit.**

3. **When one humbly listens to the Holy Spirit and to the person, there is always a blessing.** The person prayed for experiences God's love and care which always brings healing that is spiritual, often emotional, and sometimes physical.

4. **We may fall into the sin of thinking that we may bind the sovereign creator of the universe to our formulas where He can be easily manipulated.** This is not participation in Christ's healing ministry, but rather it is magic.

It is a very heady to see someone healed through one's prayers. So persistent is our sinful nature and so clever is our adversary that we may be tempted either to claim the glory for ourselves or to attempt to control this power that brings such wonderful results. *It is easy to step over the line of having a repertoire of methods the Holy Spirit may use to using these methods to manipulate the Holy Spirit.*

Falling into magic is a very real possibility that every healer must relentlessly guard against.

An example: Anointing with oil is a method recommended to us in James 5:14 - 15. In the history of the Church, oil also has been found to be highly effective in mediating God's healing power to us. But why is anointing with oil effective? (See section on Anointing with Oil in this manual.)

While the oil itself may have *medicinal* purposes, it does not have intrinsic supernatural healing powers. One falls into magic when one begins to shift the focus away from the healer, who is Jesus working through the Holy Spirit, to accord supernatural healing properties to the oil itself or to the ritual of anointing. The same may be said of the laying on of hands, the use of holy water, or the use of other symbols.

In the healing ministry of Jesus, just as there were different disorders healed, so, too, were there a variety of ways that Jesus ministered the healing. This diversity of approaches may help us to guard against the pernicious tendency to fall into formulas and routines that may hinder us from being totally dependent upon the guidance of the Holy Spirit.

C. The Three Fold Dynamic of Jesus' Healing work.

The dynamic of the Jesus cooperating with the Holy Spirit fits within the larger pattern of the three phases of Jesus' healing ministry already introduced in this manual. The actual work of physical healing will belong to Phase 2 of Engagement.

Physical Healing must be prepared for by Phase 1 which is establishing the context for the Holy Spirit to work. This often consisted of Jesus establishing the relational bridge with the person to be healed. Often with physical healing those who are sick driven by their need for healing will actively reach out to Jesus themselves and make contact. Also their friends and family would seek Jesus out on their behalf. For example in Matthew 9:27-33. First two blind men cry out, "have mercy on us, Son of David!" Then a man who was demon possessed and could not speak as brought to Jesus. After Jesus has brought the healing, there is often the move to phase three which is some form of discipleship.

The invalid at the pool of Bethesda may provide an illustration of these three phases of Jesus' work.

	John 5:2-15
Phase 1 Establishing the Context. Jesus reaches out to the invalid and establishes the context with the question, "Do you want to get well?"	2 Now there is in Jerusalem near the Sheep Gate a pool, which in Aramaic is called Bethesda and which is surrounded by five covered colonnades. 3 Here a great number of disabled people used to lie-- the blind, the lame, the paralyzed. 5 One who was there had been an invalid for thirty-eight years. 6 When Jesus saw him lying there and learned that he had been in this condition for a long time, he asked him, "Do you want to get well?"
Phase 2 Engagement with the Holy Spirit and the person. With a command Jesus heals the man and he walks.	7 "Sir," the invalid replied, "I have no one to help me into the pool when the water is stirred. While I am trying to get in, someone else goes down ahead of me." 8 Then Jesus said to him, "Get up! Pick up your mat and walk." 9 At once the man was cured; he picked up his mat and walked. The day on which this took place was a Sabbath, 10 and so the Jews said to the man who had been healed, "It is the Sabbath; the law forbids you to carry your mat." 11 But he replied, "The man who made me well said to me, 'Pick up your mat and walk.'" 12 So they asked him, "Who is this fellow who told you to pick it up and walk?" 13 The man who was healed had no idea who it was, for Jesus had slipped away into the crowd that was there.
Phase 3 Discipleship Jesus tells him to stop sinning and the man goes off testifying that it was Jesus who healed him.	14 Later Jesus found him at the temple and said to him, "See, you are well again. Stop sinning or something worse may happen to you." 15 The man went away and told the Jews that it was Jesus who had made him well. (NIV)

When facing great physical needs in Phase 2 it is easy to so focus on the physical aspects that one may overlook the other forms of healing that that the Holy Spirit may be wishing to work.

When physical healing actually does take place the next danger is to get stuck on Phase 2 and not move forward with Phase Three which is discipleship. Healing in what ever form, must be followed by the invitation to follow Jesus Christ.

IV. Physical Healing And the Theological Framework of Creation Fall and Redemption.

Recall the Theological Framework that was established at the beginning of this manual. Jesus has come into a fallen world to restore God's original vision of creation. This healing work starts from the innermost part of us, the seat of our relationship with God, and works outward to include our physical being. This process is like what Lewis called "death working backwards," as the ravaging effects of the Fall are reversed.

In this course on healing we have distinguish the following foci of Jesus' healing work. Each corresponds to dimensions of reality that were affected by the Fall and are being restored in God's Kingdom.

Spiritual Healing

This is the restoration of our fundamental relationship with God the Father. Reconciliation with God takes place through the death of Jesus Christ and through our being born again through the Holy Spirit into the new reality of the Kingdom of God (2 Corinthians 5:17–19).
This is the most basic form of healing. It is the first step in restoring us to the original environment of intimacy with God, for which human beings were created, with ready access to the Tree of Life. Being birthed into this new reality of the Kingdom of God sets in motion all other forms of healing.

Inner Healing

Inner healing is part of the process of undoing the hurtful effects of sin. This includes the results of our own sin and being sinned against. It is a process of restoring to wholeness the shattered image of God within us. As the wounding of sin is overcome we increasingly reflect the character of Jesus Christ. This is the process of sanctification, which comes from the work of the Holy Spirit within us (2 Corinthians 3:17–18).

Physical Healing

Physical healing takes place as God is restoring us to our originally intended health and immortality. Jesus Christ, the first to be resurrected from the dead, has promised eternal life to all who believe in Him. Through Jesus we are brought into the river of life. The physical healing ministry of Jesus in the New Testament, now at work through the Holy Spirit, is a harbinger of the abundant life in the Kingdom to be fulfilled in the new heaven and new earth (John 11:25–26). This form of healing will only be completed with the Resurrection, which "death shall be no more."

Relational Healing

Relational healing takes place as Jesus heals our web of fallen relationships. This starts with the most basic relationship between male and female. It then extends, in ever-expanding spheres, to include the healing of injustice between social classes and to the healing of the nations. The apostle Paul grasped the Gospel of Jesus Christ when he foresaw the healing of the three major social divisions of his society: "There is neither Jew nor Greek, slave nor free, male nor female, for you are all one in Christ Jesus" (Galatians 3:28).

Relational healing will be completed with the restoration of the Holy City, through which will flow the river of life.

This process of ever-expanding healing overcoming the effects of the Fall will be consummated in the new Heaven and the new Earth, which is Eden restored. We have already started to experience this in Jesus Christ.

Overcoming the Devil and Casting Out Evil Spirits

Jesus' work of restoring humanity and creation to God's original purposes involved the necessary warfare of overcoming and driving out the enemies of our redemption (Acts 10:37–38). Jesus came to destroy the works of the devil. Today, through the Holy Spirit, at each dimension of healing, Jesus continues to do the work of deliverance and exorcism to remove these supernatural blocks to the advancement of the Kingdom of God.

In this course we have addressed different forms of healing. Human nature, however, is like a tightly woven cloth; the separate threads may be teased out but they have their full meaning only as a woven unity. In practice, these various forms of healing are completely interwoven and interdependent. While it may be convenient to start with physical or inner healing, we are called to engage with Jesus in restoring the whole person in the whole Kingdom of God. This will involve us in all dimensions of a person's being. Only a "systems" approach within the overarching motif of the Kingdom of God is big enough to embrace the full wonder of Jesus' healing ministry. While we may be led into physical healing because of some physical need, we must be open to all the Holy Spirit may want to do. We must also take into account the deepest needs of the person which are not physical but spiritual.

The Kingdom Is *Now*, but Is Also *to Come*

The healing ministry of Jesus in all its forms must be understood as a part of what it means to be in the Kingdom of God. This Kingdom, through the Holy Spirit, is present and real now; nevertheless, it is incomplete. We still live in a world where there is sin and death. Spiritual healing, or the restoration of our relationship with God, was completed by the sacrifice of Jesus on the cross; the rest of our healing is in process. Our complete healing from the effects of the Fall awaits the fulfillment of the Kingdom of God at the end time when there will be a new heaven and a new earth.

This accounts for the disturbing phenomena of why Christians face illness, emotional wounding, loss and physical death. It also helps us understand why miracles of physical healing do happen for some, while for others healing is completed only in the resurrection. Above all, this process of healing from the inside out implies that our priority must be to bring people to Jesus Christ, who said, "I am the way and the truth and the life. No one comes to the Father except through me" (John 14:6). This is the beginning place of all the gracious healing works of God, who loves us more than we can imagine and wants us to live again in Eden. (From Let Jesus Heal Your Hidden Wounds)

Addendum
The Healing Ministry of Jesus Christ

Revised Chapter 11
February 6, 2003

Praying For Physical Healing

By Brad Long, Bob Whitaker
Revised by Cindy Strickler

The Dunamis Project

PRESBYTERIAN-REFORMED MINISTRIES INTERNATION

I.   A Model of How to Pray for the Sick (Brad Long)

How do we pray for the sick? The following is a step-by-step practical process that I have found helpful. This represents a summary of principles learned from the ministry of Jesus and from practical experience in healing ministry. In the Appendix these steps are found in outline form without commentary for use in teaching or while in ministry. Further elaboration of these steps may be found in the section which reflects on case studies.

Before You Pray

A. Interview (Listen with all of your ears!)

1. Listen to the person--What is his spoken or unspoken need?

2. Listen to God--Is God giving you an insight or a word of knowledge as the person explains his need?

3. Listen to one another--Others on the team may observe something that you have missed, or they may have received guidance.

The fundamental principle of participating with God in power ministry is to listen. Through listening to the Holy Spirit we may receive the guidance as to what to do or to speak so as to provide the connection between word and spirit and to give shape to the power of God.

Listening takes place directly in one's own heart as well as through open sharing with co-workers who may also receive guidance.

In addition to listening to God, it is imperative that one be attentive to the person for whom is being prayed. Jesus did not rely entirely upon words of knowledge. Rather, He asked questions of those for whom He prayed. For example, to the father of the epileptic, demonized boy He asked, "*How long has he had this?*" And to the man whose eyes were being healed, Jesus asked, "*What do you see?*"

The purpose in interviewing the person for whom to pray is not to get a complete medical history. Rather, the purpose is to simply determine where to lay one's hands and how to pray. One is also seeking to discern the real source of the problem. Often one may start with prayers for physical healing but may be led directly into prayers for emotional healing.

Listening with all of our ears means that we need to get past just the meaning of the words and get into the emotional tone. We must also listen for possible impressions from the Holy Spirit.

Examples:

A man once asked me to pray for his heart, but as I listened, I could sense that there was great deal of tension in his voice, suggesting that he was deeply troubled. Then I had a spontaneous image of two ganglia in his testicles. I told him the image that I had received and asked if there was not some problem other than his heart. He said that the real problem was in his testicles but that he had been embarrassed to say so. He was profoundly blessed to see that God had revealed the real problem.

A ministry team prayed for a woman who had had polio and had been left with one leg much shorter than the other and one arm nearly useless. As she talked about her physical difficulties, I could hear the anger in her voice. I also received the quiet nudging of the Holy Spirit that we needed first to deal with a heart filled with anger. So we first prayed that she would be able to forgive God for not healing her. As we prayed, she cried bitterly and gradually a sense of peace filled her. Later we laid hands on her leg, and it visibly began to grow and strength seemed to return to her arm.

We would have missed the real need of the person as well as the careful leading of the Holy Spirit if we had not listened. It is through listening that the prayer for healing, while not always resulting in physical healing, always results in blessing.

B. DIAGNOSIS

1. Is the problem physical, emotional, or both? Is there an underlying physical, emotional, or spiritual cause? This is not the time to do a complete medical history or to give medical advice. Rather, you need to know just enough to be able to pray intelligently.

2. Decide which type of prayer is most appropriate for the situation and pray as led by the Holy Spirit.

There are different types of prayer that may be used. The one chosen depends partly upon the condition of the person and how clearly the guidance is given by the Holy Spirit. Basically one may be led to do any of the things we have seen in Jesus' healing ministry. We may also be led by the Holy Spirit to do something not specifically mentioned in Scripture.

Some possibilities:

* Speaking to the condition - Originally human beings were given dominion over the earth. This has been corrupted and reduced by the fall, but in Jesus Christ it is restored to us. At times one may use this authority to speak to parts of the body that require healing, just as Jesus spoke to the wind and the waves. For example, in the case given above we spoke to the leg and commanded it to grow out. It perceptively began to grow.

* A prayer of command - This command is for the whole person to be healed. Often it involves some physical act that would be indicative of healing. Peter prayed a prayer of command with the lame man at the Gate Beautiful in Acts 3. Be careful with this one and do it only if clearly led by the Holy Spirit.

* Soaking prayer - This is not mentioned in Scripture. Most of Jesus' healings seem to have happened relatively quickly. But it is the practical experience of those involved in healing ministry that there are some conditions that seem to require extended "soaking" prayer. This may be prayer for an extended period of time by a prayer team. The prayer may last for an hour or more.

* Praying with images - Sometimes the Holy Spirit will give those praying a clear image of the person in a healed condition. If this happens, the image may be used as the basis for prayer. Pray first that God will accomplish what is suggested in the image, and then give Him thanks that He is doing it.

* Prayer of Deliverance - Sometimes one may discern that the physical problem is caused by an evil spirit. In this case one may, in the name of Jesus, cast the spirit out.

* Petitionary prayer for healing - If there is not a clear leading of the Holy Spirit as to a specific form of prayer, I believe it is always appropriate to offer up to God, in the name of Jesus Christ, the request that the person be healed.

* Prayer of blessing - There are times when a simple blessing in the name of the Father, Son, and Holy Spirit is needed. One may also ask God to bless the person in a special way, such as asking that the Holy Spirit surround the individual with an awareness of the love of Jesus Christ. I always conclude prayers for healing with a blessing.

C. Discernment of the presence of faith

1. Discern whether faith is present for the Holy Spirit to work.

2. Remove any obvious blocks to faith or people who are actively getting in the way of faith.

3. Do not condemn anyone for a lack of faith; rather trust the mercy of God.

Through faith we are able to receive God's healing. Often if faith is not present, the Holy Spirit is hindered in healing ministry. Discern if there are people present who either lack faith or who are actually taking away faith. These people should be asked to leave. Apparently this is what Jesus did before raising the little girl from the dead. First He put everyone out of the room. Their lack of faith and focus upon the obvious reason for their grief may have hindered the work of the Holy Spirit. (Mark 5:35-43)

While faith is a necessary ingredient to healing, it need not be the faith of the sick person.

One may be led to ask questions to either increase faith or to determine if it is present.

Faith is a gift. It cannot be worked up. If it is not present do not put the guilt for its absence on anyone, especially the person seeking healing. Rather, bless them and pray that God in His mercy will give what is needed.

When You Pray

A. Worship

Praise God for who He is, for what He has done, and especially for His mercy and love. Praise is the first step of expressing our faith. In praise we transcend our ourselves and our own burdens and focus upon the love, presence, and power of God. Praise is the primary way of involving the presence of the Holy Spirit.

B. Ask the Holy Spirit to come and minister

This step is really a continuation of worship. One intentionally invites the Holy Spirit to be present. Though the Holy Spirit is universally present, we are seeking His special presence and special work. It is similar to invoking the presence of the Holy Spirit before the Lord's Supper and believing that Jesus, while universally present, will be especially present in the breaking of bread.

I find that it is helpful to wait a few moments before proceeding with prayer. If one invites the Spirit to come, we should give Him a few moments to manifest His presence.

1. Move in the kairos moments

There may be special times when the Holy Spirit is moving. Be alert to such moments and listen carefully for instructions as to what to do about them. It is in the kairos moments that we find reality malleable and the Holy Spirit eager to give to us the words or actions He intends to use for the accomplishment of His purposes.

A special movement of the Holy Spirit may be discerned through a word given, a sense of quickening, or physical indications such as heat or movement.

2. Anoint with oil

According to James 5 we may anoint the sick with oil. This may be done simply and without a lot of elaborate ritual. My approach is to make the sign of the cross on the person's forehead with my forefinger, which has been dipped in oil. As I do I say, "I anoint you in the name of the Father, Son and the Holy Spirit, as a sign and a symbol of His grace towards you."

Any kind of oil may be used, but most people use olive oil. While it does not have to be especially blessed by a priest or bishop, often before anointing the person I pray a short prayer of consecration such as: "Lord, by your Holy Spirit please set this oil apart from all common usages, now to this holy use, so that it may be used as a sign of Your presence."

Anointing with oil may be effective in healing ministry for the following reasons:

 a. When led by the Holy Spirit, oil may serve as a concrete expression of our obedience.

 b. Oil may be a tangible support for our faith.

 c. Oil serves as a visible symbol of the invisible presence of the Holy Spirit.

3. Agree together in prayer

Jesus told us that wherever two or three agree on earth it shall be done for them (Matthew 18:19-20). As we pray for the sick, there is power in several people agreeing in prayer.

4. Pray in the name of Jesus

We may ask for healing or command healing in the name of Jesus.

> *"Whatever you ask in my name, I will do it, that the Father may be glorified in the Son; if you ask anything in my name, I will do it."*
> (John 14:13)

When the disciples meet the lame man at the Gate Beautiful, they commanded him in the name of Jesus of Nazareth to walk (Acts 3:1-10).

There is power in the name of Jesus Christ. It flows, not out of some magic use of the name, but out of the relationship we have with Jesus Christ.

5. Pray with laying on of hands

It was the custom of Jesus to lay on hands as He prayed for the sick. We may follow His example with great benefit.

Consider the following reflections concerning laying on of hands:

a. Laying on of hands is helpful for supporting faith as well as communicating love and concern.

b. Respect the person--always ask permission before laying on hands.

c. Generally lay hands on the afflicted area if it is medically and socially appropriate to do so.

d. Be aware of sexuality! While moving in the Spirit is spiritual, we still retain our sexuality. Members of the opposite sex should lay hands only on neutral areas. It is also best if prayer is done in a team setting rather than one-to-one.

C. Be specific

God seems to appreciate our specific petitions. In petition specifically state the problem one faces and specifically ask that it be healed. Don't pray general pious words. The person's problems are usually urgent and specific. When led by the Holy Spirit to do so, be specific when praying prayers of command. Speak to a physical condition and tell it what you want it to do.

D. Shouting is unnecessary

Increasing volume does not increase faith or authority. In fact, shouting may hinder accurate discernment as well as become an opportunity for the flesh to take over. Authority in your prayer comes from being obedient to the leading of the Holy Spirit and abiding in Jesus Christ.

E. Discernment of what the Holy Spirit is doing

Discernment is a process that may involve the following:

1. Keep Your Eyes Open

This is so you can see the effect of your prayers and can be in touch with the ministry team. This is very important. If you keep your eyes closed when you pray for a person, you are very apt to miss the signs that the Holy Spirit is working. With your eyes closed, you will also miss the visible impact that your prayers may be having on the person and, thus, lose the vital feedback to make sure that you are on track.

Once a coworker was praying for a man for healing of depression. Each time she mentioned the name of Jesus, the person's face would be distorted with a grimace suggesting the presence of a demon. Because her eyes were tightly shut, she was completely missing what was happening. Her sweet prayer for healing was off track because of a lack of feedback and discernment. Another coworker, with open eyes, detected what was going on and steered the prayer in another more productive direction.

2. Dialogue With The Person

This is a vital part of discernment, and it brings the person into the healing process.

a). At times you may want to ask, "Do you feel anything happening?" "Is the Lord saying anything to you?" This type of feedback can help immensely in discerning what is happening.

I have found that the very act of asking whether anything is happening actually increases faith and contributes to things actually happening. In this there is an element of risk for nothing may be happening. If this is the case, it must be faced.

Sometimes the person being prayed for seems to hesitate to honestly say that nothing is happening. This may come out of a desire not to embarrass the person who is praying for him. Or he may feel that it is a lack of faith to state what is obviously true.

b). It also may be helpful to explain to the person what you are doing and why. This enables the person to more actively participate in his healing. It also removes some of the unnecessary mystery from the proceedings and focuses attention on the real mystery, the living presence of Jesus Christ.

3. Dialogue With The Team

You are not the only one who can get guidance. Constantly be in touch with the team. Talk to one another about what is going on and check out their guidance and your guidance or impressions with theirs. It may be helpful to explain to the person being prayed for that this dialogue is not a lack of faith or reverence but rather a way of better cooperating with the Holy Spirit.

4. Check Out Insights, Nudges, Visions Or Words Of Knowledge

Do not assume anything, but rather, test and discern everything that comes to you or to the team. The insights, nudges, visions, or words of knowledge may be from the Lord, but on the other hand, they may not. If they are, great blessing may come and effective healing may take place. If they are not, but we assume that they are, we may seriously damage the person in our care.

Test leadings of the Holy Spirit by sharing them tentatively in the following manner:

a). Put them into question form; e.g. "Do you have a problem getting along with your brother?" Instead of "God says you hate your brother."

b). Preface them with "I think the Lord may be saying..." This gives room for discernment and leaves the person the freedom to reject the word as not relevant to their situation.

c). Describe the image, the symbol, or the picture God is using to impart knowledge to you and let the team and the person being prayed for confirm if they are actually from the Lord. This is better than enforcing a lot of authority and categorically stating that God showed you thus and such.

F. Concluding the prayer

1. Know when to stop. Sometimes it is difficult to know when to stop praying for a person. Consider the following guidelines:

a). Stop when there has been healing.

b). If there has not been a change or if there have not been signs of the Holy Spirit's special workings, it may be time to stop. If, however, things are happening keep going until the manifestations cease.

c). If one has exhausted all clear guidance, it is time to stop.

d). The Holy Spirit may come with the leading that it is time to stop for now.

2. Conclude with praise for what God has done.

3. I always conclude the prayer for healing by blessing the person in the name of the Father, Son, and Holy Spirit.

After Prayer Follow-Up

A. If there is not a change:

1.   You might arrange another time to pray.

2.   It may be helpful for them to know that most healing is progressive.

B. Give appropriate counsel to those who are healed as well as to those who are not healed.

C. Avoid giving a lot of advice.

D. Always minister the whole love of Jesus Christ to the whole person. We are praying for people, not just for physical conditions.

E. Conclude with blessing the person.

F. Help the person into the body of Christ where there can be ongoing prayer and nurture.

G. For those who pray:

1.   **Dealing with a lack of healing**: Our job is to love with Christ's love, to listen intently for the leading of the Holy Spirit, and to obey! It is God's responsibility to bless and to heal.

2.   **Dealing with evidence of healing**: Give all of the glory to Jesus and let one's faith be built up for future healing ministry.

II.   Further Reflection on Different Types of Prayer (Bob Whitaker)

A. Prayer of Command

On at least six recorded occasions, other than exorcisms, Jesus healed through a word of command. Thus in Mark 2:11 He said to the paralytic, "*Rise take up your pallet and go home.*" (See also John 5:8.) Several times He told a person to go and to do something, and as they went in obedience, the healing happened (Luke 17:14, John 4:50, John 9:7).

When my children were little, this seemed like a very practical way to help them to learn faith and to experience healing. Sometimes one of them would get up in the morning with the beginnings of a cold or a tummy-ache or even a slight fever. It seemed to me that the Lord was challenging me to take Him at His word. So my wife and I would pray for their healing and then send them off to school with words like, "Now you just trust the Lord to take that (fever, cold, sniffles) away from you on your way to school or soon thereafter." Invariably they would come home well and report that "it" went away early in the day.

The faith of children, when encouraged in this way, is astounding. There were times, however, when the condition was sufficiently serious that we were hesitant to send them off to school, and we kept them home in bed and/or called the doctor.

When it comes to serious conditions that require a person to be in a wheel chair, in braces, or on crutches, I would not dare to command them to rise and walk or to throw away their crutches unless I received an assuring word of knowledge and a strong quickening of the Spirit. Novices in healing ministry need to learn to discern the leading of the Lord, and to see small things healed before they take on paralytics. In other words, in using the prayer of command, we need to learn to walk before we run.

But we **do** need to start walking! The Lord loves us to trust Him as the centurion did and to be ready to speak the word of faith. He would rather that we err on the side of boldness than timidity. If we are motivated by love and compassion and the exhortation is rising in your heart, it is well to say, "You just go right ahead and do what you have to do; I'm praying for you and you're going to be okay." Or we may be convinced to say, "In Jesus' name, be healed."

B. Soaking Prayer

Some laundry has to soak awhile before the stubborn dirt comes out. Diseases and hurts are like that. We are much indebted to Francis MacNutt, who has helped us to see the more and less of healing and prayer. Sometimes a short prayer in faith brings quick results. More often, as in Luke 18:1-8, we have to persevere in prayer before we see results. Usually, if we pray in loving faith with the laying on of hands or anointing for some needy person, there is some degree of blessing, peace, or healing after a brief time. Quite often that small degree grows to a greater degree of healing as we continue in waiting prayer, especially when a team of two or three prays.

Guidelines:

1. As a general rule almost everyone would benefit from a period of soaking prayer every week if we had enough prayer teams with enough time.

2. If the person prayed for experiences a quickening of the Spirit[1], it is especially important that the prayer team continue to pray until the quickening leaves. This strong, pleasant heat can last twenty to thirty minutes with increasing therapeutic value the longer it lasts.

3. If there is some degree of blessing or healing in the first time of prayer, we have found it is good to meet and to pray weekly as long as benefits result. Often six or seven weeks is profitable; for diseases like cancer or MS it might be profitable for six months to a year.

4. Soaking prayer does not have to be non-stop prayer at each session. It can be interspersed with Scripture readings, sharing of relevant testimonies, singing of Christian music, and reading of inspirational healing messages. I was once part of a team who was praying for a severely crippled arthritic; we took one soda break and time out for relaxed conversation. During a two or three hour period of soaking prayer, the person was considerably freed up in the movement of her joints.

C. Speaking to the Condition

When Jesus prayed for the sick, He sometimes spoke a word of command (the "prayer of faith") to the condition. Thus, to the deaf and dumb ears and tongue of the man in Mark 7:32, He said, "*Be opened.*" In Luke 4:30, He rebuked the fever of Peter's mother-in-law. At first it sounds funny to talk this way, but on reflection it is commonplace. Mechanics pounding the stubborn bolt into place "tell it where to go." Pitchers and golfers are known to talk to the ball. Anyone present at a gambling game has heard people coax the dice to fall just so. God spoke the world into being through His Word, and that Word spoke health and salvation into being. The word from the Lord is creative and redemptive. So, as the Spirit leads, we may imitate Jesus in speaking to the condition.

Begin by practicing on yourself. Suppose you have an injured limb; speak to it daily with love and with faith--imagine seeing it becoming well, saying, "In the name of Jesus I ask you bones and muscles to come into harmony and become whole."

Talk to yourself in faith; encourage yourself, calling to mind the great healing Scriptures; repent of negative and fearful thinking; take dominion over your body and tell it to be strong in the Lord, and dare to do things that make you rely on His strength to supplant your own.

In time you will come to the place where, in praying for someone else, you will be prompted to pray the prayer of faith. For me it began with commanding headaches to go or coughs to leave. Then the temptation came to always do it that way. But that cannot be, for the healing ways of the Lord are infinitely creative. Each case is different; we have to learn in patience to act as He leads and not to rigidify our approach.

III. Practical Wisdom on How to Pray for Specific Problems

---

[1]By a quickening I mean the experience of heat coming through the laying on of hands, or electric-like waves, or vibrations or euphoria, or a sense of the presence of God or deep peace.

A. Backs And Other Painful Conditions (Bob Whitaker)

We used to refer to Silverlake Community Presbyterian Church, Los Angeles, as the church of the broken backs. It seemed that from the pastor on down through the ranks, we had a disproportionate number of back sufferers. From all of these we learned some prayer principles:

1. Back pain, or any other physical pain, normally can be relieved with prayer and laying on of hands on the painful area. Normally 5-10 minutes of prayer will take away the debilitating pain. The pain will stay away for a week or two or longer. I have no idea why it will leave for short periods in some cases and for long periods in others. There were always a few people around to pray for whoever might be in pain. I was one of the chief beneficiaries. We had a woman with terminal cancer of the liver. She was in such pain that codeine did not suffice and she hated the side effects. We could relieve her pain for a week or two at a time with prayer and laying on of hands. Finally, she died. We also prayed for the relief of toothaches for the poor until they could get proper dental care.

2. I have seldom seen back conditions permanently healed, with the exception of two severe cases of scoliosis and one herniated disc. In most cases relatively permanent relief may be found through proper diet, exercise and, most importantly, a daily walk that is long (2-3 miles) and relaxed. This, coupled with stress management, is the key. We are much too sedentary in our habits, and we are addicted to cars. We were made for walking.

Years ago I was diagnosed by an orthopedic doctor as having a herniated disc. I never had surgery. Walking and stress avoidance, plus periodic prayer for emergencies have kept me in great shape. I believe that in the case of back health, the Lord normally refuses to do for us what we must do for ourselves -- get out of the soft couches and easy chairs, and walk or swim.

Scoliosis and Herniated Discs - In these cases we asked three people who had already demonstrated a strong gift of healing to administer soaking prayer with the laying on of hands. One recipient was an older nurse who she had such severe scoliosis that she was confined to bed and a reclining chair. She had constant pain and had to sleep in a fetal position on her side. After a few times of praying once a week for about half an hour, she was able to sleep on her back and was relieved of pain. Within six to eight weeks she was up and about most of the time.

B. Cancer (Bob Whitaker)

Over the past thirty years I have visited many cancer patients, counseled and prayed for most of them, and observed their progress as we enlisted the entire church to pray lovingly and persistently for them. Many of these were considered to be terminal and most of them died within a year or two. Some of them were in parishes other than my own. I share these observations and convictions with a desire to promote healing:

1. Certainly it is true that a history of cancer in the family increases the likelihood of a person getting cancer. Everyone has inherited weaknesses of some kind which predispose them to be susceptible to certain diseases.

2. Increasingly studies indicate that a high cholesterol diet-- high in animal and dairy fats--may be a factor.

3. The incidence of cancer is especially high in the western industrialized world. This suggests that stress is a factor.

4. My strongest conviction is that deep-seated anger and/or resentment/hostility is a very big factor. I have been a close confidant and counselor to a number of people who died of cancer in middle age or in their fifties or sixties. In each case they carried some very deep anger towards someone who had hurt them deeply or was still hurting them deeply. In some cases they faced and admitted the anger, but they could not or refused to give it up. In other cases they denied the hurt and dodged any effort to deal with it.

In my experience such people do not respond well to prayers for physical healing; they need inner and/or emotional healing. In cases where they have been remarkably healed through the massive prayers of churches, they usually live only a year or so and then relapse and die of cancer. They die, I believe in most cases, because the root cause has not been dealt with through in-depth inner healing.

5. In some cases the cancer is caused by an attack of the enemy made possible by the combined despisings of many or by a curse placed on them through witchcraft. I knew of one such case in which a well-known Lutheran evangelist became deathly ill with cancer. Someone discerned that when he was evangelizing in the Orient, a curse was put on him. The curse was broken and he quickly recovered.

IV.   Some Cases Illustrating Various Principles of Healing Ministry (Brad Long)

A.   Introduction to Practical Teaching through Case Studies

I believe that the best way to learn how to cooperate with the leading of the Holy Spirit is through practical experience. In this section we will move from the theory of healing to its actual practice.

I am committed to the healing ministry of Jesus because I have had personal experiences of healing. I received emotional healing from hurts that were a result of growing up with dyslexia, a learning disability. I also received a healing of a herniated disk just before having to go in for surgery. These experiences convinced me of the reality of healing ministry.

After I began to grow in the gifts and empowering dimension of the Holy Spirit, the Lord started to use me in both emotional and physical healing. I have been immensely blessed as a result of Him allowing me to be a part of His grace and power in the lives of others.

In my experience there have been occasions when a healing took place in such a way that I knew that it was meant not only for the person healed, but it was also meant to instruct those who were praying. These were special opportunities when the Holy Spirit worked as both a teacher and a healer, almost coaching on how to participate in His gracious work.

There are some aspects of Jesus' healing work that I have not yet experienced such as raising those who were physically dead, curing cancer, or growing back missing limbs. I believe such healings are fully possible, but they are beyond my experience, and to deal with these areas, you will need to seek out teachers with that type of experience.

There are also some forms of prayer that the Holy Spirit has rarely called me to use such as commanding someone to be healed or to get up and to walk. I have tried it, but it must have been in my flesh for nothing happened. Of course I believe that the Holy Spirit works like this. But again, you will also have to seek out teachers in these areas.

In the following I share what I have experienced firsthand. I relate only those experiences that were crucial for my own learning to cooperate with the Holy Spirit's healing work. In order to protect privacy, in most cases I have not used the name of the person for whom is being prayed or the members of the prayer team.

B. The Woman Who Could Not Conceive

The following sequence of experiences had a profound effect upon me and became a turning point in my ministry.

Prelude - The Moving of God's Spirit at a *Spirit Alive Mission*

At a third year Spirit Alive mission, I taught on healing. At the commencement of this mission, the Holy Spirit seemed to be wonderfully present. Prior to the beginning of the first team meeting, I was outside walking and praying. As I prayed, I felt the Lord say to me that He was going to move clearly to show His glory on this retreat. I was also aware of the Holy Spirit moving through me.

The Spirit began to move as soon as the team meeting began. As we joined hands to pray for the mission, the woman next to me was suddenly overcome by the presence of God and rested in the Spirit. With visible effects, the power of the Holy Spirit went around the circle of people, and the power seemed to meet right at the church's pastor who broke down and wept. We later found that this was a time of an important breakthrough for him.

A startling beginning to this mission, we all had a tingling sense of expectation of the great things that God had in store for us. This experience also built our faith that Jesus was present and could work.

A Prayer Request to Become Pregnant

During a healing service one evening, as we prayed for many people, a team member came to me and burst out, "I want to get pregnant!" Startled at this request, I could manage only an "Oh!" She then explained that during the delivery of her first child she had an infection that closed her tubes. The doctor told the heartbroken couple that she would not be able to conceive again.

Prayer With the Laying On Of Hands

I invited some of the women on the team to join me in prayer. We waited upon the Lord for a while and then began to pray for healing. I asked the women to lay hands on the place where the closed tubes were. As we prayed, I felt heat and vibration in my hands but was not sure that anything was happening in the woman. Visibly nothing was happening. After a few moments of prayer in which I asked God for healing, I asked the woman if anything was happening. She said, "Yes." She felt something like heat and electricity moving through her. When we heard this, we were encouraged and prayed with even greater expectation that the Holy Spirit was at work. We continued to pray about fifteen minutes more, mostly in tongues, and she suddenly said, "My word, I am starting to itch inside and something seems to be moving inside of me!" We continued to pray.

Because many others needed prayer ministry, I left the team and periodically checked back to see what was happening. Each time the team reported that the heat was continuing, so they continued to lay on hands and to pray and praise in the Spirit. This continued for about an hour and a half. Finally the heat stopped as did the inward conviction that we should pray for her.

A Remarkable Healing

At the conclusion of our prayer time, we knew that God had done something marvelous. But because we did not yet have concrete evidence of actual healing, we did not want to jump to any conclusions. We gave thanks for the obvious evidences that God had worked and commended the results to Him.

A month or so later I received a telephone call from the woman, and she said that she was pregnant. We praised God, but we still waited. The pregnancy was a difficult one, and the baby was nearly lost.
Finally, I received a picture of a lovely baby girl. The healing was complete and authentic.

Reflections on the Healing Process

What Was the Holy Spirit Teaching Us?

1. This healing took place during a kairos moment in the life of this church.

As evidenced from the opening team meeting, the Holy Spirit was moving in this mission. There was also the base of faith and expectation. Our task was to discern the leading of the Holy Spirit and to obey.

2. The woman who asked for prayer took the initiative.

She discerned that God was at work, and she seized the opportunity to place herself where something could happen. She acted just as those who were blind or afflicted with leprosy who flung themselves right into the path of Jesus. Coming forward for prayer about a matter which was of some embarrassment was itself an expression of faith and equivalent to a verbal affirmation of faith. God honored this faith and initiative.

3. We followed the example of Jesus and laid hands on the area that needed prayer.

One needs to be very careful, however, with laying on of hands. Privacy should not be violated. Never forget that regardless of how spiritual we think we are, we are still sexual. Always ask permission before the laying on of hands, especially if it is on a sensitive area. Once I realized where the problem was, I invited a team of women to join me. They did the actual laying on of hands. We do not want to hurt or to violate the person in any way. And for ourselves, we do not want to give Satan any opportunities.

4. Sometimes the Holy Spirit will reveal to those praying what He is doing.

This revelation may come through an inward impression or through a tangible manifestation. For instance, many people experience warmth or a vibration in their hand when the Holy Spirit is moving in healing power. Others receive images that show what He is doing. At times I have had an inward image of the afflicted area bathed in light. These feelings must always be tested and verified against actual results.

Likewise, manifestations of the Holy Spirit accompanying His healing may take place within the person for whom is being prayed. He may feel heat or be aware that something in his body is moving. He may be conscious of light, or the Holy Spirit may reveal something to him that is important to the healing process.

5. **In this case I learned that it is important to directly ask the person whether anything is happening.**

If we had not asked, since neither I nor the prayer team had any special revelation that anything was happening, we would not have known that there were clear manifestations of the Spirit's work taking place within the person. We would have offered up our prayers of petition, given praise, and then prayed for someone else. We would have missed the long-term prayer that was used by God to work a miracle of healing.

It is most helpful for the discernment process to ask the person to report anything that is occurring inside of him. This may be physical sensations or thoughts or feelings that come to him. Often his response will confirm the guidance that the team has already been given. Involving the person in this type of dialogue and feedback will have the following important effects:

   a. **The working of the Holy Spirit does not depend upon some worked-up faith or hyper-emotional setting.** To stop the prayer and the praise and seriously ask whether anything is happening brings the whole process right down to reality and allows for a more accurate discernment of what the Holy Spirit may be doing.

   b. **I have found that the very act of asking builds faith, if it's not done in a critical way, but rather in an honest desire to cooperate with the Holy Spirit.** It demonstrates that those praying expect that the Holy Spirit will be doing something.

   c. **To ask this question also poses a certain amount of risk.** It may be that there is nothing happening at all. What then? I usually pray that God will heal them. If there is no further guidance I ask God to bless them and trust that He has heard our prayer. Sometimes He has healed either at that time or later.

   d. **Often the Holy Spirit may be speaking to the person for whom is being prayed. These words may include special promises, special words of guidance, and so forth.** By asking the person to share what is going on, he has the opportunity to test with the prayer team the inward guidance that he may be receiving.

6. **Sometimes it is difficult to know when to stop praying for a person.**

Often a prayer may be simple and direct. In this case, however, it went for more than an hour and a half. We kept going because the manifestations of the Holy Spirit's presence and working continued. There was also the inward awareness of not being finished. You will have to discern how long to pray case-by-case.

7. **The question of claiming healing.**

After having experienced such tangible signs of God's healing work, should this sister have claimed the promises of God's healing and have announced that she was indeed healed? There is a teaching which states that one must express in faith what he believes God has promised in His word to do. This is a misunderstanding of the nature of faith.

We are not called to have faith that we are healed and to hold on to that belief regardless of the medical facts. Rather, we are to have faith in Jesus Christ. If He heals, it is not something that we will have to believe against the evidence. Rather, the evidence will attest that we are indeed healed.

In this case we knew that Jesus loved her, cared about her and could heal her. We knew that He may well have been doing that in the heat and the itching. So, for all of this we gave thanks. But the confirmation that Jesus had indeed worked came nine months after conception with the birth of a baby.

C. Legs Lengthened

This healing took place at a Presbytery-sponsored renewal conference in West Virginia where Larry Selig, a PRRMI International Representative, and I were conducting a workshop on healing ministry.

Preparation Through Teaching

There was not any special praise or exalted moments of being caught up into the presence of God during this workshop. The atmosphere was that of a workshop, perhaps even a little clinical. At first the people were very guarded in their response and openness to the topic, and there was a mingled sense of interest and skepticism. Larry and I lectured, giving the theological and biblical basis for healing.

A Demonstration In Which A Person Was Healed

We offered to demonstrate a healing as a walk-through of the healing process. We demonstrated the steps involved in praying for the sick with the laying on of hands. I asked for a volunteer, preferably someone who did not need healing so that there would not be any expectation that something would happen.

To our surprise a women immediately came forward. She said that time was too precious to waste on dry runs and that she needed healing. She asked us to pray for her. As she came forward, she visibly looked weighted down by some burden. She also seemed to be in pain.

In a matter of fact way, Larry went through the steps while I gave the audience a running commentary on what we were doing and why. When asked the nature of the problem, she said that she had tremendous pain in her neck. Further questions revealed that she was the wife of a pastor. We began to pray for her, dealing with the physical pain and also with some emotional hurt, as we were led carefully by the Holy Spirit.

After a few minutes a striking change came over the woman's face. She brightened, and the weight was gone. She stood up, moved her head from side to side, and said that all of the pain was gone.

Once this happened the atmosphere of the group changed dramatically. One could feel faith growing. Though we still had the clinical feeling, it now was mingled with worship.

The Miracle of a Leg Lengthened

THE PRMI *DUNAMIS PROJECT*
THE HEALING MINISTRY OF JESUS

Another woman painfully walked up and asked for prayer. She said that she had a pain in her back that made walking difficult. As we prayed for her, I got the strong nudge that I should check the length of her legs. I dismissed the whole idea as hokey, a ploy of tent evangelists, but the nudging persisted. I gave in and asked another woman to come and to lift up her legs and check. One was shorter than the other by about an inch-and-a- half. I began to pray that God would heal whatever caused the difference in length. But I did not have any feelings of heat or awareness that anything was happening. All I had was the conviction that God wanted to bless this person.

In the middle of my prayer the woman interrupted and said loudly, "Oh, come now, I know this won't work! Someone else has already prayed like that for me. It can't work because I broke my leg some years ago, and it has a pin in it. It is because of that break that one is shorter than the other." Then to our amazement the woman holding the legs up said, "What do you mean it can't work. Just now your leg is growing out and is almost even." And sure enough, I could also see it visibly becoming even with the other foot. We all gave thanks and praise. The woman got up with a skeptical look on her face that quickly turned into amazement as she began to walk around. She said that for the first time in years she was walking without pain. For the next hour she walked around and felt her back. Every so often she would come over to the group and announce that she was truly healed.

Reflections on the Healing Process

What was the Holy Spirit trying to teach us?

1. **The Holy Spirit does not require a lot of music or a special atmosphere in which He can work.**

   All He needs is faith and obedience.

2. **The first healing was prelude to the second.**

   Through her obedience, the first woman who sought prayer acted on spoken prophetic words. The Holy Spirit used her to break through to the people's hearts. Until she took the risk of being obedient, it seemed that nothing would or could happen. Many times I have found that when one person is faithful and obedient, he is blessed, and his obedience prepares the way for the Holy Spirit to bless many others. To see this woman healed both physically and emotionally built the faith of the rest of the group.

3. **Notice that in the second healing no one felt anything. This was truly remarkable.**

   Even though heat and vibrations are often times signs of the Holy Spirit's presence, they are only signs. They are not the Holy Spirit Himself nor does He depend upon them in order to work.

4. **From this healing I learned my role of obedience.**

   The Holy Spirit told me to check the length of her legs. I had never done this before and felt silly doing it. After all, this was a Presbytery event--what of my reputation? But nonetheless, by the grace of God, I was obedient. And it was, I believe, that obedience that the Lord used to accomplish a great work.

   Sometimes the Lord may call you to do something about which you may feel awkward. But if it is of the Lord, it will serve some purpose and will be a part of blessing that person. Remember that sometimes Jesus did rather odd things when He prayed for healing. When He prayed for the deaf man who had a speech impediment, "...*he put his fingers into his ears, and he spat and touched his tongue; and looking up to heaven, he sighed, and said to him, 'Ephphatha,' that is, 'Be opened.'*" (Mark 7:33-35)

D. Healing Proclaimed and a Foot Healed

This healing took place at a major conference in a Pentecostal church in Taipei where around 150 people had gathered. The following is a composite of several cases of healing which took place at this meeting:

During a time of praise we became aware of the powerful presence of God. We naturally and freely began to sing in the Spirit. It was a wonderful time of being caught up into the glory and presence of God. When the singing in the Spirit was brought to a close, as if by an invisible conductor, a heavy, full silence descended upon the whole group.

I began to receive words about what the Holy Spirit was doing. Most of the words pertained to the healing of emotional hurts. I also received the urging from the Spirit to call out the term, headaches. As I spoke these words out, remarkable things began to happen. Some began to weep; others fell on the floor overwhelmed by the conviction of sin. Several announced that they experienced having their pain taken away even as the words were spoken that God was healing headaches.

Then, very clearly, the words "I am going to heal my son's left foot" flashed into my mind. This surprised me because usually words concerning physical healing do not come to me that specifically. I questioned within myself whether this was from the Holy Spirit or if it was just my imagination. But I knew that the only way I would know if it was really from the Lord was through obedience. So, I shared the word that I had received with the group.

Immediately a man came hobbling out of the congregation and said that he was the one. He said that surgery had been done on his foot, and the foot failed to heal properly. As a result he had great pain when he walked. He had endured this pain for almost six months.

A co-worker and I laid hands on his foot and began to pray. As we did, the co-worker and I both felt heat moving through our hands. We prayed a very simple prayer, "Lord, let your healing power touch our brother's foot; in the name of Jesus heal him!" When we asked the man if anything was happening, he said that he felt intense heat moving into his foot and then, with some surprise, said that the pain was completely gone. He stood up and began to praise the Lord as he joyfully walked without pain.

Reflections on the Healing Process

What was the Holy Spirit trying to teach us?

1. **Again when the Holy Spirit was moving, it was a kairos moment that followed exalted praise of Jesus Christ.**

   It has been my experience that often this type of praise both evokes the presence of God and also prepares us to welcome His presence. Often there will follow periods in which the Holy Spirit is moving to heal and to do other wonderful works that exalt Jesus Christ.

   This is not, however, a matter of working up an emotionally high-pitched atmosphere. Such must be avoided because it can get in the way of clear discernment and can give room for all types of manipulation. The praise described above is an opening up of ourselves to the presence of God. It is an invitation for Him to come.

2. **There are many ways to enter into healing ministry.**

One method is to wait for the Lord to give words. Another is to ask people to come forward to be prayed for whatever needs they may have. Waiting for the leading of the Holy Spirit and announcing whatever the He tells you He is doing is yet another way. This method is more like words of prophecy, that is, speaking out words which the Holy Spirit will use to accomplish His purpose as opposed to our prayers of petition.

At this event, many were blessed without anyone praying for them. Rather it was a time when the Holy Spirit was moving in the group, and He used the words that were given to me to do His gracious works. He also gave me a very specific word that enabled a particular individual to come forward and receive prayer for healing.

When the Holy Spirit works in this manner, it is awe-inspiring, and for the one who is receiving the guidance, it can be breathtaking as well. One feels totally vulnerable and dependent upon the Holy Spirit and must be extremely careful to speak exactly the words that the Holy Spirit gives. Do not add words that come from personal needs or which may meet the expectations of those gathered.

3. **Some different ways of hearing the Holy Spirit.**

Sometimes I know what the Holy Spirit is doing because I receive a clear mental picture of Him healing a part of the body. Sometimes words alone will come, as in the above case. At other times I have felt heat in my own body indicating the location. Sometimes there is not a word or an image. I simply look out over the people and know in my deepest self that now is the time for the Holy Spirit to act and that He will be doing a specific thing.

4. **How do we know if these things are really from the Lord?**

The section on discernment of spirits in "*In the Spirit's Power*" Dunamis Project manual gives a more complete answer to this question. But, simply put, I often test these words with a co-worker, and then I take the risk of speaking them out. I pray intently as I wait to see if anything happens. If a word is really from the Lord, it will accomplish the purpose for which it was sent. If not, I ask forgiveness and continue to listen and to practice obedience.

E. The Healing Process May Be Accelerated Through Prayer

General and profuse prayers from God's people have frequently collaborated with medical science to hasten healing.

Laura Long's Rapid Recovery From Abdominal Surgery

On July 2, 1992, Brad's wife, Laura, underwent major abdominal surgery. On several occasions people prayed for her healing with the laying on of hands. In addition, around the country intercessors were praying for her.

When she went for her post-operative check-up, the doctor said that she was two to three weeks ahead of the normal healing schedule and was doing extremely well. It seemed that the prayer may have contributed to the healing process. Medical studies show that patients who were prayed for recovered quicker than those who were not.

The Miraculous Recovery of Bob Whitaker's Granddaughter

From August 12 - 16, 1992, the Dunamis Project retreat was held in Hendersonville, North Carolina. During the retreat, the group received word that Bob Whitaker's two-year old granddaughter, Shannon, had fallen from the second floor of a building in Colorado. She was rushed by plane to a major hospital where she was diagnosed with a concussion and other serious injuries.

When the group received this news, they began an intensive and extended period of prayer for this little girl. In addition, intercessors around the country were notified.

The positive reports were immediate. Though the doctors' prognosis had been a bleak picture of a brain-damaged child who would be blind in one eye, her recovery was near perfect. One doctor called it a miracle.

Reflections on the Healing Process

What was the Holy Spirit trying to teach us?

1. **Intercession makes a difference.**

2. **Praying for healing is effective, even at a distance.**

   Jesus can heal today through prayer at a distance just as He healed the centurion's servant without stepping into the man's house.

3. **Often there is a mixture of means of God's healing.**

   In each of these cases we did not wait for God to miraculously intervene. Rather, we vigorously sought out and used all means available. This included the best medical care available.

F. Eyes Healed Without Seeking Healing

When the Holy Spirit is manifestly present, healing may take place spontaneously without anyone asking or praying for it.

An Eye Healed During a Worship Service

During a *Prayer Mountain* in Montreat, North Carolina, we entered into a time of worship led by Carla McMurry and Paul Brummer. The praise was exalted, and we felt the presence of Jesus Christ. Suddenly a man began to shout and to jump around! He kept saying, "My eyes, my eyes!"

We stopped the worship, and the man had finally settled down enough to speak clearly. He said that he had a cataract in one eye and as he was singing, Jesus came up, touched him, and suddenly his eye was perfectly clear. His vision had been restored.

Vision Restored During a Time of Silence
THE PRMI *DUNAMIS PROJECT*
THE HEALING MINISTRY OF JESUS

During a worship service at a Dunamis Project Retreat in Hendersonville, North Carolina, we came to a time when the room was filled with the sweet silence of the presence of God. The group stood in silence before the Lord. During this period, I received a nudge to lay my hand on the head of one of the older women. As I did, I experienced the power of the Holy Spirit moving through me but had no idea of what was happening.

During the testimony time prior to the retreat's closing communion service, the woman stood and said that she had some type of eye problem and was going blind. It was as though the shades were being pulled down over her vision. She then said that she did not know who had placed a hand on her as she stood silently. But as she was touched, suddenly light burst into her eyes and she was able to see more clearly than before.

Reflections on the Healing Process

What was the Holy Spirit trying to teach us?

1. **Jesus is so full of grace and love that in His presence healing occurs even if we do not know it, believe it, or ask for it.**

2. **The Kingdom of God advances with signs and wonders.**

Where the Holy Spirit is present, Jesus is present, and where Jesus is present, the Kingdom of God is alive, active, and real.

Consistently, as the Kingdom of God manifests itself in our midst, it will be attended by signs and wonders. Demons will be cast out, lives will be changed, sins will be convicted, and sickness will be healed. The Kingdom of God produced vivid evidence wherever Jesus preached. (Luke 11:20)

These signs and wonders occur for two reasons. In the face of the advancement of the Kingdom of God, the kingdom of Satan is swept away and captives are released. Secondly, the very nature of the Kingdom of God is grace, love, wholeness, peace, and life abundant. In the presence of the Kingdom of God, the nature is set free from the bondage to decay. Death is overthrown. The signs and wonders that we experience are but a foretaste of when the Kingdom shall be fully established and there shall be a new heaven and a new earth.

G. When People Were Not Healed

1.   Introduction

In the previously detailed cases, people were physically healed. However, part of my growing in the healing ministry has included some dramatic failures. From these experiences, the Holy Spirit has taught me several important lessons about His healing work.

2.   The Man in the Wheelchair at Jesus Abbey

I experienced the infilling with the Holy Spirit at Jesus Abbey in Korea. The Rev. Archer Torrey, the founder of Jesus Abbey, was my teacher and mentor. I wrote down everything he taught, underlined, and studied the Bible verses he referred to, and carefully observed how he ministered in the power of the Holy Spirit. He was the teacher and I the student.

During my stay at the Abbey a large group of Korean students arrived for a retreat. During one of the prayer services during that retreat, a young man in a wheelchair came forward for prayer.

He had a look of eager anticipation on his face, and, in Korean, Archer asked him if and what he wanted us to pray for him. The young man answered, "Of course! Please pray for healing of my crippled legs." So we laid our hands upon him. But as I did, I got a very strong nudge from the Holy Spirit who said that we were not to pray for his legs. I was puzzled and looked to Archer who was hesitant to begin. Then Archer said to me in English, "The Lord just told me that we are not to pray for this young man's legs, but we are to pray that he may be healed of all the hurts that he has received as a result of the many times that healing was prayed for him and nothing has happened. What is the Lord saying to you?" I told him that I had received similar guidance.

So we prayed as the Spirit had guided us. We asked God to come and to heal this young man's broken heart and shaken faith because he had not yet been healed. We also prayed that God would show him how he was to do the work of the Kingdom of God in whatever situation he was in, whether in a wheelchair or able to walk. As we prayed, at first the young man was surprised and then he began to weep. Gradually his tears turned into radiant joy, and it seemed that a tremendous burden lifted from him. Though he remained in the wheelchair, he got up! Later he told us that he had prayed many times for healing, but each time he had been disappointed and had felt that somehow his faith was not enough, that God did not care. However, this time, as we prayed according to the guidance received, for the fist time he felt surrounded by the love and presence of God. He felt his anger and hurt being healed, and he was sure of God's grace and calling for whatever the future held. A tremendous healing indeed took place.

Reflections on the Healing Process

What was the Holy Spirit trying to teach us?

1. Listen! Listen! Listen!

Listen to the Holy Spirit; listen to the person; listen to your co-workers. Do not jump to conclusions about what the need is or how to pray. Rather be guided by listening to the Holy Spirit! If you do, there may not always be physical healing, but there will always be a blessing.

If Archer and I had not listened and instead plunged ahead and done what we usually did, laying on of hands and praying for the sick, we would have added to this young man's burden of guilt and disappointment. We would have missed the miracle that the Holy Spirit had in mind for him, which was to restore him to usefulness in the Kingdom of God and to heal his broken heart.

Listening to the Holy Spirit and then doing what He tells us to do is the fundamental principle of the healing ministry.

2. Work together to discern the leading of the Holy Spirit.

Many times I have prayed alone for healing, and God has blessed these prayers. But I believe that it is generally God's intention to have us work as a team. Jesus did not send His disciples out alone but, rather, two-by-two. Paul was not a one-man show. He traveled with co-workers. There are many reasons for working in teams:

a. We need a check on egoism. In a team it is easier to give glory to Jesus.

b. A team provides a diversity of spiritual gifts that may be needed to minister to the whole person.

c. A team provides clearer discernment.

In the above case Archer and I were able to check the guidance that we received before moving ahead to act upon it.

3. **Sometimes God does not heal a person physically, however He always seems to move in spiritual healing.**

There seems to be a priority in God's healing work. He often seems to start with spiritual healing and then move to emotional and physical healing.

We see this illustrated in the story of the paralyzed man who was let down through the roof. First, Jesus said, *"Man, your sins are forgiven you."* It is only later, after the Scribes and the Pharisees question His authority, that He deals with the man's paralyzed body (Luke 5:17-26).

In many cases, as I have listened to the Holy Spirit, He has wonderfully healed the person's heart and emotions. Perhaps this is the Lord's priority because it is the state of the heart and the spirit that is of eternal consequence. In the eyes of God the body will soon follow the state of the heart.

4. **Sickness and death are still part of our human condition.**

We live in a fallen world, one in which the Kingdom of God has come but is not yet fully fulfilled. That is our tragic predicament. The healing that we experience, whether physical or spiritual, is a foretaste of the work that will be completed in Jesus Christ at the end of time.

3.   The Woman Who Died

I was leading a healing meeting in a church in Taiwan. During the prayer time, a very beautiful woman came forward. She was around thirty years old and was the mother of two small children. With tears she said that the doctors had just diagnosed her with cancer and that it had spread throughout her body. The doctors had given her about a month to live.

Before I began to pray with her, I invited her family to come forward, as well as, the pastor and the elders of the church. We all laid hands on her and prayed for her healing. But no sooner had I touched her than there came into my mind a vivid image of a dark cave with a cross before it and light on the other side. I knew deep inside me that she was going to die. All of my petitions died within me. Though others prayed for healing, all I could do was weep and pray in tongues. Finally I was able to commend her into the care of our gracious, ever-loving God who has defeated the powers of death. She died a few months later.

Reflections on the Healing Process

What was the Holy Spirit trying to teach us?

1. **We live in a fallen world in which there are the terrible effects of sin.**

THE PRMI *DUNAMIS PROJECT*
THE HEALING MINISTRY OF JESUS

Sometimes death will be the transition to the final healing.

2. Did I disobey?

Should I have shared with her and her family the vision that I had? I was afraid to at the time. I was afraid that it would shatter her will to live and to fight the cancer. But if I had, perhaps I would have given her even more hope to face what was ahead. I do not know.

I shared this vision with the woman's pastor, and she confirmed that it was of the Lord. The pastor may have communicated the vision to her at some other time; I do not know. In healing ministry you often face agony so deep or situations so impossible that all you can do is to fling yourself upon the mercy and grace of God. He is the only way.

Notice that all of the words died within me, and all I could do was to pray in the Spirit. In situations like this when one truly does not know how to pray, the grace of tongues is a way of letting go and letting the Holy Spirit, who intimately knows the situation as well as the mind of God, pray.

4.   Doug McMurry

The Rev. Doug McMurry, Christ Presbyterian Church, Richmond Virginia, has played a key role in the development of the Dunamis Project retreats. He is a man of solid faith and deep commitment, and he ministers effectively and powerfully to others. Yet, at nearly every retreat, he is afflicted by pain in his back because of scoliosis of the spine. He has been prayed for many times for this condition, and while there has been some healing, the condition persists.

At a Dunamis Project retreat at Lake George, New York, the Holy Spirit was moving in manifest power, and a team began to pray for Doug and his back. We anointed him with oil and laid hands on the exact location of his back where the trouble was. As we prayed, I felt the flow of the Spirit's power moving through my hands into Doug's back. When I asked Doug if anything was happening, he excitedly confirmed that he felt heat and other sensations in his back. As we continued to pray, I remember being very excited that something wonderful was about to happen to my brother.

The manifestations continued for a while longer, and then suddenly everything stopped. The heat, the sensations, the awareness of the presence of God, all stopped cold! It was as if someone had switched the current off and everything went dead. Doug was deeply disappointed as was the prayer team. But we gave thanks anyway, and prayed a prayer of blessing for Doug.

I was deeply puzzled and disturbed by this whole event, and it left me with many perplexing questions. More than anything, however, I was hurting for Doug who very much needed healing and had seemed so close to receiving it.

Reflections on the Healing Process

What was the Holy Spirit trying to teach us?

1. Sometimes there may be things in us that may block the healing work of the Holy Spirit.

Some possible blocks to healing:

a. A lack of faith - This may be in an individual or in the atmosphere.

b. Disobedience - The Holy Spirit tells people to do something that will serve as the means of His working and they do not obey.

c. Unforgiveness and emotional hurt. Many times we have found that emotional healing must take place before there is freedom to receive physical healing. Unforgiveness especially blocks God's healing grace.

d. Demonic interference. An evil spirit somehow may be getting in the way.

2. **We face the mystery of God's work in us and the world.**

As I have thought about this, I have concluded that none of the above applies to Doug's case. I do not know why Doug was not healed. I suspect that there are many cases when there is not a reason. We are simply met with the mystery of God's work among us in a fallen world. Remember what He said to us through Isaiah....,

> "*For my thoughts are not your thoughts, neither are your ways my ways, says the Lord.*"

> "*For as the heavens are higher than the earth, so are my ways higher than your ways and my thoughts than your thoughts.*" (Isaiah 55:8-9)

I also do not have any set answer as to how it is redemptive for Doug to suffer this back problem. If anything, it seems like an unnecessary burden to a person who is totally committed to following Jesus. And, besides, it is not fair. God dramatically healed me of a persistent back problem, so why not my brother who is far more mature in the faith and more useful in the Kingdom than I am? I do not know.

Yet, I do know that both Doug and I will continue to serve and praise Him regardless of whether or not it is His good pleasure to heal Doug's back. We are to remain faithful and passionately in love with Jesus Christ regardless of the vicissitudes of this mortal life. We shall also continue to pray for the sick, trusting God's grace and power to heal.

V.   Ministering To Those Who Are Not "Healed" (Bob Whitaker)

My seminary roommate was one of the most wholesome, healed individuals I have ever known. He was very loving, kind, thoughtful, helpful, unselfish, radiantly hopeful, and joyous. He was always pleasant, and became a very fine Methodist minister. Despite the efforts of many fine Christian prayer warriors and healers, however, he was never healed of the crippling effects of polio in his legs. His life still reminds me of what it means to be truly "healed" and "whole" even though physically handicapped.

Statement of Intention

If we are to pray for the physical and emotional needs of people, we must provide them with a realistic expectation of what may happen. Some churches may provide this information with a brochure that states their philosophy and practice of healing, and it may be available in the pew racks (See sample in Appendix.). Other churches may make a brief statement of expectation or give a definition of healing when inviting people to receive healing ministry. When I pray for people who are not familiar with our ministry or for those with particularly challenging infirmities, I may say something like: "Jesus is here; He is a great healer and He loves you very much. We will pray that He will heal your condition, knowing that in His wisdom He may do so very soon or much more slowly (perhaps not until heaven). We will pray knowing that He may cure you as you now desire, or He may give you a whole new perspective and power to rise above your infirmity. He may choose to heal you through means other than this time of prayer."

If the person is blind or is a paraplegic, I may remind him that such healings are rare, but if I feel so led, I will pray for a miracle, and I will encourage him to do so. I remind him, however, that the Lord may choose to heal in other ways in this life and postpone the miracle until heaven.

When Healing is Delayed

When a person has sought specific healing for a specific condition and nothing seems to happen, I encourage him to continue to pray for healing and to ask the Lord to reveal any blocks such as unconfessed sin, unforgiveness, or a need to be reconciled to someone. I also encourage him to continue to receive prayer and laying on of hands regularly, and/or anointing, and to take Communion often. I may encourage him to receive the weekly ministry of an inner healing team. I may schedule him for counseling to help work through problems.

Emily's Story

When our oldest daughter was about ten years old, she became quite sick with asthma. Though we took extra time to pray for her for healing, she continued to wheeze and cough. Then we had the elders pray and anoint her according to James 5. Still she remained sick. I kept asking the Lord what the problem was, and I kept getting a silly word in my mind; it was "paint." Finally I realized that I had been repainting the inside of the house by stages. We concluded that perhaps she was allergic to the paint, so we had her stay with a loving surrogate grandmother in the church for a few days. Sure enough, she got well! From this experience I learned to pray, "Lord, what is the problem?"

When Nothing Seems to Work

When a person has tried all of the above and is troubled about why nothing has happened, I encourage him to commit the whole matter to the Lord, to relinquish and to say, "Lord, I don't understand, but I trust you know what you're doing, and somehow, someway I'll understand. Meanwhile I trust You to work through this condition for my good and your glory. I offer it to you to use for much redemptive good. Within my limitations I'm going to seek to live an adventure of discovery and service with you." I may then refer him to lives of the saints or devotional books such as *Streams in the Desert*, which show what God has done through the lives of those who are not "healed." My favorite book which interprets life's disappointments in God's purpose is *Disciplines of Life*, by V. Raymond Edman, Harvest House Publishers, 1075 Arrowsmith, Eugene, Oregon 97402. It is a marvelous study of how God used suffering of different kinds in the lives of the great personalities of the Bible.

Crushing Disappointments

I know what it is like to believe that someone would be healed, and to publicly say so. I know what it is like to encourage a person to believe that he would be healed and to urge the whole church to believe it. I know what it is like to assure the person that the healing would take place, and then the person has died. The grief and anger was awful! But once I overcame the disappointment and sought forgiveness for presumption, I was amazed at how He redeemed my mistakes and gave the surviving family grace to rise above it with a new and hopeful perspective. In fact, I must testify that wherever there was seeming failure, God gave compensating grace. His loving presence has been most manifest where the physical miracle we pleaded for did not happen.

His Presence

Jesus' beautifully moving, lovely, gracious presence is our "exceeding great reward." The Savior, more than any of His gifts, including healing, is the ultimate all-satisfying reward for every desperate seeker. Just to have His comforting presence for a few moments is enough to live on until we see Him face-to-face and realize all of our dreams.

Abuses and Errors to Avoid (Bob Whitaker)

A. Egoism

When truly motivated by compassionate love, the exercise of healing gifts is a beautiful reflection of Christ. (This is borne out by 1 Corinthians 13 which shows us that gifts go awry without love.) But the enemy is always at work to stir up our baser instincts and to spoil the gifts of God's love. None is uglier or more ruinous than pride.

I'm reminded of the story about the woodpecker who was busy pecking away at a hole in a tree during a thunderstorm. Suddenly a bolt of lightning struck the trunk of the tree splitting it from the hole to the ground. The astonished bird was heard to exclaim as he flew away, "I didn't know there was so much power in my beak." It is very easy to be overly impressed with our spirituality and to treat the gift of God as our possession and a badge of our attainments. If miracles happen through us, if people fall to the ground while we pray, if it is noised about that we are powerful in our prayers, it can go to our heads and subtly ruin us and spoil the work of God.

Warning - The persistent theme of Scripture is, "*Everyone who exalts himself will be humbled, and he who humbles himself will be exalted.*" (Luke 14:11) God is a jealous God (a shocking truth) and repeatedly asserts this in various ways, "*My glory will I not give to another*" (Isaiah 42:8). The lesson of Scripture is that God will severely discipline the person who gets lifted up in his own heart. Often great healers fall prey to the heavy wine of people falling at their feet. They imagine themselves as demi-gods and permit themselves liberties with power, money, or sex that lead to their humiliation. None of us escapes unscathed from the pride virus.

When the seventy returned with joy, exalting in their success over sickness and demons, Jesus admonished them, "*Do not rejoice...that the spirits are subject to you, but rejoice that your names are written in heaven.*" He was saying, "Don't dwell on what happened through you, but stay excited and grateful for what has been done for you--for your eternal salvation." I think we do well to renounce any reporting of healings that happened through us. Let those who were healed testify and let us urge them to tell it so that God receives glory. As for those in healing ministry, let our motto be, "*He must increase, but I must decrease.*" (John 3:30)

B. Dishonesty

In the public healing ministry, it is easy to become success oriented. I believe that this is because many of us were raised with a lot of pressure to make a name for ourselves and to be successful in terms of visible results. This, of course, is tied in with pride and egoism. When God does not do much visibly, the temptation is to help Him and to exaggerate reports of healings. People who receive words of knowledge about others who need healing are tempted to fake it when no words come. A strong manifestation of heat while praying for someone is easily reported as a healing, when, in fact, subsequent checking usually reveals that the person was only blessed or helped.

Healings of aches, pains, and improvements of chronic conditions are sometimes reported as signs and wonders. Healers sometimes act as though they themselves are in relatively perfect health when in truth they are wounded healers struggling with real problems. Some healing evangelists act as though they have absolute answers to all problems when actually they are stumped by why it is that every formula for a cure sooner or later proves fallible. The greatest healing evangelists sooner or later have to admit that age has taken its toll of their eyes, ears, teeth, and hair despite their best prayers. Their relatives will tell you that their minds suffered, too.

It is refreshing that since the sixties when our rebel children drew a bead on all posturing, we have allowed ourselves to be more human and vulnerable. Amazingly, the public responds better to the re-discovery of healing in the church **because** we confess that we strike out alot as we learn to hit better for the Lord.

Jesus warned us that all of our secrets will eventually be revealed. Even the very private things said in the dark will be proclaimed upon the housetops (Luke 12:2-3). So we might as well be completely honest now and avoid the embarrassment later.

PART XII

Developing Healing Ministry In the Local Church

By Bob Whitaker

The Dunamis Project
Presbyterian-Reformed Ministries International

DEVELOPING HEALING MINISTRY IN THE LOCAL CHURCH

I. Context for Christian Healing

Healing happens where Jesus is powerfully present. Therefore, it can theoretically happen anywhere to anyone. But He is especially present where two or three are gathered together in His name. (Matthew 18:20) That means that where two or three are believing in all that Jesus is and all that He did, and all that He promises, and are careful to love and forgive one another as he does, and pray expectantly that He will be in their midst and act through them to save and heal -- there you will see a powerful healing climate. There the incidence of healing will be noticeable. When such people gather to listen to His Word, and recall all that He has said and done, and celebrate His goodness with joy, and pray the prayers of faith -- there healing will be contagious.

There are churches that are more or less like the above description. Let the church be the church and healing will be maximized. Where the church is not, not much will happen. Therefore, it is imperative that we pray and work for spiritual renewal in the churches so as to provide the atmosphere for healing to occur.

Where the local church resists renewal and healing we can form small cells of life where two to seven or so persons meet for sharing, prayer, Bible study, and ministering to one another's needs. Such cells can be the church until the larger congregation is permeated with life from the cell. One such cell can pray the larger congregation into life if they will faithfully pray for it and faithfully serve in humble love. It usually takes three to ten years for it to happen. Sometimes it takes longer. Some are called to this costly ministry, some are not.

Once the church is truly alive in Christ and intentionally practicing the healing ministry, she must be very careful to maintain intercessory prayer for the sick and needy. If intercessory prayer sags, the healing incidents will fall off. Many a church has organized healing services only to see them die; everything was being done decently and in order, but prayers were minimal. The same can be said for outreach and evangelism. The church lives by prayer as the body lives by breathing.

II. Introducing Healing Ministry in the Local Church

Every church is different. They have personalities as do individuals. Some are on a high plain spiritually; some are at a low ebb. Even within each church different levels of maturity and spiritual openness are present. In fact, there is usually a group who are ready to begin with healing services, and a group who look at the whole thing negatively or even fearfully. Healing can be divisive; therefore it is important to proceed with gentleness and keep the whole church together on it.

A Place to Begin

A good place to begin would be to encourage and strengthen prayer life. If there are not any prayer groups or prayer chains the aim should be to establish some. Begin with a series of sermons on the power of prayer, including illustrations about healings accomplished through prayer. For application challenge the people to commit themselves to definite experiments with prayer or to adopt some new prayer disciplines.

If the pastor is not strong on prayer, seek to have a prayer-life mission with a visiting preacher who is strong. The ideal time to do this is Lent. If none of these ideas takes, you, as an individual, can find one prayer buddy in the church who shares your concern. Begin to meet weekly, study a book on prayer together, and pray for a prayer awakening. In time draw in a third person and later a fourth. Keep at it. Without prayer healing will not get off the ground.

A Proposal to Session

A concerned person can draw up a challenge to the Session to authorize a committee to look into the healing ministry. A sample proposal is in the Appendix. The basic proposal would say:

1. The good news of the Gospel includes healing.

2. Churches are rediscovering the power of healing prayer.

3. Over 25 years ago the General Assembly encouraged steps toward a more vital healing ministry.

4. The new Directory for Worship includes a Service of Wholeness.

5. Medical costs are soaring and the needs of people were never greater.

6. We need to consider how we can more effectively minister to the whole person.

7. Let's have a balanced committee of concerned persons with strong representation from medical professions to check out what is happening and make recommendations.

Investigative Committee

I was pastoral advisor to such a committee in a large church with 24 to 30 elders. There were about six members on the committee. I guided them to read books pro and con on healing ministries in the church today. We then visited churches where healing ministry was happening--reformed, liturgical, penetecostal, etc. We interviewed healers and persons who claimed to be healed and persons who were unhappy with healing. The members of the committee got their eyes opened. I did not have to do any selling. They drew up a positive report recommending the commencement of monthly Sunday evening services of communion and healing. The Session voted to adopt the report without dissent because the committee was chaired by a very intelligent medical doctor.

Preparation

The report was circulated to the entire congregation. The pastoral staff then planned and preached a series of four sermons on the Biblical basis, philosophy, practice, and experience of Christian healing. Then Sunday evening services, described earlier in this book, were started and continue to this day, twenty years later.

Follow-Through

After the initial burst of interest, the healing service attendance began to dwindle. In time it was realized that prayer needed to be mobilized in faithful intercession. In addition, the leaders came to see that there needed to be an annual preaching mission or conference, lasting three or more days, to focus and encourage the healing ministry. These annual healing missions with outstanding guest speakers and seminars have become a highlight of the church year and attract many from other churches.

Course Correction

Soon leaders realized that healing should not be a special interest set apart for the few on Sunday nights, but part of the regular well-attended services of the church. Therefore, a core of people devoted to Sunday nights were trained in classes to be available to pray for people after Sunday morning services. These teams are publicized in the bulletin; are visible down front with name tags during the closing hymn, and the preachers encourage people to receive the ministry.

III.   Healing and the Lord's Supper

In the pioneering work of churches in the Synod of Ohio and the Order of St. Luke, it was found that an excellent way to introduce and maintain a balanced healing service was to couple it with the celebration of the Lord's Supper. This provided a secure environment and a familiar structure for those who were a bit apprehensive about being involved in a healing service. It also put the focus, not on a charismatic leader, but on the body and blood of Christ. Charismatic leaders and services can be so free and so expressive that they can be threatening to some guarded Presbyterians.

Popular - Many Presbyterians churches have followed this model. Typically they start with a once-a-month Sunday evening or mid-week service of Communion and healing. They begin with a bulletin, familiar hymns and songs, familiar liturgy, and then have a structured ministry time.

Communion Liturgy - Some churches serve the communion just as on Sunday mornings. Others innovate. We found that a camp conference style was more conducive to intimacy with the Lord and one another. We had one loaf of bread and one cup of wine (real wine with the alcohol removed) to symbolize our oneness in Christ. We passed the loaf from person to person, or broke it into quarters and passed it. We encouraged persons to speak a word of blessing as they passed it to a brother or sister. Then the leaders took the cups (we poured contents of one cup into four others) and circled around the people who were standing in a large circle or rows, while each person dipped their bread into the wine. Spontaneous singing set the stage for this, or interspersed the passing of the elements. Afterwards we had spontaneous prayers of thanks and intercession. Then we moved into teams praying for healing.

Proviso - If the communion is celebrated devotionally and evangelically, retaining the great historical ingredients such as the prayer of consecration and enough liturgy to involve the people in the action, and if there is a strong emphasis on the Lord's presence to heal when we celebrate according to 1 Cor. 11, this becomes a powerful time of fellowshipping with the Lord.

Results - Historically the early communion liturgies emphasized the healing of the Lord being communicated through the sacrament. This is still retained in the Catholic mass when the communicants all say, just before partaking, "I am not worthy to receive you, but only say the word and I shall be healed." Having celebrated communion weekly at our Wednesday night service for over five years, and then following it with individual prayers for healing, I can say without fear of contradiction that it gave us a sense of oneness in Christ and of being His body that is wonderfully satisfying. The goodness of the presence of the Lord and of communing with Him was and is more important than any individual healing or lack of healing. That became uppermost, and that is supreme.

IV. Charismatic Model of a Healing Service

In a charismatic type of healing service the leader or leaders put primary reliance on the inspiration of the Holy Spirit. A climate of praise, expectancy, and freedom is sought and prized. Bulletins are frowned upon.

Praise - Typically the service opens with a prolonged period of praise; thirty to forty minutes is about average. The song or worship leader seeks to establish a climate of relaxed informality, and may intersperse singing with inspired comments or exhortations aimed at building faith and devotion. A guitar player or several guitars who can lead well are standard; a band is even more sought after, but there are situations where a pianist who can play by ear is just as, or more, effective. Even pianists who have to have music are usable. The praise opening is in obedience to Psalm 100 and Ephesians 5:18-20. The most quoted rationale for extensive praise is Psalm 22:3, *"O Thou who inhabitest the praises of Israel"* (KJV). It is believed and experienced that as we praise God with our whole being He does indeed make His presence known.

Worship - The climax of praise is a period of intimate adoration and love, usually expressed in the more mellow and devotional type of praise music. Where the assembly is experienced in expressing spiritual gifts this period is often preceded or climaxed by singing in the Spirit.

Prophesying - Worship is normally followed by an invoking and waiting on the Spirit to prompt inspired words of edification, encouragement, comfort, or challenge. Testimonies are also encouraged, especially of healings. The sharing of the body is then often followed by teaching or preaching on the theme of healing or faith and prayer. Often visiting speakers are used for this. This part of the service is designed to prepare people to believe that the Lord is present, that He loves them, that He wills to heal them and encourages them to open up, ask and receive what He is waiting to impart.

Ministry - After about an hour or more of praise and word ministry, persons are encouraged to receive personal ministry. This may take several forms:

A. They are invited forward to stand, kneel or sit and await prayer and laying on of hands by the leader or leaders of the meeting. This may be short or lengthy depending upon the leadership. Occasionally the person ministered to will be interviewed for the encouragement of the assembly.

B. They are invited to raise their hands indicating a desire to have prayer, and ministry teams will cluster around them to pray for them. The teams may be ad-hoc or previously trained and prepared. Or ministry teams may be stationed around the room, and they go to them. Sometimes they have to wait their turn.

When we began healing services in one large Presbyterian church in the early 70's, we had elder/minister teams of two standing by chairs placed up front; persons were asked to write down their requests on cards and then come forward to sit or kneel and present the cards; the cards were later given to the prayer chain for follow through.

C. Different categories of need are instructed to go to nearby rooms or areas of the sanctuary to receive ministry. Categories might be: those needing physical healing, those needing inner healing, those desiring to be filled with the Holy Spirit. Leaders or teams who minister to the different categories of persons are then chosen because of their giftedness in those areas of need.

D. In some meetings there are persons gifted in the word of knowledge who call out persons to come forward and receive ministry. Then after these persons are ministered to (usually in a way that demonstrates God's electing grace and mercy), there is a general invitation for all to receive ministry.

E. Sometimes all present are instructed to form in small clusters, introduce themselves, share their needs and then pray for one another informally or as instructed by the leader.

Such services may last a total of two or more hours. Usually leaders tell the people to feel free to leave if they don't desire to give or receive ministry. One thing that is learned is that we need to take time to wait upon God and give Him time to work unhurriedly. Some of the most powerful healings take place late in the meeting, after many have gone home.

To God be the Glory!

THE PRMI *DUNAMIS PROJECT*
THE HEALING MINISTRY OF JESUS